Antonio Gramsci

SELECTIONS FROM

97104561

CULTUR

ANTONIO GRAMSCI
SELECTIONS FROM CULTURAL WRITINGS

edited by
DAVID FORGACS
and
GEOFFREY NOWELL-SMITH

translated by
WILLIAM BOELHOWER

LAWRENCE AND WISHART

LONDON

Lawrence and Wishart Limited
39 Museum Street,
London WC1A 1LQ

This edition first published 1985
Introductions, annotation and selection
© David Forgacs and Geoffrey Nowell-Smith, 1985
Translation © Lawrence and Wishart, 1985

Photoset by Type Practitioners Limited, Sevenoaks, Kent
Printed and bound in Great Britain by Oxford University Press

CONTENTS

*Asterisk indicates that the title is not Gramsci's, but supplied by the editors.

NOTE ON THE TEXT

The division of this volume into ten sections and our criteria of selection and arrangement require a word of explanation. Section I ('Proletarian Culture') is made up of articles taken from various Italian editions of Gramsci's early writings (the first three volumes of an eight-volume critical edition, collectively titled *Scritti 1913–1926*, in course of publication by Einaudi, Turin, have appeared at the time of going to press; elsewhere we have used the old editions). The ordering of Section I is not strictly chronological. It is divided, rather, into three parts which are in turn subdivided by theme. The aim here has been to provide a selection representative of the range and main interests of Gramsci's early cultural writings.

The remaining nine sections, all consisting of writings taken from the Prison Notebooks, posed more substantial problems of selection and grouping. Gramsci rewrote some of his first drafts of notes, in 1931–33 in Turi prison and 1934–35 in the Formia clinic (see General Introduction). The second-draft versions usually arrange the notes either into bigger and thematically more coherent bunches or into 'special notebooks' on specific themes (Risorgimento, Americanism and Fordism, etc.). While several of these special notebooks have a district thematic unity, the two which Gramsci devoted to literature (Notebook 21, 'Popular Literature' and Notebook 23, 'Literary Criticism') do not. A number of diverse thematic threads go into them, which sometimes cross-refer to each other between the two notebooks and sometimes pull apart from each other within a single notebook. In addition, many notes on literature were left in their first and only versions, scattered among the earlier miscellaneous notebooks. Given these aspects of the original text, it was clearly impossible to adopt for this translation, with its thematic slant, the arrangement of the notes in Valentino Gerratana's critical edition *Quaderni del carcere*, 4 volumes, Einaudi, Turin 1975 (hereafter referred to as Q). We were guided instead by the thematic arrangement used in the first Einaudi editions of Felice Platone (6 volumes, Turin 1948–51), particularly *Letteratura e vita nazionale* (1950, hereafter LVN) to which the majority of notes in Section II to IX of this volume correspond. Platone generally rearranged the notes on literature under the recurring headings which Gramsci gave to many of them in his manuscript (for instance 'Popular literature', 'Father Bresciani's progeny', 'Non-national-popular character of Italian literature'), adding to these a number of notes without such headings which seemed thematically assimilable to them. A later anthology by Giuliano Manacorda, *Marxismo e letteratura* (Riuniti, Rome 1975), drew on LVN for its basic outline but also interspersed cultural texts from some of the other Platone volumes and (without indication) from the early writings. We have up to a point followed the arrangements of both these editions, while at the same time making changes to the division, composition and internal ordering of the sections where these appeared to be justified on thematic grounds. The translations, however, are all from Q.

Section II ('Problems of Criticism') is based on the first part of Notebook 23 in Q with other notes on method and on Croce added from elsewhere. The remainder of Notebook 23 has been sheared off to form the nucleus of Section VIII ('Father Bresciani's Progeny'), again with other notes on the main theme added. Section IX ('Popular Literature') is based on Notebook 21, with related unique or second drafts (often headed 'Popular Literature' by Gramsci) added. The remaining notes from Notebooks 21 and 23 have been combined with a number of other notes (mostly unique drafts headed 'Italian intellectuals' or 'Non-national-popular character' by Gramsci) to form Section VI ('People, Nation and Culture'), which does not correspond either to a special notebook or to a clearly circumscribed group of notes in Gramsci's own arrangement, but which seems to be a thematically justifiable group and which is related to the layout of the second section of LVN. The remaining sections presented fewer problems of arrangement. Section V ('Language, Linguistics and Folklore') uses two special notebooks (numbers 29 and 27) as its core, supplemented with related unique drafts, and Section X ('Journalism') does the same with Notebook 24. Section IV ('Canto X of Dante's Inferno') reproduces, with one omission, a coherent sequence of notes from within a miscellaneous notebook (number 4). Sections III ('Pirandello') and VII ('Manzoni') do not correspond to distinct sections in Gramsci's layout, but the monographic character of the notes on these two authors appears to justify their being separated off. The connections they make with other groups of notes in any case remains fairly clear, and we have tried to underline them by the placing of the sections (thus, the notes on Manzoni are sandwiched between those on the non-national-popular character of Italian literature and those on 'Brescianism' in Italian literature; the notes on Pirandello follow those in Section II on the forces for change within modern literary culture). In fact in all instances the divisions of notes into sections must be regarded as provisional rather than definitive. Our thematic boundaries only correspond approximately to real thematic boundaries in Gramsci's original text, and they mainly have the pragmatic purpose of making an approach to the complex web of his cultural writings more manageable.

Each of the notes from the Prison Notebooks in Sections II to X carries a separate heading. These headings are Gramsci's original titles (usually with the generic part – e.g. 'Popular literature' – removed) except when they are within square brackets, in which case they are headings we or previous editors have supplied, either because Gramsci left that note untitled or because he used only a generic heading without a specific title. (Square brackets are also used within the text to indicate editorial interpolations.) Each note also carries a *notebook* number followed by a *paragraph* (i.e. note) number. These numbers, designated Q, correspond to those supplied by Gerratana's critical edition, not to the old notebook numbers in Roman numerals used in the contents pages of Platone's edition, which has now been superseded by Q.

A concordance table is provided at the back of this volume to facilitate cross referencing to Q and to the Platone volumes, as well as to the reprint of the latter published by Editori Riuniti in 1971. There is a similar table for the articles translated in Section I. Lower case roman numerals have been used both in these tables and the text to identify different notes or articles with the same title.

The selection and arrangement of texts was done collaboratively by both editors. The general introduction is by Geoffrey Nowell-Smith; introductions to individual sections are by David Forgacs.

ACKNOWLEDGEMENTS

The editors would like to thank the following for their help: Jennifer Lorch, Giulio Lepschy and Chantal Mouffe for providing feedback and criticisms of draft introductions to various sections of this book; Valentino Gerratana and the staff at the Istituto Gramsci in Rome for making available photocopies of the manuscript Prison Notebooks and items from Gramsci's prison library; Colin Bearne, Carmine Donzelli, Nick Jacobs, Cora Kaplan, Lino Pertile, Ardeshir Shojai, Roger Simon, Peter Stallybrass, Jennifer Stone and Mario Telò for assistance of various kinds; and to Stephen Hayward and Jeff Skelley at Lawrence and Wishart for their constant support at all stages of work on the volume. Special thanks to Rosalind Delmar and Jane Hodgkins. None of the above bears any responsibility for faults in the end product. Published sources of information for the footnotes and introductions are numerous, but the following in particular have been drawn on: the invaluable critical apparatuses in Volume IV of *Quaderni del carcere*, edited by Valentino Gerratana, and in the volumes of pre-1926 writings edited by Sergio Caprioglio; Dina Bertoni Jovine, *Storia della scuola popolare in Italia*, Turin 1954; Christine Buci-Glucksmann, *Gramsci and the State*, London 1980; Giorgio Canestri and Giuseppe Ricuperati (eds.), *La scuola in Italia dalla legge Casati a oggi*, Turin 1976; Valerio Castronovo, *La stampa italiana dall'unità al fascismo*, Bari 1970; Alberto Maria Cirese, *Intellettuali, folklore, istinto di classe*, Turin 1976; Tullio De Mauro, *Storia linguistica dell'Italia unita*, Bari 1976; Franco Lo Piparo, *Lingua intellettuali egemonia in Gramsci*, Bari 1979; Leonardo Paggi, *Gramsci e il moderno principe*, Rome 1970; Hugues Portelli, *Gramsci et la question religieuse*, Paris 1974; Paolo Spriano, *Storia del Partito comunista italiano*, Turin 1967–75 and 'L'informazione nell'Italia unita' in *Storia d'Italia*, V, *I documenti*, 2, Turin 1973.

ABBREVIATIONS OF WORKS CITED

1. Critical editions

CT   *Cronache torinesi, 1913–1917*, edited by Sergio Caprioglio, Einaudi, Turin 1980.

CF   *La Città futura, 1917–1918*, edited by Sergio Caprioglio, Einaudi, Turin 1982.

NM   *Il nostro Marx, 1918–1919*, edited by Sergio Caprioglio, Einaudi, Turin 1984.

Q   *Quaderni del carcere*, edited by Valentino Gerratana, 4 vols., Einaudi, Turin 1975.

L   *Lettere dal carcere*, edited by Sergio Caprioglio and Elsa Fubini, Einaudi, Turin 1965.

2. Other editions

SG   *Scritti giovanili, 1914–1918*, Einaudi, Turin 1958.

SM   *Sotto la Mole, 1916–1920*, Einaudi, Turin 1960.

DP   *Duemila pagine di Gramsci*, edited by Niccolò Gallo and Giansiro Ferrata, Il Saggiatore, Milan 1964, vol. I.

SC   *Scritti 1915–1921*, edited by Sergio Caprioglio, Milan 1968 (references are to the 2nd edition, Moizzi, Milan 1976).

PV   *Per la verità. Scritti 1913–1926*, edited by Renzo Martinelli, Riuniti, Rome 1974.

ON   *L'Ordine Nuovo, 1919–1920*, Einaudi, Turin 1954.

SF   *Socialismo e fascismo. L'Ordine Nuovo, 1921–1922*, Einaudi, Turin 1966.

CPC   *La costruzione del Partito comunista, 1923–1926*, Einaudi, Turin 1971.

MS   *Il materialismo storico e la filosofia di Benedetto Croce*, Einaudi, Turin 1948.

INT   *Gli intellettuali e l'organizzazione della cultura*, Einaudi, Turin 1949.

R   *Il Risorgimento*, Einaudi, Turin 1949.

MACH   *Note sul Machiavelli, sulla politica e sullo Stato moderno*, Einaudi, Turin 1949.

LVN   *Letteratura e vita nazionale*, Einaudi, Turin 1950.

PP   *Passato e presente*, Einaudi, Turin 1951.

3. Translations

SPN   *Selections from the Prison Notebooks*, edited and translated by Quintin Hoare and Geoffrey Nowell-Smith, Lawrence and Wishart, London 1971.

SPW I   *Selections from Political Writings (1910–1920)*, selected and edited by Quintin Hoare, translated by John Mathews, Lawrence and Wishart, London 1977.

SPW II   *Selections from Political Writings (1921–1926)*, translated and edited by Quintin Hoare, Lawrence and Wishart, London 1978.

LP   *Letters From Prison*, selected, translated and introduced by Lynne Lawner, Cape, London 1973.

GENERAL INTRODUCTION

I

Antonio Gramsci was arrested in Rome on 8 November 1926. His Russian wife, Julia, had just given birth in Moscow to their second child. Antonio was to spend the rest of his life in prison or in hospital. He died on 27 April 1937.

At the time of his arrest Gramsci was leader of the Italian Communist Party and was a Communist deputy in the Italian parliament. His arrest and that of a number of his colleagues took place in defiance of their parliamentary immunity and marked a new step in the imposition of fascist rule in Italy. The day after the arrest the Chamber of Deputies, ratifying a *fait accompli*, removed immunity from the deputies of all the opposition parties. On 18 November Gramsci was sentenced to five years confinement under police supervision and arrangements were made to transfer him from prison to the island of Ustica, off the coast of Sicily. There he was briefly to enjoy relatively pleasant conditions of detention, along with other 'politicals' including Amadeo Bordiga. He was also able to receive books, which were sent to him from a bookshop in Milan where his friend the economist Piero Sraffa had opened an account for him. Legislative provisions soon caught up with him, however. In January 1927 a warrant was issued by a Military Tribunal seeking his arrest and transfer to Milan, and in February the Special Tribunal for the Defence of the State entered into operation. Gramsci's trial before this tribunal began over a year later, at the end of May 1928. On 4 June of that year he was condemned to twenty years' imprisonment.

It was while awaiting trial in Milan that Gramsci formed his first plan for what were to become his *Quaderni del carcere* or Prison Notebooks. Contrary to what has sometimes been asserted, Gramsci was free to read during this period, and in fact read voraciously, though he was not permitted to take notes on his reading. As a prisoner awaiting trial he was entitled to write two letters a week to family and friends and in a letter to his sister-in-law Tatiana ('Tania') Schucht of 19 March 1927 (L, pp. 57–60, also in LP, pp. 79–81)* he expressed a wish to be able to carry out

*References to sources are explained on pp. xv and xvi.

a systematic project of intellectual work. He wrote:

> I am assailed (this phenomenon is, I think, typical of people in prison)
> by this idea: that it would be important to do something 'für ewig' [for
> eternity], according to a complex conception of Goethe's which as I
> recall much tormented the poet Pascoli too. In brief I should like,
> following a pre-established plan . . .

The plan sketched out in the letter has four parts. The first is
described as 'an inquiry into the formation of public spirit in Italy
in the last century; in other words an inquiry into the Italian
intellectuals, their origins, their groupings according to cultural
currents, their various modes of thinking, etc.' This, he says,
would be a development of his essay on the Southern Question
(see SPW II, pp. 441–62), but less superficial and written 'from
a "disinterested" point of view, "für ewig"'. Secondly he proposes
doing a study of comparative linguistics, which would in some
sense repay his debt to the academic world which he had
abandoned to take up politics. Thirdly he mentions 'a study of the
theatre of Pirandello and the transformation of Italian theatrical
taste'. Part four is 'an essay on serial novels and popular taste in
literature', an idea spinning off from his interest in theatrical
taste.

It was some time, however, before he could put into practice
this, or any, plan of intellectual work. After sentence he was
transferred to prison in Turi, near Bari in Apulia, where he
arrived on 19 July 1928 and where he was allotted a cell on his
own. Six months later, in January 1929, he finally received the
special permission necessary to allow him to write in his cell. In
a letter to Tania on 29 January (L, pp. 251–2) he announces the
permission received and declares his intention of establishing a
plan of study, for which he will require some more substantial
books than those he has been receiving thitherto. Then on 8
February 1929 he starts work on the first of his Notebooks – a
school exercise book, 15 x 20.5 cms. (8 x 6 ins.), ruled, and
marked with the prison stamp. By the time his imprisonment
ends he will have used up over thirty exercise books of this or a
similar format. In a first phase – up to August 1931 – he fills seven
notebooks with general notes on intellectual and political topics,
plus three with exercises in translation (mostly from German and
Russian).* Before leaving Turi in November 1933 he starts work

---

*Two of the Notebooks with general notes (Nos. 2 and 7) also contain some translations.

on a further ten (plus one of translations), some of which he continues to work on in the clinic in Formia, south of Rome, to which he was transferred in December of that year. Another twelve were to be started in Formia, bringing the total to thirty-three.

The opening of the first Notebook announces the plan of work alluded to in the letter to Tania of 29 January. Under 'principal arguments' he lists:

1) *Theory of history and historiography.*
2) *Development of the Italian bourgeoisie up to 1870.*
3) *Formation of Italian intellectual groups*: evolution, attitudes.
4) *Popular literature of 'serial novels' and the reasons for their continuing success.*
5) *Cavalcante Cavalcanti*: his position in the structure and the art of the *Divine Comedy*.
6) *Origins and evolution of Catholic Action in Italy and Europe.*
7) *The concept of folklore.*
8) *Experiences of prison life.*
9) *The 'southern question' and the question of the islands* [sc. Sicily and Sardinia].
10) *Observations on the population of Italy*: its composition, function of emigration.
11) *Americanism and Fordism.*
12) *The question of the language in Italy*: Manzoni and G.I. Ascoli.
13) *'Common sense'* (see 7).
14) *Types of periodical*; theory, historical–critical, of general culture (spreading of).
15) *Neo-grammarians and neo-linguists* ('this round table is square').
16) *Father Bresciani's progeny.*

Almost all these topics were to be developed, in some form or other, in this and subsequent Notebooks. Only number 8, experiences of prison life, was not pursued in the Notebooks, but it was amply represented in the letters he wrote from prison to his family.

Early in August 1931, Gramsci, whose health had never been good and had deteriorated further since his detention, underwent a severe physical crisis. Although in a letter to Tania of 10 August (L, pp. 462–3) he makes light of it, and in his next letter (17

August, L, pp. 464–7) he is again writing with his customary lucidity about intellectual topics (specifically, Dante), it is clear from his description of his symptoms in the letter of the 17th that his condition had become serious. Fearful that he now has little time left, he sets out at the beginning of Notebook 8 a new plan to follow, under the general heading 'Scattered notes and jottings for a history of the Italian intellectuals'. He starts with the observation:

> 1° Provisional character – pro-memoria – of such notes and jottings; 2° From them can be developed some independent essays, not a single organic work; 3° There cannot yet be a distinction between the principal and the secondary part of the exposition, between what would become the 'text' and what would be the 'footnotes'; 4° Affirmations are often not checked, what might be called a 'first approximation': some of them in subsequent research might [need to] be abandoned and the opposite assertion might be shown to be correct; 5° In the light of this the vastness and uncertain limits of the theme need not give a bad impression: there is no intention at all of making a giant hotch-potch of things about the intellectuals, an encyclopaedic compilation which tries to fill every possible or imaginable 'gap'.

The note continues:

> *Principal essays: General Introduction*. Development of the Italian intellectuals up to 1870: different periods – Popular literature of serial novels – Folklore and common sense – The question of the literary language and the dialects – Father Bresciani's progeny – Reformation and Renaissance – Machiavelli – The school system and national education – The position of Benedetto Croce in Italian culture up to the world war – The Risorgimento and the Action Party – Ugo Foscolo in the formation of national rhetoric – History of Catholic action: Catholic integralists. Jesuits, modernists – The medieval commune, economic-corporate phase of the state – Cosmopolitan function of Italian intellectuals up to the 18th century – Reactions to the absence of a popular-national character of culture in Italy: the Futurists – the common school and what it means for the entire organization of national culture – 'Lorianism' as a characteristic of Italian intellectuals – the absence of 'Jacobinism' in the Italian Risorgimento – Machiavelli as technician of politics or as integral politician or politician *in actu*.

Over the page, Gramsci then writes, '*Appendices*: Americanism and Fordism'; but he leaves the rest of the sheet blank and continues on the facing page:

1° *Intellectuals: Educational questions*
2° *Machiavelli*
3° *Encyclopaedic notions and cultural arguments*
4° *Introduction to the study of philosophy and critical notes on* [Bukharin's] *Popular Manual of Sociology*
5° *History of Catholic Action. Catholic integralists – Jesuits – modernists*
6° *Miscellany of various scholarly notes (Past and Present)*
7° *Italian Risorgimento* (in the sense of Omodeo's *Age of the Italian Risorgimento*, but focusing on the more strictly Italian aspects)
8° *Father Bresciani's progeny. Popular literature* (Notes on literature)
9° *Lorianism*
10° *Notes on journalism*

Over the next two years, with his health continuing to deteriorate, he continues to work to this revised programme. Wherever possible he arranged for books to be sent to him in prison, but he could not obtain all he wanted and often was forced to rely on the memory of books he had read in his youth. He also profited from conversations with other politicals in the prison at Turi. In the first years there these conversations had been frequent and had even taken the form for a while of education classes among the Communists, but political disagreements between Gramsci and the majority of the other Communist prisoners had led him to withdraw from formal discussions on politics. This was the time of the Communist International's so-called Third Period, which began in 1929 and involved a general hardening of positions in the struggle against fascism and a break with social democracy, accused of an effective equivalence with fascism. The Italian party, now led by Togliatti, supported the position of the International, and most of the Communists in prison affirmed their loyalty to the line the party was taking up. Gramsci, however, was reluctant to support it, and openly expressed his reservations, both about the line in general and about its consequences within the party, from which three members of the Political Committee were expelled in 1930. Gramsci, it seems, was unwilling to approve wholeheartedly of the expulsion of the 'three'; more importantly he made it quite clear that he could not agree with the basic premisses of the 1929 'left turn' and that in particular he did not believe that the overthrow of fascism would lead direct to the establishment of a socialist state. While these disagreements soured his relations with many of his comrades he did not, however, withdraw entirely from contact with other prisoners and even managed to continue conversations with some of them (with collusion from the warders) after a ministerial decree in late 1932 had imposed a régime of solitary confinement on the politicals in Turi.

At the end of 1932 his sentence had been commuted from twenty years to twelve, and his friends, led by Sraffa, attempted to have him released on compassionate grounds. They had just obtained permission for him to be examined by a doctor of his choice, when he underwent a second serious crisis (7 March 1933). The chosen doctor, Professor Umberto Arcangeli, visited him on 20 March. Tania was now living in Turi in order to be near him, and his brother Carlo was also permitted to visit him. (What neither of them had the courage to tell him, and he only learnt a year later, was that his mother had died the previous December.) Then in October, following an international campaign which had included the publication in France of Professor Arcangeli's report, the authorities finally agreed to Gramsci's removal to hospital – though still as a prisoner. He left Turi on 19 November 1933, taking his notebooks with him, and after a brief stay in the prison hospital at Civitavecchia, arrived at the clinic in Formia where he was to stay for nearly two years.

In Formia, Gramsci resumed work on his Notebooks, completing some that he had brought with him from Turi and starting some new ones. Although he introduces one new rubric in a Notebook of this period – No. 25, entitled 'On the margins of history (history of the subaltern social groups)' – he mostly follows the plan set forth at the beginning of Notebook 8 at the end of 1931 and concentrates especially on regrouping and revising earlier notes. In September 1934, having for a long time maintained a principled resistance to the idea of appealing for a pardon from the government, he puts in a formal request for conditional liberty, which is granted on 22 October, allowing him on the 24th briefly to leave the grounds of the clinic, in the company of Tatiana.

His further declining health, however, meant that he was forced to stay at the clinic for some time yet, while attempting to arrange a transfer to a sanatorium in Rome where he could obtain more specialized care. The transfer to the 'Quisisana' sanatorium was achieved on 24 August 1935. In April 1937 his prison sentence finally expired and he became, legally, a free man. On 25 April he underwent a severe cerebral haemorrhage and two days later he was dead. Most of his last letters had been to his children, the younger of whom he had never seen.

II

After Gramsci's death Tatiana removed the Notebooks from the clinic and held on to them until an opportunity presented itself, a year later, to send them safely to Moscow. Word about their existence and their contents began to circulate within the Communist Party and outside, but it was not until after the war that they started to appear in print. The first volume of Gramsci's writings to be published – by Einaudi in Turin – was in fact a selection of his letters (1947). Then, under the editorship of Felice Platone, came six volumes drawn from the Notebooks – *Il materialismo storico e la filosofia di Benedetto Croce* (1948), *Gli intellettuali e l'organizzazione della cultura* (1949), *Il Risorgimento* (1949), *Note sul Machiavelli, sulla politica e sullo Stato moderno* (1949), *Letteratura e vita nazionale* (1950) and *Passato e presente* (1951).

These titles – 'Historical materialism and the philosophy of Benedetto Croce', 'The intellectuals and the organization of culture', 'The Risorgimento', 'Notes on Machiavelli, on politics and on the modern state', 'Literature and national life', 'Past and present' – reflect an ordering of the material substantially derived from the headings drawn up by Gramsci in his 1931 plan. It has been argued, however, that the way the material was grouped by Platone and his colleagues does more than that, and that it prejudicially draws frontiers around areas which, in Gramsci's original conception, overlapped or were imbricated in more subtle ways. Thus the Historical Materialism volume isolates within itself all the writings on topics that are philosophical in nature; that on Machiavelli and the Modern State does the same to politics; the Risorgimento stitches up history; and Literature and National Life (which also contains, as a large appendix, the theatre reviews that Gramsci wrote for *Avanti!* in 1913–20) separates out literature and culture; etc., etc. The edition also sews together texts without any indication that they were originally separate fragments, and it hierarchizes 'text' and 'footnotes' in spite of Gramsci's injunction to the contrary.

The objections are undoubtedly well founded, but the point should not be laboured excessively as some commentators have done. In fact it is difficult to see what else the editors could or should have done at the time, when the most urgent task was to introduce Gramsci's writing to a readership avid to know what sort of ideas the Notebooks contained, what sort of topics they covered, and in what depth. It took another quarter of a century before the full scholarly labour of putting the Notebooks into a reliable order of composition and relating early drafts to subsequent revisions of the same material was eventually completed. The Critical Edition in which this labour is incorporated was edited by Valentino Gerratana and published in 1975.

The Critical Edition reproduces, word for word and with only the most trivial of emendations, the entire text of all the Notebooks written in Turi or Formia except for the Notebooks devoted purely to translation exercises and the sections of translation in the general Notebooks. The Notebooks reproduced – twenty-nine in all – are numbered in what can reliably be held to be the order in which Gramsci began to write in them, although in some cases a Notebook was returned to by Gramsci for notes on a particular topic after others had been started. Gerratana's numbering, in arabic numerals from 1 to 29, replaces the provisional numbering in roman numerals which Tania had scribbled on each Notebook when she rescued them after Gramsci's death. Within each Notebook every text is reproduced with the original title that Gramsci gave to it, which in some cases is a specific heading to the text which follows but in other cases is merely an indication of the general heading under which the text in question can be grouped.

One of the most striking features of the 1975 Critical Edition is the evidence it offers of the way Gramsci, particularly in the Formia period, reworked existing material into revised and (generally) more compact form. As explained in the Note on p. 427 of this edition, Gerratana has labelled all the texts in the Notebooks A, B or C. A designates those which were subsequently revised or rewritten with major or minor alterations, B those which were not rewritten and exist in one version only, and C the revised or rewritten version of A texts.

While no deduction can be drawn from the B texts and the fact that they were not revised – one simply cannot know or even guess whether they were to be discarded, or left unchanged, or would have been changed in due course had there been time – certain minimal inferences can be made from the texts that were revised. It is significant for example that revisions were often slight – an entire paragraph may contain no more than a couple of minor stylistic changes – and sometimes the purpose of the revision is merely to draw together in a single draft two or three notes scribbled down at different times but always intended to be connected. Apart from the evidence this gives of the extraordinarily fluent character of Gramsci's note taking, which took shape in his head and flowed as prose as soon as he put pen to paper, it can be inferred from these cases that the Notebooks, even at their most fragmentary, were always planned and that a return at a later date to previous notes was often little more than an enactment of an already existing plan – in some cases already deducible from the 'pro-memoria' headings at the top of the texts. On the other hand, however, there are cases where the rewriting or recasting seems to provide evidence of an intention to generate a new text, drawing in items previously grouped under different heads. Some of the most coherent sequences of notes in the Notebooks, such as Americanism and Fordism (SPN, pp. 279–318) or the Critical Notes on Bukharin's *Popular Manual of Marxist Sociology* (SPN, pp. 419–72), were generated in this way, with an original project enriched by the introduction of elements drawn from elsewhere.

Accounts given by comrades who were in prison with him describe him as writing without sitting down, bending over a table with his knee crooked under him on a little stool. A passage would flow and he would then revert to pacing up and down until another passage had taken shape in his head. (Reported in G. Fiori, *Antonio Gramsci: Life of a Revolutionary*, London 1970, p. 236.) At other times he would work closeted in his cell with the books and periodicals he was permitted to read next to him, sometimes transcribing or paraphrasing long passages from them with minimal interpolations of his own.

Because of the way they were composed and transmitted, the Notebooks have the character very much of what has come to be called an 'open text'. They do not have imprinted on them those features of hierarchy and directedness of argument which characterize works written for publication in book or pamphlet form. Gramsci himself makes the observation, which has already been referred to, that, as written, his notes do not – or do not yet – distinguish between what, in a more ordered work, would be the 'text' proper and what would be the 'footnotes'. No doubt, had he been in a position to revise the works for publication in some form or other, such a distinction would have been imposed. But he was never in this position, and very few of the notes are ordered in such a way as to sustain a single central argument for any distance. It is rarely possible for subsequent readers to declare with confidence what the hierarchy of argument should be, which is the main theme and which is secondary. Even if on occasion this can be done with a fair degree of confidence a situation can always be imagined in which the perspective could be reversed and the matter which appears secondary in its immediate context could be made primary in terms of another, equally legitimate and authentic, discursive theme. Thus in the notes on journalism reproduced in this volume there is a long historical 'digression' that covers such topics as the role of the para-military Royal Guard created by the Nitti government in 1920; but in the context, say, of the notes on state and civil society, this fragment of writing would not be a digression but part of a central argument.

This 'openness' of Gramsci's text to different readings, based on different hierarchizations of the argument, is particularly remarkable in the context (in which Gramsci belongs) of Marxist political writing. Most Marxist writing – and this would include Gramsci's own writing prior to prison – is highly directive. It is produced by writers – individuals or groups – with points to make, theses to prove, polemics to engage, tactics and strategies to lay down: in brief, it pursues a line. Gramsci's writings in the Notebooks are more like a network, or a web. Although there is a coherence to them, this coherence is not linear; it is established through multiple branchings out, with arguments that double back on themselves and reconnect laterally rather than in sequence. As a result the sort of univocal reading that we expect to be able to make of writings in the Marxist tradition is difficult to achieve with the Notebooks. They require a different sort of suspended attention, an openness of reading to match their openness of writing.

And yet the Notebooks are in no sense unpolitical; it is just that their political impulse, and political utility, are held at one remove from the reader by the lack of a sharply defined political context from which they can obviously be seen to spring or to which they can obviously be seen to be directed. Many of the notes, as Gramsci himself observes, have a function of 'pro-memoria': they are, as it were, notes to himself. Although the broad outlines of what was happening in the outside world were all too apparent to him – fascism, the depression, Stalinization – he had little direct knowledge of what was happening day by day in Italy or in other countries or in the international Communist movement. Nor was he in a position to intervene directly in particular conjunctures. Sitting in his cell or pacing the courtyard he could marshal arguments for a political purpose, but he had no way of knowing which arguments were most urgent to deploy. Frustrating though this must have been for him, it has advantages for readers coming later. The texts were produced under extremely difficult conditions, but one effect of this was to make them 'plural' and adaptable in a way that is rare for the classics of Marxism. Unfinished by their author, the texts are open to us because there is no point at which they could, or can, be closed off.

III

A striking and much remarked upon feature both of Gramsci's plans for his work in prison and of their eventual working out in the Notebooks is the large and indeed central place given over to literary and cultural topics. In his first announcement to Tatiana Schucht in March 1927 of the work he would like to do, he mentions four topics of which three are literary/cultural in orientation – comparative linguistics, Pirandello and Italian theatrical taste, and serial novels and popular taste in literature. Again, in the list which opens Notebook 1 in 1929, six topics out of sixteen – serial novels, folklore, the question of the language, types of periodical journalism, neo-grammarians and neo-linguists, Father Bresciani's progeny – are all concerned with culture and its diffusion. This concentration on cultural topics at the planning stage of the Notebooks and in the early period of his imprisonment is to some extent belied by the actual development of the Notebooks, in which certain projects rather fell by the wayside while others grew disproportionately. The projected study of Pirandello, for example (see Section III of this edition), never really materialised except in rather fragmentary form, whereas some topics, particularly those relating to philosophy and to the state and civil society, proved capable of a richer development.

It has been suggested that Gramsci's concentration on cultural topics at the time of his imprisonment came out of a sense of isolation from political life and a wish to do work 'für ewig' on things which took his mind off painful questions and his own powerlessness to affect the political process. There may have been an element, too, of reparation for his abandonment of humanistic studies in favour of a life of political journalism and militancy when he was a young man. While such psychological speculation contains an element of truth, it does not account for the consistency with which cultural topics are in fact handled by Gramsci throughout the Notebooks; nor does it do justice to the specificity of his thinking about cultural issues, which is above all remarkable for its refusal to divide culture from history and politics. The idea that literature was 'for ever' and politics a matter for the immediate was indeed one which Gramsci in his arguments against Croce specifically refutes.

The form of cultural production to which Gramsci devotes most attention in the Notebooks is literature. It figures there, however, not in the guise of great timeless monuments but always in the context of its reception by a readership and its absorption in particular cultures and histories. Thus Pirandello interests him not just as a playwright but as a barometer of cultural change. Dostoyevsky's novels receive attention particularly for the way they draw on serial fiction and thus reveal the interplay between 'artistic' and 'popular' culture. It is perhaps in his analysis of the tenth canto of Dante's *Inferno* (see Section IV of this edition) that Gramsci comes closest to performing a work of literary and philological criticism in the traditional sense. But even here his concern is as much with the symptomatology of the right-wing ideologues who had recently attempted interpretations of their own as it is with the work of literary analysis as such. As a former pupil of Umberto Cosmo (with whom he even attempted to communicate from prison), Gramsci was sensitive to the demands of philological scholarship, and the study of Canto X is in a sense a demonstration of how historical and linguistic methods ought to be used – in contrast to their abuse by the mediocre denizens of the official culture of the fascist period.

More remarkable, however, than his occasional forays into the world of great literature and literary scholarship, is his consistent involvement with popular literature, its production and diffusion. His concern here edges into what nowadays might be called sociology of literature, though this is a label which he himself would have repudiated, and his approach certainly makes no concession to the categorising tendency which he considered characteristic of sociological types of inquiry, whether in literature or elsewhere. Rather his approach is historical, always seeking to relate literary production to the historical process which produced it and to which it contributes. It is also political, to the extent that running throughout his reflections on literature and culture is the hidden thread of an unstated political question: what are the agencies by which culture is shaped, and to what extent can culture be guided by conscious political agency? This political thread comes to the surface most clearly in the notes on journalism reproduced as Section X of this volume, but it was present already in his pre-prison reflections, and is there, latent, in almost everything he wrote.

Partly as a consequence of this unspoken political emphasis, the concept of culture is never theoretically defined by Gramsci in the Notebooks. Culture functions loosely – and very productively – as a sort of middle term between the world of art and study on the one hand and society and politics on the other. In a way Gramsci never quite emancipated himself from a concept of culture derived from the traditional socialist thinking which provided his early cultural-political formation. For socialists of his generation, culture largely meant literature and education – which the working class were to make their own, wresting them from the hands of the bourgeoisie. The affirmative political impulse behind this conception conceals serious limitations, which Gramsci never entirely overcame. His concept of culture became richer and fuller, but it retained uncriticized residues of its original bias towards the written word as the core of cultural formation in individuals and in society. It is significant that the emerging forms of radio and cinema receive minimal attention in the Notebooks.

Nevertheless there is in the Notebooks at least an implicit theoretical concept of culture which can be seen to inform his scattered observations over a wide field. What this underlying concept is can be deduced from his procedure in approaching not just literature and art but other topics as well – philosophy, economic science, politics even. In all cases his interest is not so much in the object in itself as in the place it occupies within a range of social practices. The writings on philosophy, for example, rarely enter in detail into philosophical arguments as such; their concern is with the place of philosophical thinking and of particular philosophies within social life. In other words, with the 'culture' of philosophy. Even Gramsci's thinking on the state focuses less (as classical political theory would do) on its objective institutional features than on the way it is conceptualized, thought about, accepted or contested by different social strata in different periods. Likewise what interests him in relation to literature and art is again their culture, the place they hold generally within what he calls the 'complex superstructures' of a social formation.

The absence of an explicit theoretical definition serves Gramsci well, since it allows him to move flexibly around various manifestations of artistic, social or political activity. This flexibility has as its result the most extraordinarily rich series of observations generated on topics as diverse as Dante's *Inferno* or the role that could be played by a socialist almanac in popular culture. The richness of each observation depends however on a theoretical underpinning of other concepts which are less flexible and more systematically related. The fundamental concepts in play in Gramsci's observations on cultural themes are those which inform his writings generally – state and civil society, intellectuals, hegemony and so forth. Just as culture has only a limited autonomy from other social practices, so within Gramsci's theoretical schema its meaning is dependent on the meaning of other concepts. Gramsci is the greatest Marxist writer on culture, and the one from whom there is most to learn; but he is a theoretician of culture, or a producer of cultural theory, only to the extent that his theory in general stretches out to encompass the cultural field.

With respect to this, the selection of Gramsci's writings in the present volume, broad as it is in its range, reflects a slightly narrower sense of 'culture'. In part this is because the choice of which texts to include here was to an extent pre-determined by the fact that certain of Gramsci's theoretical writings with a bearing on cultural matters appeared in English in the 1971 volume *Selections from the Prison Notebooks*. (Other writings – on philosophy, on science, on religion – are due for publication shortly.) If – as we have maintained – it is true that the broad area of culture covered in this volume is still only a part of what for Gramsci was a single, wider field, that of the 'superstructures' in general, then it is important that this book should be read in conjunction with Gramsci's other writings, particularly those on the intellectuals, hegemony and the study of philosophy. At the same time, the writings on culture in this volume are more than an adjunct to writings available elsewhere. Much of the interest in Gramsci's thought in the English-speaking world in recent years has focused on what seemed to be the implications for the study of culture of his theoretical writings in general. With this volume we hope to make the bridge to the concrete working out of his theoretical concerns in the practice of cultural criticism.

I

PROLETARIAN CULTURE

Introduction

This section contains early writings by Gramsci from the years 1913 to 1922, a period when 'culture' in the dominant senses attaching to the word in Italian at that time (including 'education' as well as what the jargon of idealism called 'activities of the spirit' such as philosophy, art and literature) was a large part of his routine existence. In 1911 he had come to Turin from Sardinia on a scholarship of 70 lire a month and until 1915 he studied at the university for a humanities degree, taking courses in philosophy, Greek and Latin, Italian literature and modern history. He specialized in historical linguistics for a thesis he was never to complete, though he continued working on it until 1918. In late 1913 he joined the local branch of the Socialist Party (PSI) and in 1915 started full-time work as a journalist, joining the staff of the Turin socialist weekly *Il Grido del Popolo* and becoming a writer and sub-editor on the regional edition of the party newspaper *Avanti!*. Between 1916 and 1920 he contributed nearly two hundred articles to a regular theatre column in *Avanti!*, as well as writing on topical cultural and theoretical issues. He became involved in adult education within the socialist movement, lecturing to workers' cultural circles from 1916, helping to run a discussion group (1918), a workers' school (1919–20) and an Institute of Proletarian Culture (1921–22). By this time he had passed through the catalysing experiences of the First World War, the Bolshevik revolution and the 'Red Years' in Italy, developed the theory of the Factory Councils and was active in the central committee of the Communist Party (formed in January 1921) under the leadership of Amadeo Bordiga. Designated as the Party's representative to the Communist International, he left for Moscow in May 1922, where he wrote what is chronologically the last piece in this section: a letter to Trotsky in reply to a request for information on Italian Futurism, which was originally published in Russian as an appendix to the chapter on Futurism in Trotsky's *Literature and Revolution* (1923). In October 1922 Mussolini came to power and Gramsci would not return to Italy until May 1924.

'Culture' had been an important issue within the PSI since the Young Socialist Federation put it on their agenda in 1912. A debate had taken place at their congress then between 'culturists' such as Angelo Tasca (closely associated with Gramsci until 1919) who wanted to give full priority to cultural activity and theoretical propaganda in their newspaper, and 'anti-culturists' (including the young Bordiga), who called these proposals 'bourgeois' and reminded their opponents tartly that historical crises had economic causes. These criticisms accurately pinpointed the idealist thinking in the 'culturist' argument, which the young Gramsci also initially shared (see for example his 'Socialism and culture' of 1916 in SPW I, pp. 10–13). But the issue of culture in the party was more complex than this suggests, since the demand for educating the party membership was also an attempt to break the hold over the party of reformist gradualists and of the 'maximalists' who adhered to a crisis theory of capitalism's collapse. Many of the younger generation of socialists, including Gramsci and Tasca, were receptive to a set of cultural influences – the anti-positivism and moralism of Sorel, Bergson's voluntarism, the intuitionism of Croce – which played a crucial role in cutting away at the determinist tenets underpinning these twin positions of the Marxism of the Second International. After the crushing of the Turin insurrection of August 1917, Gramsci became acutely aware that the local PSI section was made up of a highly militant but essentially unorganized and theoretically unprepared membership and an impotent leadership incapable of giving any concrete direction. The problem of culture, which already in a series of articles in 1916 Gramsci had posed in terms of wresting the class privilege of 'culture' away from the ruling class by restructuring and expanding the education system, becomes from 1917 a problem also of struggling against a party leadership composed largely of middle-class intellectuals who were monopolizing theory, by creating an educated rank and file able to deliberate and elaborate strategy for themselves. To get this point across he had to try to persuade anti-intellectualist members in the party and the trade unions of the necessity of 'culture', to divest it of its associations of the schoolroom and the encyclopaedia and treat it instead as mental 'self-discipline' and a means of liberation. The first two articles included here reflect this debate.

From 1917, too, the emphasis on the class character of culture becomes more marked as Gramsci begins to pose the question of what form a specifically proletarian culture might take, how it is related to bourgeois culture and how it can be practically organized. This line of thinking is particularly evident around 1919–20, the 'Red Years', when Gramsci is active in the *Ordine Nuovo* group and instrumental in developing a theory of workers' control and a model of socialist democracy based on the Russian soviets. The slogan 'proletarian culture' had derived from Proletkult, the organization set up initially in Petrograd and Moscow in 1917–18. In the summer of 1920, between the general strike and the occupation of the factories, Gramsci invoked Proletkult as an example of an autonomous working-class cultural organization. The affiliated Institute of Proletarian Culture which he helped to set up in Turin made contact with the Moscow organization, put on lectures, drafted one issue of a magazine and invited the Futurist writer Marinetti to present an art exhibition to the workers. For Gramsci the notion of 'proletarian culture' is related to his vindication of a historically superior proletarian morality, based on productive work, collaboration and responsible personal relations, as well as his belief in a new kind of educational system in which the division between manual and intellectual labour is superseded. These views, including the important discussions of education in relation to socialism and the 'state of the Councils' (I7 and I8) in this volume), point forward to those in the Prison Notebooks on the 'new type of intellectual' (SPN, p. 9), on the need to break down and obviate a specialized bureaucratic caste by training everyone in deliberative and administrative activity (SPN, pp. 27–28), on instituting a common school curriculum which establishes 'new relations between intellectual and industrial work' (SPN, p. 33), on industrial production as the basis of a new mentality and morality and on the sexual question (SPN, pp. 304–6).

Gramsci's approach to Futurism (represented in the second part of this section by three texts written between 1913 and 1922) was uneven, but it also became bound up at a certain point with the issue of proletarian culture. At the time of the Livorno split between Communists and Socialists (1921), Gramsci is evidently attracted by the Futurists' equation of artistic modernism with industrialism and the sweeping away of *fin de siècle* bourgeois cultural residues. His treatment of Futurism as a bourgeois vanguard art produced in a phase when the proletariat is not yet able to make its own organically revolutionary art is scored through with 'productivist' ideas and is very much of a piece with his interest in Taylorism and the rationalization of factory production. By the time he wrote to Trotsky in the following year, this enthusiasm for Futurism had soured, and a prison note of 1930 entitled 'The Futurists' (Q11 §24) would be caustic: 'A group of schoolboys who escaped from a Jesuit boarding school, whooped it up in a nearby wood, and were led back under the policeman's stick.'

These early writings were, inevitably, shaped by the culture in which Gramsci was working. This was an important period of challenge and dispute within Italian high culture between different generations of intellectuals and rival centres and traditions: Futurism against academic art, cosmopolitan intellectual models like Bergson and William James against provincial traditions of study and scholarship. A younger generation of bourgeois intellectuals had emerged since 1900 whose mouthpieces were a series of periodicals produced mainly in Florence (*La Voce* 1908–16, *Lacerba* 1913–15, *L'Unità* 1911–20) with to one side Benedetto Croce's highly influential *La Critica* (1903–51). These reviews introduced much of the philosophical and artistic culture on which Gramsci drew in his formative period as a socialist militant: Bergson, Croce, Sorel, Rolland, Barbusse, Marinetti. His own *Ordine Nuovo* was also initially influenced by these models of cultural review around which intellectual vanguards had formed. In a formal sense, Gramsci broke with the culture of these reviews when some of their key collaborators (such as Papini and Prezzolini of *La Voce*) went back to their former militarist and reactionary line during the war and as he himself became more committed to Marxism: for instance in 1918 he criticized both *L'Unità* and *La Voce* for 'utopianism' and 'messianism'. Yet the heterogeneous cultural matrix which the reviews constituted influenced him deeply, often with contradictory results. The anti-positivist philosophy they represented served him as a lever with which to criticize the reformist PSI leadership and to hail the Bolshevik revolution as a 'revolution against *Capital*' (see SPW I, pp. 24–37). But it had also given him in 1916 a questionably vague notion of how historical change is culturally 'prepared' which would not be revised until he came into closer contact with Marxism and practical political work. In the same way, there are untheorized contradictions between his adoption of Croce's 'language-as-art' conception and a more socio-historical view of linguistic change (see I 3), or between a materialist account of the degeneracy of the Turin theatre and the Crocean aesthetic notion of art as the creation of 'phantasms', of pure beauty and spirit (considered radically innovative at the time), which he invokes against it (see I 20). In fact these contradictions show how Gramsci could develop an astute materialist analysis of major changes that were taking place within culture while remaining essentially locked into an idealist aesthetic. This was a period in which the apparatuses of culture had started to undergo wholesale reorganization as an effect of Italy's industrial revolution at the end of the nineteenth century. 'Mass taste' was beginning to be catered for by the extension of entrepreneurial control over the entertainment industry, the conversion of theatres for use as vaudevilles, the opening of cinemas, the takeover by business interests of artistic and musical clubs and societies. Gramsci is unhesitant in condemning these practices – for instance in his sustained attack on the Chiarella brothers' theatrical consortium (I 14–17); but the vantage point from which his criticisms are made remains at this stage that of 'art' conceived rather abstractly. It is not until the Prison Notebooks that the relations between art, culture and the social formation begin to be conceived in more concrete historical terms.

POLITICS AND CULTURE

1 For a Cultural Association

Personally, but also on behalf of many others, I approve of comrade Pellegrino's proposal for the creation of a cultural association for our Turin comrades and those resident here from outside.

Although the moment is not very favourable, I believe that it can very well be done. There are many comrades who, because of the immaturity of their convictions and because of their impatience with the painstaking work that is needed, have left the organizations, letting themselves be carried away by amusements. The association would satisfy their instinctive needs, it would provide a place of relaxation and education that would once again attract them to our political movement, our ideal.

This initiative, to which all comrades will want to give their support, may be a way to involve our comrades enrolled in distant sections, a problem never solved because of the difficulty in finding a field of common interest for carrying out an activity.

Bartolomeo Botto

The Turin edition of *Avanti!* has warmly welcomed Pellegrino's proposal and the support it has aroused. In Botto's letter there are some very interesting points which we believe it opportune to develop and present systematically to our comrades.

In Turin there is no organization whatsoever of popular culture. It is best not to speak of the Popular University.[1] It has never been alive, it has never functioned so as to respond to a real need. Its origin is bourgeois and it is based on a vague and confused criterion of spiritual humanitarianism. It has the same effectiveness as charitable institutions which believe that with a bowl of soup they can satisfy the physical needs of wretches who cannot appease their hunger and who move the tender hearts of their superiors to pity.

The cultural association which the Socialists should promote must have class aims and limits. It must be a proletarian institution seeking definite goals. The proletariat, at a certain moment of its development and history, recognizes that the complexity of its life lacks a necessary organ and it creates it, with its strength, with its good will, for its own ends.

In Turin the proletariat has reached a point of development that is one of the highest, if not the highest, in Italy. Through its political activity the Socialist section has reached a very distinct class individuality. Its economic organizations are strong. In the co-operative movement, it has succeeded in creating a powerful institution like the Co-operative Alliance.[2] It is understood,

[1] Gramsci had criticized the Popular Universities (*Università popolari:* institutes of adult education) in an *Avanti!* article of 29 December 1916 (SG, pp. 61–64, CT, pp. 673–76) because their curricula merely copied those of existing bourgeois universities, with no understanding of the different needs and background of people who had not been through secondary school. In the Prison Notebooks he compares them with 'the first contacts of English merchants and the negroes of Africa' (SPN, p. 330).

[2] The Turin Co-operative Alliance was founded in 1900 as the commercial branch of the General Workers' Association. Its headquarters were to be repeatedly destroyed by the fascists. It was disbanded in 1923.

therefore, that the need to integrate political and economic activity with an organ of cultural activity has arisen and is most strongly felt in Turin. The need for this integration will also arise and take hold in other parts of Italy. And the proletarian movement will gain in compactness and in energy for conquest.

One of the most serious gaps in our activities is this: we wait for the present moment to discuss problems and to determine the direction of our action. Out of urgency, we provide hurried solutions to problems, in the sense that not all those who take part in the movement have mastered the exact terms of the problems. Consequently, when they do follow the strategy established, they do so out of a spirit of discipline and out of the trust which they have in their leaders, more than out of an inner conviction, out of a rational spontaneity. The result is that at every important hour of history there occurs a breaking of the ranks, a giving in, internal disputes, personal issues. This also explains the phenomena of idolatry, which are a contradiction in our movement, letting back in through the window the authoritarianism that was kicked out of the door.

There is no widespread resolute conviction. There is no long term preparation that makes one ready to deliberate at any moment, that determines immediate agreements, effective and profound agreements that reinforce action.

The cultural association should see to this preparation, should create these convictions. In it one should be able to discuss in a disinterested way – that is, without waiting to be stimulated by current events – whatever interests or might one day interest the proletarian movement.

Furthermore, political and economic action presupposes moral, religious and philosophical problems which the economic and political bodies cannot discuss in their own organizations. Nor can they disseminate the proper solutions to them. Such problems are of great importance. They determine so-called spiritual crises and every so often confront us with so-called 'affairs'. Socialism is an integral vision of life: it has a philosophy, a mystique, a morality. The association would be the proper place to discuss these problems, clarify them and propagate them.

To a large extent, the question of the 'intellectuals' would also be solved. The intellectuals represent a dead weight in our movement because they do not have a specific role in it which fits their capabilities. They would find it; their intellectualism, their intelligence, would be put to the test.

By establishing this cultural institute, the socialists would deal a fierce blow to the dogmatic and intolerant mentality created in the Italian people by Catholic and Jesuit education. The Italian populace lacks the spirit of disinterested solidarity, love of free discussion, the desire to discover the truth with uniquely human means, which reason and intelligence provide. The Socialists would give an active and positive example of this. They would contribute powerfully to the creation of a new morality, freer and more open-minded than the present one, more inclined to accept their principles and goals. In England and Germany there were and are powerful organizations of proletarian and socialist culture. In England the Fabian Society, which belonged to the International, is particularly well known. Its task is to offer a forum for a thorough and popular discussion of the economic and moral problems which life brings or will bring to the attention of the proletariat. It has succeeded, moreover, in involving a large part of the English intellectual and university world in this work of civilization and liberation.

Given the environment and the maturity of the proletariat in Turin, the first core group of a distinctly socialist and proletarian cultural organization could and should arise here. Together with the party and the Labour Confederation, it would become the third organ of the movement for the vindication of the Italian working class.

Unsigned, *Avanti!*, Piedmont edition, 18 December 1917.

2 Philanthropy, Good Will and Organization

This reply to the article signed 'Most humbly' and called 'Tra la cultura e l'ignoranza' (Between Culture and Ignorance), is intended as a practical illustration of one of the major goals which the proposed cultural association should set itself.[3]

---

[3] 'Most humbly' (l'Umilissimo) was Mario Guarnieri (1886–1974), one of the three national secretaries of the Italian Metalworkers' Federation, who had contributed an article to *Avanti!* of 20 December 1917 opposing Gramsci's proposals for a cultural association: 'Whoever wishes to be cultured, be he a socialist or a worker, already has the

'Most humbly' is an organizer. I think that as such he should have clear and precise criteria on organization, more so than any other militant in the socialist movement: if it is true that the concept of organization is basic in socialist thought, it is also true that the profession, the specific activity of the organizer, bears with it a greater amount of responsibility.

I say this because 'Most humbly' writes and raises objections as a 'disorganized' person might. In other words he fails to transfer the concepts that inform his specific activity to another activity. He does not even bother to consider whether his objections might apply to his activity. Nor does he bother to consider whether those who belong to his federation, when they reflect on what he has written, might not generalize it and dissolve the organization because the workshop is sufficient to create the proletarian soul – just as the chance to buy books and reviews is sufficient for the person who wants to become 'educated', because capitalist society naturally engenders the class struggle, just as it naturally engenders class thinking and the clash between two ways of thinking, two sets of ideals.

Because of his activity, however, 'Most humbly' is convinced that the workshop is not enough, that class solidarity (if it is to take active effect and triumph) must be organized, disciplined and limited. In other words, he is convinced that nature, necessity, is only such in so far as it is transformed, through thought, into an exact awareness of ends and means. Therefore, he propagandizes the need to create specific organs of economic struggle capable of articulating this necessity, of purifying it of every sentimental and individualistic obstruction and of forming 'proletarians' in the socialist sense.

Why not transfer these concepts to cultural activity? Because 'Most humbly', like so many others in this fine country, lacks the habit of generalization, of synthesis, which is necessary if one wants complete people and not people who take each instance in isolation, of now I see you now I don't, of tomorrow yes today no, of ifs and buts, etc., etc.

---

opportunity, even though no organ of popular culture exists. According to his tastes and inclinations he can find books, newspapers, magazines. Participating in our movement contributes greatly to the development of one's intelligence. . . . If someone has the necessary requisites for developing his own culture, there is no reason to make him remain ignorant. But we should avoid wanting to make everybody cultured because, in many cases, a false culture stuffed with a bit of everything can be more harmful than simple ignorance' (Quoted in CF, p. 520).

'Most humbly' has a concept of culture that is inaccurate too. He believes that culture equals knowing a little of everything, that it equals the Popular University. I give culture this meaning: exercise of thought, acquisition of general ideas, habit of connecting causes and effects. For me, everybody is already cultured because everybody thinks, everybody connects causes and effects. But they are empirically, primordially cultured, not organically. They therefore waver, disband, soften, or become violent, intolerant, quarrelsome, according to the occasion and the circumstances. I'll make myself clearer: I have a Socratic idea of culture; I believe that it means thinking well, whatever one thinks, and therefore acting well, whatever one does. And since I know that culture too is a basic concept of socialism, because it integrates and makes concrete the vague concept of freedom of thought, I would like it to be enlivened by the other concept, that of organization. Let us organize culture in the same way that we seek to organize any practical activity. Philanthropically, the bourgeoisie have decided to offer the proletariat the Popular Universities. As a counterproposal to philanthropy, let us offer solidarity, organization. Let us give the means to good will, without which it will always remain sterile and barren. It is not the lecture that should interest us, but the detailed work of discussing and investigating problems, work in which everybody participates, to which everybody contributes, in which everybody is both master and disciple.

Naturally, for it to be an organization and not a confusion, it must interpret a need. Is this need widespread or is it that of a few? The few can begin: nothing is more pedagogically effective than an active example for revealing needs to others, for making them acutely felt. One can do without the *buffet* for the few and tomorrow one can do without it for the many. Culture understood in the humanistic sense is itself a joy and an intrinsic satisfaction. The clubs, the groups cannot suffice. They have practical needs and are themselves caught up in the vortex of current events. And then there is another reason. As well as lacking the ability to generalize, many Italians have another deficiency, which is historically due to the lack of any tradition of democratic life in our country: they are unable to carry on different activities in a single place. The majority are people of just one activity. The external separation of organizations will serve to develop the individual faculties better, for a wider and more perfect synthesis.

And there will be no shortage of problems to discuss, not least because the problems must not so much count in and for themselves, as for the way in which they are treated. But this can be dealt with another time if the proposal has really found an echo among comrades or if the proclaimed necessity of the association is not merely someone's wishful thinking.

Unsigned, *Avanti!*, Piedmont edition, 24 December 1917.

3 A Single Language and Esperanto[4]

Is there that much point in discussing just now a problem like that of a single language? If it really is a problem and not a scholastic question, I think there is. I am convinced that all man's historical activity is a unity, that thought is a unity. I thus see in the solution of any one of the problems of culture the potential solution of all the others. I believe it is useful to accustom people's minds to grasp this unity in the many facets of life, to accustom them to the organic search for truth and clarity and to applying the fundamental principles of a doctrine to every occasion.

Instransigence occurs in thought before it occurs in action, and it must be adopted for all thought as well as for all action.[5] Only when we have trained ourselves in all the difficulties of logic, to grasp all the correspondences between idea and idea and between thought and action, can we say that we are really

---

[4] This article is Gramsci's final contribution to a brief altercation with his editors on *Avanti!* in 1918 over the desirability of the PSI's promoting the study and use of Esperanto, the international language invented by L.L. Zamenhof in 1887. Earlier, Gramsci had published a reader's letter proposing the adoption of Esperanto, and had appended to it his sub-editorial comment criticizing the suggestion on grounds similar to those stated here (CF, pp. 592–95). The *Avanti!* editors opposed Gramsci by arguing that, although he was right in theory, Esperanto could still be useful in practice, and they continued to publish pieces in its favour. Gramsci replied, again anonymously, presenting himself as a student 'preparing my thesis on the history of the language, trying to apply the critical methods of historical materialism to this research as well'. He pointed out the absurdity of rejecting an idea in theory and yet supporting it in practice (CF, pp. 612–13). The debate therefore led Gramsci to make a more or less explicit attack on the backwardness and superficiality of the party's approach to cultural questions.

[5] On the political meaning of 'intransigence' in 1918 see footnote 10 below, p. 31. In one of his earlier articles on Esperanto, Gramsci had written: 'Should not intransigence be understood primarily as intransigence with wrongheaded ideas?'

ourselves, really responsible for what we do, because then we can foresee the probable repercussions of our every activity in the social and economic environment and can praise or blame ourselves for these repercussions. We will thus not leave the job of weighing up our varied activity to caprice, to the play of forces beyond our comprehension.

The advocates of a single language are worried by the fact that while the world contains a number of people who would like to communicate directly with one another, there is an endless number of different languages which restrict the ability to communicate. This is a *cosmopolitan,* not an international anxiety, that of the bourgeois who travels for business or pleasure, of nomads more than of stable productive citizens. They would like artificially to create *consequences* which as yet lack the necessary *conditions,* and since their activity is merely arbitrary, all they manage to do is waste the time and energy of those who take them seriously. They would like artificially to create a definitively inflexible language which will not admit changes in space and time. In this they come head on against the science of language, which teaches that language in and for itself is an expression of beauty more than a means of communication, and that the history of the fortunes and diffusion of a given language depends strictly on the complex social activity of the people who speak it.[6]

This anxiety for a single language has appeared in various periods and various forms. It arose under the impetus of seventeenth-century dogmatism and the eighteenth-century French Enlightenment. The aim was to give rise to the language of the bourgeois cosmopolis, the unity of bourgeois thought created by the propaganda of the Encyclopaedists. Catherine II of Russia made the state spend a stack of money for the compilation of a dictionary of all languages, the cocoon of the inter-linguistic butterfly. But the cocoon never matured, because there was no live embryo inside it.

In Italy this anxiety became a national one and was expressed in the Accademia della Crusca, purism and the ideas of

---

[6] Gramsci seems here to be invoking two different (and incompatible) 'sciences of language' – that of Croce (which saw language as the expression, like art, of individual intuitions) and a more 'sociolinguistic' conception deriving from G.I. Ascoli (1829–1907). See F. Lo Piparo, *Lingua intellettuali egemonia in Gramsci*, Bari 1979, p. 53 and the introduction to Section V below.

Manzoni.[7] The purists presented the ideal of a definitive language: that of certain writers of the fourteenth and sixteenth centuries which should be perpetuated because it was the only beautiful language, the only true Italian. But the beauty of a language is not fixed in time and space; it does not even exist. It is not the language that is beautiful but poetic masterpieces, and their beauty consists in their adequately expressing the writer's inner world. In this sense a line from the *Divine Comedy* is as beautiful as a child's expression of naïve wonder as it admires a toy.[8]

Manzoni asked himself: now that Italy is formed, how can the Italian language be created? He answered: all Italians will have to speak Tuscan and the Italian state will have to recruit its elementary teachers in Tuscany. Tuscan will be substituted for the numerous dialects spoken in the various regions and, with Italy formed, the Italian language will be formed too. Manzoni managed to find government support and start the publication of a *Novo dizionario* which was supposed to contain the true Italian language. But the *Novo dizionario* remained half-finished and teachers were recruited among educated people in all regions of Italy. It had transpired that a scholar of the history of the language, Graziadio Isaia Ascoli, had set some thirty pages against the hundreds of pages by Manzoni in order to demonstrate: that not even a national language can be created artificially, by order of the state; that the Italian language was being formed by itself and would be formed only in so far as the shared life of the nation gave rise to numerous and stable contacts between the various parts of the nation; that the spread of a particular language is due to the productive activity of the writings, trade and commerce of the people who speak that particular language. In the fourteenth and sixteenth centuries Tuscany had writers like Dante, Boccaccio, Petrarch,

[7] The reference is to some of the parties in the perennial Italian debate, the 'question of the language', on the best form of the vernacular to adopt as standard Italian (see introduction to Section V). The Accademia della Crusca published a dictionary in 1612 which listed 'pure' Tuscan words (i.e. those of the 14th century literary language, some of them obsolete) to the virtual exclusion of non-Tuscan ones. Other 'purists' followed suit. Alessandro Manzoni (1785–1873) opposed them by advocating modern educated spoken Florentine as a model.

[8] These statements draw on early Crocean aesthetics. Croce argued (*Estetica*, [1902], Bari 1965, pp. 16–17) that the difference between a simple linguistic expression and a work of art was one of quantity, not quality.

Machiavelli and Guicciardini who spread the Tuscan language. It had bankers, craftsmen and manufacturers who carried Tuscan products and the names of these products throughout Italy. Later, it reduced its productivity of goods and books and thus its linguistic productivity as well. A few years ago, Professor Alfredo Panzini published a dictionary of the modern spoken language; it shows how many Milanese words have reached as far as Sicily and Apulia. Milan sends newspapers, reviews, books, goods and commercial travellers throughout Italy and it therefore also sends some characteristic expressions of the Italian language spoken by its inhabitants.

If a single language, one that is also spoken in a given region and has a living source to which it can refer, cannot be imposed on the limited field of the nation, how then could an international language take root when it is completely artificial and mechanical, completely ahistorical, not fed by great writers, lacking the expressive richness which comes from the variety of dialects, from the variety of forms assumed in different times? But they reply: Esperanto intends to be no more than an auxiliary language, and anyway the best proof of its validity is the fact that over a million people already speak it and it allows you to dispense with interpreters at international congresses and to work quickly. They say: the Esperantists are like the man who walked in front of the philosopher who denied movement. But the comparison is inexact. The Esperantists understand each other at congresses *of Esperantists,* just as a group of deaf-mutes would understand each other at their congress by signs and nods. We would not advise someone to learn deaf and dumb language for this reason. In a congress where one had to express and communicate concepts and arguments which have a long history, which are the present moment of a process of historical becoming that has been going on for centuries, the use of Esperanto would fetter thought, it would force one into distortions and generalizations, into the strangest and most dangerous imprecisions. Furthermore, congress delegates would have to be chosen from among Esperantists, and this would introduce a criterion of selection completely extraneous to political currents and ideas. The justification of the 'movement' is thus no more than sophistry, it can only seem persuasive for a moment. And the argument for the *auxiliary* function of Esperanto collapses as well. When might Esperanto be auxiliary? And to whom? The majority of citizens carry out their activity stably in a fixed place and do not need to correspond too often by letter with other countries. Let us have no doubt about it: Esperanto, the single language, is nothing but a vain idea, an illusion of cosmopolitan, humanitarian, democratic mentalities which have not yet been made fertile and been shaken by historical critical thinking.

What attitude should the Socialists adopt towards the promoters of single languages, the Esperantists? They must simply uphold their own doctrines and fight those who would like the Party to become the official champion and propagator of Esperanto (the Milan section must still house a request from comrade Seassaro which explicitly asks for full adoption of Esperanto by the Party). The Socialists are struggling for the creation of the economic and political conditions necessary to install collectivism and the International. When the International is formed, it is possible that the increased contacts between peoples, the methodical and regular integration of large masses of workers, will slowly bring about a reciprocal adjustment between the Aryo-European languages and will probably extend them throughout the world, because of the influence the new civilization will exert. But this process can then happen freely and spontaneously. Linguistic pressures are exerted only from the bottom upwards. Books have little influence on changes in forms of speech. Books act to regulate and conserve the most widespread and oldest linguistic forms. The same thing that happens to the dialects of a nation, which slowly assimilate literary forms and lose their peculiar characteristics, will probably happen to literary languages when confronted with a language that surmounts them. But this language could be one of those existing now: that for instance of the first country to found socialism, which would become attractive and would seem beautiful because through it our civilization, asserted in one part of the world, is expressed, because in it books will be written that no longer will be critical but will be descriptive of lived experiences, because in it novels and poems will be written that will vibrate with the new life that has been established, with the sacrifices made to consolidate it and with the hope that the same will occur elsewhere.

Only by working for the coming of the International will Socialists be working for the possible coming of a single language. The attempts that one can make now belong to the realm of Utopia. They are a product of the same mentality that wanted the phalansteries and happy colonies.[9] Each new social stratum that emerges in history, that organizes itself for the good fight, introduces new currents and new uses into the language and explodes the fixed schemes established by the grammarians for the fortuitous convenience of teaching. In history, in social life, nothing is fixed, rigid or definitive. And nothing ever will be. New truths increase the inheritance of knowledge. New and ever superior needs are created by new living conditions. New moral and intellectual curiosities goad the spirit and compel it to renew itself, to improve itself, to change the linguistic forms of expression by taking them from foreign languages, by reviving dead forms and by changing meanings and grammatical functions. In this constant effort towards perfection, in this flow of liquefied volcanic matter, utopias, arbitrary acts and vain illusions like that of a present single language and of Esperanto burn up and are annihilated.

Signed A.G., *Il Grido del Popolo*, 16 February 1918.

4 Culture and Class Struggle

Camillo Prampolini's *Giustizia* is offering its readers a survey of the opinions expressed in the socialist weeklies on the controversy between the editors of *Avanti!* and the parliamentary group.[10] Its latest instalment has the jocular title 'The intrepreters of the proletariat' and it explains:

The *Difesa* of Florence and the *Grido* of Turin, the two most rigid and cultural exponents of the doctrine of intransigence, conduct

[9] i.e. the mentality of the 'utopian socialists'. Marx and Engels had remarked on Fourier, Owen and Cabet in the *Communist Manifesto*: 'They still dream of experimental realization of their social utopias, of founding little "phalanstères", of establishing "home colonies", of setting up a "little Icaria" – duodecimo editions of the New Jerusalem – and to realize all these castles in the air, they are compelled to appeal to the feelings and purses of the bourgeois.'

[10] Camillo Prampolini (1859–1930) was one of the leaders of the reformist socialists and editor of their organ *La Giustizia*. When this article was written, the PSI leadership, supported by *Avanti!* was backing the line of intransigence (i.e. refusal to collaborate with a bourgeois government) against the collaborationist parliamentary group.

broad theoretical speculations which we cannot possible summarize
and which there would in any case be little point in reproducing,
since – despite the fact that these two newspapers claim to be genuine
interpreters of the proletariat and to have the great mass with them
– our readers would not be sufficiently learned to understand their
language.

And the implacable *Giustizia*, to avoid accusations of 'malevolent
irony', quotes two passages at random from an article in the
Grido, concluding: 'It would be hard to achieve greater
proletarian clarity than this.'

Comrade Prampolini offers us an occasion to take up a
question of no small moment with respect to socialist
propaganda.

Let us admit that the article in the *Grido* was the ultimate in
difficulty and proletarian obscurity. Could we have written it
otherwise? It was in reply to an article in *La Stampa*, and the
Stampa piece had used a precise philosophical language which
was neither a superfluity nor an affectation, since every current
of thought has its particular language and vocabulary. Our reply
needed to stay on the same ground as our opponent's thought,
we needed to show that even with, indeed because of that current
of thought (which is our own, the current of thought of a socialism
which is neither scrappily put together nor childishly simple), the
collaborationist line was wrong. In order to be *easy* we would have
had to falsify and impoverish a debate which hinged on concepts
of the utmost importance, on the most fundamental and precious
substance of our spirit. Doing that is not being easy: it amounts
to fraud, like the wine merchant who passes off coloured water
as Barolo or Lambrusco. A concept which is difficult in itself
cannot be made easy when it is expressed without becoming
vulgarized. And pretending that this vulgarization is still the same
concept is to act like trivial demagogues, tricksters in logic and
propaganda.

So why Camillo Prampolini's cheap irony about the
'interpreters' of the proletariat who can't make themselves
understood by the proletarians? Because Prampolini, with all his
good sense and rule of thumb, thinks in abstractions. The
proletariat is a practical construct: in reality there are individual
proletarians, more or less educated, more or less equipped by the
class struggle to understand the most refined socialist concepts.

The socialist weeklies adapt themselves to the average level of the regional strata they address. Yet the tone of the articles and the propaganda must always be just above this average level, so that there is a stimulus to intellectual progress, so that at least a number of workers can emerge from the generic blur of the mulling-over of pamphlets and consolidate their spirit in a higher critical perception of history and the world in which they live and struggle.

Turin is a modern city. Capitalist activity throbs in it with the crashing din of massive workshops which concentrate tens of thousands of proletarians into a few thousand cubic meters. Turin has over half a million inhabitants. The human race is divided here into two classes with distinguishing characteristics not found elsewhere in Italy. We don't have democrats and petty reformists in our way. We have a bold and unscrupulous capitalist bourgeoisie, we have strong organizations, we have a complex and varied socialist movement, rich in impulses and intellectual needs.

Does comrade Prampolini think that in Turin the Socialists should conduct their propaganda on shepherds' pipes, talking idyllically about goodness, justice and Arcadian fraternity? Here the class struggle lives in all its raw grandeur, it is not a rhetorical fiction, a projection of scientific and predictive concepts into social phenomena that are still nascent and developing.

Of course, in Turin too the proletarian class is continually absorbing new individuals who are not intellectually developed, not able to understand the full significance of the exploitation to which they are subjected. For them it will always be necessary to start from first principles, from elementary propaganda. But the others? The proletarians who have already progressed intellectually and are already used to the language of socialist criticism? Who ought to be sacrificed, whom should one address? The proletariat is less complicated than might appear. They have spontaneously formed an intellectual and cultural hierarchy, and reciprocal education is at work where the activity of the writers and propagandists cannot penetrate. In workers' circles and leagues, in conversations outside the factory, the word of socialist criticism is dissected, propagated, made ductile and malleable for every mind and every culture. In a complex and varied environment like that of a major industrial city the organs of capillary transmission of opinion, which the will of the leaders would never succeed in creating and setting up, arise spontaneously.

And are we supposed to remain for ever at the Georgics, at rustic and idyllic socialism? Are we supposed to go on repeating the ABC with monotonous insistence, because there is always someone who doesn't know it?

We are reminded here of an old university professor who for forty years was meant to be running a course of theoretical philosophy on the 'final evolutionary being'. Every year he began a 'review' of the precursors of the system and he talked about Lao-tse, the old man-young boy of Chinese philosophy, the man born at the age of eighty.[11] And every year he started talking about Lao-tse again, because new students had come along and they too had to learn up on Lao-tse from the professor's lips. And so the 'final evolutionary being' became a legend, an evanescent chimera, and the only living reality for all those generations of students was Lao-tse, the old man-young boy, the child born at the age of eighty.

This is what happens to the class struggle in Camillo Prampolini's old *Giustizia:* it too is an evanescent chimera, and every week what it writes about is the old man-young boy who never matures, who never evolves, who never becomes the 'final evolutionary being', yet whom one would expect to reach fruition at last after all this slow evolution, after so much tenacious work of evangelical education.

Unsigned, *Il Grido del Popolo*, 25 May 1918.

5 Serial Novels[12]

The serial novel is, if it can be so described, a powerful factor in the formation of the mentality and morality of the people. Millions of women and young people read these fables offered

---

[11] Lao-tse (c. 604–531 B.C.), Chinese philosopher held to be the founder of Taoism. According to legend, he remained in his mother's womb for sixty years and was born with white hair. This anecdote of the professor and the Lao-tse paradox was a favourite one of Gramsci's. See below, II 15, VI and X4.

[12] This article was published in *Il Grido del Popolo* under Gramsci's editorship, but its attribution to Gramsci (originally made in SG of 1958) has been called into question by

in parsimonious doses by the big and even the small newspapers. The story runs for whole seasons at a time: the art of the novelist consists essentially in ending each instalment with an adventure that starts with an enigmatic sentence. The genre originated in the nineteenth century. By 1830 it already had astute practitioners, and it reached a kind of peak around 1840 with Alexandre Dumas, Eugène Sue and George Sand, who was very skilful at stimulating her readers' curiosity.[13] Paul Féval, Ponson du Terrail and Gaboriau continued the tradition of the serial novel.[14] Ponson was a rambling and chaotic writer but he made brilliant use of mystery effects, contriving astounding phrases for the final line of each instalment.

With Sue, Dumas, Sand and Féval, the serial novel still belongs to literature. Writing too much harms one's style, yet these are writers, and also original inventors. *The Three Musketeers* may more or less take its inspiration from previous historical novels but, in a certain sense, it has a new physiognomy. It is original. *The Mysteries of Paris* was a genuine creation: through it a new world was introduced into literary tradition.[15] Féval's novels are full of energy; he has style and occasionally he is brilliant. George Sand belongs indisputably to the history of literature.

With Ponson du Terrail and Gaboriau, literature declines (although the latter conceived a new genre, the detective novel). It is after them that the modern serial novel begins, which nearly always has a most banal form and a stupid content. It is dependent

---

Sergio Caprioglio (NM, p. 61) who suggests it is probably a translation from an untraced text by J.H. Rosny. In a theatre article of 21 April 1918 (CF, p. 994), Gramsci quoted a passage from Rosny that was almost identical to part of this article. We have chosen to keep it in this edition because of its connections with Gramsci's work on popular fiction during his imprisonment (see section IX below).

[13] Between 1840 and 1850 almost all the French novelists published their work in the daily press. Books were expensive and most readers made do with those printed in the papers, which could be cut out like coupons and collected once their format was standardized at the bottom of a page. The sudden broadening-out of the novel to a relatively mass readership was accompanied, in the case of novelists like Sue and Sand, by an interest in socialist and philanthropic subject matter. Serial novels began to appear in Italy in the 1820s, but the medium did not come into its own until the rise of the big circulation dailies in the last quarter of the nineteenth century.

[14] Paul Féval (1817–87), Pierre-Alexis Ponson du Terrail (1829–71), Émile Gaboriau (1832–73): the last two invented, respectively, the adventurer Rocambole and detective Lecoq, precursor of Conan Doyle's Sherlock Holmes.

[15] Dumas' *The Three Musketeers* was first published in 1844, and Sue's *The Mysteries of Paris* in 1842–43. For later comments by Gramsci on these novels, see Section IX below.

on the serial novel that preceded it but, with a few honourable exceptions, has completely lost all its character and style. It retains nothing from its Romantic forerunners except the clever and sensational plot, which is also carried over into theatrical works after the nauseating example of Dennery.[16] Now it is a lachrymose literature only suitable for stupefying the women, girls and youngsters who feed on it. It is also often a source of corruption. The detective novel, started in France by Gaboriau and perfected by an English author (Conan Doyle) – who took good advantage of *Murders in the Rue Morgue* and *The Purloined Letter* by Edgar Poe – has often degenerated. It may perhaps have influenced the increase in crime among adolescent loafers.

In short, the serial novel has become a rather nauseating commodity. The great majority of its suppliers no longer write their own works. They distribute 'plots' to the poor devils who have to extract an infinite number of chapters from them. They pay at two, three or four soldi a line what the newspapers will pay a lira and sometimes more for. Often, these authors also patch up novels brought to them by poor starving devils. Someone has even set up an office with a staff that makes novels to measure.

Who is responsible for this horrifying state of affairs? To some extent everybody: the public, which often has abominable tastes; the authors, who for speculation open shops for novels as one would open a haberdasher's; the newspaper editors, full of prejudices and eager to sell their papers at any cost.

Is it possible to react? Perhaps. Why could not talented writers write adventure novels in a simple style but with an elegant and engaging content? The baroque reflections and the idiotic dialogue of the fashionable serials could be substituted by reflections and dialogue which, if not astounding, might at least be intelligent. Many young people who eagerly turn out mediocre and self-styled literary novels could, with luck, write interesting popular novels. Hence, the prejudice by which the serial novel is relegated to the lower depths of literature needs to disappear. This prejudice has consigned the people, who are not always in a position to control the situation, into the hands of speculators whose activity corrupts.

As a genre the adventure novel *per se* has had ancestors in *The Odyssey*, *Robinson Crusoe* and *Don Quixote*. If fate were to bring

---

[16] Adolphe Dennery (1811–99), co-author of *Les Deux Orphelines*; see also IX 14 below.

Eugène Sue, Dumas and Féval – whose works were read with real passion – back to life, it would perform an inestimable service to the mentality of the people.

Unsigned, *Il Grido del Popolo*, 25 May 1918.

6 [Communism and Art]

In our last issue we wanted to commemorate the first centenary of the birth of Walt Whitman (31 May 1819) in the worthiest way possible: by translating and publishing one of the finest works of the great American poet, 'To a Foil'd European Revolutionaire'.

The Turin press review office relentlessly blanked out the poem. They even forced us to suppress the bibliographical note in which we offended the statutory laws and decrees of this country by writing that the poem was published for the first time in 1856 with the title 'Hymn of Liberty for Asia, Europe, Africa and America' and then republished, with additions and corrections, in 1867 and 1871 under the title 'To a Foil'd European Revolutionaire'.

The officials of public security, the lawyers and the cast-off journalists who run the office of censorship on behalf of the parliamentary-democratic-bureaucratic-police state do not need to know that Walt Whitman never was an agitator, a man of action, an 'instigator', for whom poetry was a means of revolutionary propaganda. They have committed an offence against the pure creation of artistic fantasy. As we write, we cannot quell the anger that surges through us when we recall this miserable act of censorship. Our anger is all the greater when we think that among the so-called intellectuals runs the widely held prejudice that the workers' movement and communism are enemies of beauty and art, and that the friend to art in favour of creation and the disinterested contemplation of beauty is supposedly the present regime of merchants greedy for wealth and exploitation, who perform their essential activity by barbarously destroying life and beauty. It is the regime of traffickers who appreciate genius only when it is converted into monetary value, who have raised the forging of masterpieces to a national industry, who have subjugated poetry to their laws of supply and demand. While they artificially 'launch' the literary adventurers, they let first-class artists die of starvation and desperation, those whom 'posterity will avenge since, sooner or later, real values will prevail' (a liberal-aesthetic consolation that absolves grocers, corner-shopkeepers and the officials of public security, exponents of the regime, from the crimes committed against the living creators of beauty).

No, communism will not obscure beauty and grace: one must understand the impetus by which workers feel drawn to the contemplation of art, to the creation of art, how deeply they feel offended in their humanity because the slavery of wages and work cuts them off from a world that integrates man's life, that makes it worth living. The struggle of the Russian communists to multiply schools, theatres and opera houses, to make galleries accessible to the crowds, the fact that villages and factories which distinguish themselves in the sector of production are awarded with aesthetic and cultural entertainments, show that, once in power, the proletariat tends to establish the reign of beauty and grace, to elevate the dignity and freedom of those who create beauty.

In Russia, the two people's commissars so far chosen for the office of Public Education have been an extremely fine judge of art, Lunacharsky, and a great poet, Maxim Gorky.[17] In Italy the post has been occupied successively by such masons and dealers as Credaro, Daneo and Berenini, and the power to blank out the songs of Walt Whitman is left to the officials of public security.[18]

L'Ordine Nuovo, 14 June 1919.

[17] Anatoly Lunarcharsky (1875–1933) directed Narkompros (People's Education Commissariat) from 1917 to 1929. Maxim Gorky (1868–1936) was not in fact a Commissar for Education but, at the time Gramsci was writing (1919), was collaborating closely with Narkompros.

[18] Whitman's poem, translated by Togliatti, was later published in *L'Ordine Nuovo* on 12 July 1919.

7 The Problem of the School

In opening, with this note, the discussion on the problem of the school we want to lay down the criteria with which we would like the discussion to be conducted.[19]

The problem of the school (like any other problem which concerns a general activity of the state, a necessary function in society) must be studied as part of the sphere of action of the state of workers' and peasants' councils. We are aiming to stimulate a mentality of construction, of comrades already ideally organized in the state of the Councils, already ideally active and at work in evoking all the organs of the new social life. The educational propaganda conducted so far by the Socialists has been largely negative and critical: it could not have been otherwise. Today, after the positive experiences of our Russian comrades, it can and must be otherwise if we want to ensure that their experiences have not been in vain for us. We must develop these experiences critically, paring away from them what is specific to Russia, dependent on the particular conditions in which the Soviet Republic found Russian society when it came to power. We must pick out and establish what in them is of permanent necessity to communist society, dependent on the needs and aspirations of the class of workers and peasants exploited to the same degree in all parts of the globe.

The problem of the school is at once both technical and political. In a parliamentary-democratic state there can be no technical and political solution to the problem of the school. Ministers of education are placed in office because they belong to a political party, not because they know how to administer and direct the educational function of the state. It cannot even in all honesty be claimed that the bourgeois class moulds the school to its own ends of domination. If this were to happen, it would mean that the bourgeois class had an educational programme and was carrying it out with single-minded energy: the school would then be a living thing. This is not the case. The bourgeoisie, as the

---

[19] This text was originally appended to an article, signed 'G.B.', drawing attention to the problem of education in the context of a socialist politics. In late 1919 *L'Ordine Nuovo* organized a school for workers and young intellectuals in Turin. Following Togliatti's article 'Creare una scuola' (15 November 1919) the review put on a course of twenty lectures, to which Gramsci, Togliatti and Tasca contributed, on 'Theoretical framework, historical outline, the state of the Councils'. 'Council' here corresponds to the Russian word *Soviet*.

class which controls the state, takes no interest in the school. It lets the bureaucrats make or destroy it as they are able and allows the education ministers to be chosen according to the caprice of political competition, through partisan intrigue, so as to attain a happy balance of parties in the cabinet. In these conditions the technical study of the educational problem is a pure exercise of mental chess, a matter of intellectual gymnastics rather than a serious and concrete contribution to the problem itself: when, that is, it is not a tiresome lamentation and rehashing of old banalities about the excellence of the educative role of the state, the benefits of education, etc.

In the state of the Councils, the school will represent one of the most important and essential of public activities. Indeed, to the development and success of the school is linked the development of the communist state, the advent of a democracy in which the dictatorship of the proletariat is absorbed. The present generation will be educated into the practice of the social discipline necessary for the realization of communist society, with assemblies and direct participation in deliberation and the administration of the socialist state. The school will have the task of rearing the new generations, those who will enjoy the fruits of our sacrifices and efforts, those who will reap, after the transitional period of national proletarian dictatorships, the fullness of life and development of international communist democracy. How will the communist schools carry out this task? How should the educative function of the state be organized in the overall system of the Councils? What administrative duty will need to be carried out by the primary and secondary teachers' union? How will universities and polytechnics be transformed and co-ordinated in the general cultural activity? Once the constitution is changed and the fundamental principles of the law have been altered, what character should the Faculty of Law possess? Our review numbers among its subscribers and readers a strong contingent of young students, artists and teachers of different levels who have the ability and the training to pose these problems critically and try to solve them. We appeal to their good will, to the active desire they feel for useful co-operation towards the advent of the new order of communism.

Unsigned, *L'Ordine Nuovo*, 27 June 1919.

8 [Questions of Culture]

The proletarian revolution cannot but be a total revolution. It consists in the foundation of new modes of labour, new modes of production and distribution that are peculiar to the working class in its historical determination in the course of the capitalist process. This revolution also presupposes the formation of a new set of standards, a new psychology, new ways of feeling, thinking and living that must be specific to the working class, that must be created by it, that will become 'dominant' when the working class becomes the dominant class. The proletarian revolution is essentially the liberation of the productive forces already existing within bourgeois society. These forces can be identified in the economic and political fields; but is it possible to start identifying the latent elements that will lead to the creation of a proletarian civilization or culture? Do elements for an art, philosophy and morality (standards) specific to the working class already exist? The question must be raised and it must be answered. Together with the problem of gaining political and economic power, the proletariat must also face the problem of winning intellectual power. Just as it has thought to organize itself politically and economically, it must also think about organizing itself culturally. Although through such organizations it is not yet going to be possible (no more than in the economic and political sectors) to obtain positive creative results before the system of bourgeois domination has been broken up, it should still be possible to pose the fundamental questions and outline the most characteristic features of the development of the new civilization. According to our Russian comrades, who have already set up an entire network of organizations for 'Proletarian Culture' (Proletkult), the mere fact that the workers raise these questions and attempt to answer them means that the elements of an original proletarian civilization already exist, that there are already proletarian forces of production of cultural values, just as the fact that the workers create class organizations in order to carry out their cultural activity means that these values too, unlike in the bourgeois period, will be created by the working class on the basis of organization.

Do the workers have their own 'conception of the world'? The conception of the world specific to the working class today is that of critical communism which bases historical development on the class struggle. Yet because of this very conception of the world, the working class knows that its conquest of political and economic power will mark the end of the period of class-divided societies. Will there no longer be historical development, will the machine of progress be broken once classes have been abolished and the class struggle suppressed? Many workers have undoubtedly asked this question, just as some of them have undoubtedly felt anxiety because they have been unable to find an answer. The working class, therefore, has its own 'metaphysical needs' which are proper to it alone. Even a bourgeois can conceive the world from the standpoint of the class struggle, but since he cannot but imagine this struggle as perpetual, he does not ask himself, 'And after the abolition of classes?' The abolition of the class struggle does not mean the abolition of the need to struggle as a principle of development. There will still be the struggle against the brute forces of nature, and this struggle will be applied on a scale never before seen. But what notions, what particular ways of seeing, thinking and feeling does this form of struggle, which does not set living beings against each other, presuppose in order for one to imagine the same conquering spirit in people, the same expansive energy that one finds today in the class struggle?

On this basis, then, we can begin to think that in the fullness of its autonomous historical life the working class will also have its own original conception of the world, some of whose fundamental features can already be delineated.

Tomorrow, like today, the school will undoubtedly be a crucible where the new spirits will be forged. Indeed, tomorrow the school will be immensely more important than it is now. In the various educational organizations (near home or at the workplace) in Russia, one studies up to the age of fifty. In the way schools have been organized in Russia, a Marxist principle has been applied in practice: the dominant class reflects in its social life the relations that characterize its particular modes of existence. The Russian school reflects the way of studying characteristic of the working class. The worker studies and works; his labour is study and study is labour. In order to become a specialist in his work, the worker on average puts in the same number of years that it takes to get a specialized degree. The worker, however, carries out his studies in the very act of doing immediately productive work. Industrial progress tends to annihilate the 'studies' proper to the worker in that it tends to destroy specialized trades. Having become dominant, the working class wants manual labour and intellectual labour to be joined in the schools and thus creates a new educational tradition.

One can easily foresee that when the working class wins its liberty, it will bring to the light of history new complexes of linguistic expressions even if it will not radically change the notion of beauty. The existence of Esperanto, although it does not demonstrate much in itself and has more to do with bourgeois cosmopolitanism than with proletarian internationalism, shows nevertheless, by the fact that the workers are strongly interested in it and manage to waste their time over it, that there is a desire for and a historical push towards the formation of verbal complexes that transcend national limits and in relation to which current national languages will have the same role as dialects now have.[20]

For those who have the will to solve them or to try to solve them, there are an endless number of problems of this order. Is it a waste of time to be concerned with these problems? Our Russian comrades say that not only is it not a waste of time but that, on the contrary, if the working class is not concerned with them, it means that it has not yet reached that stage of revolutionary development in which it truly understands the full implications of the notion of 'ruling class'. In order to help in this field too the working classes that have not yet liberated themselves from the political yoke of the bourgeoisie, our Russian comrades want to establish relations between the Proletkult and the proletarian cultural organizations that already exist in embryonic form throughout the world.

Unsigned, *Avanti!*, Piedmont edition, 14 June 1920.

---

[20] When Gramsci wrote this, over 80 per cent of Italians still spoke dialect for most purposes.

9 Party Art[21]

Avanti!, the national organ of the Italian Socialist Party, recalled the other day that something called art exists, that this art is a form of spiritual activity which, because of its universal character, can and must interest the workers, and that a proletarian party is failing in a part of its task if it does not try to initiate its readers into an understanding of it. Said organ of the Italian Socialist Party recalled, indeed, that a proletarian paper cannot limit its action, in the field of art, to publishing the stories of, say, Italo Toscani, or reports by 'Vacirca' on the colour that the Baltic Sea takes on in the winter months or that of the Russian countryside in the summer.

It recalled, did *Avanti!*, that there exists a world of vast dimensions within which the mind of the proletariat still needs to be given a guiding hand, if it is to acquire the necessary competence to distinguish values from non-values and to understand in what quarters there exists an effort to create original work and to give shape to a new world of forms worthy to stand alongside those created in past ages and expressive at the same time of the greater profundity acquired by the modern spirit in reflection about itself and thus about the world as a whole. *Avanti!* recalled all these things, and therefore concerned itself with the fine art exhibition at the Valentino gallery.

The *Ordine Nuovo*, at the time, concerned itself with such things too, and did so with the aim described above; it called bread bread, wine wine, and housepainters housepainters, quite freely, as is right for people concerning themselves with art and, if we are not mistaken, for someone writing for the workers.

We did not find, among the pictures on show at the Valentino, anything worthy of being signalled to the workers' attention for its intrinsic value. And we said so. And it seemed all the more necessary to say so, quite frankly, given the build-up to the exhibition and given that the same thing had happened with this exhibition as has been happening in Turin for some time now in

---

[21] This article was a reply to a note in *Avanti!* criticizing a review in *L'Ordine Nuovo* of an art exhibition at the Valentino gallery in Turin. (The review, by Piero Gobetti, is reprinted in his *Scritti storici, letterari e filosofici*, ed. Paolo Spriano, Turin 1969, pp. 623–25.) *L'Ordine Nuovo* had by this time become a Communist party paper, following the Livorno split (January 1921), and the Socialist *Avanti!*'s attack had been aimed at the paper itself rather than at Gobetti personally.

relation to all artistic manifestations: the invasion of the sharks into the field of art, the industrialization of art for the sharks' benefit.

The Fine Art Promotion Society [*Promotrice di belle arti*], which used to be run by a group of artists, and with artistic aims, has fallen into the hands of the Turin sharks – the FIAT, AMMA and Lega Industriale lot,[22] who are the same lot as have also for example taken over the Orchestral Society and are everywhere introducing and trying to make prevail their clumsy and coarse spirit of businessmen and traders of human freedom. And we are not alone in saying so: in protest against this fact Turin's best known artists have refused to take part in the Valentino exhibition; to take a few names in no particular order, people like Grosso, Bosia, Casorati, Ferro, Alciati, Ollivero and so on. That is the position taken by the best artists.

But what does *Avanti!* do? *Avanti!* did not send anyone to the exhibition, but it used another criterion of judgement. It thought: the *Ordine Nuovo* gave a bad review to the exhibition; the *Ordine Nuovo* is Communist; therefore we must say the opposite of the *Ordine Nuova*, in order to spite the Communists.

So here is *Avanti!* publishing a report which reads just like one of the communiqués that the government and the sharks are wont to distribute to their captive organs. The communiqué heaps praise on the exhibition, says that it is better than the one in Rome (which showed pictures by artists of the calibre of Soffici, Previati, Segantini and Fattori); it is fulsome in its compliments to the organizing committee (the committee of sharks which drove out the artists), it says nice things all around about everyone and everything, and finally – the only real purpose of the publication – it throws out an insult in the direction of the *Ordine Nuovo*.

Poor *Avanti!*, obliged by its pique to publish such stuff, stuff which even the *Lady's Weekly* would have thrown in the waste bin! Better, better by far, the stories of Italo Toscani or the semi-poetic reports of 'Vacirca' on the colour of the Baltic Sea in winter and the Russian countryside in summer. At least the sharks have

---

[22] The Lega Industriale, constituted in Turin in 1906, was the first Italian employers' organization, nucleus of the later Confindustria. AMMA (Associazione tra gli industriali metallurgici, meccanici e affini) was an association of engineering employers, also based in Turin.

nothing to do with these. And besides, a little 'purism', at least in art, is not a bad thing.

Unsigned, *L'Ordine Nuovo*, 8 May 1921.

FUTURISM

10 The Futurists

The Italian intellectual hen-house is all of a flutter. It is no longer enough to cry shame. People thrust their hands in their hair: there's no more religion! They shriek in finely turned sentences: the world is going to wrack and ruin! The second millennium that will mark the end of this putrid humanity is approaching!

One of these people has even found the words in the dictionary to incite his fellow believers to defend with pistol and dagger the sacrilegiously violated Manes!

The Futurists! For the good Italians they could be no more than a number played at a café concert, a substitute for the fleas trained at fairground booths, and now here is someone who is threatening to take them seriously, to study and understand them! Yes, things are really, really bad!

What an amazing man Giovanni Papini is![23] He only had to blaspheme the goddess Rome and bring upon his head the howls and jeers of the stupid journalistic rabble still fresh from having intoned on the rustic pipes the classical Tripolitan clang of the trumpets, in order to produce in the conscience of those who still had a spark of intelligence left in some secret fold of their brains

---

[23] Giovanni Papini (1881–1956) played a leading role in the Florentine reviews (see introduction to this section) founding, with Giuseppe Prezzolini, *Leonardo* (1903–8), subediting Enrico Corradini's nationalist *Il Regno* (1903–6), and acting as a key contributor and editorial impresario on *La Voce*. He broke with the latter in 1913 to found *Lacerba*, in which he aimed to give more space to art and literature. *Lacerba* was the organ of Florentine Futurism from 1913–14; it then transferred its emphasis to politics and became a mouthpiece for intervention, folding in 1915 after Italy entered the war. The war shocked Papini into a sense of guilt which contributed to his conversion to Catholicism around 1919. He wrote a popular *Story of Christ* (1921), became a fascist, was nominated to the Accademia d'Italia, and wrote a pious eulogy of the regime, *Italia mia* (1939). See also Gramsci's notes on Papini in VIII 5 below.

a reaction against the general state of degradation.[24]

Besides, the Futurists were bound to be recognized. Given the present appalling poverty of artistic production, it was inevitable that whoever worked for a belief, for an idea, had to prevail.

It is generally acknowledged that literature had become a pimp of the newspapers, with their respective shareholders. Hidden away on the third pages and distilled in fixed doses, its task was to procure in the days of prosperity a tranquil digestion for the bellies of the respectable bourgeoisie. Palazzeschi, Govoni and Buzzi are in this situation the best that contemporary poetry can offer history, and because of them all the millions of imbeciles who soil paper will be absolved by future generations. They will be read even when the volumes of the Benellis, the Zuccolis, the Moschinos and Tumiatis will make excellent material for sausage-makers and provide magnificent clothes-racks for provincial tarts.[25]

So far, the Futurists have had no intelligent critic: that is why no one has paid any attention to them. If a few Crocean journalists had written a couple of articles on the subject, who knows who many discoverers of America there would now be!

Instead, Papini himself, in his rather good articles,[26] has tried only to establish the ethical and historical reasons why the Futurists have been derided; Prezzolini, G. S. Gargàno and others have tried to show that the innovations of Futurism are not

---

[24] In a Rome theatre on 21 February 1913, Papini, on Marinetti's invitation, delivered a speech attacking Rome, Christianity and Benedetto Croce. The text was published in *Lacerba* on 1 March as 'Il discorso di Roma'. The 'howls and jeers' Gramsci mentions probably refer to the outraged reactions of the press and public reported in brackets in the text of the speech. Those sectors of the Italian press representing the expansionist interests of finance capital (*La Stampa, Corriere d'Italia, L'Idea Nazionale*, etc.) had compaigned since 1910 for Italian colonization of Tripolitania. The campaign had borne fruit in the form of the Libyan war of 1911–12.

[25] Palazzeschi, Govoni and Buzzi were Futurists (on Palazzeschi see footnote 35 below). The writers they are contrasted with here used conventional genres (erotic novel, historical drama) or – in the case of Sem Benelli – traditional forms in experimental ways. Benelli's dramas of intrigue in the classic eleven-syllable verse line had been 'taken seriously' by Ettore Cozzani in *Il Giornale d'Italia* in 1911 – hence Gramsci's sarcastic reference below.

[26] As well as 'Il discorso di Roma,' Papini had published in *Lacerba* 'Il significato del futurismo' (1 February 1913), 'Contro il futurismo' (15 March) and 'La necessità della rivoluzione' (15 April) prior to this article of Gramsci's. All Papini's *Lacerba* articles on Futurism, charting his critical exchange with Boccioni and break with the movement (1914), were collected in *L'esperienza futurista*, Florence 1914 (reprinted in his *Opere* volume II, *Filosofia e letteratura*, Milan 1961).

exactly new. [27] True, very true, but why not tell us why they are artists and not rustic entertainers?

Marinetti's latest piece, which to most people and perhaps even to some of his friends seemed like buffoonery, the penultimate Catherine wheel of a highly talented fanatic, should alone have caused discussion and consideration if, as has been proclaimed, there really were in Italy all that interest in artistic things, because it is linked to the new tendency in the most modern contemporary art, from music to cubist painting. The experiment of 'Adrianopoli assedio orchestra' is a form of linguistic expression that finds its perfect counterpart in the pictorial forms of Ardengo Soffici or Pablo Picasso. [28] It, too, is a splitting of the image into planes. The image does not appear to the imagination diluted into adverbs or adjectives, gently unwinding into conjunctions and prepositions, but as a successive or parallel or intersecting series of noun-planes with clearly defined limits. It is to be seen if Marinetti has given real artistic life to this form of expression of his, but whoever has taken Sem Benelli's revolution in the technique of the hendecasyllable seriously has no right to sneer faun-like at Futurist prose.

Preparations for a resistance have already begun: pity, though, that these poor people are not really able to use their shotguns and daggers!

Unfortunately, as Papini said, the eagles left Rome to conquer the world and the geese stayed behind to guard it. But the croaking and the fluttering of the geese is by now no longer taken seriously. As soon as it was discovered, the trick was undone. Along the way, the pistols and daggers were turned into a triumphal outburst: *God has suffused them with a spirit which has stunned them!* The battle is really too uneven. Every fortnight the gelatinous group of new romantics content themselves with publishing another effigy of St George with the old stabbed

---

[27] Giuseppe Prezzolini, 'Futurismo vecchio e nuovo', *La Stampa*, 4 April 1913 and 'Alcune idee chiare intorno al futurismo', *La Voce* V (1913) n. 15; G.S. Gargàno, 'Poesia futurista', *Il Marzocco* XVIII (1913) n. 18.

[28] F.T. Marinetti, 'Adrianopoli assedio orchestra', *Lacerba* I (1913) n. 6, p. 50. Ardengo Soffici (1879–1964), painter and writer, had been art critic on *La Voce* before leaving with Papini to found *Lacerba* and produce Futurist poetry. Soffici had met Picasso, Apollinaire and Max Jacob while in Paris from 1903 to 1907. As early as 1911 he began to defend the virtues and values of a 'healthy' rural Italy, influenced Papini in this direction and under fascism collaborated again with Papini in the Catholic periodical *Frontespizio*. See also VIII 19 below.

dragon, but it is only stabbed on paper.[29] Such jelly melts in the rays of the sun and inevitably turns back into stock for pasta, the heritage of illustrious ancestors. Art is too harsh an Angelica for backs weakened by smothering the confessional grille with kisses.[30] With all their unseemliness, with all the swelling of muscles revealing the effort, the newcomers have too much vitality to be forced to withdraw by the whispers and murmurs of the gossipers.

Signed 'alfa gamma', *Corriere Universitario*, 20 May 1913.

11 Marinetti the Revolutionary

This incredible, enormous, colossal event has happened, which, if divulged, threatens completely to destroy all the prestige and reputation of the Communist International: during the Second Congress in Moscow, comrade Lunacharsky, in his speech to the Italian delegates (a speech given, mark you, in Italian, excellent Italian even; so that any suspicion of a dubious interpretation must *a priori* be rejected), said that in Italy there lives a revolutionary intellectual by the name of Filippo Tommaso Marinetti. The philistines of the workers' movement are extremely shocked. It is now certain that to the insults of being called 'Bergsonian voluntarists, pragmatists and spiritualists' will be added the more deadly one of 'Futurists! Marinettians!'[31] Since such a fate awaits us, let us see if we can raise ourselves to a self-awareness of our new intellectual position.

Many groups of workers looked kindly towards Futurism

[29] An allusion to the Bologna-based review *San Giorgio. Giornale dei nuovi romantici* (1912–13) which had published an attack on the Futurists in its issue of February 1913.

[30] Angelica is the free-spirited and inconstant lady pursued by Orlando and Rinaldo in the chivalric poems of Boiardo and Ariosto.

[31] The PSI reformists accused the *Ordine Nuovo* group of 'Bergsonian voluntarism'. An unsigned article which appeared in *L'Ordine Nuovo* three days before this one had remarked on the 'curious case of seeing the name of a school of philosophy becoming something like an insulting epithet. Do you no longer know how to answer your opponent? Tell him he's a voluntarist or a pragmatist or – make the sign of the cross – a Bergsonian. The effect is guaranteed'. The article, 'Bergsoniano', is in SF, pp. 12–13, although its attribution to Gramsci has since been questioned.

(before the European war). It happened very often (before the war) that groups of workers would defend the Futurists from the attacks of cliques of professional 'artists' and 'littérateurs'. This point established, this historical observation made, the question automatically arises: 'In this attitude of the workers was there an intuition (here we are with the word intuition: Bergsonians, Bergsonians) of an unsatisfied need in the proletarian field?' We must answer: 'Yes. The revolutionary working class was and is aware that it must found a new state, that by its tenacious and patient labour it must elaborate a new economic structure and found a new civilization.' It is relatively easy to outline right from this moment the shape of the new state and the new economic structure. In this absolutely practical field, we are convinced that for a certain time the only possible thing to do will be to exercise an iron-like power over the existing organization, over that constructed by the bourgeoisie. From this conviction comes the stimulus to struggle for the conquest of power and from it comes the formula by which Lenin has characterized the workers' state: 'For a certain time the workers' state cannot be other than a bourgeois state without the bourgeoisie.'[32]

The battlefield for the creation of a new civilization is, on the other hand, absolutely mysterious, absolutely characterized by the unforeseeable and the unexpected. Having passed from capitalist power to workers' power, the factory will continue to produce the same material things that it produces today. But in what way and under what forms will poetry, drama, the novel, music, painting and moral and linguistic works be born? It is not a material factory that produces these works. It cannot be reorganized by a workers' power according to a plan. One cannot establish its rate of production for the satisfaction of immediate needs, to be controlled and determined statistically. Nothing in this field is foreseeable except for this general hypothesis: there will be a proletarian culture (a civilization) totally different from the bourgeois one and in this field too class distinctions will be shattered. Bourgeois careerism will be shattered and there will be a poetry, a novel, a theatre, a moral code, a language, a painting and a music peculiar to proletarian civilization, the flowering and

---

[32] Lenin, *State and Revolution*, London 1933, p. 76: 'Consequently, for a certain time not only bourgeois rights, but even the bourgeois state remains under Communism, without the bourgeoisie!' See also the translation in *Collected Works*, Volume 25, p. 471.

ornament of proletarian social organization. What remains to be done? Nothing other than to destroy the present form of civilization. In this field, 'to destroy' does not mean the same as in the economic field. It does not mean to deprive humanity of the material products that it needs to subsist and to develop. It means to destroy spiritual hierarchies, prejudices, idols and ossified traditions. It means not to be afraid of innovations and audacities, not to be afraid of monsters, not to believe that the world will collapse if a worker makes grammatical mistakes, if a poem limps, if a picture resembles a hoarding or if young men sneer at academic and feeble-minded senility. The Futurists have carried out this task in the field of bourgeois culture. They have destroyed, destroyed, destroyed, without worrying if the new creations produced by their activity were on the whole superior to those destroyed. They have had confidence in themselves, in the impetuosity of their youthful energies. *They have grasped sharply and clearly that our age, the age of big industry, of the large proletarian city and of intense and tumultuous life, was in need of new forms of art, philosophy, behaviour and language.* This sharply revolutionary and absolutely *Marxist* idea came to them when the Socialists were not even vaguely interested in such a question, when the Socialists certainly did not have as precise an idea in politics and economics, when the Socialists would have been frightened (as is evident from the current fear of many of them) by the thought that it was necessary to shatter the machine of bourgeois power in the state and the factory. In their field, the field of culture, the Futurists are revolutionaries. In this field it is likely to be a long time before the working classes will manage to do anything more creative than the Futurists have done. When they supported the Futurists, the workers' groups showed that they were not afraid of *destruction*, certain as they were of being able to create poetry, paintings and plays, like the Futurists; these workers were supporting historicity, the possibility of a proletarian culture created by the workers themselves.

Unsigned, *L'Ordine Nuovo*, 5 January 1921.

12 [A Letter to Trotsky on Futurism][33]

Here are the answers to the questions you put to me on Italian Futurism.

The Italian Futurist movement completely lost its character after the war. Marinetti is not particularly active in it. He has got married and prefers to devote his energies to his wife. At present, monarchists, communists, republicans and fascists participate in the movement. A political weekly has recently been founded in Milan with the title *Il Principe* which supports or tries to support the same theses that Machiavelli preached for Italy in the Cinquecento, namely that the struggle between the local parties which would result in the collapse of the nation could be stopped by an absolute monarch, a new Cesare Borgia who could decapitate all the leaders of the belligerent parties. Two Futurists edit the magazine – Bruno Corra and Emilio Settimelli. Marinetti, although arrested during the patriotic demonstration in Rome in 1920 for a violent speech against the king, contributes to the weekly too.

The most prominent representatives of pre-war Futurism have become fascists, with the exception of Giovanni Papini who has become a Catholic and has written a history of Christ.[34] During the war the Futurists were the most tenacious proponents of a 'war to the victorious end' and of imperialism. Only one Futurist, Aldo Palazzeschi, was against the war. He broke with the movement, and although he was one of its most interesting writers, he has ended in literary silence.[35]

Marinetti, who had always wholeheartedly praised war, published a manifesto in which he tried to prove that war was the only means of purging the world. He took part in the war as a

---

[33] Originally published in L. Trotsky, *Literatura i revolutsiya*, Moscow: Krasnaya Novy, 1923, pp. 116–18, with the title 'Comrade Gramsci's letter on Italian Futurism'. The letter is omitted from the English translation of Trotsky's book and has been translated for this edition by Colin Bearne. On the circumstances surrounding its composition, see the introduction to this section.

[34] See footnote 23 above.

[35] Aldo Palazzeschi (1885–1974) joined the Futurists in 1909 and contributed a Futurist manifesto to *Lacerba* in early 1914. Three months later he broke with the movement ('Dichiarazione', *La Voce*, 1914, n. 8) and, with Papini and Soffici, signed the counter-manifesto 'Futurismo e marinettismo' which arrogated the name 'Futurist' to the *Lacerba* group alone by defining Marinetti and the other original Futurists (minus Carrà) as rule-bound, propagandistic and bizarre rather than genuinely original.

captain of an armoured car brigade and his latest book, *The Iron Alcove*, is an ecstatic hymn to armoured cars in war. Marinetti has written a pamphlet, *Beyond Communism*, where he sets forth his political doctrines, if one can call the sometimes witty but always strange fantasies of this man doctrines.[36] Before my departure the Turin section of Proletkult invited Marinetti to an exhibition of Futurist paintings in order to explain what it meant to the working-class members of the organization. Marinetti accepted the invitation willingly, and after visiting the exhibition together with the workers he was satisfied to have been convinced that the workers understood Futurist art far better than the bourgeoisie.[37] Before the war, Futurism was very popular among the workers. The magazine *Lacerba*, with a circulation of 20,000 copies, had 80 per cent of its distribution among workers. During numerous Futurist meetings in the theatres of the largest Italian cities, workers defended Futurists against young semi-aristocrats and bourgeois who came to blows with them.

Marinetti's Futurist group no longer exists. Marinetti's former magazine *Poesia* is now run by a certain Mario Dessy, a totally insignificant man both intellectually and in organizational ability. In the south of Italy, especially in Sicily, quite a few very small Futurist magazines are published to which Marinetti sends articles, but these magazines are edited by the students who think Futurism is the same as ignorance of Italian grammar. The hard core of the Futurists are the artists. There is a permanent Futurist art gallery in Rome, organized by a failed photographer, one Anton Giulio Bragaglia, a cinema and theatre agent. Giacomo Balla is the best known of the Futurist artists. D'Annunzio never made any public pronouncements on Futurism. One must bear in mind that from the outset Futurism had a distinct anti-D'Annunzio character: one of Marinetti's first books had the title 'Les Dieux s'en vont, et D'Annunzio reste' [The gods depart, and D'Annunzio remains]. Although during the war the political programmes of Marinetti and D'Annunzio coincided on all points, the Futurists remained anti-D'Annunzian. They had been almost totally uninterested in the

[36] The texts Gramsci is referring to are *Guerra sola igiene del mondo* (Milan 1915), *L'Alcova d'acciaio* (Milan 1921) and *Al di là del comunismo* (Milan 1920).

[37] *L'Ordine Nuovo* reported this event on 3 April 1922 (article by Mario Sarmati).

Fiume movement, though they later took part in the demonstrations.[38]

It could be said that after the conclusion of the armistice the Futurist movement entirely lost its character and split up into different trends created and formed during the upheaval of the war. Nearly all the young intelligentsia have become reactionary. The workers, who had seen in Futurism the elements of a struggle against academic Italian culture, fossilized and remote from the popular masses, had to fight for their freedom with weapons in their hands and had little interest in the old arguments. In the big industrial centres the programme of Proletkult, aimed at educating workers in the fields of literature and art, absorbs the energy of those who still have the desire and the time to occupy themselves with these problems.

8 September 1922.

THEATRE CRITICISM

13 Theatre and Cinema

They say that the cinema is killing the theatre. They say that in Turin the theatrical firms have kept their houses closed during the summer months because the public is deserting the theatre and thronging to the cinemas. The new film industry has sprung up and caught on in Turin. In Turin luxurious cinemas have been opened, with few equals in Europe, and are always crowded out.

There would seem to be some basis to the sad observation that the audience's taste has degenerated and that bad times are round the corner for the theatre.

[38] Gabriele D'Annunzio (1863–1938), major figure in *fin de siècle* culture as novelist, poet, dramatist and nationalist publicist. In September 1919 he led a 'legion' of army veterans to occupy Fiume on the coast of Dalmatia, whose Italian-speaking population had become citizens of the new state of Yugoslavia by the Treaty of London. The action was widely supported by bourgeois and petty-bourgeois 'patriots'. Premier Nitti was unable to act decisively and the international impasse lasted until the Treaty of Rapallo (1920), the withdrawal of the legionnaires and the cession of Fiume to Italy (1923). The venture has been widely viewed as a dress-rehearsal for fascism: plans had been made for an invasion and seizure of power on the mainland, a corporatist constitution was drafted, and Mussolini followed the episode in his *Popolo d'Italia* with enthusiasm, coupled with private doubts as to the ripeness of the conjuncture.

We, however, are thoroughly convinced that these complaints are founded on a jaded aestheticism and can easily be shown to depend on a false assumption. The reason for the success of the cinema and its absorption of former theatre audiences is purely economic. The cinema offers exactly the same sensations as the popular theatre, but under better conditions, without the choreographic contrivances of a false intellectualism, without promising too much while delivering little. The usual stage presentations are nothing but cinema. The most commonly staged productions are nothing but fabrics of external facts, lacking any human content, in which talking puppets move about variously, without ever drawing out a psychological truth, without ever managing to impose on the listener's creative imagination a character or passions that are truly felt and adequately expressed. Psychological insincerity and lame artistic expression have reduced the theatre to the same level as the pantomime. The sole aim is to create in the audience the illusion of a life which is only outwardly different from everyone's normal life. Only the geographical horizon, the social environment, of the characters is changed, all the things which in life are subjects for the picture postcard, for visual curiosity, not for artistic curiosity or the curiosity of fantasy. And nobody can deny that in this respect the film is incontrovertibly superior to the stage. It is more complete and more varied. It is silent; in other words it reduces the role of the artists to movement alone, to being machines without souls, to what they really are in the theatre as well. It is ludicrous to take it out on the cinema. Talking about vulgarity, banality, etc., is feeble rhetoric. Those who really believe that the theatre has an artistic function should instead be happy with this competition. It serves to precipitate things, to bring the theatre back to its true character. There is no doubt that a large proportion of the public needs to be entertained (to relax by shifting its field of attention) with a pure visual distraction. By becoming an industry, the theatre has recently tried to satisfy this need alone. It has become quite simply a business, a shop dealing in cheap junk. It is only by accident that they put on productions that have an eternal universal value. The cinema, which can fulfil this function more easily and more cheaply, is more successful than the theatre and is tending to replace it. The theatrical firms and companies will eventually realize that they need to change tack if they want to stay in being. It is not true that the public is deserting the theatres. We have seen theatres that were empty for a large number of productions fill up, become suddenly crowded for a special evening when a masterpiece was exhumed or even more modestly, a typical work of a past style, but which had a particular quality of its own. What the theatre now offers as an exception must become the rule. Shakespeare, Goldoni, Beaumarchais may indeed require active effort to be properly staged but they are also beyond any banal competition. D'Annunzio, Bernstein, Bataille will always be more successful in the cinema. The grimace and the physical contortion find in the film material more appropriate to their expression. And the useless, boring and insincere rhetorical tirades will once again become literature, nothing but literature, dead and buried in books and libraries.

Avanti!, Piedmont edition, 26 August 1916.

14 The Theatre Industry [i]

At the Politeama Chiarella: variety shows, Cuttica, Spadaro and company. At the Carignano Theatre: the living miracle or professor Gabrielli who outwits all the great names of science. At the Alfieri: the sixtieth performance of Luigi Maresca's operetta company. The operettas, variety shows, and vaudevilles of Carosio and Cuneo, and such living phenomena as Fregoli, Petrolini, Cuttica, Spadaro and Titina.[39] Turin has become a fair, Barnum has become the tutelary god of the aesthetic activity and taste of its citizens.

Barnum or the theatrical consortium: Barnum or the trust of the Chiarella brothers. The animating spirit is the same: that of the person who piles up money, who is blind, deaf, and insensitive to everything that is not a source of gain. If tomorrow it is proved to be more expedient to use the theatres to retail peanuts and iced drinks, the theatre industry will not hesitate an instant to become

---

[39] Varieties and vaudevilles were increasingly staged in Italian theatres from the end of the 19th century. Primo Cuttica impersonated army types. Odoardo Spadaro was an impressionist and comic singer. Ettore Petrolini (1886–1936) was one of the great Italian comic actors of stage and screen. Achille and Giovanni Chiarella had taken over the Politeama Chiarella on the death of their impresario father in 1907 and rapidly began controlling other Turin playhouses.

an outlet for peanuts and drinks, while keeping the adjective 'theatrical' in the firm's title.

Only one thing is really surprising: that the military authorities – so inquisitorial when it comes to requisitioning the schools or the People's Theatre of Corso Siccardi, or the Teatro Regio, which only admit those companies that really want to offer the audience works of theatre, of use for aesthetic education and the satisfaction of a valuable need – should spare the theatres managed by the Chiarella firm, which have now lost their artistic genuineness and serve only to exploit the pretensions of vulgar amusement.

Turin's theatrical trust has gone a little too far in its industrial ability. The city is now completely cut off from the rest of Italian theatrical life. Only rarely do two or three of the major theatre companies turn up for an exceptional season. Turin provides large audiences for variety shows, it has an insatiable thirst for questionable locales. The theatre industry has begun to compete with the variety show and seeks to corner the most lucrative category of this audience. In this way it pursues its monopolistic goal. The major companies are reserved for the provinces, the small centres, where the actors are naturally paid less, because the theatres are smaller and the takings are lower. Monopoly triumphs. The big city theatres stay profitable, even if they house shows of an inferior quality, because out of 500,000 people there is always going to be a certain number who will go to them all the same. Variety artists are paid less and capital grows fat. In the small centres a big name is needed to draw the crowds. The artists are paid less because it is a secondary market, and capital gets fat in like manner. The large companies are breaking up and the actors are being forced to turn to the cinema to make a living. But the theatre industry, now a monopoly, does not care. Business prospers just the same because there is no room for competition, because the aesthetic level has been lowered. As a result, the people crowd to see Petrolini or Cuttica while no one misses the artistic performances of Ermete Zacconi and Emma Gramatica.

In Turin, however, the industrial activities of the trust have overstepped the limit. It would not be a bad thing if another autocracy were set up against the autocracy of monopolized capital. What overriding reason can there now be to go on treating the theatres of the Chiarella firm as if they are untouchable, while the educational theatres are considered extremely touchable, as was the Teatro Regio?

Petrolini, Cuttica, Spadaro and associates used to have their natural environment. What overriding reason can go on allowing the city of Turin to become a fief of the variety show? It is painful to have to admit that in a great city good custom must be re-established by an authoritarian measure. Yet unfortunately this is the case. Monopolistic excesses can only be stopped by state intervention.

Avanti!, Piedmont edition, 28 June 1917.

15 The Theatre Industry [ii]

We have received the following letter from Mr Giovanni Chiarella:

I appeal to your sense of fairness to correct the various inaccuracies contained in the article 'The Theatre Industry' which appeared in your newspaper on the 28th of this month. The ill-informed columnist asserts that our firm has harmed the development of Turin's artistic theatre by excluding or by limiting the presentation of good companies.

Well, here are the names of the companies who performed in our theatres from October 1916 to the present: theatre companies: Tina Di Lorenzo and Armando Falconi; Lyda Borelli and Ugo Piperno; Emma Gramatica; Ermete Novelli; Talli, Melato, Betrone, Gandusio; Ruggero Ruggeri; Alfredo De Sanctis; Dina Galli and Amerigo Guasti; Carini, Gentilli, Baghetti, Dondini; Sichel and associates; Sainati; Tempesti; Musco; Tina Bondi. Operetta companies: Lombardo no. 1; Città di Milano; Lombardo no. 2; Maresca; Vannutelli.

There are, therefore, 14 theatre companies and 5 operetta companies: a total of 19 major companies. Almost all those that the war has left standing have alternated in our theatres in the space of nine months. Do you call this cutting a city off from the theatrical movement?

One must add the opera season to the shows given by established companies. Since last September, twenty-one operas were more than respectably performed in our theatres.

I shall not mention the various lectures, concerts, and French companies. Faced with this important presence of major shows, which can always be documented, the ill-informed columnist attacks us because in June we took the liberty of bringing Fregoli and Cuttica to the Politeama Chiarella and Gabrielli to the Carignano. Either because he is unaware of the facts or because he has forgotten them, the columnist would like to accuse us of having cut Turin off from the theatrical movement, reducing it, he says, to housing only two or three good companies. With concrete data, it has been easy for us to deny this. As for being unscrupulous businessmen, we may reply by affirming without fear of being contradicted that in no top-ranking city like Turin have the prices remained so reasonable. It is well known that our theatres are constantly open, entirely free of charge, to all works of charity.

To reply to another inaccuracy, we may add that in no city as in Turin has requisitioning been so pitiless towards the theatres, since three private firms, not counting the municipal Teatro Regio, were occupied by the military authorities, namely the Balbo, the Vittorio Emanuele and the Torinese.

Trusting to your impartiality for the publication of this letter, I remain, etc.

Mr Chiarella parades the names of the major companies that have passed through his theatres from October 1916 to June 1917 and the string of names would seem to prove him right. If he had included in his calculations the last two years, he would have been even righter. But we did not want to put on trial the entire history of the industrial activities of the Chiarella firm. We wanted to note a trend in this activity which has become apparent in 1917, which has intensified in the quarter from April to June, and which we fear is now tending to become an established business arrangement. Our anxiety has valid grounds. Many people in Turin go to public shows. We state this fact, without trying to explain it in any way. This increasing attendance at such shows has caused an indecorous expansion of the most inferior theatre houses. The Chiarella firm, which has a monopoly of the city's theatres, is contributing to this lowering of the level of general taste. There is a noticeable trend, in the business criteria of the firm, to exploit this mania for the variety show, instead of directing it towards better types of shows. Between April and June, the Chiarella theatres have housed only one theatre company for an ordinary season and this was, by a remarkable coincidence, the company of Sichel, whose plays are on the same level as the variety shows. In the month of April, there were also other companies, but for extraordinary performances: Musco, 5 days; Talli-Melato, 15 days; Novelli, 5 days. During this quarter, the city's theatres have predominantly housed variety shows and operettas: two months of the Maresca company, performances by the Lombardo company, the city companies of Milan and Paris; then Petrolini at the Alfieri, cinema at the Alfieri, Zambi at the Scribe, Gabrielli at the Carignano, Fregoli and Cuttica at the Chiarella. During the two months of May and June, only ten performances by a respectable, if not major, theatrical company – that of Tina Bondi.

Mr Chiarella says that we have accused him of being a profiteer. He is simply a businessman, who finds a monopoly the surest way of attaining his ends. Business under monopolistic conditions is fatally deformed, just as the business of his theatrical industry is. Monopolies even lead to the destruction of economic values, and are responsible for the growth of twisted and harmful forms of speculation: harmful, of course, for the community, not for the capitalist and therefore harmful not only in the short term. The trust of the theatrical consortium has already excluded Ermete Zacconi from Turin's theatres. Now Emma Gramatica has also been ostracized. Because of it, the theatre companies are slowly breaking up since, if they want to live and work, they must suffer the extreme humiliation of the agreements, interferences and repertoires that the consortium imposes. The theatre has a great social importance. We are concerned by the degeneration which threatens it at the hands of the industrialists and we would like to react against this as best we can. There is a large public that wants to go to the theatre. The industry is slowly conditioning it to prefer the inferior, indecorous show to one which represents a positive need of the spirit.

Given this attitude of ours, we ask Mr Chiarella to believe that we have no intention of contributing towards the requisitioning of his theatres. It seems to us that it is his firm itself which is inviting such a measure. The Balbo, the Torino and the Vittorio were requisitioned precisely because for quite some time they had no longer opened their doors to theatrical performances worthy of the name. The Vittorio Theatre, managed by the Chiarellas, closed on 23 October after a theatrical season of the Bisini equestrian circus, and until the day it was requisitioned, it only opened rarely for a few second-rate opera shows. This is the danger of monopolized industry: it makes money, even when it devalues itself in a certain market, even when it destroys its values, because it makes them up in other markets, without worrying about the disorder it creates or the morbid tendencies it causes. And there is no way to do so by economic means. We would be happy if the protest of the newspapers served some purpose. If after this the Chiarella trust wants us to speak of their concessions to charity performances, we would not have any problem: except that the discussion would be lengthy and . . . dangerous!

Avanti!, Piedmont edition, 4 July 1917.

16 The Chiarella Brothers Again

Mr Giovanni Chiarella has sent us a second letter full of recriminations which fail to change our views. He wants us to inform our readers that the Musco and Novelli companies held acting courses that began in March and continued through April, so it appears they did not come to Turin only for five days. He wants it known that in the same month of April the Talli company ran their show for 28 nights. Naturally, this does not alter the fact that during the months of May and June the Chiarella theatres hosted predominantly low-grade shows, while during the same period in Milan, Rome, Bologna, and Florence the theatres offered quite different fare. We were not the only ones to point this out. Other Turin newspapers repeated what we had written.

As for the deleterious work of the trusts, Chiarella appeals to the Italian actor-managers.[40] In order for our observations not to appear unfounded, we will quote a passage of the open letter with

---

[40] The actor-manager (*capocomico*) was usually the principal actor of a theatre company doubling as its artistic director and business manager. Travelling companies were the norm in early twentieth-century Italy.. Bad economic conditions had prevailed in the theatre throughout the nineteenth century, with minimal wages and unpaid rehearsals for company members. Costumes, travel and the transport of luggage and props were usually charged to the companies themselves. The mutual obligations of company members and company owners were regulated by a labour contract; those of company members and theatre owners by a performance contract. An iniquitous system of 'owner's deductions' (*prelevazioni*), which remained in force till the mid-thirties, gave the theatre owner a right to the takings from a given number of tickets stipulated in the performance contract before dividing the rest with the manager of the company. The increasing capitalist organization of the theatre as well as its growing technical complexity widened the gap between the

which Marco Praga, president of the Italian Society of Authors, announced a conference of actor-managers for 9 July:

> We have heard many reports, which deserve to be listened to whether they come from the highest authorities or the most humble.
>
> Some actor-managers say: such is the state of things that the activity of our industry has been made too difficult, too risky, if not downright impossible. Unusually onerous contracts have been forced upon us. People who have no right are interfering in the formation of companies. The itinerary of the companies is compulsory and is subordinated, not to the interests of art and the theatre industry, but to the sole interest of those who hold in their power the utilization and availability of the principal theatres of the major cities. There have been bitter controversies and painful debates on this subject which have not yet come to an end.
>
> The actors say: long years of struggle had given us equitable hiring contracts, with the abolition of certain obsolete clauses which were extremely dangerous for us, and the concession of guarantees which assured us a modest income and gave us the security we absolutely need to exercise our art to the maximum. And then, suddenly, everything was taken away again, in a period of crisis such as the Italian theatre has never known. We are forced to choose between living a life of hardship and anxiety, or abandoning the theatre to take refuge on that silent stage which cannot satisfy our self-esteem but which offers us a less uncertain and less arduous livelihood.
>
> Some theatre owners or directors say: it is not the mania for monopoly that guides us, the mania for centralizing the theatrical industry in our hands, nor is it a hegemony for our profit alone that we wish to create. Rather, it is the desire and the need to discipline the functioning of this theatre industry, a discipline that cannot be harmful. Indeed, the art can only benefit from it.
>
> Finally, other theatre owners and directors say: we could and we would like to, offer more favourable contracts to the actor-managers and we do not fear legitimate competition among theatres of the same city. But, for reasons that are all too obvious, we must go with the tide. We must conform to the directions and advice of those who control the greatest number of theatrical interests, nor can we act without the consent and mediation of the agencies.

Furthermore, one need only recall the letters sent by Ermete Zacconi (to whom Chiarella also appeals in his letter) to the press

---

actors (many of whom were driven to find better-paid work in the new film industry) and the company manager. The figure of the professional director (*regista*) started to emerge and a move began in the inter-war years towards stable theatre companies and state subsidies.

on various occasions and the recent campaign of the trust's newspapers against Emma Gramatica.[41]

It is this which concerns us more than all the statistics, all the calendars that Chiarella uses to back himself up, since he cannot deny the facts, which in Turin go by the names of Petrolini, Bambi, Cuttica, Spadaro and Gabrielli, while in other cities they go by the names of dramatic companies. That the Chiarellas are trying to reconcile the desire to avoid a deficit with the fulfilment of a high artistic ideal is something we would like to see in reality and not just in a generic statement written for the newspaper. The reality of these last two months has been such as to justify our comments. The rest is inconclusive hair-splitting.

Finally, Mr Chiarella proposes to submit his charitable services to the examination and judgement of the arbiters of the press. We do not see the importance of this. In order that Mr Chiarella may rest assured and in order to avoid a series of wholly pleonastic disputes and annoyances, we are willing to recognize that Mr Chiarella has done everything that he could, as a businessman, for charity!!

Avanti!, Piedmont edition, 8 July 1917.

17 The Theatre Industry [iii]

A few days ago, the representatives of the three categories concerned with the theatre business – the owners, the play and operetta managers, and the contracted employees – held a conference. It was patronized by the president of the Society of Authors and its purpose was to seek a peaceful settlement of the disputes that have arisen between the trust of the theatre owners and those who work for the theatre. A waste of time. The questions were not settled, the owners did not budge an inch. Nevertheless, Mr Giovanni Chiarella will go on appealing to the Italian managers to bear witness to his enlightened patronage.

The actor-managers demanded a straightforward return to the

[41] Ermete Zacconi (1857–1948) and Emma Gramatica (1875–1965) were leading serious actor-managers. Zacconi championed a naturalistic style of acting. Gramatica (see also I 20 and 21 below) played many female leads including Ibsen's Hedda Gabler and Nora Helmar and Shaw's Candida and Saint Joan.

contract conditions that existed before the trust was set up: 1) abolition of the 3 per cent fee on the takings of each show, imposed by the trust in favour of the Paradossi agency: 2) abolition of owner's deductions: all saleable seats in the theatres should be entered on the daily balance-sheets to the joint profit of the managers and the theatre owners, thus eliminating the disadvantage of having a part of the takings go to the owners alone;[42] 3) proportional division for each show of the total annual rent on boxes, rents which at present go entirely and exclusively to the owners; 4) heating charged to the theatre owners; 5) evening tax charged to the owners; 6) for the operetta companies, the expenses of the orchestra charged to the theatre owners.

The owners did not accept any of these proposals, even though they were accompanied by these two compensations: 1) extension to all theatres of the 10 per cent increase on the price of special boxes and seats already charged in many theatres: this increased revenue to be made over exclusively to the owners in order to compensate them for the price increase of coal and the increase in the theatre tax; 2) a 5 per cent reduction of the percentage on the takings of the evening performances made over until now to the actor-managers. The owners, instead, made counter-proposals that were intended to create friction between the actor-managers and the contracted employees. They did not succeed. If the convention served any purpose at all it was to have brought closer together the three categories that are directly damaged by the trust: the authors, the managers and the contracted employees. The managers conceded to the latter a new labour-hire contract: a single contract, annual pay without dead periods.

Certainly, this agreement will not be sufficient to break up the trust and prevent its operations, harmful for art and usurious with regard to those who work. The trust has ways of retaliating which only state intervention could put a stop to. It can underhandedly boycott the actors and open its theatres only to cinema shows and to Petrolini, Cuttica and Gabrielli. Mr Giovanni Chiarella flew into a rage of indignation when we pointed out the first effects of monopolistic industrialism in Turin. Other newspapers are now writing the same things, after the experience of the Milan conference. And they use precisely that language which, according to Chiarella, I used to accuse him of unscrupulous

---

[42] On owner's deduction, see footnote 40 above.

business dealings. We quote here a passage from one of these articles, taken from a newspaper which, while taking a protectionist stance towards industry proper, happens to have a laissez-faire and anti-monopolistic attutide to the theatre industry, the only one it studies and dissects with non-administrative criteria:

> The theatre owners have formed a consortium along commercial and industrial lines: they protect only their own interests. They care nothing for art. It would be naïve to suppose that all of a sudden they are going to turn into a group of patrons or into people who realize that they are not speculating in footwear.
>
> Besides having brought about an increase in owner's deductions, even in provincial theatres outside the consortium, and besides having raised the price of theatres, the trust has also ended up by looking after its own interests badly, driven as it is by its intrinsic needs.
>
> In its eagerness to lay hands on as many theatres as it can, it has bought and continues to buy second- and third-rate theatres which are completely unremunerative and which remain closed for most of the year. And so it dreams up those stupid expedients – cinema shows, visionists, sporting events, Petrolini, and the like – which diminish even the secondary importance of these places, corrupting their audiences and reducing the theatres to all-purpose halls, like the upstairs rooms of cafés: for weddings, banquets, dancing parties and so forth. Indeed, it is precisely the criterion of the café owner that inspires the consortium, which is always on the look-out for the type of show or individual that pleases the public. And tomorrow, logically, it would entertain any quality of show if there were no laws on public morality, on gaming and other wretched activites. It is easy to guess the state of dramatic art, when it is at these people's mercy.
>
> With the exception of two companies, which are favoured because they draw the crowds, the others, which would also attract people if they could perform during the best seasons, are forcibly excluded from any chance to do good. And since commercial and artistic values rarely coincide, the consortium favours the former to the total detriment of the latter, quite apart from the fact that it weighs on the actor-managers in a way that makes it difficult for them to manage the company. It also forces them to put on performances that titillate the basest tastes of the public, even in the theatres frequented by cultured and intellectual people who are ready to respond to any beautiful spectacle.

Avanti!, Piedmont edition, 17 July 1917.

18 Continuation of Life

Entering and exiting. These two words should be abolished. One does not enter or exit: one continues. I am beginning to admire the industrial genius of the Chiarella brothers. I am beginning to believe that theirs are the only criteria possible in Turin. Turin has the theatre it deserves: it is the mirror of its soul, of its life.

Sichel, who plays the part of the moron and always repeats the same gestures, the same idiotic catch-phrase, and still has them rolling in the aisles, is the *serious person,* the *pater conscriptus*, the commendatore Usseglio of Turin life. The city council is not sufficient: at the Carignano they have opened a branch office. Fiction takes over life: there is no longer fiction and life, only the gelatinous reality of Turin, and everything becomes dull grey, everything becomes flat and vulgar.

Cyrano becomes Serafino Renzi. They have reopened the Balbo Theatre so that Cyrano could perform in this latest make-up of his. The juggler has dressed up as Cyrano and slobbers poetry and waves the plume of his hat. It is the Cyrano of Porta Palazzo, the Cyrano who writes for the newspapers, who everyday racks his castrated flea's brain and invents new plots and discovers, denies and reconfirms new meetings and nominates new generals to the 55 thugs and whirls about in circles, proud and full of self-admiration. Cyrano of the Scribe Theatre, Cyrano of Serafino Renzi, under your plume, under the vulgarity of your latest make-up, you continue the exploits of Francesco Repaci, you continue the exploits of Mario Gioda. You too have opened a branch office at Porta Palazzo. We will see you in the moonlight strolling with Donvito, your Roxane, drooling long tales of romantic intrigue, unearthing conspiracies and then rubbing your hands with glee: let them prove that it is not true, let them prove that it is a fabrication. Poor Cyrano, how much disgust for your make-believe and for your life which has slid in the oily smoothness of the crowded latrines. The Chiarella brothers really have a touch of genius. They have taken you by the nose and they exhibit you in their shop window. They know how to do business. Turin, you have the theatre you deserve.

Sichel, Renzi, *Trovatore, Pagliacci*, the operetta that is all laughs. A gelatinous reality: the sneer and the sentimental groan, the fiction of sweetened falsity and the life of your blind alleys – Cyrano giving his arm to the policeman, the libertarian anarchist writing a defence of the police commissioner. The theatre is merely the continuation of your life, and your life is all written in the police's black book.[43]

Avanti!, Piedmont edition, 11 September 1917.

19 Contrasts

A riding instructress, an adulterous wife, a simple-minded girl, a deaf and grotesque husband, two elegant and stupid young men, an utterly crude swindler. These seven characters play at chasing and hoodwinking each other. They mouth innumerable stupidities; their lives are a massive stupidity. Sichel and company repeat the stupidities very well, with such self-assured immersion in the roles as to make it clear that they would not be able to mouth intelligent things nearly so well. The place is swamped in idiocy. There is a palpable atmosphere of bestiality in the auditorium of the Alfieri. It emanates from the laughing faces, from the gleaming eyes, from the short and nervous bursts of laughter of the audience. It spreads thick and heavy from the actors, from the stage. Not even a shiver of humanity, of spirituality. And yet, these spectators are not crude lumps of flesh and blood wrapped in skin. They are moved, they are able to be moved. During the intervals, huddled together in the small smoking-room, they go quiet, they freeze and crush back against the walls to let past a young man in dark glasses and army uniform, reeling on the arm of a friend, unsure of spatial relations, as one still is when one has recently been plunged into

[43] This article was written at the time of the anti-socialist witch-hunt in Turin which followed the riots, strikes and anti-war protests of 22–26 August 1917 (see footnote 23 on p. 396). Giuseppe Sichel (1849–1934) was a comic actor. Serafino Renzi played in crime dramas. Cyrano and Roxane are protagonists of Rostand's *Cyrano de Bergerac*. Porta Palazzo is the Turin market. Leopoldo Usseglio was mayor of Turin, rumoured to have fled to his country villa during the agitation. Francesco Répaci (1891–1951) was a former socialist lawyer who had broken with the party and wrote for Mussolini's militarist *Popolo d'Italia*. In 1921 Gramsci wrote of Répaci that 'after the events of August 1917 he explicitly invited the police to put the entire Turin staff of *Avanti!* behind bars' (SC, p. 270). Pietro Donvito was the Turin police commissioner responsible for the arrest of socialists. On Mario Gioda, also a contributor to the *Popolo d'Italia* and butt of Gramsci's polemics in this period, see footnote 1 on p. 345. On Sichel, see also LVN 250–52 (now in CT 808–9). On Renzi's theatre company as the 'theatrical reflection of the serial novel', see L, p. 59.

the dark with one's eyes burned by a burst of exploding gases, by a puff of poison gas. A veil of melancholy makes these spectators pale. They can feel humanity, they can understand pain, they can take on an expression of seriousness, they can feel their eyes veiled by a deep sadness. And yet, when the curtain rises and the ridiculous caricatures of the men and women on the stage put their machine in motion once again, the faces relax into dull-witted gaiety and the atmosphere of bestiality increases and grows heavy. One stupidity follows another, piling up into huge rubbish heaps, gawkily overflowing. Boorishness triumphs absolutely over intelligence, it spreads in the applause, and deepens in satisfied tittering. It continues to haunt our steps in the putrid vapours of the evening, in the fogginess of approaching autumn.

Avanti!, Piedmont edition, 3 October 1917.

20 Emma Gramatica

The theatre, as a practical organization of people and tools of trade, has not escaped from the coils of the capitalist maelstrom. But the practical organization of the theatre as a whole is a means of artistic expression. One cannot upset it without upsetting and ruining the expressive process, without sterilizing the 'linguistic' organ of the theatrical performance.

Industrialism has determined its essential moments. The theatrical company, as a working team governed by relations like those which existed between the master and his disciples in medieval art, has been dissolved. In place of the disciplinary bonds generated spontaneously by teamwork – work of a particular nature because its aims are those of artistic creation – there are 'bonds' that tie the manager to the wage-earners, like those between the gallows and the hanged man. The laws of competition have rapidly carried out their work of fragmentation. The actor is now an individual in conflict with his fellow workers, with the 'master', who has become a mediator, and with the industrialist of the theatre. Once unleashed, this sordid speculation has known no bounds. The peculiar nature of the work to be done has itself become a corrosive reagent. Excelling in wages goes hand in hand with excelling in the company, in managing and decision-making, in the freedom of choosing for oneself the most popular parts so as to stand out like a funerary monument in a cemetery of common graves. Theatrical technique has been upset as a result. Production has 'easily' adapted to the new conditions – easily in the sense that the balance has been reached at a shoddy level of companies, public and playwrights. There is talk of the depravity of taste, the decadence of customs and artistic dissolution. The origin of these showy phenomena is to be sought solely in the changing economic relations between the theatrical impresario, now a businessman who belongs to a trust, the actor-manager, now a middleman, and the actors subjugated to the slavery of wages.

There is little resistance to this rage of competition and speculation. Besides, resistance is difficult. There were a few who tried to save at least a part of the freedom of artistic expression among the cries and avid shrieking of the capitalist market. Emma Gramatica is certainly among these few, and this is a sign of her personality and artistic will. It would have been mad and childish to rebel. The time of romantic adventures and quixotic audacity is over. Besides, this is only possible for individual initiatives, not for businesses that require a team of individuals. Rebelling would only have meant being immediately deprived of a greater chance for expression. But there is adaptation and adaptation. Gramatica has kept her own freedom of movement and choice. There is a continuous search, a continuous struggle in her activity: there is life. She can discover unexplored areas, and enlarge the sphere of her sensibility and her experiences. She never falls into a routine. She has not become a mere employee who has applied the Taylor method to the plastic expression of life, who has reduced to a mechanism – complicated, expert, made up of 20,000 movable parts but a mechanism all the same – that which is unpredictable and irrepressible in her: expression.

At least in Turin, where the theatre industry functions like an implacable scourge, Gramatica is the only one in recent years who has 'produced' something new, who has aroused from within herself new creatures that quiver with love and hate or go through the daily toil of living in forms that are not worn down and dulled by the habit and routine of the trade – which is regulated by the law of minimum effort. She has tried, she has dared. They say that she even risked some capital, without being sure of getting it back, in order to present artistic phantasms that otherwise would never have set foot on the Italian stage. The irresistible and irrepressible creative principle that moulds a personality and shapes a character according to its own laws, the laws of beauty, lives and operates in her incessantly and also conditions her practical activity.

Avanti!, Piedmont edition, 1 July 1919.

21 Morality and Standards (Ibsen's 'A Doll's House' at the Carignano)

For her gala performance, Emma Gramatica brought Nora, the protagonist of Henrik Ibsen's *A Doll's House*, to life again before a full house of gentlemen and ladies. The play was evidently new to most of the audience. But if most of them warmly applauded the first two acts, they were bewildered and deaf to the third, and applauded weakly: only one curtain call, more for the great actress than for the superior creature that Ibsen's fantasy brought into the world. Why was the audience deaf? Why was it not moved to sympathy before the profoundly moral act of Nora Helmar, who gives up her home, her husband and her children to look for herself on her own, to dig down and find in the depths of her own self the strong roots of her moral being, to fulfil the duties that everyone has towards themselves even before having them towards others?

The drama, if it is to be truly such and not a pointless iridescence of words, must have a moral content. It must depict a necessary collision between two inner worlds, two conceptions, two moral lives. If the collision is necessary, the drama immediately takes hold of the minds of the spectators. They relive it in all its wholeness, in its most elementary as well as its more specifically historical motivations. By reliving the inner world of the drama, they also relive its art, the artistic form that has given concrete life to the world, that has made that world solid in a living and sure portrayal of human individuals who suffer, rejoice and struggle incessantly to go beyond themselves, to better the moral fibre of their historical personalities immersed in the present life of the world. Why, then, was the audience – the gentlemen and ladies who yesterday evening saw the sure, necessary, humanly necessary, unfolding of Nora Helmar's spiritual drama – not moved at a certain point to sympathize with her, instead of remaining bewildered and almost disgusted by the conclusion? Are they immoral, these ladies and gentlemen, or is the humanity of Henrik Ibsen immoral?

Neither the one nor the other. What happened was simply that our standards rebelled against a more spiritually human morality. Our standards (and I mean the standards that constitute the life of the Italian public), which are the traditional moral garb of our high and petty bourgeoisie, made up for the most part of slavery, submission to the environment, a hypocritical masking of man the animal, a bundle of nerves and muscles sheathed in a voluptuously itchy skin, rebelled against another standard, a superior, more spiritual and less animal tradition. Another standard, whereby woman and man are no longer just muscles, nerves and skin, but are essentially spirit; whereby the family is no longer just an economic institution but is above all a moral world in process, completed by the intimate fusion of two souls which find in each other what each individually lacks; whereby the woman is no longer just the female who nurses her newborn and feels for them a love made up of spasms of the flesh and palpitations of the heart, but is a human creature in herself, with her own awareness, her own inner needs, a human personality entirely her own, and the dignity of an independent being.

The standards of the high and petty Latin bourgeoisie rebel, they cannot comprehend a world of this kind. The only form of female liberation which our standards allow us to grasp is that of the woman who becomes a *cocotte*. The *pochade* really is the only dramatic female action that our standards comprehend; the attainment of physical and sexual freedom. The circuit of nerves, muscles and sensitive skin remains closed in on itself.

A great deal has been written recently about the new spirit that the war has kindled in bourgeois Italian women. Rhetoric. The abolition of the institution of the husband's authorization was exalted as a proof of the recognition of this new spirit. But the institution considers the woman as part of an economic contract, not as a universal humanity. It is a reform which affects the bourgeois woman as holder of a property and does not change relations between the sexes, nor even dent the surface of behavioural standards. These have not and could not have been changed, not even by the war. The woman of our countryside, the woman with a history, the woman of the bourgeois family remains as before a slave, without any deep moral life, without spiritual needs, submissive even when she seems rebellious, even more the slave when she discovers the only freedom that is allowed her, the freedom of coquetry. She remains the female who feeds the newborn, the doll who is the more dear the more stupid she is, the more beloved and extolled the more she renounces herself and the duties which she should have towards herself, in order to devote herself to others, whether they be her family or the sick, the human waste which charity gathers up and maternally succours. The hypocrisy of charitable sacrifice is another face of this inner inferiority of our standard of behaviour.

Our standard. A standard which is important in our present history, because it is that of the class which is the protagonist of this history. Alongside it, however, another standard is being formed, one that is more ours because it is that of the class to which we belong. A new standard? Simply one that is more closely identified with universal morality, that adheres entirely to it because it is deeply human, because it is more spiritual than animal, more of the spirit than of economics, than of nerves and muscles. Potential *cocottes* cannot understand the drama of Nora Helmar. Proletarian women, women who work, those who produce something more than pieces of new humanity and voluptuous shivers of sexual pleasure can understand it because they live it daily. Two proletarian women whom I know, for example, understand it, two women who have had no need either of divorce or of the law to find themselves, to create a world where they would be better understood and more humanly themselves. Two proletarian women who, with the complete consent of their husbands, who are not gentlemen but simple workers without hypocrisy, have abandoned their families and have gone with the man who best represented their other half. They have gone on in the old familiar way without thereby creating those licentious situations which are a network more typical of the high and petty bourgeoisie of the Latin countries. They would not have laughed coarsely at the creature Ibsen's fantasy has brought into the world because they would have recognized in her a spiritual sister, the artistic evidence that their act is understood elsewhere because it is essentially moral, because it is the aspiration of noble souls to a higher humanity, whose standard is the fullness of inner life, the profound excavation of one's personality and not cowardly hypocrisy, the tickling of sick nerves, the fat animality of slaves who have become masters.

Avanti!, Piedmont edition, 22 March 1917.

22 'Non amarmi così!' by Fraccaroli at the Carignano[44]

Witty people are a very important part of modern social life, and they are very popular. They replace truth, seriousness and profundity with a quip that makes people laugh. The ideal of their spiritual life is the elegant drawing-room, its fatuous and brilliant conversation, its measured applause and the veiled smile of its habitués. They reduce all life to the clever mediocrity of drawing-room life: a lot of words, amiable scepticism, and a light sprinkle of melancholy sentimentalism. The wit has become even more important through the latest incarnation of drawing-room life, namely the offices of the bourgeois newspapers. Here the wit has enlarged the circle of his audience and has made everything a source of humour – politics, war, pain, life and death – thereby winning much applause and earning a pile of money. Arnaldo Fraccaroli, who is one of the best liked of Italy's wits, has, in his latest comedy *Non amarmi così!*, offered a very brilliant example of how the wit renders down serious things for the amusement of his clients.

The general theme is this: on discovering that her husband does not understand her, a wife rebels, becomes withdrawn, and begins to examine her inner self. A theatrical genius, Ibsen, would give this drama the definitive seal of his poetic fantasy. But Ibsen was not a wit: he was an artist who deeply experienced the life of his characters. Consequently, he was not popular in the drawing-rooms and their debased enlargement, the theatres. Arnaldo Fraccaroli has corrected Ibsen, making him pleasant and lovable, latinizing him. Fraccaroli's Margherita is much easier to understand than Nora. The reasons for the conflict between

---

[44] 'Don't love me that way'. Arnaldo Fraccaroli (1883–1956), comic dramatist. Gramsci also reviewed his play *Mimí* (LVN pp. 302–3) and his one-acter *Ma non lo nominare* (LVN pp. 389–90).

husband and wife in Fraccaroli are within reach of everyone in face powder. Margherita loves her husband badly, she is the tiresome doll because she loves Luciano too much, smothers him with too many kisses, never leaves him alone and – the crux of the profound paradox – because she makes his life too easy, cleaning his pens and making sure that he finds his umbrella, overcoat and boots always in the right place and at the right moment. Luciano says that Margherita is boring and the drama precipitates. Margherita does not leave the marital home. The wit finds that this solution would be an exaggeration and the drawing-room abhors exaggerations. Margherita is a complicated modern soul (who moves towards a happy ending). She gets an idiot to court her, but not to make her husband jealous: not for nothing is she a complicated soul. The courtship of the idiot serves to conceal another fictional lover whose personality, thanks to these general complications, remains immersed in mystery and the deepest darkness. And it is this darkness, this mystery, that leads to the happy ending, to the reconciliation of the two souls. Between them there remains the background of mystery, the immanent threat of a new drama, to strengthen them, to make them become wise. 'Husbands, don't play with loaded guns' is the profound truth that Fraccaroli instills in the soul and the consciousness of his audience, and the path is eased by an infallible lubricant: divine melancholy, with fleecy clouds on the horizon and the pallid rays of the sun that glimmer and whiten the faces of the heroes.

The wit has achieved his goal. He has found in the Carignano theatre the drawing-room of those idiots most prepared to understand and applaud him. The wit is always a lucky man. Even if his wit has passed through all the paper filters of the international warehouse and has kept their mould and smell: from the filters of Ibsen to those of Pierre Wolf and his *Marionettes*.

Avanti!, Piedmont edition, 18 April 1917.

23 'Anfisa' by Andreyev at the Carignano[45]

For the bourgeois who has fed well and has three hours to kill between dinner and bedtime, a play is something in between a digestive and an aphrodisiac. For the critic, a play is a contrast of 'character types', of puppets playing at life. Andreyev's *Anfisa* is neither of these things. It hits the bourgeois who wants to digest his dinner like a blow to the stomach, the critic scans it in vain for his puppets. The dramatic quality of *Anfisa* lies in the way it exacerbates to the point of absurdity, laceration and crime an initially simple contrast of passions.

At its centre is a man, Fyodor Kostomarov, a lawyer, proud, vain, sensual, a great mind in the eyes of his provincial town. He plays the superman, but a provincial superman: he insults his opponents in a courtroom address, slaps those who do not greet him in the street, is a ladykiller, has contempt for common morality, but is no more original than a libertine. All in all, he is someone who wants to dominate while keeping his feet on the ground. He is shaken by a crisis, which arises more from external conflicts than from an inner dissent and which causes him to lose his self-control, making him both uncertain and brutal, violent and frightened.

Around him, three female figures, or rather one single figure in all of them: the being who lives on the love and domination of a man, who lives on them to the point of sacrifice, loss of self, hatred, crime.

Kostomarov's wife, betrayed, neglected, asks her sister Anfisa to stay. The latter, a widow, arrives with an undisclosed reputation for authority, and her sister hopes that she will restore her husband's affection and fidelity by admonitions and exhortations and perhaps by inspiring a new feeling in him. But he has been in love with Anfisa since the day he married her sister, and Anfisa loves him too. The doubly culpable feelings of the husband and the sister-in-law are aggravated by the strange situation in which they find themselves. Are these feelings going to be purified and to triumph as something primordial which needs no justification, which will not let itself be subdued, which is valid in itself and is everything? The play writhes for four acts,

---

[45] Leonid Nikolaevich Andreyev (1871–1919), dramatist and short-story writer. *Anfisa* (1909) established his reputation outside Russia.

through a few months of life, and ends with a crime. I say 'writhes', and I do not mean it as a condemnation. On the contrary, the action is perfect. If there is something to be criticized it is the tension which does not let up at all from the first to the last speech, giving the impression of a perfect logicality and a development fully in accordance with the laws of life. But the anguished writhing in which the dramatic manner and the limitations of ordinary existence are surpassed, which reaches tragedy and poetry, is that of a few people caught in the coils of a fate which, although spun by their own passion, appears no less as something of great tragic weight. It is totally explicable, from Anfisa's first repulse to her fall, to the promises of her lover and his petty desire for revenge and the exacerbation of passion and jealousy in the woman. A totally human process of development leads to tiredness in the man and hatred in the woman, to his insults against love and hers against pride, to the violent scene where Anfisa, in front of the whole assembled family, accuses Fyodor of having betrayed his wife and having taken his sister-in-law as a lover, and of now seeking a new lover in the third sister, young, naïve, unaware. It is totally human and it all unfolds deftly and quickly, but you feel that a whirlpool of passion has opened which draws these people in like straws, that a wound has been cut which cannot heal over because human forces and feelings are at work to widen and deepen it all the time.

The crime which ends the play, with Anfisa poisoning to death the man she loves and hates, in fact hangs over the action from the first scenes. It could be called an act of destiny if it were not something which comes so clearly from inside these people.

In this respect Andreyev has written a bourgeois drama: he has not just introduced a tragic event or a few tragic elements into an ordinary environment, but has tried to obtain a transfiguration of the environment by an exacerbated contrast of passions. If he is to be reproached for something, it is for having put too much emphasis on this, bringing in, for example, secondary elements which serve to create and pile up a sense of diffuse dramaticality and uncertainty, but which are only weakly connected to the main action. They remain implicit and are not explained by that action. One such instance is the figure of the grandmother who has poisoned her first husband, who plays deaf and haunts the protagonist.

But here too this reproach would only be valid if the dramatic work were not a work of art, of poetry, subject to no logic other than the fantasy of the poet, which possesses its own law which he must exclusively obey. We should acknowledge that life itself is not logical but is full of elements that cannot be weighed on the scales of reason. We should acknowledge above all that Andreyev has given life to a tragic tableau in which the figure of the grandmother, by the very uncertainty of her role, is an essential element. If she were to speak and if we had a clear idea of who she was, we would not only lose a dramatic element of incomparable evocative power but also an intuitive element which is inseparable from the rest of the work of art. The same goes for many other details and for their prominence and degree of finish.

The company performed all this with dramatic perfection. If a certain heaviness hangs over the play, this defect was accentuated by the style of acting, in particular that of Maria Melato. It was a style with too many traces of cinema acting about it, and although it kept the audience absorbed, in the end it tired them. Thus some scenes seemed to drag because of excessive tension, and thus after three acts which were well brought off and got a good number of encores one heard a few hisses at the end.

Yet we confess that the bourgeois audience in the theatre was not the most suitable for watching and listening to the work of art. Its undiluted truth must, we fear, have seemed like a blow to their stomachs.

Let us hope, then, that this play finds a better audience, less refined, more immediately sincere, nearer to appraising and suffering the impetuous anguish of the tragedy. We wish it a proletarian audience.

Avanti!, Piedmont edition, 14 November 1920.

24 'Pensaci, Giacomino!' by Pirandello at the Alfieri

This play of Luigi Pirandello's is a total outburst of virtuosity, literary ability, and verbal glitter. The three acts run on a single track. The characters are photographed more than examined psychologically. They are portrayed externally more than through an inward recreation of their moral being. This, besides, is the characteristic of Luigi Pirandello's art which captures the grimace more than the smile of life, the ridiculous more than the comic. He observes life with the physical eye of the literary man more than with the sympathetic eye of the artist and he deforms it through an irony that is more professional habit than sincere and spontaneous vision.

The inner lives of the characters are frighteningly poor in this play, as is true of those in the short stories, novels and other plays by the same author. They are only pictorial or, better, picturesque: caricatures with a glazing of melancholy, it too a physical grimace more than passion. The protagonist of the comedy is an old schoolmaster, wizened through thirty-four years of teaching natural history: a wreck of humanity, a piece of rubble, no longer possessing any human characteristics, except for his physical outline. The cause of the action, the only one that might surprise, is the following. For many years Professor Toti has served the state. Having been paid so miserably that he has not been able to raise a family, he now wants to avenge himself on the government. Before dying, he wants to take a wife, a very young one. In this way, he can leave her his right to a pension and thus make the government pay the young widow, in all those years of pension entitlement, all that money he was not able to have, all the money he never had to live life properly, to be a man and not a teaching machine. The desire to play this dirty trick on the government becomes for Professor Toti the consuming reason for the few years of life that are left to him. But since he is not a wicked man, he does not want his wife to suffer. Therefore, he allows her to be almost completely free. He helps his substitute carry out his marital duties, loves him like a son, and moves towards his goal, totally impervious to the gossip of the town, the reproaches of the head of the school, and the ridicule of which he himself is the object. Giacomino, the wife's lover, would like to get free of the situation in which he is entangled. Professor Toti goes to Giacomino's house, he takes his little boy back there, he gets rid of all obstacles, dismayed relatives, moralistic priests, and defends the cause of his wife. Finally, he succeeds in leading Giacomino back to the path of duty, to fulfil his obligations as the husband of the young wife of the employee who wants to avenge himself on the government without thereby creating other victims.

The comedy was very successful. Angelo Musco made

Professor Toti an admirable theatrical creation by his sincerity, restraint and acting ability.

Avanti!, Piedmont edition, 24 March 1917.

25 'Liolà' by Pirandello at the Alfieri

The new three-act play by Luigi Pirandello was not a success at the Alfieri. It did not even meet with that success a play needs to make it a profit. In spite of this, though, *Liolà* remains a fine play, perhaps the best that the Sicilian dialect theatre has created. The failure of the third act, which caused the work to be momentarily withdrawn, was due to extrinsic reasons: *Liolà* does not end in the traditional way, with a knifing or a marriage. Therefore, it was not received enthusiastically. But it could not have ended any other way than it did and therefore it will eventually find favour.

Liolà is the best product of Luigi Pirandello's literary energy. In it Pirandello has managed to shed his rhetorical habits. He is a calculated humorist, which means that all too often the initial intuition of his works is submerged in a rhetorical swamp of unconsciously sermonizing morality and pointless verbosity. *Liolà*, too, has gone through this stage, when he was called Mattia Pascal, the protagonist of a long ironic novel entitled *Il fu Mattia Pascal* published around 1906 in *Nuova Antologia* and then reprinted by Treves. Pirandello subsquently reworked his creation and *Liolà* is the result.[46] The plot is the same, but the artistic phantasm has been completely renewed. It has become homogeneous and pure representation, entirely freed of all those moralizing and factitiously humoristic trappings which had weighed it down. *Liolà* is a farce, but in the best sense of the word; a farce which goes back to the satyr dramas of ancient Greece and which has its pictorial equivalent in the vascular figurative art of the Hellenistic world. One is led to believe that the dialect art as expressed in these three acts by Pirandello is linked to the ancient popular art tradition of Magna Grecia, with its buffoons, its

---

[46] *Il fu Mattia Pascal* first appeared in serial form in the Rome periodical *Nuova Antologia* from April to June 1904. The plot of *Liolà* reworks an episode narrated in chapter IV of this novel.

pastoral idylls, its country life full of Dionysian frenzy, a great part of which has remained in the rural tradition of modern Sicily, where this tradition has been kept most alive and sincere. It is a naïve and coarsely honest life in which the bark of the oak trees and the water of the fountains still seem to palpitate. It is an efflorescence of naturalistic paganism where life, all life, is beautiful, work is joyful and irresistible fecundity springs from all organiç matter.

Mattia Pascal, the melancholic modern man, cross-eyed, a spectator of life who is at times cynical, bitter, melancholic, and sentimental, becomes Liolà, the man of pagan life, full of physical and moral robustness because he is a man, because he is himself, simple vigorous humanity. And the plot is renewed, it becomes life, it becomes truth. It also becomes simple, while in the first part of the original novel it was contorted and ineffective. Uncle Simone rants because he wants an heir who will justify his tenacious labour of accumulating a fortune. He is old and accuses his wife of being sterile. She does not realize that Simone wants any heir whatever, he wants a child at all costs and is willing to pretend that he is the father. A niece of his who has understood the old man's state of mind, and who has become pregnant by Liolà, suggests to Simone that he become the father by giving out that the child is his. The old man agrees. It comes as a blow to his legitimate wife, who feels humiliated because she has not done the same. To get the upper hand she follows suit. Now, Uncle Simone legally has a son. But it is Liolà who gives life to these new lives and to the comedy. It is Liolà who is always full of songs, whose entrance on stage is always accompanied by a Bacchic chorus of women and by his other three natural children who are like little satyrs obeying the impulse of dance and song, imbued with music and dance like the primitive creatures of the satyr plays. Liolà wanted to marry Tuzza, Simone's niece, before the trick of the heir was devised. Now that there is a legal heir, Tuzza would like to be married. But not Liolà, who does not want to give up his singing, the dancing of his children, the Dionysian life of joyful work. Tuzza's dagger is wrenched from her hands which, however, know no hate or revenge. But the audience needed blood or a marriage, and so did not applaud.

Avanti!, Piedmont edition, 4 April 1917.

26 'Così è (se vi pare)' by Pirandello at the Carignano

The truth in itself does not exist, it is nothing but the highly personal impression that each individual draws from a certain fact. This statement may be (indeed, certainly is) nonsense, the pseudo-wisdom of a wit who wants to score superficial merriment from incompetent listeners. But that does not matter. The statement can give rise to a drama all the same: plays do not have to be based on very logical reasons. Pirandello, though, has not managed to make a drama out of this philosophical statement. It remains an external thesis, a superficial opinion. A number of facts unfold, a few scenes follow upon each other. The only reason for their existence is the gossipy curiosity of a petty provincial environment. But not even this is a real reason, a necessary and sufficient one, for a play. Nor is it enough for the artistic and vivid creation of characters, living people with a fantastic, if not a logical, meaning. Pirandello's three acts are simply a fact of literature, without any dramatic connection, without any philosophical connection. They are purely a mechanical accumulation of words that create neither a truth nor an image. The author has called them a parable: the term is exact. The parable is a mixture of the demonstration and the dramatic representation, of logic and fantasy. It can be an effective means of persuasion in practical life, but it is a monster in the theatre because in the theatre allusions are not enough. In the theatre a demonstration is embodied, living people and allusions no longer suffice. Metaphorical suspensions must descend to the concreteness of life. In the theatre the virtues of style are not enough to create beauty. What is necessary is the complex construction of deep inner intuitions of feeling that lead to a collision, a struggle, that unravel into an action.

The demonstration fails in Pirandello's parable. The truth in itself does not exist. There is only one's interpretation of it, and this interpretation is true when there is enough evidence to permit men of good will to arrive at it. There are only two witnesses to the fact that gives rise to the parable, and they are parties to the fact itself. The audience sees only their external behaviour, their visible appearance which is based on motives that remain unexplored. Three characters, survivors of the Marsica earthquake, arrive in a small provincial town: a husband, a wife and an old woman. Their lives are engulfed in mystery and this mystery excites gossip in the town. Questions begin to be asked and authorities are called in. But no results. The husband maintains one thing, the old woman another. The former claims that the latter is mad. Who is right? Mr Ponza says that he is the widower of a daughter of Mrs Frola. He says he has remarried and keeps Mrs Frola with him (in the same town, but in a different house) only out of pity because the poor thing, who has gone mad over the death of her daughter, believes that the second Mrs Ponza is her daughter, still living. Mrs Frola maintains that at a certain time in his life Ponza lost his reason. According to her, during that period his wife was taken from him and he thought she was dead. Afterwards, he would not live with her again until they had simulated another marriage, giving her a new name and believing her to be another person. Taken separately, both these people seem wholly lucid. When they are put together, however, they necessarily contradict one another, although they both behave as if they are putting on an act out of compassion for the other. What is the truth? Which of the two is mad? There is no documentary evidence. Since the town they come from has been destroyed by the earthquake, all the potential informants are dead. Ponza's wife makes a brief appearance but the author, enchanted by his demonstration, makes her into a symbol. She is truth appearing in a veil, and she says, 'I am both one and the other, I am what I am believed to be.' Simply a logical catch. The author has only hinted at the real drama: it lies in the two pseudo-insane characters who do not however portray their real lives, the inner necessity of their external attitudes, but are presented as pawns in a logical demonstration. A monster, therefore, not a demonstration, not a drama. More the residual product of a ready wit and considerable stagecraft.

The actors were Melato, Betrone, Paoli and Lamberti, who performed with enthusiasm and a skilful handling of dialogue. Little applause at the end of each act.

Avanti!, Piedmont edition, 5 October 1917.

27 'Il piacere dell'onestà' by Pirandello at the Carignano

Luigi Pirandello is a 'stormtrooper' of the theatre. His comedies are so many hand grenades that explode in the brains of the spectators, bringing down banalities, wrecking feelings and ideas. Luigi Pirandello has the great merit of producing at least flashes of life that deviate from the usual schemes of tradition, and yet they cannot begin a new tradition, they cannot be imitated, they cannot establish a fashionable stereotype. There is in his plays an effort of abstract thought that always seeks a concrete representation, and when it succeeds, it results in something unusual for the Italian theatre: works of an exceptional plasticity and clarity of fantasy. This is the case with the three acts of *Il piacere dell'onestà*. In it Pirandello depicts a man who lives a life of thought, life as a plan, life as 'pure form'. He is not an ordinary man this Angelo Baldovino. Judging from appearances, he has led a bad life and is now a wreck. In reality, he is merely a man towards whom society has committed the injustice of being a place where the 'pure form' is adjusted to the rest of reality. In the play Baldovino inserts himself in a favourable environment and lives his own life. He becomes the lawful husband of a young noble lady who has been made pregnant by a married man. He accepts his part, imposing duties of honesty on himself and others, and develops his ideas. But he immediately becomes a burden. His thought materializes by itself but upsets his surroundings and reaches this deadlock which was foreseen by Baldovino but is paradoxical for the others: Marquis Fabio, the seducer, must become a thief for the 'pure form' to develop according to its logic, and Baldovino must appear to be the thief. It remains clear to all those involved, however, that the real thief is the marquis and that one has to accept the consequences of contracts where logic and the will of one bent on respecting it are essential ingredients. Having arrived at this point of break-up and psychological dissolution, the play takes a dangerous and somewhat confused turn. Emotional reactions gain the upper hand. The real knavery of Marquis Fabio acquires a humorous and catastrophic obviousness. Baldovino's reputed wife becomes his real and impassioned wife. Baldovino is neither a rogue nor a gentleman, but only a man who wants to be both and who really is capable of being a gentleman, a worker, because these words are only the contingent attributes of an absolute created and nourished by thought and the will alone.

Pirandello's play received increasing applause because of the force of persuasion present in the imaginative development of the plot. Ruggero Ruggeri played the part of Baldovino, Vergani was the young lady, later Mrs Agata Baldovino, Martelli was Marquis Fabio. Together with Pettinello and Mosso they were an excellent acting ensemble and this helped bring out the play's clipped and foreshortened dialogue.

Avanti!, Piedmont edition, 29 November 1917.

28 'Il giuoco delle parti' by Pirandello at the Carignano

In the first act of *Il giuoco delle parti*, Luigi Pirandello has the 'wife' personify the physics of life as conceived by the sculptors and painters of post-cubist Futurism: the inner life of the spirit is a breaking-up of volumes and planes that continue in space, not a limitation rigidly defined in lines and surfaces. The 'husband', on the other hand, is firmly centred in a reasoning self, smoothed and polished like a pure concept, which turns around on an axis, a silent spinning-top made to rotate on a plane of glass by a will freed of any contingent conditioning. Clearly, the two creatures cannot establish relationships of affectionate coexistence. The husband is impervious to the vibratile planes and volumes of his wife, and she, unable to extend herself into her husband, feels limited by him, since it is her nature to extend herself into all the spiritual lives and territories of the world. She suffers, raves and strives to liberate her own self, which inevitably seeks to destroy its uncoercible opposite. The pure concept triumphs over the vibratile protoplasm. Classical philosophy triumphs over Bergson, contingencies submit to the will of the Socratic spinning-top. Since the play is in the eternal triangle mould, there is a 'lover', but the lover does not personify any idea. He is unresponsive matter, opaque objectivity, the 'fool' of life who is logically led to get himself killed so that the dialectic of contraries may finally end in the tears of the pure concept and the savage howl of protoplasm in motion. Humanity, in other words, which we are amazed to find is still there in this frenzy of philosophical squibs worthy of a provincial schoolmaster. To put it banally, the wife wants to get rid of her husband. Insulted as a wife, she want him to fight a duel. He does not see things this same way and he constructs the triumph of logical reason over the contingencies put in his way by nature external to his self. He accepts this duel to the death and then does not fight, forcing the lover, who is the real husband, to fight and get himself killed. For him, pure concept, life is a mechanical game, and one must try to anticipate and arrange the roles *a priori*, always ending in checkmate.

This play is not one of Pirandello's best. The game element has become an external mechanism of dialogue, a purely literary effort of pseudo-philosophical verbalism. The mutual incomprehension of the stage puppets was projected on to the theatre: a complete domain of windowless and doorless monads; incommunicable and unbending: the author, the characters and the audience.

Avanti!, Piedmont edition, 6 February 1919.

29 'La ragione degli altri' by Pirandello at the Carignano

Home is where the children are. Family life cannot be founded on mere sexual relations. It cannot be founded on law or conventional ideas of duty or sentimental motives of devotion. Only one elementary, and therefore constant and irrepressible, bond exists: the children. And only where children are can there be a home.

The logic of this principle (brought to the point of absurdity: even if the children are of another woman, even if their natural mother is obtained on loan) substantiates Pirandello's play. He abandons the literary and . . . philosophical motives of plot and dramatic dialogue and bases the action on one of humanity's primordial motives, the most profound and instinctive. The drama proves to be atrocious and skeletal in the third act: two opposing women are struggling for the possession of a child, one because she is the mother, not in order to keep her lover; the other because she wants her husband's daughter in her home, in order to appear to her husband as a mother and with this illusory motherhood reconstruct or build a family, to give a morality to love. It is an atrocious and cruel struggle because the mother will have to give up her child in order to ensure it a future, the name of her father, wealth, a home. The play is performed without oratorical blandishments, without mawkishness, without grandiloquent scenes and it aims, therefore, to hit all the sentimental habits of the audience, which reacts with all its petty-bourgeois prejudices bristling. But has Pirandello succeeded in developing the drama to the full? One has the uncomfortable impression, in the first two acts, of effort and of inescapable torment settling into the prolix insistence on useless details. The fundamental motive is vaguely hinted at but does not direct or indicate the development of the action. The third act seems too crude a revelation, too offensive to . . . good taste and good manners.

There are no further performances.

Avanti!, Piedmont edition, 13 January 1920.

II
PROBLEMS OF CRITICISM

Introduction

Gramsci's prison writings (dating from 1929 to 1935 and represented in this and the remaining sections of this volume) reflect the break with immediately tactical issues imposed by his imprisonment after 1926. Their scope however remains political, since all Gramsci's theoretical and historical work in prison is linked to the problem of how to win power now that the prospect of an imminent socialist revolution is in abeyance in the West, fascism is installed in power and international capitalism is developing structurally new characteristics and extensive ideological defences.

The theoretical questions Gramsci asks in the following notes are straightforward: What are the preconditions for a genuinely new art and culture? What is the relation between progressive tendencies in high culture and the formation of a new culture? What kinds of intellectual attitude and organization block or promote its formation? How is cultural change related to economic and political change and how can it be rationally organized and accelerated? What kind of criticism is best able to pose and resolve these problems? Gramsci in other words is not dealing with 'literary criticism' in the narrow sense but with questions of cultural analysis and strategy. Two central figures act as co-ordinates on his discussion: Francesco De Sanctis and Benedetto Croce.

De Sanctis (1817–83) had been an important influence on Gramsci's thinking since his student days. Risorgimento democrat, southerner, educational reformer, literary historian and critic, towards the end of his career De Sanctis powerfully overlaid his political, moral and aesthetic ideas into a single set of preoccupations. In his 1872 inaugural lecture, 'Science and Life', he criticized the positivist 'science' of the liberal ruling class of newly united Italy for its failure to incorporate the interests of the popular classes, to merge with the 'life' of the nation. De Sanctis favoured a progressive and expansive bourgeoisie which could overcome the separation between the state and the nation and (a nod here in the direction of the Paris Commune) check the class-divisive threat of incipient socialism. The divorce between science and the people was parallelled in De Sanctis's other writings by his contrast between the self-interested 'particularism' of Guicciardini in politics and the expansive political involvement of Machiavelli, between the Renaissance as a surface cultural reform and the Reformation as a mass cultural movement from below, between an instructional and dogmatic kind of education and a democratic one based on interaction between teachers and taught. Gramsci takes over many of these ideas and transposes them into a socialist key: for instance in his description of hegemony as a relation between intellectual strata and popular masses. In his literary criticism and his aesthetics De Sanctis drew on Hegel, developing the theme of a 'sinking' (*calarsi*) of ideas into art, of abstract content into a particular concrete form. This sinking both described in Romantic terms the process of literary composition and acted as a criterion of value in determining what was an authentic work of art. A work was fully realized if its content had been fully elaborated and sunk into form, but not if either the content or the form remained in a raw or superfluous state and unassimilated to the other. This aesthetic precept became closely related to De Sanctis's political and cultural theme of the merging of science with life. He came to view Italian literary history as a cycle of separations and fusions between intellectual activity and popular life. The seventeenth-century baroque poets had for example been detached stylistic hedonists whereas the late nineteenth-century naturalist novelists had engaged with popular life and social problems. De Sanctis identified moral and political involution or regress with the first of these tendencies and regeneration and progress with the second.

Croce (1866–1952) came from the same Neapolitan intellectual stable as De Sanctis, and produced the first major edition of the latter's writings. He also stood squarely within the Hegelian tradition and his range of interests was remarkably wide, yet he lacked De Sanctis's democratic commitment and adopted more the role of professional philosopher and savant. Whereas the keynote of De Sanctis's later work had been the overlaying of disciplines and themes and their linkage with political actuality, the keynote of Croce's philosophy was the demarcation of distinctions between disciplines (ethics, politics, economics, aesthetics, historiography, logic) and the policing of their boundaries. In his aesthetic theory, Croce took over De Sanctis's views on the fusion of content and form as well as a belief that art was qualitatively different from conceptual or logical thought without being inferior to it. But he broke substantially with De Sanctis in his concern to theorize the specificity of the aesthetic as a distinct category of spiritual activity. He had defined art in 1902 by distinguishing it from what was not art (conceptual thought, moral or utilitarian acts, physical facts) and despite making a number of modifications to this theory at successive stages (1908, 1918, 1928) he had kept this basic distinction, as well as that between 'history of art' and 'history of culture'. 'History of art' was, in Croce's definition, the history of individual works: in his view the only proper kind of aesthetic history. 'History of culture' was the history of tendencies, genres, artists' lives, intellectual 'background', ideas about art and so forth: things which for Croce had no 'reality' or value for explaining individual works of art and their beauty but which possessed some significance and interest in their own right as cultural facts and ideas. In making such a theoretical separation between the 'artistic' and the 'cultural' (one which subsequently became a virtual orthodoxy in Italian criticism), Croce exemplified the procedure of his 'dialectic of distincts' in which two categories or disciplines could be separated at one level while still circulating under a higher unity. In addition to distinguishing art from culture and history in this way, Croce's system distinguished art from politics, since art was a spiritual activity while politics was a practical one, a matter of 'passion' having no immediate connection with the spiritual sphere.

Gramsci saw Croce as corresponding to the current conjuncture of 'restoration-revolution'. Just as in his philosophy he etherealized real struggles and conflicts into a purely speculative dialectic, so in his historical writing the liberal Croce omitted the moments of struggle and concentrated on those of restoration and reform. 'It might be one of the numerous paradoxical aspects of history', Gramsci wrote, ' . . . that Croce, with his own particular preoccupations, should in effect have contributed to a reinforcement of fascism – furnishing it indirectly with an intellectual justification' (SPN, p. 119). He insisted on the need for an 'Anti-Croce' as an equivalent to Engels's 'Anti-Dühring', exposing the political practices that underlay Croce's thought and overturning it into praxis (SPN, p. 371). Gramsci's relation with Croce's thought is in reality a complex one of appropriation and transformation more often than one of simple rejection. In Notebook 10, devoted to Croce's philosophy in relation to Marxism, he performs a double operation. On the one hand, he seizes on the importance of Croce's focus on 'ethico-political history': on culture, the historical function of the traditional intellectuals, consent, civil society. Croce had criticized historical materialism for deifying the economy and treating the ethico-political sphere as a merely phenomenal superstructure reared up over it and Gramsci acknowledges the force of this critique of vulgar Marxism. On the other hand, he criticizes Croce's inaccurate identification of all Marxism with this position as well as the purely speculative notion Croce has of the ethico-political sphere. He also opposes to Croce's dialectic of distincts a real dialectic grounded in praxis. In his treatment of literature and culture, too, Gramsci's relation with Croce's thought is ambiguous. After the democratic militancy of De Sanctis's criticism and that of *La Voce*, Croce's represents a stabilization of bourgeois high culture, a phase of historical 'serenity' and detachment which must be broken up. Gramsci takes over Croce's distinction between history of art and history of culture but he tends constantly to tip the scales in his concrete analyses towards history of culture, politics, praxis. He is less concerned with why a work is beautiful in a fine art sense than with why it is read, what feelings it arouses and how it can act as an instrument of consent in the elaboration of a new culture. Nevertheless he is evidently concerned not to relinquish the aesthetic as a distinct category.

These notes also reflect a more immediate context of discussions among Italian writers and critics which Gramsci followed in the literary journals he received in prison. In 1932–33 a debate took place between two groups dubbed 'contentists' and 'calligraphists' on how literature could best be made to suit the life of the time. The 'contentists' argued that the new period should be expressed with a new subject matter. The 'calligraphists' (in effect formalists) retorted that form was also content so that they too were producing a historically new content by working on form. As Gramsci notes, the debate was little more than a gang war between two literary coteries bent on defending their respective territories. It reflected the cultural immobility of two kinds of traditional literary intellectual. The 'contentists' rallied a more militant type who wanted to see the 'new mentality' and 'revolutionary' thrust of fascism expressed in literature. The 'calligraphists' exemplified an attitude of aloofness from politics and a defence of 'pure' literary values and the national tradition. Several of them were writers who had been associated with *La Ronda* (1919–22), the Rome review that had epitomized this stance during the crisis years before the fascist seizure of power. The literary wrangle which these groups engaged in, like the other debates Gramsci mentions in this and subsequent sections ('Super-country' and 'Super-city', 'Constituting an epoch'), was a telling illustration of the resistance to any fundamental change which kept this area of civil society inert and prevented a new kind of relation between intellectuals and a mass public from arising. Since, Gramsci argues, the fascist transformation of the state had not been accompanied by a revolution in the relations of production or a real transformation of civil society, the various 'contentists' and 'calligraphists' could not effect any real changes in culture and were bound to remain limited to their voluntaristic slogans or their formalism. He stresses that a new literature or art cannot simply be created on demand, or 'from above', by decree. It can only be an *effect* of a new culture, and the latter is not an abstraction but a very concrete process involving the formation of new strata of intellectuals with a new mentality and a new educative relationship with popular masses of readers.

1 Back to De Sanctis

'Let us return to De Sanctis!' What does this slogan of Giovanni Gentile's mean, what can and what should it mean? (See, among other things, the first number of the weekly *Il Quadrivio*.)[1] Does it mean 'to return' mechanically to those concepts on art and literature that De Sanctis developed or does it mean to assume an attitude toward art and life similar to the one assumed by De Sanctis in his day? Having established his attitude as 'exemplary', one should see: 1) what its exemplariness consisted of; 2) what current attitude corresponds to it, that is, what current moral and

---

[1] Giovanni Gentile, 'Torniamo a De Sanctis', in *Quadrivio* I, 1 (6 August 1933). In Gramsci's first draft (also 1934), this was part of a single note (Q 17 § 38) with 'Connection of problems' and 'An early note by Luigi Pirandello' (VI 1 and III 5 respectively in this edition).

intellectual interests correspond to those which dominated the activity of De Sanctis and gave it a definite direction.

It cannot be said that the life of De Sanctis, although essentially coherent, was 'rectilinear', as is commonly thought. During the last phase of his life and activity, De Sanctis turned his attention to the 'naturalist' or 'verist' novel.[2] In Western Europe this form of the novel was the 'intellectualist' expression of a more general movement of 'going to the people'. It was a populist expression of several groups of intellectuals towards the end of the last century, after the democracy of 1848 had disappeared and after large masses of workers had emerged with the development of large urban industry. As for De Sanctis, one should recall his essay 'Science and Life', his going over to the parliamentary Left and his fear of attempted reaction masked under a ceremonious rhetoric.[3]

An opinion of De Sanctis's: 'There is no fibre because there is no faith, and there is no faith because there is no culture.'[4] But what does 'culture' mean here? Undoubtedly, it means a coherent, integral and nationwide 'conception of life and man', a 'lay religion', a philosophy that has become 'culture', that is, one that has generated an ethic, a life-style and an individual and civil pattern of behaviour. This above all required the total unification of the 'educated class' and that is why De Sanctis founded the Philological Circle, which aimed at the 'union of all the educated and intelligent men' of Naples.[5] In particular, it required a new attitude towards the popular classes and a new concept of what is 'national', different from that of the Right, broader, less exclusive

---

[2] *Verismo* was a late 19th century literary movement pioneered by the Sicilians Giovanni Verga (1840–1922) and Luigi Capuana (1839–1915), who followed the French naturalists' conception of writing as a scientific record of reality unhindered by moral or stylistic self-expression. In two late essays on Zola, De Sanctis noted that his application of positivist science to the novel had helped him supersede older realist modes and analyse people and environments more acutely. But he also argued (in line with his 'science-life' theme) that Zola's art was suffused with moral ideals despite the author's claims to clinical impassivity. ('Studio sopra Emilio Zola', 1878; 'Zola e l'"Assommoir"', 1879: in F. De Sanctis, *Opere*, Volume XIV, Turin 1972.)

[3] 'La scienza e la vita' (1872) in De Sanctis, *Opere*, Volume XIV. On this essay, see the introduction to this section. De Sanctis, who had been education minister in the moderate (Right) governments of Cavour and Ricasoli in 1861–62, moved to the Left around 1864 and called for a genuine two-party system.

[4] 'La coltura politica' (1877) in De Sanctis, *Opere*, Volume XVI, Turin 1970, p. 102.

[5] The phrase is from a letter of 27 April 1877 to Guglielmo Capitelli. The Naples Philological Circle was an adult education institute founded in 1877 to promote the study of foreign languages and culture among the local bourgeoisie.

and, so to speak, less 'police-like'.[6] It is this side of De Sanctis's activity that should be illuminated, an element, moreover, that was not new but represented the development of seeds already present from the beginning of his career in literature and politics.

Q 23 § 1.

2 Art and the Struggle for a New Civilization

The artistic relationship brings out, especially in relation to the philosophy of praxis, the fatuous naïvety of the parrots who think that with a few brief and stereotyped formulas they possess the key to open all doors (those keys are actually called 'picklocks').[7]

Two writers can represent (express) the same socio-historical moment, but one can be an artist and the other a mere scribbler. To try to deal with the question just by describing what the two represent or express socially, that is, by summarizing more or less thoroughly the characteristics of a specific socio-historical moment, hardly touches at all upon the artistic problem. All this can be useful and necessary, indeed it certainly is, but in another field: that of political criticism, the criticism of social life, involving the struggle to destroy and to overcome certain feelings and beliefs, certain attitudes toward life and the world. This is not the criticism or the history of art, nor can it be presented as such – except at the expense of creating confusion and a retarding or stagnation of scientific concepts: in other words a failure precisely to pursue the intrinsic aims of cultural struggle.

A given socio-historical moment is never homogeneous; on the contrary, it is rich in contradictions. It acquires a 'personality' and is a 'moment' of development in that a certain fundamental activity of life prevails over others and represents a historical 'peak': but this presupposes a hierarchy, a contrast, a struggle.

[6] The Right (*destra storica*) was the moderate party in power from 1860 to 1876.

[7] The original draft of this note (Q4 § 5) includes a first paragraph which links the discussion of Marxist art theory to Gramsci's analyses of Bukharin's *Popular Manual of Sociology* and Croce's *Historical Materialism* (see SPN, pp. 378 ff and the note 'On art' in SPN, pp. 471–72) as well as explaining the allusion to 'parrots': 'In some respects one could make the same critique of certain tendencies (perhaps the most widespread) in historical materialism that historicism has made of the old historical method and philology. The latter had led to new naïve forms of dogmatism, interpretation was replaced by a more or less accurate external description of phenomena and particularly by the perpetual repetition of "we are followers of the historical method!"' The remainder of the draft parallels the revised version reproduced here.

The person who represents this prevailing activity, this historical 'peak', should represent the given moment; but how should one who represents the other activities and elements be judged? Are not these also 'representative'? And is not the person who expresses 'reactionary' and anachronistic elements also representative of the 'moment'? Or should he be considered representative who expresses all those contrasting forces and elements in conflict among themselves, that is, the one who represents the contradiction of the socio-historical whole?

It could also be said that a critique of literary civilization, a struggle to create a new culture, is artistic in the sense that a new art will be born from the new culture, but this appears to be a sophism. At any rate, it is perhaps on the basis of such presuppositions that one can best understand the relationship between De Sanctis and Croce and the controversy over form and content. De Sanctis's criticism is militant, not 'frigidly' aesthetic; it belongs to a period of cultural struggles and contrasts between antagonistic conceptions of life. Analyses of content, criticism of the 'structure' of works, that is, the logical, historical and topical coherence of the mass of artistically represented feelings, are connected to this cultural struggle.[8] The profound humanity and humanism of De Sanctis, which even today make this critic so congenial, would seem to consist precisely in this. It is good to feel in him the impassioned fervour of one who is committed, one who has strong moral and political convictions and does not hide them nor even attempt to. Croce succeeds in distinguishing these various aspects of the critic which in De Sanctis were organically united and fused. Croce has the same cultural motives as De Sanctis, but at a time when these are in a period of expansion and triumph. The struggle continues; but it is a struggle for a refinement of culture (a certain type of culture) and not for its right to live: romantic fervour and passion have subsided into a superior serenity and an indulgence full of *bonhomie*. Even in Croce, though, this position is not permanent. A new phase follows in which cracks appear in the serenity and indulgence, and acrimony and a barely repressed anger emerge:

[8] For criticism of 'structure' (a Crocean term which Gramsci is applying back to De Sanctis) see the introduction to Section IV, 'Canto X of Dante's Inferno'.

[9] This passage probably involves a recollection of Croce's article of 1915, 'Religione e serenità', which argued that philosophy could provide more consolation and serenity than

a defensive, not an aggressive and impassioned phase, hence not to be compared with that of De Sanctis.[9]

In short, the type of literary criticism suitable to the philosophy of praxis is offered by De Sanctis, not by Croce or by anyone else (least of all by Carducci).[10] It must fuse the struggle for a new culture (that is, for a new humanism) and criticism of social life, feelings and conceptions of the world with aesthetic or purely artistic criticism, and it must do so with heat and passion, even if it takes the form of sarcasm.

More recently the De Sanctis phase has had an equivalent, albeit at a lower level, in the phase represented by the magazine *La Voce*. De Sanctis fought for the creation, *ex novo*, of an advanced national culture in Italy and against traditional rubbish, rhetoric and Jesuitism (Guerrazzi and Father Bresciani).[11] *La Voce* struggled only to spread that same culture at an intermediate level, against such things as provincialism. This review was an aspect of militant Crocism because it sought to democratize what had been necessarily 'aristocratic' in De Sanctis and had

religion. Although Croce repeatedly maintained that philosophy and the practical sphere (politics, etc.) were mutually distinct (see introduction to this Section), Gramsci detected slidings in Croce from the one to the other sphere. Remarking on an altercation between Croce and Lunacharsky at Oxford in September 1930 (where Croce had argued that a Marxist aesthetic was impossible since historical materialism was based on 'a hidden God, the Economy, which pulls all the strings and which is the only reality amid the appearances of morality, religion, philosophy, art and so on'), Gramsci comments that Croce 'in spite of his Olympian serenity (is) dozing off a little too often' (LP, p. 189): Croce had replaced his earlier considered treatment of Marxism with this reductionist caricature and 'his judgement, more than a historical-philosophical judgement, is nothing else but wilfulness with a practical end in view' (ibid.). Croce's intervention against Lunacharsky 'must be interpreted not as the judgement of a philosopher but as a political act of immediate practical significance' (Q 10 II § 41).

[10] Giosue Carducci (1835–1907), poet and critic who attempted to promote a classical revival in poetry and taste. Metrical experimentation with 'barbarous' verse-forms played an important part in his writing. Politically, he evolved away from republicanism to monarchism after the Unification. His criticism set close textual analyses in historical 'contexts'. He disliked De Sanctis's historicism and aesthetic system. Croce admired Carducci's taste and skill as a textual critic but deplored his lack of a philosophy of art. The critics of the later *Voce* (1914–16) had defended Carducci against both De Sanctis and Croce because of his concentration on the text.

[11] Francesco Domenico Guerrazzi (1804–73), Risorgimento democrat (member of the revolutionary government of Tuscany in 1849) and historical novelist. De Sanctis criticized his novel *Beatrice Cenci* in 1855 for its abstractness, mechanical characters and hyperbolical language. Guerrazzi compared unfavourably for De Sanctis with the liberal Catholic Manzoni (see Section VII below), whom he considered a great realist artist despite his politics. On Bresciani, see the introduction to Section VIII. Gramsci refers in a prison letter to Guerrazzi and Bresciani as left and right variants of the same bitterly sectarian type of historical novel (L, pp. 335–36).

remained 'aristocratic' in Croce.[12] De Sanctis had to form a cultural General Staff. *La Voce* wanted to extend the same cultural tone to the junior officers, and therefore had a function. It worked on the substance and it stirred up a number of artistic currents in that it helped many people to rediscover themselves. It aroused a greater need for inwardness and a sincere expression of it, even if no major artist came out of the movement.

(Raffaello Ramat writes in *L'Italia Letteraria*, 4 February 1934: 'It has been said that in tracing the history of culture it is at times more useful to study a minor writer than a great one. This is partly true. In the case of the great writer the individual comes out on top and acquires a quality of timelessness: it can then happen (and indeed it has) that features peculiar to this individual are attributed to an entire age. With the minor writer, on the other hand, provided he is aware and self-critical, the dialectical moments of that particular culture can be discerned more clearly because they are not unified as in the great writer.')

The problem referred to above finds a confirmation *per absurdum* in Alfredo Gargiulo's article 'Dalla cultura alla letteratura' in *L'Italia Letteraria*, 6 April 1930 (this is the sixth part of a panoramic study entitled '1900–1930', which will be republished in book form and will be useful to keep in mind for 'Father Bresciani's progeny'[13]). In this series of articles Gargiulo

---

[12] On *La Voce*, see the introduction to Section I, 'Proletarian culture', above. Gramsci's use of the term 'militant' here picks up a specific Italian sense of the phrase 'militant culture' or 'militant criticism', used in the years around the First World War to describe the culture of the little reviews and cafés as opposed to the 'academic' and specialist culture of the universities. Croce was an ambiguous figure in this context, since he too represented (with *La Critica*) a new, dynamic culture of the young intellectuals against the professorial old guard, yet at the same time he was becoming the leader of a new intellectual establishment himself. Croce both contributed to the key organ of 'militant' culture, *La Voce*, and came under attack from *Voce* writers like Papini (for his philosophical casuistry) and Renato Serra (for his over-systematized aesthetics).

[13] 'Father Bresciani's progeny' is Gramsci's tag for a series of critical notes on Italian literary culture: see Section VIII below. Gramsci received *L'Italia Letteraria* weekly in prison. It was founded by Umberto Fracchia (1889–1930) in 1925 with the title *La Fiera Letteraria* (see VIII 13). It changed its name in April 1929 and ran till 1936 under the editorship of Giovanni Battista Angioletti (1896–1961). Initially part of the involutionary tendency to retreat from politics into literary culture after the demise of *La Voce*, the review aimed explicitly to reconstitute the function of the 'intellectual class' as spiritual guide of the nation while rejecting the polemical militancy of the Florentine reviews, favouring an open exchange of ideas and defending an authority and autonomy of art. In the debate between 'contentists' and 'calligraphists' in 1932–33 (see introduction to this Section and the note '"Contentism" and "calligraphism"' below, II 15), it principally represented the 'calligraphists'. It also aimed to be less élitist than the little Florentine reviews (its circulation was higher and it promoted 'book fairs' – see IX 13) and its contributors were

(one of the many young men without 'maturity') gives proof of total intellectual exhaustion. He has become completely absorbed into the *Italia Letteraria* gang and in the article cited has made his own this judgement of G.B. Angioletti's in his preface to the anthology *Scrittori nuovi* [New Writers] compiled by Enrico Falqui and Elio Vittorini: 'The writers in this anthology, then, are new not because they have discovered new forms or have celebrated new *subjects*; on the contrary they are new because they have an idea about art that is different from that of the writers who preceded them. Or, to come straight to the point, because they *believe* in art, while the others believed in many other things that had nothing to do with art. Thus, such novelty can allow for traditional forms and old content but cannot accept deviations from the essential idea of art. This is not the place to repeat what that idea is. Allow, me, though, to recall that the new writers, by carrying out a revolution (!) which will not be the less memorable (!) for having been silent (!), *intend above all to be artists*, where their predecessors were content to be moralists, preachers, aesthetes, psychologists and hedonists.'

The argument is not very clear or ordered. If anything concrete is to be drawn from it, it is merely this tendency to theorize the baroque.[14] This conception of the artist is a new 'watch your language' when speaking, a new way to construct little 'conceits'. Those who construct such little conceits – not images – are the poets most revered by the 'gang', led by Giuseppe Ungaretti (who, moreover, writes in a pretty Frenchified and unseemly way).[15]

That the *Voce* movement could not have created artists is, *ut sic*, evident. But by fighting for a new culture, for a new way of life, it also indirectly promoted the formation of original artistic temperaments, since in life there is also art. The 'silent revolution' which Angioletti speaks of was only a series of café confabulations and mediocre articles for a standardized newspaper and lightweight provincial reviews. The caricature of

heterogeneous, including the ex-editor of *La Voce*, Prezzolini, and a young creative writer like Elio Vittorini (1908–66) who moved to the fascist 'left' in the thirties and then joined the clandestine PC[d,]I.

[14] 'Secentismo' in the original: see footnote 103 on p. 272.

[15] Gramsci classifies the poet Giuseppe Ungaretti (1888–1970) as a 'Brescianist' and his opinion of him is consistently negative (see VI 33 and VIII 21). Ungaretti studied in Paris from 1912 to 1915, read Laforgue and Mallarmé, was in contact with avant-garde circles and wrote some of his early verse in French (the collection *La Guerre*, 1919).

the 'high priest of art' is not a great novelty even if the ritual has changed.

Q 23 § 3.

3 Art and Culture

It seems evident that, to be precise, one should speak of a struggle for a 'new culture' and not for a 'new art' (in the immediate sense). To be precise, perhaps it cannot even be said that the struggle is for a new artistic content apart from form because content cannot be considered abstractly, in separation from form. To fight for a new art would mean to fight to create new individual artists, which is absurd since artists cannot be created artificially. One must speak of a struggle for a new culture, that is, for a new moral life that cannot but be intimately connected to a new intuition of life, until it becomes a new way of feeling and seeing reality and, therefore, a world intimately ingrained in 'possible artists' and 'possible works of art'.

Although one cannot artificially create individual artists, this does not therefore mean that the new cultural world for which one is fighting, by stirring up passions and human warmth, does not necessarily stir up 'new artists'. In other words, one cannot say that Tom, Dick and Harry will become artists, but one can say that new artists will be born from the movement. A new social group that enters history with a hegemonic attitude, with a self-confidence which it initially did not have, cannot but stir up from deep within itself personalities who would not previously have found sufficient strength to express themselves fully in a particular direction.

Therefore, one cannot talk about a new 'poetic aura' being formed – to use a phrase that was popular a few years ago. 'Poetic aura' is only a metaphor to express the ensemble of those artists who have already formed and emerged, or at least the process of formation and emergence which has begun and is already consolidated.

Q 23 § 6.

4 Adelchi Baratono[16]

In the second issue of the review *Glossa Perenne* (which was edited by Raffa Garzia and started publication in 1928 or 1929), Baratono wrote an article on 'Novecentismo'[17] which sounds as if it is full of backhanded remarks. For instance: 'The art and literature of a time can only and must (!) only be that which corresponds to the life (!) and taste of the time, and to deplore the way they are, since it would not serve to change their inspiration and form, would thus also be contrary to any historical (!) and therefore correct (?) criterion (!) of judgement.'

But are the life and taste of an age something monolithic or are they not rather full of contradictions? And in this case how does one verify the 'correspondence'? Was it Berchet or Father Bresciani who 'corresponded' to the period of the Risorgimento?[18] Plaintive and moralistic disapproval would certainly be idiotic, but one can be critical and judge without crying. De Sanctis was a resolute advocate of the national revolution, yet he was a brilliant critic not only of Bresciani but of Guerrazzi too. Baratono's agnosticism is nothing but civil and moral cowardice. If it were true that a value judgement of one's contemporaries is impossible due to a lack of objectivity and universality, critics would have to shut up shop; but Baratono is only theorizing his own aesthetic and philosophical impotence and his own cowardice.

Q 23 § 20.

5 Literary Criticism. [Paul Nizan]

See Argo's polemical article against Paul Nizan ('Idee d'oltre confine') in the March 1933 issue of *Educazione Fascista*, concerning the conception of a new literature that should arise

[16] Adelchi Baratono (1875–1947), taught philosophy and had been a Socialist parliamentary deputy. In 1934 he published an introduction to aesthetics, *Il mondo sensibile*. Gramsci had already attacked him in an article of 1922 (SF, pp. 445–47; see SPN, p. 389, footnote).

[17] See VIII 14.

[18] Giovanni Berchet (1783–1851) was a leading Italian romantic and a political democrat. The verse he wrote in exile circulated semi-clandestinely in Italy around 1848. On Bresciani's reaction against the 1848 revolutions and De Sanctis's judgement, see the introduction to Section VIII.

from an integral moral and intellectual renewal.[19] Nizan seems to pose the problem well by beginning with a definition of an integral renewal of cultural premises, thus limiting the very field to be investigated. Argo's only valid objection is this: the impossibility of going beyond a national and autochthonous stage of the new literature and the 'cosmopolitan' dangers of Nizan's conception. From this point of view, many of Nizan's criticisms of groups of French intellectuals should be reconsidered: the *Nouvelle Revue Française*, 'populism' and so on, including the *Monde* group;[20] not because his criticism is politically off-target, but because the new literature must necessarily manifest itself 'nationally', in relatively hybrid and different combinations and alloys. One must examine and study the entire current objectively.

Besides, one must keep the following criterion in mind when dealing with the relationship between literature and politics: the literary man must necessarily have a less precise and definite outlook than the politician. He must be less 'sectarian', if one can put it this way, but in a 'contradictory' way. For the politician, every 'fixed' image is *a priori* reactionary: he considers the entire movement in its development. The artist, however, must have 'fixed' images that are cast into their definite form. The politician

[19] This article, signed pseudonymously 'Argo', discusses Nizan's piece 'Littérature révolutionnaire en France' which had appeared in *La Revue des Vivants* of September-October 1932 (reprinted in Paul Nizan, *Pour une nouvelle culture*, edited by Susan Suleiman, Paris 1971, pp. 33–43). Nizan (1905–1940) had joined the PCF in 1927. He was to leave the party in 1939 in protest at its support of the Nazi-Soviet pact. The victim of a smear campaign after his death, his reputation was rehabilitated by Sartre and others in the sixties.

[20] Nizan argued that populism was a 'new exoticism' which reassured the bourgeois reader as to the weakness of the proletariat while giving him 'an agreeable sense of his human charity'. (For Gramsci's views on populism in France, see IX 12). He also attacked 'left' petty-bourgeois humanitarian authors and those writers 'tempted by the Revolution but not daring to take the final step' (Guéhenno, Malraux, Berl, etc.), held back as they were 'by old dreams of spiritual transformation'. *Monde* was a review founded in 1928 by Henri Barbusse with PCF support. It came under attack at the International Congress of Revolutionary Writers at Kharkov for 'right deviationism' because Barbusse had opened it up to the collaboration of non-party writers. Nizan (who calls *Monde* 'a social-democratic and radical socialist paper playing a role of dangerous confusion') was making his criticisms from the point of view of the Association of Revolutionary Writers and Artists (which then included internationally Aragon, Buñuel, Dos Passos, Lukács, Anna Seghers, etc.) for which his article was a platform: 'To struggle concretely against imperialism, the war, fascism, the social-democratic traitors, to defend the Soviet Revolution. To describe the proletariat no longer in a "humane" but in a revolutionary way'. After the Comintern turn of April 1934 which sanctioned the Popular Front strategy, the line of *Monde* and that of the Association fused, and Nizan himself published criticism in *Monde* after returning from Moscow in 1935.

imagines man as he is and, at the same time, how he should be in order to reach a specific goal. His task is precisely to stir men up, to get them to leave their present life behind in order to become collectively able to reach the proposed goal, that is, to get them to 'conform' to the goal. The artist necessarily and realistically depicts 'that which is', at a given moment (the personal, the non-conformist, etc.). From the political point of view, therefore, the politician will never be satisfied with the artist and will never be able to be: he will find him always behind the times, always anachronistic and overtaken by the real flow of events. If history is a continuous process of liberation and self-awareness, it is evident that every stage (historical and in this case cultural) will be immediately surmounted and will no longer hold any interest. It is this, it seems to me, that must be kept in mind when evaluating Nizan's opinions about various groups.

From the objective point of view, though, just as Voltaire is still 'current' for certain strata of the population, so can these literary groups and the combinations which they represent be, and indeed, are. In this case, 'objective' means that moral and intellectual renewal does not develop simultaneously in all of the social strata. On the contrary, it is worth repeating that even today many people are Ptolemaic and not Copernican. There are many 'conformisms', many struggles for new 'conformisms' and various combinations of that which already exists (variously expressed) and that which one is working to bring about (and there are many people who are working in this direction). It is a serious error to adopt a 'single' progressive strategy according to which each new gain accumulates and becomes the premiss of further gains. Not only are the strategies multiple, but even in the 'most progressive' ones there are retrogressive moments. Furthermore, Nizan does not know how to deal with so-called 'popular literature', that is, with the success of serial literature (adventure stories, detective stories, thrillers) among the masses, a success that is assisted by the cinema and the newspapers.[21]

---

[21] Argo's article included a paraphrase of the following observation by Nizan on popular literature: 'Finally, there is the question of the public. We should have no illusions about it: the French proletariat does not read. They are not responsible, it is the fault of their masters. Still less do they read books which could give them a revolutionary consciousness. The bourgeoisie lavishes on the proletariat detective stories, erotic or sentimental stories, sport and cinema papers, papers full stop: if one defines a literature by the public that reads it, proletarian literature in France includes *Fantômas, Fatala, Froufrou, Le Miroir des Sports, Detective, Police Magazine* and the *Petit Parisien*' (op. cit., pp. 36–37).

And yet, it is this question that represents the major part of the problem of a new literature as the expression of moral and intellectual renewal, for only from the readers of serial literature can one select a sufficient and necessary public for creating the cultural base of the new literature. It appears to me that the problem is this: how to create a body of writers who are, artistically, to serial literature what Dostoyevsky was to Sue and Soulié or, with respect to the detective story, what Chesterton was to Conan Doyle and Wallace. With this aim in mind, one must abandon many prejudices, but above all it should be remembered not only that one cannot have a monopoly but also that one is faced with a formidable organization of publishing interests.

The most common prejudice is this: that the new literature has to identify itself with an artistic school of intellectual origins, as was the case with Futurism. The premiss of the new literature cannot but be historical, political and popular. It must aim at elaborating that which already is, whether polemically or in some other way does not matter. What does matter, though, is that it sink its roots into the humus of popular culture as it is, with its tastes and tendencies and with its moral and intellectual world, even if it is backward and conventional.

Q 15 § 58.

6 Constituting an Epoch

In *Nuova Antologia* of 16 October 1928, Arturo Calza writes:

> One must realize that from 1914 to the present, literature has not only lost the audience that nourished it (!) but also the one that provided it with subject matter. In other words, in our European society, which is now passing through one of those stormy moments of spiritual and moral crisis that prepare (!) the way for profound renewal, the philosopher and thus also, necessarily, the poet, novelist and dramatist see in their midst a society 'in evolution' rather than one settled and consolidated into a definitive (!) scheme of moral and intellectual life; somewhat vague and ever changing customs and ways of life rather than firmly established and organized ones; seeds and buds rather than blossoms and ripe fruit. Consequently, as the distinguished editor of *La Tribuna* (Roberto Forges Davanzati) has written recently and as other newspapers have repeated and even

'intensified', 'we live in the midst of the greatest artistic absurdity, among all kinds of styles and experiments, *without any longer being able to constitute an epoch*'.[22]

What a waste of ink from Calza and Forges Davanzati. So it is only now that there has been a historical crisis? Is it not rather the case that precisely during periods of historical crisis passions, interests and feelings become red-hot and one has literary 'romanticism'? The arguments of the two writers limp and rebel against the disputants. How is it that Forges Davanzati fails to see that the inability to constitute an epoch cannot be limited to art but invests all of life. The absence of an artistic order (in the sense this expression can be held to possess) is connected to the absence of a moral and intellectual order, in other words the absence of an organic process of historical development. Society is turning upon itself, like a dog trying to catch its tail, but this apparent movement is not development.

Q 23 § 47.

7 Croce and Literary Criticism

Is Croce's aesthetics becoming normative, is it becoming a 'rhetoric'? One would have to read his *Aesthetica in nuce* (the article on aesthetics in the latest edition of *Encyclopaedia Britannica*). There it is stated that the main task of modern aesthetics is 'the reassertion and defence of the classical as against romanticism: the synthetic, formal theoretical element which is the *proprium* of art, as against the affective moment, which it is the business of art to resolve into itself'.[23] Apart from the aesthetic concerns of Croce, this passage shows what his 'moral' preoccupations are, that is, his 'cultural' and therefore

[22] Roberto Forges Davanzati (1880–1936) had been a leading Nationalist before Mussolini came to power. After the Italian Nationalist Association (ANI) merged with the fascist party in 1923, he took over the former liberal paper *La Tribuna* and fused it in 1925 with the ANI's *L'Idea Nazionale*, wrote a widely-used fascist school handbook, *Il Balilla Vittorio* (1934), and broadcast a nightly radio propaganda programme, 'Cronache del regime' (1934–36). Gramsci describes him elsewhere in the notebooks as 'a character-type from an intellectual farce . . . the "superman" portrayed by a stupid novelist or dramatist and at the same time this novelist or dramatist himself' (Q10 II § 49).

[23] B. Cr., 'Aesthetics', *Encyclopaedia Britannica*, 14th edition, 1929, Volume I, p. 269. Gramsci probably found this passage quoted in Natalino Sapegno's review of *Aesthetica in nuce* in *Pègaso*, II 12 (December 1930) pp. 758–59.

'political' preoccupations. One might ask if aesthetics, as a science, can have any other task besides that of elaborating a theory of art, beauty and expression. Here aesthetics means 'the concrete act of criticism', but should this act of criticism not simply criticize – i.e. make concrete application of the history of art to 'individual artistic expressions'?

Q6 § 124.

8 Ethico-political History

Definition of the concept of ethico-political history.[24] Note that ethico-political history is an arbitrary and mechanical hypostasis of the moment of hegemony, of political leadership, of consent in the life and activities of the state and civil society. This formulation which Croce has made of the historiographical problem reproduces his formulation of the aesthetic problem. The ethico-political moment is in history what the moment of 'form' is in art; it is the 'lyricism' of history, the 'catharsis' of history.[25] But things are not so simple in history as in art. In art the production of 'lyricism' is perfectly located in a personalized cultural world, in which one can admit the identification of content and form and the so-called dialectic of distincts in the unity of the spirit. (It is only a question of translating speculative language into historicist language, that is, of finding out if this speculative language has a concrete instrumental value which is superior to preceding instrumental values.) But in history and in the production of history the 'individualized' representation of

---

[24] This note is taken from Gramsci's main notebook on Croce's philosophy. Croce's 'ethico-political' history aimed to be an integral history in which intellectual and cultural activity and the activity of the state were treated as a unity. Croce thus contrasted it with three kinds of historiography: (a) positivist – a merely factual narration of external events, a 'chronicle'; (b) Hegelian – which conceived of the state as the only true ethical reality, above the moral life of individuals; (c) Marxist – which treated economic life as the only real historical substance and moral and cultural life (i.e. the superstructures) as mere appearance or illusion. See *Etica e politica*, Bari 1931, p. 274 ff.

[25] For this concept, see 'The term "catharsis"' in SPN, pp. 366–67. Croce himself suggested this analogy between his aesthetic and historiographical concepts, arguing that ethico-political history distinguishes the moral from the passionate (shorthand for politics in Croce) just as the 'history of poetry' (aesthetic criticism) distinguished the poetic from the practical. See 'Storia etico-politica e storia della poesia' in *Discorsi di varia filosofia*, Volume I, Bari 1945). Croce's identification of poetic value with the individualized 'lyrical' moment was a characteristic of his so-called second aesthetic (1908).

states and nations is a mere metaphor. The 'distinctions' that need to be made in such representations are not and cannot be presented 'speculatively' without the risk of falling into a new form of rhetoric and into a new kind of 'sociology' which, for all its 'speculative' nature, would be no less an abstract and mechanical sociology. They exist as distinctions of 'vertical' groups and as 'horizontal' stratifications, as diverse, coexisting and juxtaposed civilizations and cultures connected by state coercion and organized culturally into a contradictory and at the same time 'syncretistic' 'moral conscience'. At this point what is needed is a critique of the Crocean idea of the political moment as a moment of 'passion' (a permanent and systematic 'passion' is inconceivable), of his negation of 'political parties'[26] (which are precisely the concrete manifestation of how inconceivable permanent passion is, proof of the intrinsic contradiction of the 'politics-passion' concept) and, therefore, of the inexplicability of permanent armies and of the organized existence of civil and military bureaucracy, and the need for Croce and Crocean philosophy to be the matrix of Gentilean 'actualism'.[27] In fact, only in an ultra-speculative philosophy like actualism do these contradictions and inadequacies of Crocean philosophy find a formal and verbal composition. At the same time, however, actualism reveals in a more evident way how unconcrete the philosophy of Croce is, just as 'solipsism' shows the inherent weakness of the subjective-speculative conception of reality. That ethico-political history is the history of the moment of hegemony can be seen from a whole series of Croce's theoretical writings (and not only from those contained in the volume *Etica e politica*). A concrete analysis needs to be made of these writings. One can see this particularly from a number of scattered points on the concept of the state. For example, Croce has argued

[26] Croce denied political parties an effective historical function since ethico-political history (the sphere where parties operate) was composed of individual moral impulses, not collective efforts. If parties really fulfilled the function of collectively embodying opposing ideologies they would, Croce held, 'drain energy from individual variations and reduce people to flocks'. In reality, parties allowed individuals (party leaders, notably) to express their own personalities and moral ideals. ('I partiti politici', in *Etica e politica*, pp. 233–41).

[27] Giovanni Gentile (1875–1944) had been Croce's key collaborator on *La Critica*. His philosophy of 'pure act' or 'actualism' was a radical dilution of both Hegel and Croce which subordinated culture and moral life to action. Gentile became the principal philosopher of fascism. He accentuated the role of the state in the Hegelian tradition, subordinating to it both civil society and the family. He was shot by partisans during the Resistance.

somewhere that it is not always necessary to seek the 'state' where official institutions would seem to indicate, since it might sometimes be found instead in revolutionary parties.[28] This assertion is not paradoxical according to the state-hegemony-moral conscience conception, because it can in fact occur that in a specific emergency the moral and political leadership of the country in a given situation is exercised not by the legal government but by a 'private' organization and even by a revolutionary party. But it is not difficult to show in what an arbitrary way Croce generalizes this commonsense observation.

The most important problem to discuss in this paragraph is this: whether the philosophy of praxis excludes ethico-political history, whether it fails to recognize the reality of a moment of hegemony, treats moral and cultural leadership as unimportant and really judges superstructural facts as 'appearances'. One can say that not only does the philosophy of praxis not exclude ethico-political history but that, indeed, in its most recent stage of development, it consists precisely in asserting the moment of hegemony as essential to its conception of the state and to the 'accrediting' of the cultural fact, of cultural activity, of a cultural front as necessary alongside the merely economic and political ones. Croce commits the serious error of not applying to his criticism of the philosophy of praxis the methodological criteria that he applies to his study of much less important and significant philosophical currents. If he were to employ these criteria, he would be able to discover that the judgement contained in his attribution of the term 'appearance' to superstructures is none other than a judgement of their 'historicity' expressed in opposition to popular dogmatic conceptions and therefore couched in a 'metaphorical' language adapted to the public to whom it is destined. The philosophy of praxis thus judges the

---

[28] See for example Croce's *Cultura a vita morale* (Bari 1926) pp. 24–25: 'The point is to look in the real world for *where the true state really is in a determinate historical moment*; where the ethical force really is. For if the state is concrete ethicality, it does not hold that this ethicality is always embodied in the government, the sovereign, the ministers, the parliamentary chambers and not rather in those who do not take a direct part in government, the opponents and enemies of a particular state, the revolutionaries.' Cf. *Etica e politica* p. 279: the object of ethico-political history should be 'not just the state and the expansion of the state but also what is outside the state, whether it co-operates with it or whether it struggles to modify, overthrow and replace it. . . . Since this movement as a whole could be considered the real life of the state in its highest sense, we will not stand opposed to the word [state], so long as the fact is understood in this way. Indeed this is precisely why we prefer the term "ethico-political" to "moral", which is somewhat vapid.'

reduction of history to ethico-political history alone as improper and arbitrary, but does not exclude the latter. The opposition between Crocism and the philosophy of praxis is to be sought in the speculative character of Crocism.

Q 10, I § 7.

9 [Educative Art]

'Art is educative in so far as it is art, but not in so far as it is "educative art" because in the latter case it is nothing and nothing cannot educate. Of course, it seems that we all agree in wanting an art which resembles that of the Risorgimento and not, for example, the period of D'Annunzio. Actually, however, if one thinks about it, this desire does not imply a preference for one kind of art over another but for a certain moral reality over another. In the same way, someone who wants a mirror to reflect a beautiful person rather than an ugly one does not hope for a mirror different from the one in front of him, but for a different person.' (Croce, *Cultura e vita morale*, pp. 169–170; from the chapter 'Fede e programmi', 1911).

'When a work of poetry or a cycle of poetic works is formed, it is impossible to continue that cycle by the study, imitation and variation of those works: by doing so, one only obtains what is called a school of poetry, the *servum pecus* of the imitators. Poetry does not generate poetry; there is no parthenogenesis. There must be an intervention of the male element, that which is real, passionate, practical and moral. The greatest critics of poetry warn one not to resort to literary prescriptions but, as they say, to "remake man". Once man is remade, the spirit renewed and a new life of affections has emerged, from this will arise, if at all, a new poetry' (Croce, *Cultura e vita morale*, pp. 241–242; from the chapter 'Troppa filosofia', 1922).

The observation can be appropriated by historical materialism. Literature does not generate literature, and so on; that is ideologies do not create ideologies, superstructures do not generate superstructures other than as an inheritance of inertia and passivity. They are not generated through 'parthenogenesis' but through the intervention of the 'male' element, history, and the revolutionary activity which creates the 'new man', that is, new social relations.

From this one also deduces another fact: through this change the old 'man' also becomes 'new', since he enters into new relationships, the primitive ones having been overturned. Whence the fact that one can witness the 'swansong' of the old man (who is negatively renewed) before the 'new man' (positively formed) has created poetry: and this swansong can often be of great brilliance. The new unites with the old, the passions become incomparably red-hot, etc. (Is the *Divine Comedy* not somewhat of a medieval swansong which yet looks forward to the new age and the new history?)

Q 6 § 64.

10 Criteria of Literary Criticism

Is the concept that art is art and not 'willed' and directed political propaganda in itself an obstacle to the formation of specific cultural currents that reflect their time and contribute to the strengthening of specific political currents? It seems not; indeed it seems that such a concept poses the problem in more radical terms, those of a more efficient and conclusive criticism. Given the principle that one should look only to the artistic character of the work of art, this does not in the least prevent one from investigating the mass of feelings and the attitude towards life present in the work of art itself. Indeed, one need only consult De Sanctis and Croce himself to see that this is accepted by modern currents in aesthetics. What is excluded is the idea that a work is beautiful because of its moral and political content and not for its form, with which the abstract content is fused and becomes one.[29] Furthermore, one should examine whether a work of art

[29] Compare the passage in a letter from Gramsci to his wife Julia of 5 September 1932: 'the statement that you ascribe to me, "To love a writer or an artist is not the same thing as to have respect for him", is certainly incorrect. Could I have ever written something so . . . banal? I would certainly have thought twice about making a similar remark. The thought of those plays inspired by universal philistinism in which themes such as "love without respect" and "respect without love" are treated in relation to marriage would surely have been enough to inhibit me. Perhaps I made a distinction between aesthetic enjoyment and a positive value judgement of artistic beauty, i.e. between enthusiasm for a work of art in itself and moral enthusiasm, by which I mean a willing participation in the artist's ideological world – a distinction which seems to me just and necessary. I can admire Tolstoy's *War and Peace* from an aesthetic point of view without agreeing with the ideological contents of the book. If both factors coincided, Tolstoy would be my vade mecum, my *livre de chevet*. This holds also for Shakespeare, Goethe and Dante' (LP, pp. 245–46).

might not have failed because the author was diverted by external practical (that is, artificial and insincere) preoccupations. The crucial point of the polemic seems to be this: X 'wants' to express a definite content in an artful way and fails to create a work of art. The artistic failure of this work shows that in X's hands that particular content was unpliable and refractory (since he has proven to be an artist in other works that he has really felt and experienced). It also shows that his enthusiasm was fictitious and externally willed, that in that specific case he was not really an artist, but a servant who wanted to please his masters. There are, then, two sets of facts: one aesthetic (to do with pure art), the other politico-cultural (that is, frankly political). The possibility of coming to deny the artistic character of a work can help the political critic proper to demonstrate that, as an artist, X does not belong to that particular political world. And since his personality is prevalently artistic, that world does not have any influence on him at a deep and intimate level, and does not exist for him. As far as politics is concerned, therefore, X is play-acting, he wants to be taken for what he is not, etc., etc. The political critic, then, denounces him as a 'political opportunist', not as an artist.

When the politician puts pressure on the art of his time to express a particular cultural world, his activity is one of politics, not of artistic criticism. If the cultural world for which one is fighting is a living and necessary fact, its expansiveness will be irresistible and it will find its artists. Yet if, despite pressure, this irresistibility does not appear and is not effective, it means that the world in question was artificial and fictitious, a cardboard lucubration of mediocre men who complain that those of major stature do not agree with them. The very way of posing the question can be an indication of the firmness of such a moral and cultural world. In fact, so-called 'calligraphism'[30] is nothing but the defence thrown up by petty artists who opportunistically assert certain principles but who feel incapable of expressing them artistically (i.e., in their own proper sphere of activity) and drivel on about pure form which is its own content, etc., etc. The formal principle of the distinction and the unity in circulation of the spiritual categories, abstract though it is, allows one to grasp

---

[30] The Italian word is *calligrafismo* which refers, generally, to excessive concern with good style in writing and here in particular to the thirties debate between 'contentists' and 'calligraphists' (see II 15 and the introduction to this Section).

the actual truth[31] and to criticize the arbitrariness and pseudo-life of those who are not prepared to put their cards on the table or who are simply second-rate individuals whom chance has placed in positions of authority.

Q 15 § 38.

11 For a New Literature (Art) through a New Culture

See the chapter in B. Croce's volume *Nuovi saggi sulla letteratura italiana del Seicento* (1931), where he deals with the Jesuit academies of poetry and likens them to the 'schools of poetry' created in Russia (Croce most likely took his lead as usual from Fülöp-Miller).[32] Why does he not liken them to the painters' and sculptors' workshops of the fifteenth and sixteenth centuries? Were they, too, 'Jesuit academies'? And why should what happened with painting and sculpture not also happen with poetry? Croce does not take into account the social element that 'wants to have' its own poetry, an element 'without a school' – in other words, one that has not appropriated a 'technique' and a single kind of language: what we are dealing with here is a 'school' for adults which educates taste and creates 'critical' feeling in a broad sense. Does a painter who 'copies' a painting by Raphael belong to a 'Jesuit academy'? He 'immerses' himself in Raphael's art as deeply as he can, seeks to recreate it for himself, and so on. And why could workers not be given exercises in versification? Will that not serve to educate the ear to the musicality of verse?[33]

Q 6 § 133.

[31] On these basic principles in Croce's thinking (the distinction of categories and the assertion that they circulate under the unity of the spirit) see the introduction to this Section.

[32] The reference is to chapter 12 of Croce's book. René Fülöp-Miller's *Geist und Gesicht des Bolschevismus* (Vienna 1926: translated as *The Mind and Face of Bolshevism*, London-New York 1927) was a mainly hostile survey of Soviet life which, among other things, launched the concept of 'collective man'. The chapter on 'The Mechanizing of Poetry' informed readers about the Bryusov Institute, where writers, translators and critics were trained in three-year courses. The prison censors at Turi had for a long time refused Gramsci's request to have this and other 'suspect' books. On Croce and Fülöp-Miller, see also LP, p. 235.

[33] Compare Gramsci's 1918 article on the director Virgilio Talli in his *Avanti!* theatre column (LVN, pp. 328–30): 'Talli has brought back to life, with wonderful precision, the artistic families of the fifteenth century in which there were the master and his pupils, and the master carried out his educative work in a dense atmosphere of humanistic

12 [Individualism and Art]

In his article, 'Art and Religion', in *L'Italia Letteraria*, 1 January 1923, Luigi Volpicelli notes:

> They (the people), we might note in passing, have always loved art more for its non-artistic qualities than for its essentially artistic ones; and perhaps precisely for this reason they are so diffident towards contemporary artists who, by seeking only what is purely artistic in art, end up being enigmatic, unintelligible and the prophets of a few initiates.

This observation is both meaningless and without foundation. Certainly the people want an 'historical' art (if one does not care to use the word 'social'), that is, they want an art expressed in terms that are culturally 'comprehensible' or, what amounts to the same thing, in universal or 'objective' or 'historical' or 'social' terms. They do not want 'artistic neology', especially if the 'neologist' is also an idiot.[34]

It seems to me that the problem should always be posed on the basis of this question: 'Why do poets write? Why do painters paint?' (Remember Adriano Tilgher's article in *L'Italia che scrive*.) Croce roughly replies, more or less: 'In order to recall their own works' – given that according to Crocean aesthetics the work of art is already and only 'perfect' in the artist's brain.[35] In a certain

collaboration, from which sprang the infinite world of beauty of the Renaissance. These masters are often nothing outside their school and the tradition they create and develop: their nature is not so much that of individual creators as of educators and revealers. Their greatness and perfection is in their pupils, who rapidly rise to fullness, because the master has saved them any scattering of energy in arbitrary attempts, in useless experiments. The school is for the spirit what the Taylor method is for the mechanical gestures of the body: economy of experiments and effort, acceleration of spontaneous evolution, organization of the intellect.'

[34] Gramsci's Italian terms *neolalismo* and *neolalico* (from a compound Greek root meaning 'new-speaking') are translated here as 'neology' and 'neologist'. As he himself makes clear in II 17, he takes the term from linguistics, where it refers to 'a pathological expression of individual language', and applies it to cliques and verbal innovators in literature.

[35] Gramsci returns in several places to this view of Croce's and to Tilgher's article criticizing it (see SNP, p. 461; II 20 and 23 below; on Tilgher see also the introduction to Section III 'Pirandello'). Croce argued: 'It is clear that the poem is complete as soon as the poet has expressed it in words which he repeats to himself. When he comes to repeat them aloud, for others to hear . . . or sets them down in writing or print, he has entered upon a new stage, not aesthetic but practical, whose social and cultural importance need not, of course, be insisted upon. So with the painter.' ('Aesthetics', *Encyclopaedia Britannica*, 1929, Volume I, p. 266). Tilgher understood Croce to mean that the artist only 'objectified' in order to recall his 'phantasm' (i.e. the intuited image), a view which he rejected by arguing that the shapeless phantasm was only given a clear form by the act of objectification (writing, painting, etc.) itself. Tilgher none the less concluded that artistic

sense this could be roughly admitted, but only roughly and in a certain sense. In fact, one falls back on the question of 'man's nature' and of 'what is the individual?' If one cannot think of the individual apart from society, and thus if one cannot think of any individual who is not historically conditioned, it is obvious that every individual, including the artist and all his activities, cannot be thought of apart from society, a specific society. Hence the artist does not write or paint – that is, he does not externalize his phantasms – just for his own recollection, to be able to relive the moment of creation. He is an artist only insofar as he externalizes, objectifies and historicizes his phantasms. Every artist-individual, though, is such in a more or less broad and comprehensive way, he is 'historical' or 'social' to a greater or lesser degree. There are the 'neologists' or 'jargonists', those who alone are able to relive the memory of the creative moment (and usually it is an illusion or the recollection of a dream or a fancy); then there are others who belong to more or less large cliques (who have a corporate jargon); and finally, those who are universal, in other words 'national-popular'. Croce's aesthetics has been responsible for many degenerations in art and it is not true that these have always occurred against the intentions and spirit of the Crocean aesthetic itself. For many degenerations, yes, but not for all, and especially not for the fundamental one of anti-historical (or anti-social or anti-national-popular), expressive and artistic 'individualism'.

Q 14 § 28.

13 Criteria of Method

It would be absurd to claim that the literature of a country is capable of producing a *Betrothed* or a *Sepolcri* once a year or even

---

creation was 'a island defended by high walls against the waves of practical life' (Adriano Tilgher, 'Perché l'artista scrive, o dipinge, o scolpisce, ecc.?' in *L'Italia che scrive* XII (1929) 2, pp. 31–32). In his first note on this article, Gramsci calls it 'typical of the logical inconsistency and moral levity of Tilgher who, after "knocking down" Croce's theory on this in a banal manner, presents it again point for point at the end of the article as his own, in a fantastic and aestheticist form. Tilgher says that, according to Croce, "the physical objectification . . . of the artistic phantasm serves an essentially mnemonic purpose". This argument needs to be looked at. What does Croce mean in this case by "memory"? Does it have a purely personal, individual value or also a group value? Is the writer only preoccupied with himself or is he also historically led to think of others?' (Q 2 § 103).

every ten years.[36] That is why normal critical activity cannot but have a predominantly 'cultural' character. It cannot but be a criticism of 'trends', if it is not to become a continuous massacre.

And in this case, how does one choose the work to be massacred and the writer who is to be proven unartistic? This appears to be a negligible problem, yet, from the viewpoint of the modern organization of cultural life, it is fundamental. A consistently negative criticism, based on slashing evaluations and demonstrations of 'non-poetry' rather than of 'poetry', would become tedious and revolting. The 'choice' would look like a man-hunt or else could be considered 'fortuitous' and therefore irrelevant.[37]

It seems clear that criticism must always have a positive function, in the sense that it must point out a positive value in the work being studied. If this aspect cannot be artistic, perhaps it can be cultural, in which case the individual work (except in rare instances) will not be as important as groups of works placed in series according to cultural tendency. On the question of choice: other than the critic's intuition or the systematic study of all literature (a colossal and almost impossible undertaking for a single individual), the simple criterion appears to be that based on the 'success' of a book, in two senses – 'success with readers' and 'success with publishers'. In some countries where intellectual activities are controlled by governmental organs, this success with publishers is still significant because it indicates the cultural direction that the state would like to give to the nation.

The same problems are presented if one uses the criteria of Crocean aesthetics: since 'fragments' of poetry can be found everywhere, the critic should know 'everything' in order to be able to reveal the 'pearl' in the mire, whether it be *L'Amore Illustrato* or a strictly specialized scientific work. In reality, every critic feels he belongs to an organization of culture that functions as a unit. Whatever escapes one critic will be discovered and pointed out by another. Even the proliferation of 'literary prizes' is nothing but a relatively well organized collective

---

[36] On Manzoni's *The Betrothed*, see Section VII, below. On Foscolo's poem 'Dei Sepolcri' ('On Tombs') see VI 20.

[37] Distinguishing between 'poetry' and 'non-poetry' became a basic litmus-test in Croce's criticism. A series of his critical readings had the title *Poesia e non poesia* (1923). See also the introduction to Section IV.

'recommendation' (with varying degrees of fraud) by militant literary critics.

It should be pointed out that in certain periods of history, the greatest creative minds of a nation can be absorbed in practical work. During such periods all of the best human energies are, in a certain sense, concentrated in work at the base and one cannot yet talk about superstructures. According to what Cambon says in the introduction to the French edition of Henry Ford's autobiography, a whole sociological theory has been constructed on this basis in America, to justify the absence in the United States of a flourishing of artistic and humanistic culture.[38] This theory, if it is to have at least a semblance of justification, must be able to point to an extensive creative activity in the practical field, even if the following question remains unanswered: if this 'creative-poetic' activity exists and is vital, stirring up all of man's vital forces, energies, will and enthusiasms, how is it that it does not stir up literary energy and create an epic? If this does not occur, one can legitimately suspect that only 'bureaucratic' energies are involved, not universally expansive forces but brutal and repressive ones. Is it possible to believe that the slaves who were whipped into building the pyramids saw their work in a lyrical light? What needs to be pointed out is that the forces which direct this huge practical undertaking are not only repressive with respect to instrumental work (which is understandable), but are universally repressive. This is typical and explains why in America for example, a certain literary energy can be observed in those who reject the organization of a practical activity which is passed off as 'epic' in its own right. Still, the situation is worse where there is not even a certain large-scale practical activity which will 'come about' and produce artistic activity in turn in due course.

In reality, every innovative force is repressive with respect to its adversaries, but, as an unleashing of latent forces, it strengthens and exalts them. In this sense such a force is expansive and its peculiar character undoubtedly lies here. Regardless of the name

[38] Victor Cambon, preface to Henry Ford, *Ma vie et mon oeuvre* (original edition *My Life and Work*, 1922), Paris 1926, pp. vii-viii: 'The most honoured work in any age has always attracted the leading minds of the age. When under the Medici it was painting and sculpture, the greatest brains devoted themselves to it. Leonardo da Vinci and Michelangelo embraced all forms of knowledge, including technical, but they were first and foremost painters and sculptors. The great navigators of the reign of Elizabeth, the bold pioneers like the Frenchman Lassalle would today be railwaymen.'

they assume, restorations, especially those of the present epoch, are universally repressive: 'Father Bresciani' and Brescianist literature predominate. The psychology behind such an intellectual expression is based on panic, on a cosmic fear of unintelligible demoniac forces which can only be controlled by a universally repressive force. The memory of this panic (in its acute phase) lasts a long time and governs people's wills and feelings. Freedom and creative spontaneity disappear. Resentment, the spirit of revenge and a purblind stupidity dressed up in mellifluous jesuitical language remain. Everything becomes practical (in the worst sense), everything is propaganda, controversy and (in a mean, narrow and often ignoble and revolting form) implicit negation, as in *L'Ebreo di Verona*.[39]

The question of the young writers of a given generation. Certainly, when judging a writer's first book, one must consider the author's 'age', since this will always also be a cultural judgement: the unripe fruit of a young man can be appreciated as a promise and encouraged. Withered fruit, however, is not promising, even if it seems to have the same taste as unripe fruit.

Q 23 § 36.

14 [The Writer's Attitude]

From an article by Paolo Milano in *L'Italia Letteraria*, 27 December 1931:

'The value given to the content of a work of art can never be too great, wrote Goethe. An aphorism like this may come to mind when one considers the *effort*, set in motion (sic) so many generations ago and still being made, *to create a tradition* of the modern Italian novel. What society, or rather what class, should be depicted? Do not the most recent attempts consist in the desire to get away from the folk characters who occupy the stage in the works of Manzoni and Verga? Cannot these partial successes be related to the difficulties and uncertainty in choosing a setting (idle haute-bourgeoisie, common people, peripheral bohemia)?'[40]

This passage is staggering because of the mechanical and

---

[39] On Bresciani and *L'Ebreo di Verona*, see the introduction to Section VIII.

[40] Milano's article is a review of a novel by Umberto Barbaro, *Luce fredda*. The italics in the quotation are Gramsci's.

external way in which the questions are posed. Is it really the case that 'generations' of writers have *coldly* attempted to find a setting to describe without thereby manifesting their 'ahistorical' character and their moral and emotional emptiness? In any case, 'content' does not just mean the choice of a given environment: what really matters for the content is the *attitude* of the writer and his generation towards this environment. Attitude alone determines the cultural world of a generation and an age and thus its style. In Manzoni and Verga, too, it is the writers' attitude towards their 'folk characters' which is decisive, and not the characters themselves, and this attitude is antithetical in the two of them.

In Manzoni it is one of Catholic paternalism, an implicit *irony*, which indicates the absence of a deep instinctive love for those characters. It is an attitude dictated by an external feeling of abstract duty decreed by Catholic morality, but corrected and enlivened by a pervasive irony. Verga's is an attitude of cold, scientific and photographic impassiveness, dictated by the canons of *verismo*, applied more rationally than by Zola.[41]

Manzoni's attitude is the more widespread in the literature depicting 'folk characters'; one need only recall Renato Fucini.[42] It is still superior, but it is balanced on a razor's edge and in lesser writers it degenerates into the stupidly and jesuitically sarcastic attitudes of 'Brescianism'.

Q8 §9.

---

[41] On Manzoni's paternalism see Section VII below. On Verga, see footnote 2 above. Zola, in *Le roman expérimental* (1880), suggested that novelists should adopt the processes of empirical observation applied in medicine by Claude Bernard. Verga's theoretical statements echoed this idea. Compare another note by Gramsci: 'The following point should be studied: whether French naturalism, in its claims to scientific and experimental objectivity, did not already contain, in general, the ideological position which underwent extensive subsequent development in Italian naturalism or provincial realism and particularly in Verga: the country people are seen with "detachment", as "nature" emotionally extrinsic to the writer, as drama, etc. It is the position of Hagenbeck's *The Animals and I*. The "naturalist" claim to experimental objectivity of the French writers, which had a polemical origin in opposition to aristocratic writers, was grafted in Italy on to a pre-existing ideological position, as is apparent from *The Betrothed*, where there is the same "detachment" from the people, a detachment barely veiled by a benevolent ironic and caricatural smile' (Q 23 § 56).

[42] Renato Fucini (1843–1921), Tuscan regionalist writer, author of the short-story collections *Le veglie di Neri* (1884) and *All'aria aperta* (1887).

15 Non-National-Popular Characteristics of Italian Literature: ['Contentism' and 'Calligraphism']

Controversy between 'contentists' and 'calligraphists' in *L'Italia Letteraria, Tevere, Il Lavoro Fascista* and *Critica Fascista*. It seemed from his references to the subject that Gherardo Casini (the editor of *Il Lavoro Fascista* and co-editor of *Critica Fascista*) would at least formulate the problem in a critically accurate way, but his article in the issue of *Critica Fascista* of 1 May 1933 is a disappointment.[43] He fails to define the relationships between 'politics' and 'literature' in the field of science and the art of politics, just as he fails to define them in the field of literary criticism. He is unable to indicate practically how a struggle for the triumph of a new culture or civilization can be planned or conducted or how a movement towards it can be aided. Nor does he say how it is possible that a new civilization, said to exist already, can fail to have its own literary and artistic expression, to penetrate the sphere of literature, while historically the opposite has always occurred. Every new civilization, as such (even when held back, attacked and fettered in every possible way), has always expressed itself in literary form before expressing itself in the life of the state. Indeed its literary expression has been the means with which it has created the intellectual and moral conditions for its expression in the legislature and the state.

Since no work of art can be without a content, can fail to be connected to a poetic world and this poetic world to a moral and intellectual world, it is evident that the 'contentists' are simply the bearers of a new culture, a new content, while the 'calligraphists' are the bearers of an old content, an old or different culture (setting aside for the moment any immediate question of the value of these contents or cultures, although in fact it is precisely the value of contrasting cultures and the superiority of one over the other that resolves the contrast). The problem thus concerns the 'historicity' of art, 'historicity and perpetuity' at the same time, and it concerns research into whether the raw politico-economic fact, the fact of force, has undergone or can undergo further elaboration which is expressed in art, or whether, rather, it is a question of the purely economic which cannot be elaborated artistically in an original way, since the preceding elaboration

---

[43] Gherardo Casini, 'Elementi politici di una letteratura' in *Critica Fascista* XI (1933) 9, pp. 161–62. On this debate, see the introduction to this Section. See also VIII 27.

already contains the new content, which is only new in a chronological sense. Since every national complex is an often heterogeneous combination of elements, it may happen that its intellectuals, because of their cosmopolitanism, do not coincide with the national content, but with a content borrowed from other national complexes or even with a content that is abstract and cosmopolitan. Thus Leopardi can be described as the poet of the despair created in certain minds by eighteenth-century sensationalism, which in Italy had no corresponding development of material and political forces and struggles as it did in the countries where it was an organic cultural form.[44] When, in a backward country, the civil forces corresponding to the cultural form assert themselves and expand, not only are they certain not to create a new and original literature but there will – naturally enough – emerge a 'calligraphism', a generic and widespread form of scepticism about any serious and profound passionate content. 'Calligraphism' will thus be the organic literature of those national complexes which, like Lao-tse, are born eighty years old,[45] without fresh and spontaneous feelings, without 'romanticisms', but also without 'classicisms', or else with a mannered romanticism in which the initial crudeness of the passions is that of an artificially rejuvenated old man trying to relive his youth rather than a stormy virility or masculinity, while their classicism will be likewise mannered, in other words precisely a 'calligraphism', a mere form like the livery of a majordomo.[46] We will have the phenomena of 'Super-country' and 'Super-city', and the prefix [i.e. 'extreme', 'excessive'] will always be more significant than it might seem.

It should also be noticed that no serious preparation has gone

[44] The materialist ideas of the writer Giacomo Leopardi (1798–1837) were influenced by Locke, Condillac and Destutt de Tracy. Sensationalism is the belief that all ideas in the mind stem from physical sensations. In the letter to Julia quoted in footnote 29 above, Gramsci noted, with reference to Leopardi's pessimism: 'In Leopardi, we find the crisis marking the transition to modern man in a very dramatic form: old transcendental concepts are being criticized and discarded, while a new, secure, moral and intellectual *ubi consistam* has not yet been found' (LP, p. 246).

[45] The allusion is to Italy – see V 1. On Lao-tse see also I4 and X8.

[46] The passage echoes De Sanctis: 'The essence [of my idea of realism] is that more room should be given in art to man's animal and natural forces, we should expel the "*rêve*" and replace it with action if we want to become young again, form the will, retemper the fibre. The realism which resembles an orgy is a poetry of impotent and depraved old men, not a restoration of youth' (Appendix to 'Zola e l' "Assommoir"' *Opere*, Volume XIV, pp. 455–56).

into the conduct of the discussion: maybe Croce's theories should be accepted, maybe they should be rejected, but either way one should know them properly and quote them correctly. Here they are referred to by ear, 'journalistically'. It is evident that, in Croce, the 'artistic' moment, as a category, even if it is presented as a moment of pure form, does not presuppose any calligraphism or negate any contentism, any energetic breakthrough of a new cultural element. Nor does the concrete activity of Croce as politician count, his attitude towards this or that current of passions and feelings. As an aesthetician, Croce vindicates the lyrical character of art, even if as a politician he vindicates and struggles for the triumph of one particular programme. Indeed, it seems undeniable that with his theory of the circling of the spiritual categories Croce presupposes a strong 'morality' in the artist, even if he considers the work of art as an aesthetic fact and not a moral one. That is, he considers one moment of the circle, and not another, as the object in question. For example, in the economic moment he includes 'brigandage' along with stock-exchange transactions, but as a man he would not seem to be working for the development of 'brigandage' any more than for stock-exchange business (and it might be said that, in accordance with his political stature, his attitude is not without repercussions on the stock exchange).[47] This frivolity of the discussion and the less than excessive care of the disputants in mastering the precise terms of the problem does not exactly suggest that the problem is vital and of great importance. It is more a controversy between petty and mediocre journalists than the 'birth pangs' of a new literary civilization.

Q 15 § 20.

16 [Languages of the Arts]

De Sanctis says somewhere that before writing an essay or lecturing on a canto of Dante, for example, he would read the canto aloud several times and learn it by heart. We recall this in order to support the observation that the artistic element of a work cannot be appreciated at first reading, except on rare

[47] Croce defined the economic fact as 'man's practical activity considered in itself, independent of any moral or immoral determination' (*Materialismo storico ed economia marxistica* [1900] Bari 1968, p. 219).

occasions (we shall see which) and often not even by major specialists such as De Sanctis. The first reading allows only an introduction into the writer's emotional and cultural world, and even this is not always true, especially for non-contemporary writers whose emotional and cultural world is not that of the present. A poem by a cannibal on the joys of a sumptuous banquet of human flesh may be considered beautiful, and require in order to be appreciated artistically, without 'extra-aesthetic' prejudices, a certain psychological distance from present culture.

But the work of art also contains other 'historicist' elements besides its determinate emotional and cultural world. These elements are its language, understood not just as purely verbal expression which grammar can photograph in a given time and place, but as a sum of images and modes of expression which fall outside grammar. These elements appear more clearly in the other arts. Japanese looks immediately different from Italian, but the same does not hold for the language of music, painting and the figurative arts in general. Yet these differences of language also exist and they are the more striking the more one descends from the artistic expressions of artists to those of folklore, where the language of these arts is reduced to its most autochthonous and primordial element (remember the anecdote of the artist who drew the profile of a negro and the other negroes scoffed because the painter had only reproduced 'half his face').

From the historical and cultural point of view, though, there is a great difference between the linguistic expression of the written and spoken word and the linguistic expressions of the other arts. Literary language is strictly tied to the life of national masses and it develops slowly and only molecularly. One might say that every social group has a 'language' of its own, yet one should still note that (rare exceptions apart) there is a continuous adhesion and exchange between popular language and that of the educated classes. This is not true of the languages of the other arts, for which one can note at present two phenomena: 1) the expressive elements of the past, one can say of the entire past, are still alive in them, at least in far greater quantities than in literary language; 2) a cosmopolitan language is rapidly formed in them that absorbs the technical-expressive elements of all the nations which respectively produce great painters, writers, musicians, etc. Wagner has given as many linguistic elements to music as the whole of German literature throughout its history. This is because the people rarely participate in the production of these languages, which belong to an international élite, whereas they can quite quickly (as a collectivity, not as individuals) come to understand them. All this is to indicate that in reality purely aesthetic 'taste', even if it can be considered primary as the form and activity of the spirit, is not so practically – i.e. in chronological terms.

It has been said (for example by Prezzolini in *Mi pare . . .*)[48] that the theatre cannot be called an art, but a mechanistic amusement: the reason being that the audience cannot take an aesthetic interest in the play performed, since they are only interested in the plot (or something of the sort). This observation is wrong because in the theatrical performance the artistic element does not reside only in the play as a work of literature. The writer is not the only creator. The author intervenes in the theatrical performance with words and stage directions that limit the freedom of the actor and the director. In reality, though, in performance the literary element becomes the occasion for new artistic creations, which, once complementary and critical-interpretative, are now becoming increasingly important: the interpretation by the individual actor[49] and the scenic ensemble created by the director. It is true, however, that only repeated readings can let one enjoy the play as the author made it. The conclusion is this: a work of art is the more 'artistically' popular the more its cultural, moral and emotional content adheres to national morality, culture and feelings – these being understood not as something static but as a continually developing process. Immediate contact between reader and writer is made when the unity of form and content for the reader can presuppose a unity of poetic and emotional worlds. Otherwise, the reader must begin to translate the 'language' of the content into his own language. The situation is rather like that of someone who has learned English in a Berlitz speed course and then reads Shakespeare: the effort of literal comprehension, achieved with the constant aid of a mediocre dictionary, reduces the reading to no more than a pedantic school exercise.

Q 6 § 62.

[48] Giuseppe Prezzolini, *Mi pare.* . . . Florence 1925, pp. 73–79.

[49] Gramsci's manuscript, followed by Gerratana's critical edition, reads 'autore' (author) here. We have followed the emendation of LVN to 'attore' (actor).

17 Neology[50]

Neology as a pathological expression of individual language (vocabulary). But cannot the term be used in a more general sense, to indicate a whole series of cultural, artistic and intellectual manifestations? What are all the literary and artistic schools and clubs if not manifestations of cultural neology? The most widespread and multifarious cases of neology take place in periods of crisis.

Language and languages. Every cultural expression, every moral and intellectual activity, has its historically specific language: this language is also called 'technique' and 'structure'.[51] If a writer started using a personally arbitrary language (if he became a 'neologist' in the pathological sense of the word) and if others were to imitate him (each with an arbitrary language), the situation would be described as Babel. One does not have the same impresson for musical, pictorial and plastic language (technique). (This point deserves more thought and examination.)

From the viewpoint of cultural history, and thus also of cultural 'creation' (not to be confused with artistic creation, but to be related to political activities; and, indeed, it is in this sense that one can speak of a 'cultural politics'), there is a difference between literary art and the other forms of artistic expression (figurative, musical, orchestral) which should be defined and clarified in a theoretically justified and comprehensible way. 'Verbal' expression has a strictly national-popular-cultural character: a poem by Goethe, in the original, can only be understood and fully relived by a German (or by one who has 'become German'). Dante can only be understood and relived by an educated Italian, etc. But a statue by Michelangelo, a piece of music by Verdi, a Russian ballet or a painting by Raphael can be understood almost immediately by anyone in the world, even by the non-cosmopolitan, even if they have not gone beyond the narrow circle of a province in their own country. Still, the matter is not as simple as it might appear on the surface. The artistic emotion that a Japanese or a Laplander feels when in front of a

---

[50] See footnote 34 above, p. 111.

[51] On Croce's concepts of 'technique' and 'structure', see respectively the introductions to Section V, 'Language, linguistics and folklore' and Section IV 'Canto X of Dante's Inferno'.

statue by Michelangelo or when listening to a tune by Verdi is certainly an artistic emotion. (The same Japanese or Laplander would remain insensitive and deaf if he listened to a poem by Dante, Shelley or Goethe being read aloud, or else would admire the art of the speaker as such.) Nevertheless, the artistic emotion of the Japanese or Laplander will not be of the same intensity and quality[52] as the emotion of an average Italian, still less that of a cultured Italian. This means that alongside or rather beneath the cosmopolitan expression of musical, pictorial and other types of language, there is a deeper cultural substance, more restricted, more 'national-popular'. And that is not all: the grades of this language are different; there is a national-popular grade (and often, before this, a provincial-dialect-folklore grade), then the grade of a determinate 'civilization' which can be empirically determined by religious tradition (for example Christian, but separated into Catholic, Protestant, Orthodox, etc.) and also, in the modern world, by a determinate 'politico-cultural current'. During the war, for example, an English, French or Russian orator could speak in his own language to an Italian audience about the devastations caused by the Germans in Belgium; if the audience sympathized with the orator, they listened closely and 'followed' him. It is true that in oratory the words are not the only element: there are also gestures, tone of voice and so on, a musical element that communicates the leitmotiv of the predominant feeling, the principal passion, and the orchestral element: gesture in the broad sense, which scans and articulates the wave of feeling and passion.

These observations are indispensable for establishing a cultural politics and they are fundamental for a cultural politics of the popular masses. They explain the current international 'success' of the cinema and, earlier, of the opera and music in general.[53]

Q 23 § 7.

---

[52] Gramsci's manuscript and the critical edition read 'colore' (figuratively: 'quality') here. LVN, however, emends to 'calore' (warmth).

[53] See the three notes on opera in 'Popular literature' below, IX 22–24.

18 Sincerity (or Spontaneity) and Discipline

Is sincerity (or spontaneity) always a merit and a value? Only if disciplined. Sincerity (and spontaneity) means the maximum degree of individualism, even in the sense of idiosyncrasy (in this case originality is equal to idiom). An individual is historically original when he gives maximum prominence to social being, without which he would be an 'idiot' (in the etymological sense, which is however not far from the common and vulgar sense).[54] There is a romantic meaning attached to such words as originality, personality and sincerity, and this meaning is historically justified in that it springs from an attempt to counteract a certain essentially 'jesuitical' conformism, an artificial and fictitious conformism created superficially for the interests of a small group or clique, and not for those of a vanguard.

There is also a 'rational' form of conformism that corresponds to necessity, to the minimum amount of force needed to obtain a useful result. The discipline involved must be exalted and promoted and made 'spontaneous' or 'sincere'. Conformism, then, means nothing other than 'sociality', but it is nice to use the word 'conformism' precisely because it annoys imbeciles. This does not mean that one cannot form a personality or be original, but it makes matters more difficult. It is too easy to be original by doing the opposite of what everyone else is doing; this is just mechanical. It is too easy to speak differently from others, to play with neologisms, whereas it is difficult to distinguish oneself from others without doing acrobatics. Today people try to be original and to have a personality on the cheap. Prisons and mental asylums are full of original men with strong personalities. What is really difficult is to put the stress on discipline and sociality and still profess sincerity, spontaneity, originality and personality. Nor can one say that conformism is too easy and reduces the world to a monastery. What is 'real conformism', what is the most useful and freest form of behaviour that is 'rational' in that it obeys 'necessity'? In other words, what is 'necessity'? Everyone is led to make of himself the archetype of 'fashion' and 'sociality', to offer himself as the 'model'. Therefore, sociality or conformism is the result of a cultural (but not only cultural) struggle; it is an 'objective' or universal fact, just as the 'necessity'

[54] 'Idiot' and 'idiom' derive from the same Greek root – 'idios' (private, one's own).

on which the edifice of liberty is built cannot but be objective and universal. Liberty and free will, etc.

In literature (art), sincerity and spontaneity are opposed to calculation or mechanical procedures. This, too, can be a false conformism or sociality, that is, a tendency to settle down into customary and received ideas. There is the classical example of Nino Berrini who 'catalogues' the past and seeks to be original by doing what is absent from the files. Berrini's principles for the theatre are as follows: 1) the length of the work: determine the average length, basing it on those works which have been successful; 2) the study of endings: which ones have been successful and have won applause; 3) the study of combinations: for example, in the bourgeois sexual drama involving husband, wife and lover, see what combinations are exploited the most and, through elimination, 'invent' new combinations discovered in this mechanical way. In this way Berrini found that a drama must not have over 50,000 words, that is it must not last beyond a specific time. Every act or principal scene must culminate in a given way and this way is studied experimentally, according to an average of those feelings and stimuli that have been traditionally successful. Undoubtedly, with these criteria a box-office catastrophe is impossible.[55] But is this 'conformism' or 'sociality' in the sense explained above? Of course not. It is an accommodation to what already exists.

Discipline also means a study of the past, since the past is an element both of the present and the future. It is not, though, an 'idle' element, but a necessary one in that it is a language, an element of a necessary 'uniformity' and not of an 'idle' and slothful uniformity.

Q 14 § 61.

19 Cultural Themes: 'Rationalism' [i]

Romantic conception of the innovator. According to this concept the innovator is someone who wants to destroy everything that exists, without worrying about what will happen afterwards since

---

[55] Gramsci reviewed three plays by Berrini (1880–1962) in his *Avanti!* theatre column (see LVN, pp. 230–31. 366–67, 379). The critical edition suggests that Berrini's 'principles' enumerated here were remembered by Gramsci from private conversations. See also the mention of Berrini in the note on Pirandello, III 1.

one already knows that in a metaphysical sense every destruction is creation, indeed one only destroys what is then replaced by a new creation. Alongside this romantic idea goes a 'rational' or 'enlightenment' idea, the belief that everything which exists is a 'trap' set by the strong for the weak, by the cunning for the poor in spirit. The danger comes from the fact that in an 'enlightenment' way the words are taken literally, materially. The philosophy of praxis versus this way of seeing things. The truth of the matter is that everything which exists is 'rational', it has had or has a useful function. The fact that what exists has existed, has been justified, because it 'conforms' to the way of living, thinking and acting of the ruling class, does not mean that it has become 'irrational' because the dominant class has been stripped of its power and its strength of influence over the whole of society. A truth which is forgotten is that what exists has had its justification, it has been useful, rational and has 'facilitated' historical development and life. It is true that at a certain point this stops being the case, that certain forms of life change from being means of progress into a stumbling block, an obstacle. But it is not true 'over the whole area'. It is true where it is true, namely in the highest forms of life, the decisive ones, those that mark the peak of the progress, etc. But life does not develop uniformly; it develops by partial advances, by peaks, by a 'pyramidal' growth, so to speak. Hence it is necessary to study the history of each way of life, its original 'rationality' and, once this has been recognized, to ask whether this rationality still exists in each individual case, insofar as the conditions on which it was based are still present. What one tends to ignore is that these ways of life appear to the people who live them as absolute, as something 'natural', as they put it, and to indicate their 'historicity' is of itself a formidable step, to show that they are justified so long as certain conditions exist, but when these conditions change they are no longer justified and become 'irrational'. Hence the argument against certain ways of living and acting takes on an odious, persecutory character, it becomes a question of 'intelligence' or 'stupidity', etc. Intellectualism, pure enlightenment thinking, against which one must struggle relentlessly. We can deduce: 1) that every fact has been 'rational'; 2) that it should be opposed when it is no longer rational, no longer in conformity with its ends, but is dragging itself along with the sluggishness of habit; 3) that it is wrong to suppose that just because a way of living, acting or thinking has become 'irrational' in a given environment it has thereby become irrational everywhere and for everyone and is only kept alive by malice or stupidity; 4) that it is nonetheless true that when a way of thinking, living and acting has become irrational somewhere, this is of the greatest importance and should be clarified in every possible way. Thus one starts by modifying habits, which will facilitate substantial changes once conditions have changed; it will make habitual behaviour less 'sluggish'. Another point to establish is this: the fact that a way of living, acting, feeling has been introduced into the whole of society because it is that of the ruling class does not of itself mean that it is irrational and should be rejected. On close inspection one can see that there are two aspects to every fact: one which is 'rational', i.e. economical or in conformity with its ends, and one which is 'fashionable', a particular expression of the former, rational aspect. It is rational to wear shoes, but the particular style of one's shoes will be determined by fashion. It is rational to wear a shirt collar because you can thus frequently change that part of the shirt which gets dirty most easily, but the cut of your collar will depend on fashion, etc. One can see, in other words, that when the ruling class 'invents' a new utility which is more economical and more suitable to given conditions or given ends, it has at the same time stamped 'its own' particular form on this invention, this new utility. One has to be stubborn and blind to confuse permanent utility (when it is permanent) with fashion. By contrast, the task of the moralist, the creator of ways of behaving, is to analyse ways of being and living and to criticize them, shearing off what is permanent, useful, rational, in conformity with a desired end (so long as that end lasts) from what is accidental, snobbish, apish, etc. It can be useful to create an original 'fashion' on the basis of the 'rational', a new form which can arouse interest.

The error of the way of thinking we have mentioned can be seen from the fact that it has limitations. For instance, no one (unless they are mad) is going to advocate that people should no longer be taught to read and write because reading and writing were undeniably introduced by the ruling class, because writing serves to spread certain kinds of literature or to write blackmail letters or the memoranda of spies.

Q 14 § 67.

20 Popular Literature: [Rationalism (ii)]

Questions of names. It is evident that in architecture 'rationalism' means simply 'modern'. It is also evident that 'rational' is nothing other than a way of expressing the beautiful according to the taste of a given period.[56] That this has happened in architecture before happening in other arts is understandable because architecture is 'collective' not only as an 'occupation' but also in terms of 'judgement'. One could say that 'rationalism' has always existed, that there have always been attempts to reach a given end according to a given taste and according to technical knowledge of the resistance and adaptability of the 'material'.

To what extent and in what way the 'rationalism' of architecture may be spread to the other arts is a difficult question which will be resolved by a 'criticism of the facts' (which does not mean that intellectual and aesthetic criticism is useless, since it prepares for the criticism of the facts). It is true that architecture, in itself and through its (immediate) connections with the rest of life, seems to be the most reformable and 'disputable' of the arts. A picture or a book or a statuette can be kept in a 'private' place for one's personal taste, but this is not possible with an architectonic construction. One should also recall indirectly (for the part which is relevant here) Tilgher's observation that the work of architecture canot be compared to other works of art because of such things as its 'cost' and its bulk.[57] To destroy a constructive work, to make and remake it, by trial and error, is not a recommended procedure for architecture.

Q 14 § 2.

---

[56] Architecture was being widely discussed in the Italian press at the time Gramsci wrote this and the following note on rationalism (1933). Rationalist architecture in Italy drew on the work of Gropius and Le Corbusier, aiming to scale the proportions and functions of a building to the human body and eliminate redundant decoration. Between 1931 and 1937, several projects for major public buildings were assigned to the rationalists Giuseppe Pagano and Giuseppe Terragni.

[57] See the article cited in II 12 and footnote 35 above, Tilgher writes (p. 32): 'passing finally to architecture, the testing ground – in Giuseppe Rensi's felicitous phrase – of every aesthetic, Croce's theory seems decisively to fall down. Who can believe that costly and imposing buildings are put up for no other purpose than to counteract the shortcomings of our memory?'.

21 Popular Literature: [Rationalism (iii)]

It is right that the study of function is not sufficient – though it is necessary – for the creation of beauty. Moreover, 'function' itself is a source of dispute in that the idea and the fact of function is individual and gives rise to individual interpretations. Nor can it automatically be assumed that 'decoration' is not 'functional', meaning 'decoration' in the broad sense – everything which is not strictly 'functional' like mathematics. At the same time 'rationality' leads to 'simplification', which is a considerable step in itself. (Struggle against the aesthetic of the baroque which is characterized precisely by the predominance of the externally decorative over the 'functional' element, albeit in the broad sense of a function which includes the 'aesthetic function'.) It is a considerable step to come to admit that 'architecture is the interpretation of that which is practical'. Perhaps this could be said about all the arts, that they are a 'determinate interpretation of that which is practical', once every 'inferior and Judaic' or flatly bourgeois meaning is stripped from the expression 'practical'. (It should be noted that in many languages 'bourgeois' just means 'flat, mediocre, selfish', in other words, it has assumed the meaning which the expression 'Judaic' once had. Nevertheless, these problems of language are important because language = thought. The way one speaks indicates not only the way one thinks and feels, but also the way one expresses oneself, the way one makes others understand and feel.) Certainly, for the other arts the questions of 'rationalism' are not posed in the same way as for architecture. Still, the 'model' of architecture is useful, since one must admit *a priori* that the beautiful is always such and presents the same problems no matter what the particular formal expression of it may be. One could say that it is a matter of 'technique', but technique is nothing other than expression and the problem re-enters its initial circle with different words.

Q 14 § 1.

22 Popular Literature: ['Functional' Literature]

What in literature corresponds to 'rationalism' in architecture? Clearly, literature based on a plan or on a pre-established social course, in other words, 'functional' literature. It is strange that rationalism is acclaimed and justified in architecture and not in the other arts. There must be a misunderstanding. Is it perhaps that architecture alone has practical aims? This certainly looks like being the case because architecture is used to build houses; but this is not the point: it is a question of 'necessity'. One might say that houses are more necessary than the products of the other arts, meaning by this that everybody needs a house, while the products of the other arts are necessary only for intellectuals, for the cultured. One should then conclude that it is precisely the 'practical' people who propose to make all the arts necessary for everybody, to make everybody 'artists'.

Social coercion again! How people do blather against this coercion! Nobody sees that it is merely a word! Coercion, direction and planning are nothing more than a terrain for selecting artists. They are to be chosen for practical purposes, in a field in which will and coercion are perfectly justified. As if there has not always been some form of coercion! Just because it is exerted unconsciously by the environment and by single individuals, and not by a central power or a centralized force, does it cease to be coercion? Ultimately, it is always a question of 'rationalism' versus the individual will. Therefore, coercion is not the issue, but whether we are dealing with an authentic rationalism, a real functionalism, or with an act of the will. This is all. Coercion is such only for those who reject it, not for those who accept it. If it goes hand in hand with the development of the social forces, it is not coercion but the 'revelation' of cultural truth obtained by an accelerated method. One can say of coercion what the religious say of predestination: for the 'willing' it is not predestination, but free will. In fact there is opposition to the concept of coercion because it involves a struggle against intellectuals, especially traditional and traditionalist intellectuals who are prepared at most to concede that innovations can be brought in little by little, gradually.

It is curious that in architecture rationalism is contrasted with 'decorativism', which is called 'industrial art'. Curious but correct. In fact, any artistic manifestation that is meant to satisfy the taste of individual wealthy buyers, to 'embellish' their lives as they say, should always be called industrial. When art, especially in its collective forms, aims to create a mass taste, to elevate this taste, it is not 'industrial', but disinterested: i.e. it is art.

The concept of rationalism or 'functionalism' in architecture seems to me to be rich in consequences and princples for cultural politics. It is no accident that the concept arose in the present period of 'socialization' (in the broad sense) and of attempts by central forces to organize the great masses against the remnants of individualism and the aesthetics of individualism in cultural politics.

Q 14 § 65.

23 The New Architecture

The special objective character of architecture. In reality, the 'work of art' is the 'project' (the sum total of the designs and plans and calculations with which people other than the architect, 'the artist-planner', produce the building): an architect can be judged a great artist on the basis of his plans even without having materially built anything. The relation between the project and the material building is the same as that between the 'manuscript' and the printed book. The building is the social objectification of the art, its 'diffusion', the chance given to the public to participate in its beauty (when it is such), just like the printed book.

Tilgher's objection to Croce's idea about 'memory' as the cause of artistic objectification does not hold. The architect does not need the building to 'remember', but the plan.[58] Croce's 'memory' too is only to be treated as a relative approximation in the problem of why painters paint, writers write, etc., and are not satisfied with constructing phantasms for their personal use and consumption: and it should be borne in mind that the architect's plan is always more 'approximate' than the manuscript, the painting etc. The writer too introduces innovations in each edition of his book (or modifies when correcting the proofs, like Manzoni). In architecture the question is more complex because the building is never fully completed in itself but must go through a series of adaptations in relation to the 'panorama' in which it is inserted (and one cannot make second editions of it as easily as one can with a book). But the most important point to be noted today is this: that in a rapidly developing civilization, in which the urban 'panorama' must be very 'elastic', a great architectural art cannot be born because it is harder to conceive buildings for 'eternity'. In America they calculate that a skyscraper must not

[58] See footnote 57 above.

last more than 25 years because they presume that in 25 years the entire city 'may' change its appearance. In my opinion, a great architectural art can be born only after a transitory phase of a 'practical' kind, in which one seeks to attain the maximum satisfaction of the elementary needs of the people with maximum conveniences, understood in the broad sense, i.e. not only with regard to the single building, the single dwelling or the single assembly hall for large masses, but with regard to an architectonic complex, with streets, squares, gardens, parks and so on.

Q 3 § 155.

24 Justification of Autobiography [i]

One justification can be this: to help others develop in certain ways and towards certain openings. Autobiographies are often an act of pride: one believes one's own life is worth being narrated because it is 'original', different from others, etc. Autobiography can be conceived 'politically'. One knows that one's life is similar to that of a thousand others, but through 'chance' it has had opportunities that the thousand others in reality could not or did not have. By narrating it, one creates this possibility, suggests the process, indicates the opening. Autobiography therefore replaces the 'political' or 'philosophical essay': it describes in action what otherwise is deduced logically. Autobiography certainly has a great historical value in that it shows life in action and not just as written laws or dominant moral principles say it should be.

Q 14 § 59.

25 Justification of Autobiography [ii]

The importance of details is that much greater the more actual reality in a country differs from appearances, deeds from words, the people who act from the intellectuals who interpret these actions. I have already pointed out elsewhere that in certain countries the constitutions are modified by laws, the laws by rulings, the application of the rulings by their written form.[59] The

---

[59] The reference is back to a passage in Q 8 § 180: 'People are judged by what they do, not by what they say. Constitutions > laws > rulings: it is the rulings – and indeed their application (by means of circulars) – that indicate the real political and juridical structure of a country and a state.'

person who executes the 'law' (the ruling) is enrolled in a certain social class, of a certain cultural level, selected through a certain salary, etc. In fact the law resides in this executor, the way in which it – the law – is executed, especially because there are no organs of control and sanction. Now, only through autobiography does one see the mechanism at work, in the way it actually functions which very often does not correspond at all to the written law. Yet history, in its broad outlines, is based on written law: and when new facts arise, which overturn the situation, a lot of vacuous questions get thrown up, or at least documentation is found to be lacking on the 'molecular' way in which the change was prepared up to the moment when it actually exploded. Certain countries are especially 'hypocritical'; that is, in certain countries what one sees and what one does not see (because one does not want to see, or because whenever one does see it it seems an exception or 'picturesque') are particularly contrasting. And it is precisely in these countries that memoir writers are few in number or autobiographies are 'stylized', strictly personal and individual.

Q 14 § 64.

26 Some Criteria of 'Literary' Judgement

A work can be valuable: 1) because it expounds a new discovery that advances a specific scientific activity. There are, though, other factors that are valuable besides absolute 'originality'. It may be: 2) that already known facts and subjects have been chosen and arranged on the basis of a more adequate and convincing order, connection or criterion than say any previous one. The structure (the economy, the order) of a scientific work can be 'original' in itself. 3) Already known facts and subjects have given rise to 'new' subordinate but none the less important considerations.

Evidently, a 'literary' judgement must take into account the aims a given work set itself: the act of creation and scientific reorganization, the divulgation of facts and subjects known to a specific cultural group, a particular intellectual and cultural level, and so on. Therefore, there is a technique of divulgation that must be adapted to and reworked according to the particular case. In the eminently practical act of divulgation, one must see if the means conform to the end, which is a question of the technique used. But the process of examining and evaluating the 'original' fact and subject, or the 'originality' of the facts (concepts, the inter-relationships of ideas) and the subject, is also very difficult and complex and requires very extensive historical knowledge.

One should note the following criterion in Croce's chapter on Loria: 'It is one thing to throw out a casual observation that is left to fall without any further elaboration, and another to establish a principle with an awareness of the fecundity of its consequences. It is one thing to enunciate a generic and abstract idea, and another to think it out properly and concretely. Finally, it is one thing to invent, and another to repeat something at second or third hand.'[60]

There are the extreme cases: that of the person who discovers that there is nothing new under the sun and that the world is the same everywhere, even in the realm of ideas; and that of the person who finds 'originality' everywhere and claims that every rechewing is original because the saliva is different. Consequently, critical activity must be based on the ability to make distinctions, to discover the difference underlying every superficial and apparent uniformity and likeness, and on the ability to discover the essential unity underlying every apparent contrast and superficial differentiation.

(Although the author's explicit aims must be considered when judging his work, this does not mean therefore that some other real contribution of the author should be omitted or disregarded or depreciated, even if it is in opposition to the ostensible aim. The fact that Christopher Columbus intended to go 'in search of the great Khan' does not diminish the value of his real voyage and discoveries for European civilization.)

Q 23 § 5.

27 Methodological Criteria

The critical examination of a 'dissertation' may involve: 1) seeing if the author has rigorously and coherently deduced *all* of the consequences inherent in his initial premises or viewpoint: there

---

[60] Croce, *Materialismo storico*, p. 26.

may be a lack of rigour, or of coherence, or there may be tendentious omissions; or again there may be a lack of scientific 'imagination' (that is, the ability to see the full fecundity of the principle adopted); 2) evaluating the starting point (or viewpoint) and premisses, which may be completely rejected or limited or shown to be no longer valid historically; 3) discovering if the premisses are homogeneous or if, through the author's inability or inadequacy (or his ignorance of the historical state of the question), they are contaminated, contradictory, heterogeneous and historically incompatible. Therefore, critical evaluation can have different cultural (or even politico-polemical) ends: it can aim at demonstrating that as an individual someone is a hopeless nonentity; that the cultural group to which he belongs is scientifically irelevant; that although he 'thinks' or claims he belongs to a cultural group, he is deceived or wishes to deceive; that he makes use of the theoretical premisses of a respectable group in order to draw tendentious and particularistic deductions, etc.

Q 14 § 5.

III
PIRANDELLO

Introduction

In an early plan of the Prison Notebooks contained in a letter of 19 March 1927, Gramsci reports to Tania Schucht that as well as intending to work on the intellectuals, linguistics and serial literature he is going to write 'a study of Pirandello and the transformation of theatrical taste he represented and helped determine. Did you know that long before Adriano Tilgher, I discovered and helped popularize Pirandello's work? I wrote enough about Pirandello from 1915 to 1920 to form a book 200 pages long, and at that time my comments were original and went against the tide: Pirandello was either good-naturedly tolerated or openly derided' (LP, p. 80). The project was not carried far in practice, and this section groups the handful of notes on Pirandello that Gramsci wrote. They can be read as a theoretical development of the early *Avanti!* reviews of Pirandello's plays (see Section I), to which he refers in the letter, since they extend both his critique there of the schematic and artificial qualities of some of the plays as well as restating the point about them being cultural 'hand grenades' (I 27) and echoing the enthusiasm for the 'folkloric' *Liolà* in Sicilian dialect (I 25). Gramsci had stopped producing his *Avanti!* theatre column in 1920, a year before Pirandello's *Six Characters in Search of an Author* was first staged.

In 1922, Adriano Tilgher, a writer on pragmatist and relativist philosophy who was working as a drama critic in Rome, published a chapter on Pirandello in his *Studi sul teatro contemporaneo* which interpreted all the plays as variations on a single theme, the conflict between 'Life' and 'Form'. This formulation, which gave rise in the twenties to the critical label 'Pirandellism', neatly linked together various elements in Pirandello's work: the conflict between spontaneous action and socially constrained behaviour in the individual, the difference between what people feel themselves to be and the way others see them, the disparity between the flux of lived experience and the fixity of art. Tilgher's essay provoked a critical debate in Italy not least because it offered an alternative to Croce's negative judgement of

Pirandello at a time when Croce's influence as a critic was at its apogee. By driving a wedge between art and conceptual thought, Croce's aesthetics was unable to accomodate a philosophical theatre. Croce consequently played down Pirandello's importance as an artist and scorned his 'pseudo-philosophy' of relativism. Pirandello himself welcomed Tilgher's essay. He started using the Life versus Form idea both in explaining his earlier work (for instance in a preface he added to *Six Characters* in 1925) and in writing his new work. Tilgher, for his part, dissociated himself politically from Pirandello soon after the latter rallied to the Fascist Party in 1924. When, in 1927, he attacked Pirandello's work for its increasing sterility (the result, he claimed, of Pirandello's over-eager acceptance of his formulas) Pirandello in turn began to react against Tilgher's definitions, objecting that they made his work seem wholly cerebral and claiming in effect that 'Pirandellism' had itself become a 'Form' which occluded the genuine 'Life' of his art.

Gramsci in the thirties was able to take advantage both of the established critical polarization between Tilgher and Croce as well as of more recent discussions in the literary journals aimed at reassessing the respective weight and interaction of the aesthetic and the philosophical in Pirandello's work. On the surface, his own views move somewhere in between Tilgher's and Croce's, since he dissents from Tilgher's definition of Pirandello's intellectualism and looks for where poetry and art are to be found in his work (he finds them in one instance, à la Croce, in the form of 'fragments'), but at the same time he does not, like Croce or the Crocean critic Italo Siciliano, treat the aesthetic as the only measure of this work's value or see its aesthetic and philosophical moments as irrevocably separated. In fact, the questions Gramsci raises here about the stage play as something aesthetically and culturally composite open up an entirely different perspective on Pirandello's theatre.

1 Father Bresciani's Progeny: Pirandello

Pirandello does not belong in this category of writers. Far from it. I'm putting him under this head in order to group together the notes on literary culture.[1] A special essay will have to be written on Pirandello, using all the notes I wrote during the war, when Pirandello was attacked by the critics who were not even able to summarize his plays and who enraged some of the theatre-going public. (Remember the reviews of *L'innesto* in the Turin newspapers after the first performance and the offers of collaboration made to me by Nino Berrini.)[2] Remember that Pirandello removed *Liolà* from the repertory because of the hostile demonstrations of the young Turin Catholics on the second night. See the article in *La Civiltà Cattolica* of 5 April 1930, 'Lazzaro ossia un mito di Luigi Pirandello'.

Pirandello's importance seems to me to be more of an intellectual and moral, i.e. cultural, than an artistic kind. He has tried to introduce into popular culture the 'dialectic' of modern philosophy, in opposition to the Aristotelian-Catholic way of conceiving the 'objectivity of the real'. He has done it as it can be done in the theatre and in the way Pirandello himself is able to do it. This dialectical conception of objectivity appears acceptable to the audience because it is acted out by exceptional characters and thus has a romantic form, that of a paradoxical struggle against common sense and good sense. But could it be otherwise? Only in this way do the plays of Pirandello display less of the character of 'philosophical dialogues', which they nevertheless still possess to a fair extent, since the protagonists too often have to 'explain and to justify' their new way of conceiving reality. Besides, Pirandello himself does not always steer clear of a real solipsism, since in him the 'dialectic' is more sophistry than dialectic.

Q6 § 26.

2 Italian Literature: Pirandello

I have noted elsewhere how in a critico-historical judgement of

---

[1] Gramsci used the 'tag' heading 'Father Bresciani's progeny' (*I nipotini di padre Bresciani*) for 70 different notes. As well as serving to label the trend in literature he dubs 'Brescianist' (see Section VIII and introduction), the tag was also used in the earlier notebooks over notes which he later re-categorized as 'Popular literature' or 'Non-national-popular', and thus appears to have been a rather elastic signifier at this stage (1930–32). A single heading in the 1932 schema opening Notebook 8 in fact reads '*Father Bresciani's progeny. Popular literature* (Notes on literature)'.

[2] There is no record of this 'offer of collaboration' by Berrini during Gramsci's days as theatre critic of *Avanti!* On Berrini see also II 18.

Pirandello the 'history of culture' element must prevail over that of the 'history of art'. In other words, the cultural value of Pirandello's literary activity prevails over its aesthetic value. In the general picture of contemporary literature, Pirandello has been more effective as an 'innovator' of the intellectual climate than as a creator of artistic works. He has done much more than the Futurists towards 'deprovincializing' the 'Italian man' and arousing a modern 'critical' attitude in opposition to the traditional, nineteenth-century 'melodramatic' attitude.

The question, though, is even more complicated than it appears from these jottings. It takes this form: not only must the poetic values of Pirandello's plays (and the theatre is his most apt terrain, the most complete expression of his poetico-cultural personality) be isolated from his prevalently intellectual-moral and cultural activity, but they must undergo a further limitation. Pirandello's artistic personality is manifold and complex. When he writes a play, he is expressing 'literarily', with words, only a part of his artistic personality. He 'must' integrate the 'literary draft' into his activity as actor-manager and director. Pirandello's plays acquire their full expressiveness only in so far as the 'acting' is directed by Pirandello the actor-manager, in so far, that is, as Pirandello has provoked a definite theatrical expression in his given actors and Pirandello the director has created a specific aesthetic relationship between the human complex of the actors and the material apparatus of the scene (lighting, colours, *mise-en-scène* in the broad sense).[3] In other words, Pirandello's plays are closely tied to the physical personality of the writer and not only to their 'written' artistic-literary values. When Pirandello dies (that is, if Pirandello ceases to be active, not only as a writer but as an actor-manager and director), what will remain of his plays? A vague 'plot-outline' that can be compared in a sense to the scenarios of pre-Goldoni theatre and theatrical 'pre-texts', not that of eternal 'poetry'.[4] One might say that this is what happens to all theatrical works and in a sense this is true. But only in a

[3] Pirandello became artistic director of one of the first major stable theatre companies in Italy, the Teatro d'Arte in Rome, in 1925, staging his own and other writers' work. The company received a state subsidy but was dissolved with a large deficit in 1928.

[4] The *scenario* or *canovaccio* was a skeletal performance outline used by actors of the Commedia dell'arte (sixteenth to eighteenth century) upon which they elaborated their dialogues, gags and routines. Carlo Goldoni (1707–93) began from 1737 a reform of the Italian theatre, by using full written scripts and individualized characters in place of scenarios and standardized types.

sense. It is true that a Shakespearian tragedy can be given various theatrical interpretations by different actor-managers and directors, that every Shakespearian tragedy can become a 'pre-text' for theatrical performances of varying originality. The fact remains, though, that the tragedy 'printed' in book form, and read individually, has an independent artistic life which can detach itself from the theatrical performance. It is poetry and art even outside a theatre and a performance. This does not happen with Pirandello. For the most part, his plays live aesthetically only if 'performed' in the theatre with Pirandello as actor-manager and director. (All this should be taken with a good deal of discernment.)

Q9 § 134.

3 Theatre of Pirandello [i]

Perhaps Pirandello is right in being the first to protest against 'Pirandellism' and to maintain that so-called Pirandellism is an abstract construction of would-be critics, not sanctioned by his plays themselves, a convenient formula that often hides tendentious cultural and ideological interests which they do not want to admit explicitly. Pirandello has certainly always been attacked by the Catholics. Remember that *Liolà* was withdrawn from the repertory after the uproar staged by the young Catholics at the Alfieri theatre in Turin on the instigation of *Il Momento* and its tenth-rate drama reviewer, Saverio Fino.

The pretext for attacking *Liolà* was the play's supposed obscenity,[5] but the Catholics are in fact opposed to all Pirandello's theatrical works because his conception of the world, whatever this may be, whatever philosophical coherence it may have, is undoubtedly anti-Catholic in a way that the 'humanitarian' and positivistic conception of the bourgeois and petty-bourgeois *verismo* of traditional theatre was not. In fact, it does not seem possible to attribute a coherent conception of the world to Pirandello, to extract a philosophy from his plays. Thus

---

[5] Gramsci's manuscript is not clearly legible here, and we have preferred the reading of LVN, 'oscenità', to that of the critical edition, 'oscurità'. In a 1916 article on Saverio Fino, Gramsci claimed that 'the philosopher's stone of his drama criticism is pornography and holiness of intentions' (CT, p. 119; SM, p. 32). *Liolà*, first performed in Rome in November 1916, opened in Turin on 3 April 1917. See Gramsci's review, I 25 above.

Pirandello's theatre cannot be said to be 'philosophy'. Yet there are definitely points of view in Pirandello that can be generically connected to a conception of the world, one that can be approximately identified with subjectivism. But the problem is: 1) Are these points of view presented in a 'philosophical' way, or do the characters live them as an individual way of thinking? In other words, is the implicit 'philosophy' explicitly only 'culture' and individual 'ethicality', that is to say, is there, at least to a certain extent, a process of artistic transfiguration in Pirandello's plays? Again, is the reflection always the same, and of a logical nature, or are the positions always different, and of a fantastic nature? 2) Are these points of view necessarily bookish, erudite, taken from individual philosophical systems, or are they not, rather, present in life itself, in the culture of the time and even in the lowest level of popular culture, folklore?

This second point seems to me fundamental and it can be resolved by a comparative study of the different plays, those conceived in dialect where a rural 'dialectal' life is depicted and those conceived in literary language where a supradialectal life of national and even cosmopolitan bourgeois intellectuals is depicted. Now, it seems that in the dialect plays Pirandellism is justified by ways of thinking which are 'historically' popular and folkish, dialectal. We do not, in other words, seem to have 'intellectuals' disguised as common people, common people who think like intellectuals, but a historically and regionally real Sicilian people who think and act the way they do precisely because they are common people and Sicilians. Just because they are not Catholics, Thomists and Aristotelians does not mean that they are not common people and Sicilians. Just because they cannot be familiar with the subjectivist philosophy of modern idealism does not mean that there can be no 'dialectical' and immanentist currents in the popular tradition. If this were demonstrated, the whole castle of Pirandellism, the abstract intellectualism of Pirandello's plays, would collapse, as it appears it must.

I do not think, however, that the cultural problem of Pirandello's theare is exhausted in these terms. In Pirandello we have a 'Sicilian' writer who manages to conceive rural life in 'dialectal' and folklore terms (even if his folklore is not the one influenced by Catholicism, but one which has remained 'pagan' and anti-Catholic under the superstitious Catholic husk), and who is at the same time an 'Italian' and a 'European' writer. In Pirandello we have, moreover, the critical awareness of being simultaneously 'Sicilian', 'Italian' and 'European', but herein lies his artistic weakness along with his great 'cultural' significance (as I have noted elsewhere). This 'contradiction', which is deep-seated in Pirandello, has been explicitly expressed in some of his fiction (in a long story, I think *Il turno*, he describes a meeting between a Sicilian woman and a Scandinavian sailor, between two 'provinces' which historically are so far apart).[6] But what really matters is this: Pirandello's critico-historical sense may have led him, in the cultural field, to overcome and dissolve the old traditional, conventional theatre with its Catholic and positivistic mentality, a theatre putrefied in the mildew of regional life or of grey and abjectly banal bourgeois settings. But has it given rise to fully realized artistic creations? We can admit that Pirandello's intellectualism is not that identified by vulgar criticism (whether that of tendentious Catholic origin or that of dabblers like Tilgher), but is Pirandello free of all intellectualism? Is he not more a critic of theatre than a poet, more a critic of culture than a poet, more a critic of national-regional life than a poet? To put it another way, where is he really a poet, where has his critical attitude become artistic content-form and not just an 'intellectual polemic' – one of logic, albeit not that of a philosopher but the polemic of a 'moralist' in the superior sense? To me it seems that Pirandello is an artist precisely when he is a dialect writer and I feel that *Liolà* is his masterpiece. But of course, many 'fragments' in his 'literary' plays should be pointed out as very beautiful.

Literature on Pirandello. For the Catholics: Silvio D'Amico, *Il teatro italiano* (Treves, 1932) and a few notes in *La Civiltà Cattolica*. D'Amico's chapter on Pirandello was published in *L'Italia Letteraria*, 30 October 1932, and has created a lively controversy between D'Amico himself and Italo Siciliano in *L'Italia Letteraria* of 4 December 1932. Italo Siciliano is the author of an essay, 'Il teatro di L. Pirandello', which would seem to be fairly interesting precisely because it deals with Pirandello's 'ideology'. For Siciliano, Pirandello the 'philosopher' does not exist, his so-called 'philosophy' is a 'melancholy, variegated and

---

[6] The story is in fact *Lontano* (in Pirandello, *Novelle per un anno*, Milan 1949, pp. 93–137). In prison Gramsci had an edition (Milan 1915) of *Il turno* and *Lontano* in the same volume.

contradictory heap of rusty commonplaces and decrepit sophisms', while 'the famous Pirandellian logic is an empty and defective dialectical exercise' and 'the two together (logic and philosophy) make up the dead weight, the ballast that drags down – at times fatally – an artistic work of undoubted power'. For Siciliano, 'Pirandello's laborious intellectual convolutions have not been turned into lyricism or poetry, but have remained unelaborated; and since they are not deeply lived but a veneer, unassimilated and at times incompatible, they have harmed, fettered and suffocated the real poetry of Pirandello.' Siciliano, it seems, was reacting to the criticism of Adriano Tilgher, who had made Pirandello 'the poet of the central problem', presenting as Pirandello's 'artistic originality' what was a simple cultural element, one which should be kept subordinate and examined in cultural terms. For Siciliano, the poetry of Pirandello does not coincide with this abstract artistic content, so that this ideology is completely parasitical. At least this is how it appears, and if it is so, it does not seem correct. It can be granted that this cultural element is not the only one in Pirandello; anyway this is a matter of textual verification. It can also be granted that this cultural element is not always transformed artistically. But it still remains to be seen: 1) whether it has become art at certain moments; 2) whether, as a cultural element, it has not had a function and significance in changing the audience's taste by deprovincializing and modernizing it, and whether it has not changed the psychological inclinations and the moral interests of other playwrights by joining with the best of Futurism in the task of destroying the petty-bourgeois and philistine culture of the late nineteenth century.

D'Amico's ideological position towards 'Pirandellism' is expressed in these words:

> With all due respect to those philosophers, from Heraclitus onwards, who think the contrary, it is most certain that, in an absolute sense, our personality is always one and the same, from birth to the hereafter. If each of us were 'many', as the Father says in *Six Characters*, each of these 'many' would be able neither to enjoy the benefits nor to pay the debts of the 'others' that he carries within him. Yet the unity of consciousness tells us that each of us is always 'that one' and that Paul must redeem the sins of Saul because even after becoming 'another' he is always the same person.

This way of posing the question is pretty stupid and laughable, and besides one should see whether humour is not the predominant element in Pirandello's art, whether the author does not amuse himself by raising certain 'philosophical' doubts in unphilosophical and narrow minds in order to make fun of subjectivism and philosophical solipsism. The traditions and philosophical education of Pirandello are rather 'positivistic' and French Cartesian in origin. He studied in Germany, but in the Germany of pedantic philological scholarship, which certainly does not derive from Hegel but from positivism.[7] In Italy he has taught stylistics and humour, not, clearly, according to neo-Hegelian idealist tendencies but along positivist lines. For this very reason it must be accepted and established that the Pirandellian 'ideology' does not have bookish and philosophical origins but is linked to lived historico-cultural experiences with a minimum contribution of a bookish nature. It is possible that Tilgher's ideas reacted on Pirandello, that Pirandello, accepting Tilgher's critical explanations, has ended up by conforming to them. In this case, it will be necessary to distinguish between the Pirandello prior to Tilgher's interpretation and the later one.

Q 14 § 15.

4 Theatre of Pirandello [ii]

One should see how much of Pirandello's 'ideology' is, so to speak, of the same origin as that which seems to form the nucleus of the 'theatrical' writings of Nikolai Evreinov.[8]

For Evreinov theatricality is not only a particular form of artistic activity, that which is technically expressed in theatre in the literal sense. For him 'theatricality' is present in life itself, it is an attitude peculiar to man in that man tends to believe and to

---

[7] Pirandello studied at the University of Bonn from 1888 to 1891, graduating with a thesis on the phonetics of his native dialect.

[8] Nikolai Evreinov (1879–1953), Russian dramatist and theatre director. His theatrical experiments included parodies of the naturalistic staging of Stanislavsky, e.g. *The Fourth Wall*, 1915, and an enactment of the idea of the division of human personality into discrete identities, e.g. *The Theatre of the Soul*, 1912. His theoretical works, e.g. *The Theatre in Life*, argued that theatrical transfiguration was a primordial instinct, that life is a continuous 'theatre for oneself' organized in various forms by individuals and societies. Gramsci drew the information in this note from a review of Evreinov's *Theatre of Eternal War* in *L'Italia Letteraria* IV (1932) no. 31.

make others believe that he is different from what he is. Evreinov's theories should be considered carefully because it seems to me that he has grasped a precise psychological trait that ought to be examined and investigated further. There are several forms of this kind of 'theatricality' in this sense: one is that familiar form, conspicuous when exaggerated, which is called 'histrionics'; but there are others which are no worse or are less bad and some which are normal and also meritorious. In reality everyone tends, in his own way, to create a character for himself, to control certain impulses and instincts, to acquire certain 'social' forms, from snobbery to the observing of conventions to politeness and so on. Now what is the meaning of 'one's real nature', from which one tries to appear 'different'? 'One's real nature' can be taken to be the sum of one's animal impulses and instincts, and what one tries to appear is the social-cultural 'model' of a certain historical epoch that one seeks to become. It seems to me that 'one's real nature' is determined by the struggle to become what one wants to become.

As I have noted elsewhere, Pirandello is critically a Sicilian 'villager' who has acquired certain national and European traits, but who feels these three elements of civilization to be juxtaposed and contradictory within himself. From this experience has come his attitude of observing the contradictions in other people's personalities and then of actually seeing the drama of life as the drama of these contradictions.

Besides, the practice of describing, satirizing and caricaturing the provincial who wants to appear 'transformed' into a 'national' or European-cosmopolitan character is an element not only of Sicilian dialect theatre (*Aria del continente*)[9] but of all Italian dialect theatre and also of the popular novel. It is nothing other than a reflection of the fact that a national-cultural unity of the Italian people does not yet exist, that 'provincialism' and particularism are still deeply rooted in their customs and in the way they think and act. What is more, there is no 'mechanism' for raising life collectively from the provincial level to the national and European level. Hence the 'sorties', the individual raids made towards this end, assume low, 'theatrical', absurd and caricatural forms.

Q 14 § 21.

[9] A play by Nino Martoglio (1870–1921), reviewed by Gramsci in 1916 (see CT, pp. 779–80; LVN, pp. 236–37).

5 An Early Note by Pirandello[10]

Published in *Nuova Antologia*, 1 January 1934, and written by Pirandello in 1889–90, when he was a student at Bonn:

> We complain that the drama is missing from our literature. Many things are said on the matter and many others proposed – encouragements, exhortations, indications, projects – a mere waste of energy. They do not see where the real canker lies and they do not want to. A conception of life and man is lacking. And yet, we have time to give to the epic and the drama. Ours is an arid and stupid Alexandrianism.

Yet perhaps this note of Pirandello's does no more than echo discussions among German students on the general need for a *Weltanschauung* and is more superficial than it appears. At any rate, Pirandello has created his conception of life and man, but it is 'individual', incapable of national-popular diffusion. It has, however, had a great deal of 'critical' importance in corroding old theatrical customs.

Q 23 § 2.

---

[10] This note was originally drafted in the same paragraph as the first drafts of 'Back to De Sanctis' (II 1) and 'Connection of problems' (VI 1). Although retitled by Gramsci as a separate paragraph, it also followed 'Back to De Sanctis' in its later version at the beginning of Notebook 23. The thematic link between the notes is clearly that of the lack of a 'conception of life and man' as observed and dealt with respectively by De Sanctis and Pirandello.

IV

CANTO X OF DANTE'S INFERNO

Introduction

Gramsci planned a series of notes on the tenth canto of Dante's *Inferno* in his schema of 8 February 1929. Several letters to Tania record his progress with the project, the most detailed being that of 20 September 1931 (L, pp. 489–93; partly in LP, pp. 208–10). The notes, contained on the first pages of Notebook 4, were written in 1931–32.

In Canto X, Dante meets the souls of two Florentines, Farinata degli Uberti and Cavalcante dei Cavalcanti, who are being punished in the sixth circle of Hell for the heresy of Epicureanism. Farinata had been a leader of the Florentine Ghibellines who routed Dante's old faction, the White Guelphs, in 1260. Farinata's family was in turn persecuted and driven from Florence after his death. Cavalcante was the father of Dante's friend, the poet Guido Cavalcanti. The physical punishment of the Epicureans, who denied the afterlife expecting oblivion in the tomb, is to be placed in flaming sepulchres where they can never rest. The greater part of the canto consists of a dialogue between Dante and Farinata about Florentine politics. Into this dialogue is embedded a scene of some sixty lines with Cavalcante, who asks Dante why Guido is not with him. Dante replies, referring to Guido in the preterite tense 'ebbe' ('had'), which Cavalcante takes to mean that his son is dead. Dante's intended meaning was different – Guido is in fact still alive – but he says nothing to resolve the ambiguity and Cavalcante collapses in despair back into the tomb. After about fifteen lines of the dialogue resumed with Farinata, in which the latter predicts the fate that will befall the Whites and Dante's own exile in 1302 (the action of the poem is set back in 1300), Dante asks him to solve a problem which has been troubling him: how is it that the souls in this circle, who see so clearly into past and future, are blind to matters of the present? How is it, in other words, that Cavalcante did not know that Guido was still living? Farinata explains that the Epicureans in Hell are like long-sighted people – they see well at distances but not close to. In their lives they fixed their gaze on material things close to them. Their mental punishment therefore consists in having this immediate vision taken away from them. Dante then asks Farinata to tell Cavalcante that Guido still lives and that his perplexity over this problem had been the reason for his silence earlier.

In the letter of 20 September, Gramsci notes that Dante criticism had traditionally concentrated its analysis of this canto on two separate areas: a problem of interpretation in the first part – that of what or whom Guido's 'disdain' refers to in line 63 – and Farinata's predictions in the second. He was seeking to show, by contrast, that 'the importance of the second part lies especially in the fact that it illuminates Cavalcante's drama' in the first. 'Canto X is traditionally the canto of Farinata . . . I maintain that two dramas are represented in this canto – Farinata's and Cavalcante's, not just Farinata's.' Gramsci, in other words, convinced that the canto was a unity, was trying to overcome any tendency to fragment it, whether by philological or historical scholars who broke it up into a series of discrete 'problems', or by aesthetic critics who isolated the strongly expressive figure of Farinata from the surrounding context and the moral and theological doctrine. The latter tendency was particularly manifest in the critical approaches of De Sanctis and Croce, both bound in different degrees to a romantic aesthetic. De Sanctis, with his concept of authentic poetry as abstract ideas fully 'sunk' into concrete images, and Croce, with his identification between poetry and lyric expression, were both compelled by their outlooks to misrecognize a kind of writing like Dante's, based on quite different poetic principles such as eloquence, levels of style and schematic allegory and treating an often deliberately abstract and conceptually difficult subject-matter. Both critics coped with this disparity between their modern aesthetic criteria and Dante's medieval text by driving a wedge into the text itself. De Sanctis, making another variation on his science-life theme, distinguished its cold, abstract and generic allegorical message from the 'living', concrete and individualized poetic vehicles of this allegory (characters and images), and he highlighted the dramatic or passionate moments of the poem, at times wilfully against the grain of Dante's moral-theological framework itself. Gramsci noted how, in his essay of 1869, 'Il Farinata di Dante', De Sanctis had registered a falling-off in Farinata from a 'heroic' to a merely 'pedagogical' stature in the second half of the canto. Croce, in *La poesia di Dante* (1920) applied a distinction between the 'structure' of the text, i.e. its conceptual and practical levels – abstract ideas and moral or political doctrines, and its 'poetry', the aesthetic or lyrical level. His book consequently took the form of a fragmentary reading of the *Divine Comedy*, stringing together its lyrically accentuated moments and skipping most of the doctrine. Gramsci engages critically with this De Sanctis-Croce line by arguing that in Canto X 'poetry' cannot be severed from 'structure'. Taking Cavalcante's despair in the first part of the canto as a dramatic or lyrically heightened moment ('marked by an unutterable intensity' as he says in the 1931 letter) and Farinata's explanation of the Epicureans' limited perception in the second part as a doctrinal moment ('structural' in Croce's terms, since its function is to explain part of the system of divine justice, not to express an individualized feeling), Gramsci wants to show that these two moments are intimately connected. Farinata's retrospective explanation of Cavalcante's blindness to the present works like a stage-direction which 'instructs' the reader to set in motion the full extent of Cavalcante's drama. As Gramsci says, 'it gives the reader all the essential elements with which to relive it' (L, p. 491). 'Poetry' and 'structure' are therefore completely interdependent in this instance.

Gramsci believed that his reading of Canto X would 'deal a mortal blow to Croce's argument about poetry and structure in the *Divine Comedy*' (L, p. 491), and in 1931 he got Tania to forward the outline of his interpretation to Umberto Cosmo, his former professor at Turin and a Dante scholar. In his reply (transcribed in full in L, pp. 593–94 and in part by Gramsci himself in Q 4 § 86, though not reproduced here), Cosmo approved the outline but was sceptical as to whether Gramsci's reading in fact vitiated Croce's approach. He thought Gramsci's views needed to be backed up with other examples and he sent him suggestions for further reading. But Gramsci, who had mentioned to Tania at the start of the project that his library resources in prison were quite inadequate for making it a thorough piece of research, felt by now that it was not worth the trouble to buy the issues of periodicals recommended by the diligent Cosmo in order to 'write something for my own sake, to pass the time' (L, p. 590). This was not simply a 'disclaimer': Gramsci's distaste for the professionalized literary scholarship exemplified by Dante specialists was genuine enough and his

Dante project was a minor one in comparison with other more important projects in the notebooks. The recognition from Cosmo that his interpretation was relatively novel and worthwhile was 'sufficient, for my human condition as a prisoner, for me to distil a few pages of notes which I need not reject a priori as a waste of time' (ibid).

Yet the fact remains that he kept his Dante project on the agenda for three years, referred to it in five letters and devoted these notes to it. Their importance in relation to his prison writings as a whole perhaps lies partly in the way they continue the wrenching away from a Crocean idea of art. The notes demonstrate clearly Gramsci's concern with language in its material aspect as against Croce's idealist conception of language as intuition-expression (see Section V) and of reading as 'affective' immediacy. The core of Gramsci's critique of Vincenzo Morello's reading here is precisely that it fails to interpret the letter of Dante's text, and Gramsci's analogy in these notes between Farinata's 'doctrinal' speech and a theatrical stage-direction reveals very clearly how he sees interpretive reading as a process not only of decoding the elements of a text but also of reconstructing meaning from an elliptical message, a process in which the reader must engage dynamically with the whole of a given text.

1 ['Structure' and 'Poetry']

The question of 'structure and poetry' in the *Divine Comedy* according to Benedetto Croce and Luigi Russo. Vincenzo Morello's reading as *corpus vile*. Fedele Romani's reading of Farinata. De Sanctis.[1] Question of 'indirect representation' and of stage directions in drama: do the latter have artistic value? Do they contribute to the representation of the characters? Inasmuch as they limit the actor's freedom of choice and lead to a more concrete description of the given character, certainly. See Shaw's *Man and Superman* with John Tanner's handbook as an appendix:

---

[1] See Benedetto Croce, *La poesia di Dante*, Bari 1920, particularly Chapter 2; Luigi Russo, 'Critica dantesca', *Leonardo* III (1927) 12, pp. 305–11; Fedele Romani, 'Il canto X del "Inferno",' *Giornale Dantesco* XIII (1906) 1; Francesco De Sanctis, 'Il Farinata di Dante' in *Opere* Volume V, ed. Sergio Romagnoli, Turin 1967, pp. 653–80 (translated as 'Farinata' in J. Rossi and A. Galpin (eds.) *De Sanctis on Dante*, Madison 1957). On Morello's reading, see IV 5 below.

an intelligent actor can and must use this appendix as a guide for his own interpretation.[2] The picture at Pompeii of Medea killing the children she had by Jason: Medea is depicted with her face blindfolded. The painter is not able to or does not want to depict that face.[3] (There is, however, the case of Niobe, but in sculpture: to cover her face would have meant to take away the specific content of the work.) Cavalcante and Farinata: father and father-in-law of Guido. Cavalcante is the one punished in the circle. No one has observed that if the drama of Cavalcante is not taken into consideration, one does not see the torment of the damned in that circle being *enacted*. The *structure* ought to have led to a more exact aesthetic evaluation of the canto, since every punishment is represented in act. De Sanctis noticed the harshness contained in the canto by the fact that all at once Farinata changes character. After having been *poetry*, he becomes *structure*, De Sanctis explains; he acts as Dante's guide. The poetic depiction of Farinata has been admirably re-created by Romani: Farinata *is a series of statues*. Then Farinata acts out a *stage direction*. Isidoro Del Lungo's book on Dino Compagni's *Cronica*: the date of Guido's death is established in it.[4] It is strange that scholars did not think first of using Canto X for approximating this date (or has someone done so?). But not even Del Lungo's reckoning served to interpret the figure of Cavalcante or to explain the function that Dante makes Farinata fulfil.

[2] '*The Revolutionist's Handbook and Pocket Companion* by John Tanner' appendix to G.B. Shaw, *Man and Superman* (London 1903). Tanner is the Don Juan figure in Shaw's play. Compare Gramsci's remarks on stage directions in the letter to Tania on Canto X of 20 September 1931: 'The latest innovations brought to the art of the stage with its process of giving increasing importance to the producer, raise the question [of the artistic importance of stage directions] increasingly starkly. The author of the play struggles with the actors and the producer through his stage directions, which allow him to delineate his characters better. The author wants his division to be respected and the interpretation of his play by the actors and the producer (who are at one and the same time translators from one art into another and critics) to be in accordance with his conception. In G.B. Shaw's *Man and Superman*, the author appends a handbook written by the protagonist, John Tanner, in order to delineate the figure of the protagonist more clearly and get a greater fidelity to his image from the actor. A work of theatre without stage directions is more a lyrical work than a representation of living people in a dramatic clash; the stage direction has partly incorporated the old soliloquies etc. If in the theatre the work of art results from the collaboration of the writer and the actors aesthetically united by the producer, the stage direction has an essential importance in the creative process, in that it restricts the freedom of actor and producer. The whole structure of the Divine Comedy has this supreme function, and although the distinction [of poetry and structure] is a valid one to make, one needs to be very cautious with it in each case' (L, p. 492).

[3] See IV 3.

[4] See IV 4.

What is Cavalcante's situation, what is his torment? Cavalcante sees into the past and into the future, but does not see in the present, in a specific zone of the past and future in which the present is included. In the past Guido is alive, in the future Guido is dead; but in the present? Is he dead or alive? This is Cavalcante's torment, his gnawing worry, his only dominant thought. When he speaks, he asks after his son. When he hears 'ebbe', the verb in the past tense, he presses for an answer. And as the answer is slow to come, he no longer doubts: his son is dead. He disappears into the flaming tomb.

How does Dante represent this drama? He suggests it to the reader, he does not represent it. He gives the reader the elements for reconstructing the drama and these are given by the structure. There is, nevertheless, a dramatic part and it precedes the stage direction. Three cues: Cavalcante appears, not upright and manly like Farinata, but humble, downcast, perhaps on his knees, and asks uncertainly about his son. Dante's reply is almost indifferent and he uses the verb that refers to Guido in the past. Cavalcante immediately seizes this fact and lets out a desperate cry. He has doubt, not certainty. He demands other explanations, with three questions in which there is a gradation of his states of mind: 'Come dicesti: egli *ebbe*?' – 'Non vive egli ancora?' – 'Non fiede gli occhi suoi lo dolce lume?'[5] In the third question there is all of Cavalcante's paternal tenderness. Generic human 'life' is seen in concrete terms, in the enjoyment of light, which the damned and the dead have lost. Dante is slow in replying and it is then that Cavalcante ceases to doubt. Farinata, however, does not stir. Guido is his daughter's husband, but at that moment this feeling has no power over him. Dante stresses this strength of mind in him. Cavalcante collapses, but Farinata's countenance remains the same, he does not move his neck or turn his body. Cavalcante falls on his back, Farinata makes no gesture of prostration. Dante analyses Farinata negatively to suggest the (three) movements of Cavalcante, the distortion of the face, the head sinking and the back bending. Something has also changed in Farinata, though. His continuation is no longer so haughty as his first appearance.

Dante does not question Farinata only to 'inform' himself, he does so because he has been struck by Cavalcante's

[5] *Inferno* X, 67–69 ('What did you say? He had? Is he no longer alive? Does the sweet light not strike his eyes?').

disappearance. He wants the knot which prevented him from answering Cavalcante to be untied. He feels guilty towards Cavalcante. The structural passage is not only structure, then, it is also poetry, also a necessary element of the drama that has taken place.

Q 4 § 78.

2 Criticism of the 'Unexpressed'?

The observations that I have made might give rise to an objection: that this is a criticism of the unexpressed, an account of the non-existent, an abstract investigation of plausible intentions that were never given concrete poetic embodiment, but of which we have external traces in the mechanism of the structure. Something like the position that Manzoni often adopts in *The Betrothed*: as when Renzo thinks about the black braid of Lucia after having wandered in search of the river Adda and the border: 'And contemplating the image of Lucia – we will not venture to describe his feelings: the reader knows the circumstances, and can picture them for himself'.[6] Here, too, it could be a question of trying to 'picture' a drama, when we know the circumstances.

The objection has a semblance of truth. While one cannot imagine Dante setting limits to his expression for practical reasons (as is the case with Manzoni, who decided on the grounds of 'Catholic morality' not to speak of sexual love or to represent the passions in their fullness), a limit could have been imposed by the 'tradition of poetic language' (Ugolino, Myrrha, etc.)[7] – though not one that Dante always respects – 'reinforced' by his special feelings for Guido. But can one reconstruct and criticize a poem other than in the world of concrete expression and historically produced language? It was not a 'voluntary' element

---

[6] Manzoni, *The Betrothed* (Chapter 17), translated by Archibald Colquhoun, London 1951, p. 250.

[7] The letter of 20 September 1931 makes it clear that Gramsci is referring here to other instances of that technique of ellipsis in Dante, where instead of communicating an emotionally intense event directly he gives a 'stage-direction' enabling the reader to 'relive' it. 'Ugolino's . . . expression "Poscia più che il dolor poté il digiuno" ("Then famine did what sorrow could not do": *Inferno* XXXIII, 75) is an example of this kind of technique. the popular imagination understands it as a veil thrown over the image of father devouring son' (LP, p. 209). Similarly, Dante refers to Myrrha's incestuous love for her father, which had been explicitly consummated in Ovid's version of the story in *Metamorphoses* X, in an elliptical and euphemistic way (*Inferno* XXX, 37–39).

'of a practical and intellective character', therefore, that *clipped* Dante's wings. He 'flew with the wings he had', so to speak, and he did not renounce anything voluntarily. On the question of Manzoni's artistic neo-Malthusianism, see Croce's little book[8] and Giuseppe Citanna's article in *La Nuova Italia* of June 1930.

Q 4 § 79.

3 [Pliny and Lessing]

Pliny states that in painting the scene of the sacrifice of Iphigenia, Timanthes of Sicyon had portrayed Agamemnon veiled.[9] Lessing, in the *Laokoon*, was the first (?) to see in this artifice not the artist's inability to depict the father's sorrow but his deep conviction that only with this veiled figure (whose face is covered by his hand), and not with the portrayal of a face in agony, could he have given such a grievous expression of infinite sadness.[10] In the Pompeian representation of the sacrifice of Iphigenia, which is composed in a different way from Timanthes' painting, the figure of Agamemnon is also veiled.

These different representations of the sacrifice of Iphigenia are described by Paolo Enrico Arias in the *Bollettino dell'Istituto Nazionale del dramma antico di Siracusa* (summarized in *Il Marzocco* of 13 July 1930).

In the paintings at Pompeii there are other examples of veiled figures: for example Medea killing her children. Has the question been treated by other writers after Lessing, whose interpretation is not entirely satisfying?

Q 4 § 80.

[8] Croce, *Alessandro Manzoni. Saggi e discussioni*, Bari 1930.

[9] See Pliny, *Natural History* Book XXXV, 73–74 (Loeb edition, London 1968, Volume IX, p. 315).

[10] See Lessing, *Laokoon*, Oxford 1965, p. 67: 'Was er nicht malen durfte, liess er erraten' ('What he might not paint he left to conjecture'). Gramsci recalled this observation of Lessing's from Pietro Toesca's art history lectures at Turin University in 1912 (see LP, p. 209).

4 [Guido Cavalcanti's Death]

The date of Guido Cavalcanti's death was critically established for the first time by Isidoro Del Lungo in his work *Dino Compagni e la sua Cronica*. Of this work, the 'third volume, containing the historical and philological notes to the complete work and the text of the *Cronica* based on the Laurentian Ashburnham Manuscript', was published in 1887. Volumes I and II were finished in 1880 and published shortly thereafter. It is worth checking whether in establishing the date of Guido's death, Del Lungo relates this date to Canto X. If I remember right he does not. On the same subject, one should consult these other books by Del Lungo: *Dante nei tempi di Dante*, Bologna 1888; *Dal secolo e dal poema di Dante*, Bologna 1898; and especially *Da Bonifazio VIII ad Arrigo VII: pagine di storia fiorentina per la vita di Dante*, which is a revised, corrected and in places enlarged edition of part of the work on *Dino Compagni e la sua Cronica*.

Q 4 § 81.

5 Guido's Disdain

In 'La lingua nei tempi di Dante e l'interpretazione della poesia' (*Marzocco*, 14 April 1929), G.S. Gargàno's review of Enrico Sicardi's posthumous books, *La lingua italiana in Dante* (Optima, Rome, 1929), Gargàno quotes Sicardi's interpretation of Guido's 'disdain'. The passage, writes Sicardi, should be interpreted like this: 'I am not making this journey of my own free will; I am not free to come or not to come. I have been led here by him who is standing there waiting for me and *with whom* your Guido disdained to come here, i.e. to come in his company.' Sicardi's interpretation is one of form, not of substance. He does not pause to explain the nature of this 'disdain' (disdain for the Latin language or for Virgil's imperialism or the other explanations given by the interpreters). Dante was bestowed with 'grace' from Heaven: how could the same grace have been accorded to an atheist? (This is not right: for by its very nature 'grace' cannot be limited for any reason.) According to Sicardi, in the line 'Forse cui Guido vostro ebbe a disdegno' ['which' (or 'whom') perhaps your Guido held in disdain] the 'cui' clearly refers to Virgil; it is not an object complement but one of those pronouns which lack the case-marker 'con' ['with']. And the object of 'ebbe a disdegno'? It is to be found in the preceding 'da me stesso non vegno' ['I don't come of my own will'] and is, let us suppose, either the noun 'venuta' ['coming'] or, if one prefers, an object clause: 'venir' ['to come'].

At a certain point in his review, Gargàno writes: 'Guido's friend tells the poor *disappointed* father that he does not see his son walking through Hell alive.' *Disappointed?* The word is too weak: is it Gargàno's or is it taken from Sicardi? The problem of just why Calvante should actually expect Guido to come with Dante into Hell has been ignored. Because of his 'altezza d'ingegno'?[11] Cavalcante is not moved by 'reason' but by 'passion'. There is no reason why Guido should accompany Dante. There is only the fact that Cavalcante wants to know whether at that moment Guido is alive or dead and thus get out of his torment. The crucial word in the line 'Forse cui Guido vostro ebbe a disdegno' is not 'cui' or 'disdegno', but only *'ebbe'*. The 'aesthetic' and 'dramatic' accent on the line falls on 'ebbe', and it is the source of Cavalcante's drama, interpreted in the stage directions of Farinata. And there is the 'catharsis'. Dante corrects himself and takes Cavalcante out of his torment. In other words, he interrupts his punishment in *action*.

Q 4 § 82.

6 Vincenzo Morello[12]

'*Dante, Farinata, Cavalcante*' (octavo, 80 pp., Mondadori 1927). Contains two essays: 1) 'Dante e Farinata. Il canto X dell'Inferno letto nella "Casa di Dante" in Roma il XXV aprile MCMXXV'; 2) 'Cavalcanti e il suo disdegno'. The card bearing the publisher's blurb says 'Morello's interpretations will provide material for discussions among scholars, since they depart completely from traditional readings and arrive at new and different conclusions.' But did Morello have any background preparation for this work

---

[11] 'Se per questo cieco/carcere vai per altezza d'ingegno/mio figlio ov'è? perché non è ei teco?' ('If it is because of high intellect that you go through this blind prison, where is my son? Why is he not with you?') *Inferno* X, 58–60.

[12] Vincenzo Morello (1860–1933), right-wing nationalist publicist, wrote for *La Tribuna* under the pseudonym 'Rastignac'. Gramsci had written a fiercely polemical article on him in *Il Grido del Popolo* in 1918 (see SG, pp. 179–80). On Morello's pseudonym, see also IX 9.

and this study? He starts his first essay: 'The criticism of the last thirty years has explored the fountain-heads (!) of Dante's poem so deeply that the most obscure meanings, the most difficult references, the most abstruse allusions and even the innermost details of the characters in the three canticles can be said to have been penetrated and clarified.' How nice to be so easily satisfied. And it is very convenient to work on this kind of assumption: it lets one off the tiring task of individually filtering out and looking closely at the results reached by historical and aesthetic criticism. Morello goes on:

> Thus, *after the necessary research*, we can now read and understand the *Divine Comedy* without any longer getting lost in the mazes of the old conjectures which incomplete historical information and *insufficient intellectual discipline* vied with each other in constructing and making impossible to unravel.

Morello, then, is supposed to be one of those who has done the *necessary research*: it will not be hard to show that his reading of Canto X is superficial and that he has not understood the most apparent letter of the text. According to Morello, Canto X is 'pre-eminently political' and 'for Dante, politics is as sacred as religion.' Therefore 'a stricter discipline than ever' is required in interpreting Canto X so as not to substitute one's own tendencies and passions for those of others and so as not to abandon oneself to the most unusual aberrations. Morello says that Canto X is pre-eminently political, but he does not and cannot demonstrate it because it is not true. The tenth canto is political as all of the *Divine Comedy* is, but it is not pre-eminently political. But Morello finds this assertion convenient because it saves him from tiring his brain. Since he considers himself a great politician and a great political theorist, it is going to be easy for him to make a political interpretation of Canto X after having flicked through it in the first edition he has found to hand, using the general notions put about on Dante's politics which every good journalist of repute must have a smattering of, as well as a number of index cards about.

The pages where Morello deals with the relations between Farinata and Guido Cavalcanti (p. 35) show that he has only superficially read Canto X. Morello wants to explain why Farinata is unmoved during 'the *episode*' of Cavalcante. He recalls Foscolo's view that this indifference shows the strong fibre of the man, who 'does not let domestic feelings distract him from thinking about the new calamities in his country.' And he recalls De Sanctis's opinion that Farinata remains indifferent because 'Cavalcante's words reach his ears but not his mind, which is wholly preoccupied with a single thought: the badly learnt art'.[13] For Morello there may 'perhaps be a more convincing explanation.' Namely: 'If Farinata does not change his appearance, nor move his neck, nor bend his body, as the poet will have it, it is, perhaps, not because he does not feel or care about the suffering of others but because *he does not know Guido*, just as he did not know Dante, and because he is not aware that Guido has taken his daughter in marriage. He died in 1264, three years before the Cavalcantis returned to Florence and when Guido was seven. Guido was betrothed to Bice when she was nine (1269), five years after Farinata's death. *If it is true that the dead cannot know about the living by themselves, but only by means of the souls who come near them or from angels or devils*, Farinata can be unaware of his kinship with Guido and remain indifferent to his fortunes, if no soul or angel or devil has brought him news about them. *And this does not seem to have occurred.*' The passage is staggering in numerous respects and reveals the inadequacy of Morello's intellectual discipline. 1) Farinata himself overtly and clearly says that the heretics of his group are unaware of things 'when they come near or are', not always; and it is in this, as well as in the flaming tomb, that their specific punishment consists 'for having wanted to see into the future'. It is only in this case that 'unless others tell us' they remain in ignorance. Thus Morello has not even read the text well. 2) It is amateurish to go looking for the intentions of the characters in a work of art beyond what is conveyed by the letter of the text. Foscolo and De Sanctis (especially De Sanctis) do not depart from critical seriousness. Morello, however, really thinks about Farinata's concrete life in Hell beyond Dante's canto, and even thinks it improbable that, in their spare time, devils or angels could have informed Farinata of what he did not know. It is the mentality of the man of the people who, after reading a novel, would like to know what all the characters did later on (whence the success of serialized adventures). It is the mentality of Rosini who wrote *The Nun of*

---

[13] Ugo Foscolo, 'Discorso sul testo della Divina Commedia' (1825) CXLI, in *Opere* Volume IX, part 1, Florence 1979, p. 424; *De Sanctis on Dante* (cit) p. 82.

Monza[14] or that of all the scribblers who write continuations of
famous works or develop and amplify partial episodes.

That there is a close relationship between Cavalcante and
Farinata in Dante's poetry is evident from the letter of the canto
and its structure. Cavalcante and Farinata are close to each other
(some illustrators even imagine them as being in the same tomb).
Their two dramas are tightly interwoven and Farinata is reduced
to the structural function of explicator in order to make the reader
penetrate Cavalcante's drama. Explicitly, after the '*ebbe*', Dante
contrasts Farinata and Cavalcante in the physical-statuesque
terms which express their moral positions. Cavalcante *falls*,
collapses and no longer appears outside. Farinata 'analytically'
neither changes his expression, nor moves his neck nor turns his
body.

But Morello's failure to understand the letter of the canto also
emerges when he deals with Cavalcante (pp. 31 ff.). 'This canto
also expresses the drama of the family under the laceration of the
civil wars. Yet it is not expressed by Dante and Farinata, but by
Cavalcante.' Why 'under the laceration of the civil wars'? This is
Morello's own bizarre addition. The double element, family-
politics, is contained in Farinata, and politics holds him upright
when the family disaster of his daughter is impressed upon him.
But in Cavalcante the sole dramatic element is the love of his son
and he collapses as soon as he is sure his son is dead. According
to Morello, Cavalcante 'asks Dante *weeping*: – Why is my son not
with you? – Weeping. This weeping of Cavalcante's can really be
called the lamentation of the civil war.' This is idiotic and it
follows from the claim that Canto X is 'political *par excellence*'.
And further on: 'Guido was alive at the time of the mystical
journey; but he was dead when Dante was writing. Thus Dante
was in fact writing about a dead person, *even though, for the
chronology of the journey, he had* to tell the father the opposite', etc.
This passage shows how Morello has barely skimmed the
dramatic and poetic content of the canto and has literally glided
over the letter of the text.

Morello's superficiality is full of contradictions because he
then goes on to dwell on Farinata's prediction, without stopping
to think that if these heretics can know the future, they must know

---

[14] Giovanni Rosini's (1776–1855) *La monaca di Monza. Storia del secolo XVII*, first
published in 1829 and reprinted throughout the nineteenth century, was a popular
continuation of the story of the nun Gertrude in Manzoni's *The Betrothed*.

the past, since the future always becomes past. This does not lead him to reread the text and ascertain its meaning.

But even Morello's so-called political interpretation of Canto X is incredibly superficial. It is nothing but a return to the old question, was Dante a Guelph or a Ghibelline? For Morello, Dante was essentially a Ghibelline and Farinata is 'his hero', only that he was a Ghibelline in the manner of Farinata, more of a 'politician' than a 'party-man'. One can turn this argument any way one likes. In fact, Dante, as he himself says, 'was a party unto himself'.[15] He was basically an 'intellectual' and his sectarianism and partisanship were more intellectual than political in the immediate sense. Besides, Dante's political position could only be established by a highly detailed analysis not only of all his own writings but also of the political divisions of his time, which were very different from those of fifty years earlier.[16] Morello is too caught up in literary rhetoric to be able to have a realistic conception of the political attitudes of the men of the Middle Ages towards the empire, the papacy and their Communal republic.

What is amusing about Morello is his 'disdain' for the commentators whom he dips into here and there, as on p. 52, in the essay 'Cavalcanti e il suo disdegno', where he says that 'the prose of the commentators often alters the meaning of the lines'. Look who's talking!

This essay 'Cavalcanti e il suo disdegno' belongs precisely to that hack literature on the *Divine Comedy*, pointless and space-

[15] *Paradiso* XVII, 69.

[16] Gramsci deals elsewhere with the political side of Dante as an intellectual of the period of the communes, the economic-corporate phase of transition from the medieval to the modern world. A note on the politico-cultural significance of Dante's use and theoretical justification of the Italian vernacular against Latin is reproduced below (see V 13). Gramsci sees Dante's political thought (as expressed in his tract *De monarchia* and as can be gleaned passim from the *Divine Comedy*) as containing a progressive element insofar as it desires to restrict the temporal influence of the Church and invest centralized power in a lay Empire, but as looking back to the Middle Ages in that it conceives of this centralized power as transcending and neutralizing the communal factions (Ghibellines-Guelphs, Whites-Blacks). See Q 6 § 85: Dante's is 'not a political doctrine, but a political utopia, coloured with reflections of the past. (. . .) Above the internal communal struggles, Dante dreams of a society superior to the commune, superior both to the Church which supports the Blacks and to the old empire which upheld the Ghibellines, he dreams of a form able to impose a law above factions etc. He is one who has been defeated by the war between classes who dreams of the abolition of this war under the aegis of an arbitrary power.' In this respect, Gramsci establishes a contrast with Machiavelli: 'Dante ends the Middle Ages (a phase of the Middle Ages), whereas Machiavelli indicates that a phase of the Modern World has already managed to elaborate its problems and the related solutions in a way which is already very clear and elaborated.'

wasting with its conjectures, subtleties and flights of the intellect produced by people who, just because they have pens in their hands, think they are entitled to write about anything, unreeling the idle imaginings of their mediocre talents.

Q4§83.

7 The 'Renunciations of Description' in the 'Divine Comedy'

From an article by Luigi Russo, 'Per la poesia del Paradiso dantesco' (in *Leonardo* of August 1927), I take a few observations on Dante's 'renunciations of description' which, however, have a different origin and explanation than in the episode of Cavalcante. Augusto Guzzo had raised the question in an article ('Il Paradiso e la critica del De Sanctis') in the *Rivista d'Italia* of 15 November 1924, pp. 456–79. Russo writes:

> Guzzo speaks of the 'renunciations of description' that are frequent in the Paradiso ('Qui vince la memoria mia lo ingegno' – 'Se mo' sonasser tutte quelle lingue' etc.) and he believes this is a proof that where Dante cannot transfigure the earth celestially he 'forgoes description of the celestial phenomenon rather than overturn, invert, violate the experience with an abstract and artificial fantasy' (p. 478). Now, here too Guzzo, like other Dante scholars, is trapped in a psychological evaluation of several verses of this kind that recur in the Paradiso. A typical case is that of Vossler who once used these 'renunciations of description' of Dante's as if they were confessions of imaginative impotence to conclude that, on the poet's own admission, the last canticle is inferior. Recently, in his critical reappraisal, he referred, however, precisely to those renunciations to ascribe a religious value to them, almost as if from time to time the poet wished to point out that this is the realm of the transcendental absolute (*Die Göttliche Komödie*, 1925, II Band, pp. 771–2). To me it seems that the poet never succeeds in being so expressive as in these confessions of expressive impotence, which must in reality be considered not in their content (which is negative), but in their lyrical tone (which is positive and at times hyperbolically positive), This is poetry of the ineffable and one should not mistake poetry of the ineffable for poetic ineffability.

According to Russo, one cannot speak of renunciations of description in Dante. They are, in a negative form, full and sufficient expressions of everything that is really in motion within the poet.

In a note Russo mentions one of his studies, 'Il Dante del Vossler e l'unità poetica della Commedia' in volume XII of *Studi Danteschi*, edited by Michele Barbi, but the Vossler reference must be to do with the attempts to order the three canticles into an artistic hierarchy.

Q4 § 84.

8 [The Blind Tiresias]

The interpretation given in these notes of the figure of Cavalcante was indicated in 1918 in a 'Sotto la Mole' entitled 'The Blind Tiresias'.[17] The note published in 1918 was occasioned by a story in the newspapers about a young girl from a small Italian town who went blind after having predicted that the war would end in 1918. Its relevance is evident. In literary tradition and folklore the gift of foresight is always related to the present infirmity of the seer, who, while he sees into the future, does not see into the immediate present because he is blind. (Perhaps this is linked to the concern with not disturbing the natural order of things. That is why seers are not believed, like Cassandra. If they were believed, their predictions would not come true, since, once alerted, men would act differently and events would unfold differently from the prediction.)

Q4 § 85.

9 ['Rastignac'][18]

Since one should not give the slightest importance to the solemn task of advancing Dante criticism or contributing one's own little stone to the edifice of commentaries and clarifications of the divine poem etc., the best way of presenting these observations on Canto X seems precisely to be a polemical one – to demolish a classic philistine like Rastignac and demonstrate, in drastic and

[17] 'Il cieco Tiresia, *Avanti!* Piedmont edition, 18 April 1918. The article is reprinted in SM, pp. 392–93, CF, pp. 833–35 and in the notes on pp. 2663–5 of the critical edition (Q).

[18] On 'Rastignac' alias Vincenzo Morello, see V6 and footnote 12 above.

explosive albeit demagogic fashion, that the representatives of a subaltern social group can scientifically and in their artistic taste get the better of intellectual pimps like Rastignac. But Rastignac counts for precious little in the official cultural world! It does not take much skill to reveal his ineptitude and worthlessness. All the same, his lecture was given at the Casa di Dante in Rome. Who runs this Casa di Dante in the eternal city? Do the Casa di Dante and the people in charge of it also count for nothing? And if they count for nothing, why does high culture not eliminate them? And what did the Dante scholars think of the lecture? Did Barbi speak of it in his reviews in *Studi Danteschi* to point out its deficiencies? Anyway, it is nice to be able to seize on a man like Rastignac and use him as a ball in a solitary football game.

Q 4 § 87.

V

LANGUAGE, LINGUISTICS AND FOLKLORE

Introduction

Language and linguistics have recently come to be seen not as a marginal subject in the Prison Notebooks but as occupying a central place in their overall theoretical construction. This revaluation stems largely from the argument of Franco Lo Piparo in *Lingua intellettuali egemonia in Gramsci* (Bari 1979) that Gramsci's concept of hegemony was influenced by models for describing linguistic change in terms of 'radiations of innovations' from high-prestige to lower-prestige speech communities. These models, originating in the nineteenth century, had been developed in the Italian school of 'neolinguistics' (later 'spatial linguistics'), principally by Matteo Giulio Bartoli (1873–1946) who taught at the University of Turin and had supervised Gramsci's unfinished thesis in historical linguistics. In opposition to the positivist neogrammarians, who saw sound changes as governed by 'exceptionless' laws, the neolinguists described language change as a process in which a dominant speech community exerted prestige over contiguous subordinate communities: the city over the surrounding countryside, the 'standard' language over the dialect, the dominant socio-cultural group over the subordinate one. Bartoli developed a set of 'areal norms', according to which the earlier of two given linguistic forms would be found in a peripheral rather than a central area, an isolated rather than an accessible area, a larger rather than a smaller area. Using these norms, the linguist could reconstruct and predict the diffusion of innovations. Lo Piparo's thesis is that Gramsci conceived of the relations between intellectuals and the people, between a hegemonic culture and a subaltern culture, in substantially the same way as neolinguistics had described the relations between areas – as relations of direction through the exercise of prestige securing active consent, rather than as relations of domination by coercion and passive consent. Although he does not deny that Gramsci's use of the term 'hegemony' may have been decisively influenced, as has been widely argued, by the meanings it had acquired in Russian political discourse, he does claim that the characteristic sense it took on in Gramsci's writing was strongly conditioned by his background and interest in linguistics.

For Gramsci linguistic relations are not only representations and historical traces of past and present power relations but are also paradigms for other relations of cultural influence and prestige: elaborated philosophical conceptions of the world over unelaborated folkloric ones (see the last notes in this Section), high over popular literature (see Section IX), the network of a press emanating from a homogeneous cultural centre (see Section X). Thus Gramsci's interest in the way linguistic change occurred over a whole area, radiating out from a 'source of diffusion', and the way this process could be accelerated by a rational intervention in education became an interest in the way a political party as 'collective intellectual' could exert its attraction through capillary organizations, breaking up existing hegemonic relations and constructing new ones with the popular classes over whole diffuse cultural areas.

Language and literacy were already important political questions in Italy before Gramsci wrote. At the time of the Unification in 1861, only a tiny proportion of the population, possibly as little as 2½ per cent, actually spoke 'Italian', a language which was historically the dialect of medieval Florence adopted as a written language by educated minorities in the sixteenth century for reasons of its cultural prestige (Dante, etc.) and developed thereafter in differing forms in the various regions. Most Italians spoke one of a very large number of dialects, whose survival was the result of the persisting political and cultural fragmentation of the peninsula after the break-up of the Roman Empire. Political unification brought a demand for linguistic standardization by the liberal ruling class and language instruction was introduced into the new state school curriculum under the provisions of the 1859 Education Act. The practical effects of this Act on the diffusion of a common language were however severely restricted at first by inadequate funding for elementary schools and the permanent absenteeism (47% of the 6–11 age group in 1906) of children of poorer families. Attendance at middle and secondary schools was limited to 4% of the 11–18 age group in 1911 and was still under 15% in 1931.

Italian was generally taught prescriptively in 'grammar lessons' and teachers tended to favour over-literary and affected Tuscan forms and a use of the language which abstracted from a personal point of view. At the same time dialect was stigmatized as substandard. Working-class speakers who became bilingual experienced a marked gap between their two codes: Italian as the language of the classroom, of written communications and 'official' interactions; dialect for personal, local, informal exchanges.

The Education Act of 1923, which replaced the 1859 legislation, embodied the diametrically opposed liberal and idealist thinking of Croce and his former associate Giovanni Gentile, who was the education minister responsible for the new law. In his *Estetica* of 1902, Croce had identified language with creative self-expression and treated communication as its merely subordinate practical realization. Prescriptive or normative grammar was, in Croce's view, 'impossible' because a spiritual activity like language could not be 'summed up' and transmitted by a practical technique. The effect of this thinking on Gentile's legislation was reactionary. No provision was made for the normative teaching of Italian. In effect, as Gramsci points out, it was a policy which condemned to illiteracy a great number of working-class and peasant children, keeping them confined to their spoken dialects. As he argues elsewhere, the Gentile reform reinforced class divisions because its laissez-faire attitude ensured that only children from educationally advantaged backgrounds, already culturally homogenized with the school system, would do well (SPN, p. 41).

Gramsci's discussion of 'normative grammar' needs to be seen in the light of this legislation. If working-class children, who were dialect speakers, were denied access to the culturally more advanced language (the language of a society undergoing political unification, urbanization, industrialization) then they were deprived in relation to those who had access to it. The point was not to coerce them to speak in a particular way. When a hegemonic language established itself they would naturally begin to adopt it once they became exposed to its influence. But the process could be accelerated by normative language teaching. Gramsci sees both Italian and the dialects as 'conceptions of the world' and the difference between them as one of 'cultural, politico-moral emotional environment'. The dialects, however, are also the linguistic sediments of earlier social formations with localized and primitive cultures whereas Italian is 'technically superior' and belongs to a more advanced formation. Gramsci's views on linguistic change and education thus assume that there will be a necessary interaction between language and dialect *and* a necessary elevation out of the dialects into a common monolingualism. Yet it may be questioned to what extent he is correct in ascribing a 'technical' superiority to the language used by the dominant sectors of a historically specific culture, in other words in his correlation between a particular language and 'abstract' or 'elaborated' functions of language.

All these considerations, including the problems, are 'mapped' onto the notes on folklore. Language and folklore were assimilated to each other by Gramsci as instances of what he called 'spontaneous philosophy' (see SPN, pp. 322 ff), and he treats folklore here with analytical paradigms – spatial area, stratification in time and space, dominance and subordination – that he had derived from Bartoli's neolinguistics. Just as each language is 'an integral conception of the world' (VI 9), so all folklore is 'a conception of the world and life' (V 14). But just as the language-conception is 'fossilized and anachronistic' for those who only speak a dialect, so the folklore-conception is 'not elaborated and systematic' for those people who live it. These notes of Gramsci's are of considerable importance for understanding his way of conceiving ideology and what he meant by a process of 'intellectual and moral reformation'. The latter would need to overcome 'local particularisms' (V 8) through relations of hegemony, and this would involve a wholesale cultural transformation.

1 The Question of the Language and the Italian Intellectual Classes

Development of the idea that Italy embodies the paradox of a very young and a very old country at the same time (like Lao-tse born at the age of eighty).[1]

The relation between the intellectuals and the people-nation studied in terms of the language written by the intellectuals and used among them and in terms of the function of Italian

---

[1] On Lao-tse, see I 4. See also II 15 and X 4.

intellectuals in the medieval cosmopolis because of the papacy
having its seat in Italy (the use of Latin as a learned language is
bound up with Catholic cosmopolitanism).

Literary Latin and vulgar Latin. The Neo-Latin dialects
develop from vulgar Latin not only in Italy but throughout the
European area dominated by Rome. Literary Latin crystallizes
into the Latin of scholars, of the intellectuals – so-called 'middle-
Latin' (see Filippo Ermini's article in *Nuova Antologia*, 16 May
1928). In no way can it be compared to a spoken, national and
historically living language, though neither should it be mistaken
for a jargon or an artificial language like Esperanto. In any case,
there is a split between the people and the intellectuals, between
the people and culture. (Even) religious books are written in
middle-Latin, so even religious discussions are out of reach of
the people, although religion is the most important element of
culture. The people *see* religious rites and *hear* exhortatory
sermons, but they cannot follow discussions and ideological
developments, which are monopolized by a caste.

The vernaculars are written down when the people regain
importance. The oath of Strasbourg (after the battle of Fontaneto
between the successors of Charlemagne) has remained because
the soldiers could not swear in an unknown language without
thereby invalidating their oath. In Italy, too, the first traces of the
vernacular are the oaths and testimonies of witnesses from the
people for establishing the ownership of monastic lands
(Montecassino).[2] At any rate, it can be said that from 600 A.D.
in Italy, when one can presume that the people no longer
understood learned Latin, up to 1250, when the vernacular
begins to flourish (i.e. for more than 600 years), the people could
not understand books and were unable to participate in the world
of culture. The rise of the communes enables the vernaculars to
develop and the intellectual hegemony of Florence unifies the
vernacular, it creates an illustrious vernacular.[3] But what is this
illustrious vernacular? It is the Florentine dialect elaborated by

[2] The Strasbourg oaths – generally cited as the earliest known example of written French
– were oaths of alliance sworn in 842 by Louis the German and his followers in French
(*romana lingua*) and Charles the Bald and his followers in German (*teudisca lingua*). The
placiti cassinesi – early instances of Italian vernacular texts dating from 960–63 – were
sworn testimonies of three monasteries dependent on Montecassino.

[3] 'Illustrious vernacular' (*vulgare illustre*) is a phrase used in Dante's treatise on language
and style *De vulgari eloquentia* to denote an ideal unitary Italian which acts as a centre of
attraction for the various regional vernaculars.

the intellectuals of the old tradition: it is Florentine in its vocabulary and phonetically but it is Latin in its syntax. Moreover, the victory of the vernacular over Latin was not easy: learned Italians, with the exception of poets and artists in general, wrote for Christian Europe and not for Italy. They were a concentration of cosmopolitan, not national, intellectuals. The fall of the communes and the advent of the principate, the creation of a ruling caste removed from the people, crystallizes this vernacular in the same way that literary Latin had been crystallized. Once again, Italian is a written not a spoken language, a language of scholars, not of the nation. There are two scholarly languages in Italy, Latin and Italian, and the latter ends by gaining the upper hand and triumphs completely in the nineteenth century with the separation of the lay intellectuals from those of the Church[4] (even today the clergy continue to write books in Latin but today, too, the Vatican is increasingly using Italian in Italian affairs and will end up doing the same for other countries, in line with its current nationalities policy).

Anyway I think the following point should be established: the crystallization of the illustrious vernacular cannot be separated from the tradition of middle-Latin and it represents a similar phenomenon. After a brief interlude (the communal liberties) when there is a flourishing of intellectuals who came from the popular (bourgeois) classes, the intellectual function is reabsorbed into the traditional caste, where the individual elements come from the people but where the character of the caste prevails over their origins. In other words, it is not a stratum of the population which creates its intellectuals on coming to power (this occurred in the fourteenth century), but a traditionally selected body which assimilates single individuals into its cadres (the typical example of this is the organization of the ecclesiastical hierarchy).

In a complete analysis other elements should be taken into account. I believe that for many questions the national rhetoric of the last century and the prejudices that it embodied have not even stimulated preliminary investigations. Thus: what was the exact area in which the Tuscan language was used? I think that in

---

[4] After the brief alliance (neo-Guelphism) between liberal nationalism and Catholicism in 1843–48, Gramsci registered the split between clerics and lay intellectuals, with the passage to 'Jacobinism' of ex-neo-Guelphs like Gioberti (see VI 18) and clerical opposition to the liberal and democratic formulas of unification.

Venice, for example, the Italian introduced was already elaborated by scholars on the Latin model and original Florentine never entered (in that Florentine merchants did not make real spoken Florentine heard there as they did, for instance, in Rome and Naples; the language of politics continued to be Venetian). The same was true for other centres (Genoa, I believe). There is still no history of the Italian language along these lines: historical linguistics is still far from historical in this respect. For the French language there are such histories (Brunot's – and Littré's – seems to be of the type I have in mind, but I do not remember). I feel that if language is understood as an element of culture, and thus of general history, a key manifestation of the 'nationality' and 'popularity' of the intellectuals, this study is not pointless and merely erudite.

Ermini's article is interesting for the information it provides on the importance that the study of 'middle-Latin' has acquired (this term, which should, I think, mean 'medieval' Latin, seems rather inappropriate and could cause errors among non-specialists). I could use this article for an initial bibliography, along with other pieces by Ermini (who is a middle-Latin specialist). On the basis of his investigations, Ermini states that 'in place of the theory of two separate worlds, that of Latin, which is in the hands of scholars alone and dies out, and that of Neo-Latin which arises and takes on life, one should substitute the theory of the unity of Latin and the perennial continuity of the classical tradition.' This can only mean that the new Neo-Latin culture was strongly influenced by the culture preceding it, not that there was a 'national-popular' unity of culture.

But perhaps for Ermini middle-Latin has precisely its literal meaning, that of the Latin which stands half way between classical and humanistic Latin. Humanistic Latin undoubtedly marks a return to the classical, whereas middle-Latin has unmistakable characteristics of its own. Ermini sets the beginning of middle-Latin towards the middle of the fourth century, when the alliance is formed between classical culture (!) and Christian religion, when 'a noble pleiad of writers, deserting the schools of rhetoric and poetry, feels a quickening desire to link the new faith with ancient beauty (!) and thus give life to the first Christian poetry.' (It seems to me correct to trace middle-Latin back to the first blooming of Christian Latin literature, but the way its genesis is described seems to be vague and arbitrary: for this point see Marchesi's history of Latin literature.)[5] Middle-Latin would therefore have been contained between the middle of the fourth century and the end of the fourteenth century, between the beginnings of Christian inspiration and the spread of Humanism. These thousand years are subdivided by Ermini as follows: *first age*, that of *origins*, from the death of Constantine to the fall of the Empire in the West (337–476); *second age*, that of barbarian literature, from 476 to 799, i.e. until the restoration of the Empire by Charlemagne, which is truly a time of transition in the continuous and progressive Latinization of the barbarians (exaggeration: it was the period of formation of a stratum of Germanic intellectuals who write in Latin); a *third age*, that of the Carolingian renaissance, from 799 to 888, up to the death of Charles le Gros; a *fourth*, that of *feudal literature*, from 888 to 1000, up to the pontificate of Sylvester II, when feudalism, a slow transformation of pre-existing ordinances, opens a new era; a *fifth*, that of scholastic literature, which goes up to the twelfth century, when knowledge is gathered into the great Schools and philosophical thought and method fertilizes all the sciences; and a *sixth* , that of *erudite literature* , which runs from the beginning of the thirteenth to the end of the fourteenth and already points to decline.

Q3 § 76.

2 Bellonci and Crémieux[6]

La Fiera Letteraria of 15 January 1928 summarizes a rather stupid and blundering article published by G. Bellonci in *Il Giornale d'Italia*. In his *Panorama* Crémieux writes that in Italy there is no modern language. This is correct in a very specific sense: 1) there is no concentration of the unitary educated class whose members write and 'always' speak a 'living' unitary language, one that is equally diffused among all the social classes and regional groups

[5] Concetto Marchesi, *Storia della letteratura latina*, Messina 1925–27.

[6] Goffredo Bellonci (1882–1964), principal literary critic of *Il Giornale d'Italia*, was a former nationalist influenced as a critic by Croce. Benjamin Crémieux (1874–1944), French critic who specialized in Italian literature, was responsible for introducing the work of Svevo and Pirandello into France. Gramsci possessed a copy of his *Panorama de la littérature italienne contemporaine* (Paris 1928) in prison. Crémieux later took part in the French Resistance, was captured, and died in Buchenwald.

of the country: 2) because of this there is a noticeable distance between the educated class and the people. The language of the people is dialect, backed up by a jargon that tends towards Italian, a jargon which is to a great extent the dialect translated mechanically. Furthermore, the various dialects have a strong influence on the written language because the so-called educated class also speaks the national language on certain occasions and dialect in the family, where speech is most vivid and closest to immediate reality. On the other hand, however, reaction to the dialects causes the national language to remain at the same time somewhat fossilized and pompous, and when it tries to be informal it breaks up into so many refractions of the dialects. This process affects the tone of speech (the *cursus* and the music of the period) which characterizes the regions, the vocabulary, morphology and above all syntax. Manzoni rinsed his personal Lombard-influenced vocabulary in the river Arno, less so his morphology and hardly at all his syntax, which is more ingrained in one's style, in one's personal artistic form and in the national essence of the language.[7] In France, too, something similar is found in the contrast between Paris and Provence, but to a much lesser, almost negligible extent. In a comparison between A. Daudet and Zola it was discovered that Daudet makes practically no use of the etymological remote past tense which is replaced by the imperfect. In Zola this occurs only incidentally.

Against Crémieux's affirmation Bellonci writes: 'Until the sixteenth century linguistic forms descend from above, from the seventeenth century onwards they rise from below.' A gross mistake, due to his superficiality, the absence of a critical perspective or an ability to make distinctions. It is precisely up till the sixteenth century that Florence exerted its cultural hegemony, along with its commercial and financial hegemony (Pope Boniface VIII said that the Florentines were the fifth element of the world), and that there was a unitary linguistic development from below, from the people to the educated class. This development was reinforced by the great Florentine and Tuscan writers. After the decline of Florence, Italian increasingly became the language of a restricted caste which had no live contact with an historical speech. Is this not the question posed

---

[7] 'Rinsing in the Arno' was Manzoni's metaphor for his replacement of Milanese with Florentine words in the final (1840) reworking of *The Betrothed*. See footnote 11 on p. 295.

by Manzoni, that of returning to a Florentine hegemony using state means, but rejected by the more historicist Ascoli who does not believe in cultural hegemonies imposed by decree and not supported by a deeper and more necessary national function.[8]

Bellonci's question, 'Would Crémieux deny that a Greek language exists' (he must mean 'existed') 'because it has Doric, Ionic and Aeolic varieties?', is merely comical. It shows that he has not understood Crémieux and does not understand anything about these problems. He argues with bookish categories, such as language, dialect, 'varieties', etc.

Q 23 § 40.

3 Giulio Bertoni and Linguistics

One ought to write a critical demolition of Bertoni as linguist, for the attitudes he has recently expressed in his *Manualetto di linguistica* and in the small volume published by Petrini (see the passage published in *La Nuova Italia* of August 1930).[9] I think one can demonstrate that Bertoni has succeeded neither in providing a general theory of the innovations which Bartoli has brought to linguistics nor in understanding the nature of these innovations and their practical and theoretical importance.

Besides, in the article he published a few years ago in *Leonardo* on linguistic studies in Italy,[10] he in no way distinguished Bartoli from the ordinary ranks. Indeed, through an effect of contrasts he placed him in the second rank, unlike Casella who, in his recent article in *Il Marzocco* on the *Miscellanea* for Ascoli, underlines Bartoli's originality.[11] In Bertoni's article in *Leonardo* one should

---

[8] On Manzoni and Ascoli, 'A single language and Esperanto', I3.

[9] Bertoni's *Linguaggio e poesia* (Rieti 1930) was mentioned in this issue of *La Nuova Italia* but no extracts were quoted. The '*Manualetto*' referred to here is Bertoni and Bartoli's *Breviario di neolinguistica* (Modena 1925), divided into a theoretical part ('Principi generali') by Bertoni and a technical part ('Criteri tecnici') by Bartoli. There was little connection between Bartoli's methodological criteria ('spatial norms', etc.) for classifying linguistic areas and Bertoni's neoidealist view of language as a 'divine and human activity . . . which links words together and winds through them'. On Bartoli, see the introduction to this Section.

[10] G. Bertoni, 'Nuovi orientamenti linguistici' in *Leonardo* II (1926) 2.

[11] Mario Casella 'L'eredità dell'Ascoli e l'odierna glottologia italiana' in *Il Marzocco* XXXV (1930) 27.

note that *Campus* comes over as being actually superior to Bartoli, when Campus's studies on the Aryo-European velars are nothing but straightforward applications of Bartoli's general method and thus derived from suggestions made by Bartoli himself. It was Bartoli who disinterestedly pointed out Campus's value and has always tried to put him in the top rank. Bertoni, perhaps not without academic malice, in an article like the one in *Leonardo* in which he had practically to count the words he would devote to each scholar, has arranged things in such a way that Bartoli is placed in a nook. It is an error on Bartoli's part to have collaborated with Bertoni on the compilation of the *Manualetto*: his error and also his scientific responsibility. Bartoli is esteemed for his concrete studies: by leaving Bertoni to write the theoretical part, he leads students astray and puts them on the wrong track – in this case modesty and disinterestedness become a fault.

In addition to failing to understand Bartoli, Bertoni has not even understood the aesthetics of Croce, in the sense that he has not managed to derive from Crocean aesthetics rules for research and for the construction of the science of language. He has done nothing but paraphrase, praise, and lyricize certain impressions. He is essentially a positivist who goes weak-kneed in the face of idealism because it is more fashionable and allows one to be rhetorical. It is astonishing that Croce has praised the *Manualetto*, without seeing or pointing out Bertoni's inconsistencies.[12] My impression is that Croce has sought to give benevolent recognition to the fact that in this branch of studies, where positivism reigns, there is an attempt to open the way to idealist approaches. I do not feel that there is any relationship of immediate dependence between Bartoli's method and Crocism. The relationship is with historicism in general, not with a particular form of historicism. Bartoli's innovation lies precisely in this: that he has transformed linguistics, conceived narrowly as a natural science, into an historical science, the roots of which must be sought 'in space and time' and not in the vocal apparatus in the physiological sense.

Bertoni ought to be demolished not only in this field: his image as a scholar has always been intellectually repugnant to me. There is something false about it, something insincere in the literal sense of the word – besides his prolixity and his lack of

---

[12] Croce's review appeared in *La Critica* XXIV (1926) 3, pp. 181–82.

'perspective' in dealing with historical and literary values.

In 'linguistics' Vossler is a Crocean, but what does Bartoli have in common with Vossler and what relationship is there between Vossler and that which is commonly called 'linguistics'? In this regard, remember Croce's article 'This round table is square' (in *Problemi di estetica*), the criticism of which should be the starting point for establishing the exact concepts in this question.[13]

Q3 § 74.

4 Linguistic Problems: Giulio Bertoni

There is an amazingly benevolent review of Bertoni's book *Linguaggio e poesia* (Bibliotheca editrice: Rieti 1930, 5 Lire) by Natalino Sapegno in *Pègaso* of September 1930. Sapegno is not aware that Bertoni's theory that the new linguistics is a 'subtle analysis which discriminates poetic words from functional words' is anything but a novelty because it goes back to an ancient rhetorical and pedantic view in which words are divided into 'ugly' and 'beautiful', poetic and non-poetic or antipoetic, etc., in the same way that languages were divided into beautiful and ugly, civil or barbaric, poetic and prosaic. Bertoni adds nothing to linguistics, other than old prejudices. It is quite remarkable that these stupidities should have got the seal of approval from Croce and his pupils. What are words when they are cut off and abstracted from the literary work? No longer an aesthetic element but an element of the history of culture and it is as such that the linguist studies them. And how does Bertoni justify 'the naturalistic analysis of languages, as a physical fact and as a social fact'? As a physical fact? What does this mean? That man too, besides being an element of political history, must be studied as a biological fact? That one must make a chemical analysis of a painting? That it would be useful to examine the amount of mechanical effort it cost Michelangelo to sculpt his Moses?

It is astonishing that these Croceans fail to recognize all this and it serves to point out the confusion which Bertoni has helped to spread in this field. Sapegno even writes that this investigation of Bertoni's (into the beauty of individual words in isolation: as if

---

[13] See V 7 below. Karl Vossler (1872–1949), neo-idealist linguist who followed Croce by dissolving linguistics into stylistics, which he treated as a branch of aesthetics.

the most 'stale and mechanized' word did not regain in the concrete work of art all of its freshness and primitive simplicity) 'is difficult and delicate, but not therefore any the less necessary: because of it, linguistics, instead of being a science of language aimed at discovering relatively fixed and certain laws, will begin to become the history of language, attentive to particular facts and to their spiritual significance.' And again: 'The core of this argument (of Bertoni's) is, as anyone can see, a concept of Crocean aesthetics that is still alive and fertile. But Bertoni's originality consists in having developed and enriched it in a concrete direction, a concept which Croce himself had only indicated or perhaps started to follow, but never purposefully or all the way.' If Bertoni 'has revived Crocean thought' and even enriched it, and if Croce recognizes himself in Bertoni, then Croce himself ought to be re-examined and corrected. But it seems to me that Croce has simply been very indulgent towards Bertoni because he has not thoroughly examined the issue and for 'didactic' reasons.

Bertoni's research is partly a return to old etymological systems: '*sol quia solus est*'; how beautiful it is that the sun implicitly contains in itself the image of solitude in the immense sky and so on; 'how beautiful it is that in Apulia the dragonfly, with its little wings in the form of a cross, is called "*la morte*" (death)', and so on. Remember in a work by Carlo Dossi the story of the schoolmaster who explains how words are formed: 'In the beginning a piece of fruit fell, making the sound "*pum!*", and so we have the word "*pomo*" (apple).' 'And if a pear had fallen?' young Dossi asks.[14]

Q 6 § 20.

5 Linguistics: [Pagliaro]

Antonino Pagliaro, *Sommario di linguistica arioeuropea*, Part I, *Cenni storici e quistioni teoriche* (Libreria di Scienze e Lettere, Dr G. Bardi: Rome, 1930) in 'Pubblicazioni della Scuola di Filologia Classica dell'Università di Roma, Serie seconda: *Sussidi e materiali*, II.ɪ '. On Pagliaro's book, see the review by Goffredo Coppola in *Pègaso* of November 1930.

[14] Carlo Dossi, *L'altrieri* (1868), part III of the chapter 'Panche di scuola'.

The book is indispensable for seeing the recent progress made in linguistics. It appears to me that much has changed (judging from the review) but that the basis on which linguistic studies can be situated has not been found. Croce's identification of art and language has permitted some degree of progress and has enabled certain problems to be solved and others to be declared non-existent or arbitrary. Linguists, though, who are essentially historians, find themselves faced with another problem: is the history of languages possible outside of the history of art and, in turn, is the history of art possible?

But linguists study languages precisely in so far as they are not art, but the 'material' of art, a social product and the cultural expression of a given people, etc. These questions either remain unresolved or are resolved by going back to a tarted-up version of old-style rhetoric (cf. Bertoni).

For Perrotto[15] (for Pagliaro too?) the identification of art and language has led to the recognition that the problem of the origin of language is insoluble (or arbitrary?), that it would mean asking why man is man (language = imaginative capacity or thought). I find this imprecise; the reason why the problem cannot be solved is because documents are unavailable – that is why it is arbitrary. Beyond a given historical limit, one can draw up a hypothetical, conjectural and sociological history, but this is not 'historical' history. He argues further that this identification enables one to determine what an error is in language, what is non-language. 'An error is an artificial, rationalistic, willed creation which does not take hold because it reveals nothing, it is peculiar to the individual outside of society.' It seems to me that in this case one should say that language = history, and non-language = the arbitrary. Artificial languages are like jargons. It is not true that they are absolutely non-languages because they are useful in some ways: they have a very limited socio-historical content. But the same is true of dialects in relation to the national-literary language. Yet dialect too is language-art. But between the dialect and the national-literary language something changes: precisely the cultural, politico-moral-emotional environment. The history of languages is the history of linguistic innovations, but these innovations are not individual (as is the case in art). They are

---

[15] The critical edition suggests that this is a mistake for the name Coppola, recorded correctly at the beginning of this note.

those of a whole social community that has renewed its culture and has 'progressed' historically. Naturally, they too become individual, yet not in the artist-individual, but in the individual as a *complete*, determinate historical-cultural element.

In language too there is no parthenogenesis, language producing other language. Innovations occur through the interference of different cultures, and this happens in very different ways: it still occurs for whole masses of linguistic elements as well as happening in a molecular way (for example: as a 'mass', Latin altered the Celtic language of the Gauls, while it influenced the Germanic language 'molecularly', by lending it individual words and forms). There can be interference and a 'molecular' influence within a single nation, between various strata, etc.; a new ruling class brings about alterations as a 'mass', but the jargons of various professions, of specific societies, innovate in a molecular way. In these innovations artistic judgement takes the form of 'cultural taste' and not artistic taste, for the same reason that one prefers brunettes or blondes and that aesthetic 'ideals', related to specific cultures, change.

Q6 § 71.

6 Linguistics: [Sicardi]

Importance of Enrico Sicardi's book *La lingua italiana in Dante* published by Optima, Rome, with a preface by Francesco Orestano. I read G.S. Gargàno's review of it ('La lingua nei tempi di Dante e l'interpretazione della poesia') in *Il Marzocco* of 14 April 1929. Sicardi stresses the need for studying the 'languages' of various writers if one hopes to arrive at an accurate interpretation of their poetic world. I do not know if everything Sicardi says is correct, and especially whether it is 'historically' possible to study the 'particular' language of individual writers, since an essential document is missing: a large body of evidence about the spoken language in the times of these writers. Still, Sicardi's methodological reminder is correct and necessary (remember in Vossler's book *Positivismo e idealismo nella scienza del linguaggio* his aesthetic analysis of La Fontaine's fable about the crow and the fox and the erroneous interpretation of '*son bec*', due to his ignorance of the historical value of '*son*').[16]

Q5 § 151.

7 Croce's Essay 'This Round Table is Square'[17]

The essay is wrong even from the Crocean point of view (that of Croce's philosophy). The very use that Croce makes of the proposition shows that it is 'expressive', and therefore justified. The same can be said for any 'proposition', even if it is not 'technically' grammatical, which can be expressive and justified inasmuch as it has a function, even if only a negative one (to demonstrate a grammatical 'error' one can use an ungrammatical form). The problem, then, must be formulated in another way, in terms of 'discipline in the historicity of language' in the case of 'ungrammatical expressions' (which are an absence of 'mental discipline', neology, provincial particularity, jargon, etc.) or in other terms (in the case given in Croce's essay the error comes from this, that such a proposition can appear in the descriptions of a 'madman' or an abnormal person, and acquire absolute expressive value; how else can we represent someone who is not 'logical' except by making him say 'illogical things'?). In reality, everything that is [not] 'grammatically correct' can also be justified from the aesthetic and logical point of view if one sees it as an element of a broader and a more comprehensive representation, rather than within the particular logic of the immediately mechanical expression.

The question that Croce wants to raise, 'What is grammar?', cannot be solved in his essay. Grammar is 'history' or 'a historical document': it is the 'photograph' of a given phase of a national (collective) language that has been formed historically and is

[16] Vossler's aesthetic analysis of La Fontaine's fable contained the claim that 'son bec' ('far from frequent in French') instead of 'dans le bec' in the line 'Tenait en son bec un fromage' evokes an 'image of calm and full possession, so that the latter loss of the cheese will appear so much the more painful'. (*Positivismo e idealismo nella scienza del linguaggio*, Bari 1908, pp. 224–37). Gramsci's point is that in seventeenth century French the possessive pronoun in such cases was still normal usage.

[17] The essay 'Questa tavola rotonda è quadrata' (1905) is in Croce's *Problemi di estetica* [1910] Bari 1966, pp. 172–76. This sentence had been used by the German linguist Steinthal to show that a well-formed sentence could be illogical and thus to illustrate the difference between grammar and logic. Croce endorsed Steinthal's argument and maintained in addition that the sentence was also aesthetically unacceptable. A logically contradictory statement could not, Croce said, be expressive (aesthetic), because expressiveness depends on the internal coherence of the thing or things expressed. He concluded that grammar, unlike logic and aesthetics, was not a science but merely a set of descriptive rules. In a letter to Tania of 12 December 1927 requesting a copy of the Bertoni-Bartoli *Breviario*, Gramsci says he wants to write 'a dissertation on the theme and with the title: "This round table is square" . . . it is no small question if you consider that it means: "What is grammar?"' (L, pp. 157–58).

continuously developing, or the fundamental traits of a photograph. The practical question might be: what is the purpose of such a photograph? To record the history of an aspect of civilization or to modify an aspect of civilization?

Croce's claim would lead one to deny that a picture depicting, among other things, a . . . siren, for example, has any value. In other words, one would have to conclude that every proposition must correspond to the *true* or to *verisimilitude*.

(The proposition can be non-logical in itself, contradictory, but at the same time 'coherent' in a broader context.)

Q 29 § 1.

8 How Many Forms of Grammar Can There Be?

Several, certainly. There is the grammar 'immanent' in language itself, by which one speaks 'according to grammar' without knowing it, as Molière's character produced prose without knowing it.[18] Nor does this point seem useless because Panzini (*Guida alla Grammatica italiana*, 18° migliaio) seems not to distinguish between this 'grammar' and the 'normative', written one which he intends to speak about and which seems to be for him the only possible grammar there can be. The preface to the first edition is full of inanities, which are however significant in someone who writes (and is considered a specialist) on grammatical matters, like the statement 'we can write and speak even without grammar'.

Besides the 'immanent grammar' in every language, there is also in reality (i.e., even if not written) a 'normative' grammar (or more than one). This is made up of the reciprocal monitoring, reciprocal teaching and reciprocal 'censorship' expressed in such questions as 'What did you mean to say?', 'What do you mean?', 'Make yourself clearer', etc., and in mimicry and teasing. This whole complex of actions and reactions come together to create a grammatical conformism, to establish 'norms' or judgements of correctness or incorrectness. But this 'spontaneous' expression of grammatical conformity is necessarily disconnected, discontinuous and limited to local social strata or local centres. (A peasant who moves to the city ends up conforming to urban

---

[18]   The character is M. Jourdain in *Le Bourgeois Gentilhomme* Act II scene 4.

speech through the pressure of the city environment. In the country, people try to imitate urban speech; the subaltern classes try to speak like the dominant classes and the intellectuals, etc.)

One could sketch a picture of the 'normative grammar' that operates spontaneously in every given society, in that this society tends to become unified both territorially and culturally, in other words it has a governing class whose function is recognized and followed. The number of 'immanent or spontaneous grammars' is incalculable and, theoretically, one can say that each person has a grammar of his own. Alongside this actual 'fragmentation', however, one should also point out the movements of unification, with varying degrees of amplitude both in terms of territory and 'linguistic volume'. Written 'normative grammars' tend to embrace the entire territory of a nation and its total 'linguistic volume', to create a unitary national linguistic conformism. This, moreover, places expressive 'individualism' at a higher level because it creates a more robust and homogeneous skeleton for the national linguistic body, of which every individual is the reflection and interpreter. (Taylor system and self-education.)

Historical as well as normative grammars. But it is obvious that someone who writes a normative grammar cannot ignore the history of the language of which he wishes to propose an 'exemplary phase' as the 'only' one worthy to become, in an 'organic' and 'totalitarian' way, the 'common' language of a nation in competition and conflict with other 'phases' and types or schemes that already exist (connected to traditional developments or to the inorganic and incoherent attempts of forces which, as we have seen, act continuously on the spontaneous 'grammars' immanent in the language). Historical grammar cannot but be 'comparative': an expression that, analysed thoroughly, indicates the deep-seated awareness that the linguistic fact, like any other historical fact, cannot have strictly defined national boundaries, but that history is always 'world history' and that particular histories exist only within the frame of world history. Normative grammar has other ends, even though the national language cannot be imagined outside the frame of other languages that exert an influence on it through innumerable channels which are often difficult to control. (Who can control the linguistic innovations introduced by returning emigrants, travellers, readers of foreign newspapers and languages, translators, etc.?)

Written normative grammar, then, always presupposes a 'choice', a cultural tendency, and is thus always an act of national-cultural politics. One might discuss the best way to present the 'choice' and the 'tendency' in order to get them accepted willingly, that is, one might discuss the most suitable means to obtain the goal; but there can be no doubt that there is a goal to be reached, that adequate and suitable means are needed, in other words that we are dealing with a political act.

Questions: what is the nature of this political act, and is it going to raise oppositions of 'principle', a *de facto* collaboration, opposition to the details, etc.? If one starts from the assumption of centralizing what already exists in a diffused, scattered but inorganic and incoherent state, it seems obvious that an opposition on principle is not rational. On the contrary, it is rational to collaborate practically and willingly to welcome everything that may serve to create a common national language, the non-existence of which creates friction particularly in the popular masses among whom local particularisms and phenomena of a narrow and provincial mentality are more tenacious than is believed. In other words, it is a question of stepping up the struggle against illiteracy. There is already *de facto* opposition in the resistance of the masses to shedding their particularistic habits and ways of thinking, a stupid resistance caused by the fanatical advocates of international languages. It is clear that with this set of problems the question of the national struggle of a hegemonic culture against other nationalities or residues of nationalities cannot be discussed.

Panzini does not even remotely consider these problems and, as a result, his publications on grammar are ambiguous, contradictory and wavering. For example, he does not ask what is the centre from which linguistic innovations are presently diffused from below; yet this is a problem of no small practical importance. Florence, Rome, Milan. On the other hand he does not even ask if (and where) there is a spontaneous centre of diffusion from above, i.e. in a relatively organic, continuous and efficient form, and whether it can be regulated and intensified.

Q 29 § 2.

9 Sources of Diffusion of Linguistic Innovations in the Tradition and of a National Linguistic Conformism in the Broad National Masses

1) The education system; 2) newspapers; 3) artistic writers and popular writers; 4) the theatre and sound films; 5) radio; 6) public meetings of all kinds, including religious ones; 7) the relations of 'conversation' between the more educated and less educated strata of the population (a question which is perhaps not given all the attention it deserves is that of the 'words' in verse learnt by heart in the form of songs, snatches of operas, etc. It should be noted that the people do not bother really to memorize these words, which are often strange, antiquated and baroque, but reduce them to kinds of nursery rhymes that are only helpful for remembering the tune); 8) the local dialects, understood in various senses (from the more localized dialects to those which embrace more or less broad regional complexes: thus Neapolitan for southern Italy, the dialects of Palermo and Catania for Sicily).

Since the process of formation, spread and development of a unified national language occurs through a whole complex of molecular processes, it helps to be aware of the entire process as a whole in order to be able to intervene actively in it with the best possible results. One need not consider this intervention as 'decisive' and imagine that the ends proposed will all be reached in detail, i.e. that one will obtain a *specific* unified language. One will obtain a *unified language*, if it is a necessity, and the organized intervention will speed up the already existing process. What this language will be, one cannot foresee or establish: in any case, if the intervention is 'rational', it will be organically tied to tradition, and this is of no small importance in the economy of culture.

Manzonians and 'classicists'. They had a type of language which they wanted to make prevail. It is not correct to say that these discussions were useless and have not left traces in modern culture, even if the traces are modest. Over the last century a unified culture has in fact been extended, and therefore also a common unified language. But the entire historical formation of the Italian nation moved at too slow a pace. Every time the question of the language surfaces, in one way or another, it means that a series of other problems are coming to the fore: the formation and enlargement of the governing class, the need to establish more intimate and secure relationships between the governing groups and the national-popular mass, in other words to reorganize the cultural hegemony. Today, we have witnessed various phenomena which indicate a rebirth of these questions: the publications of Panzini, Trabalza-Allodoli, Monelli, columns in the newspapers, intervention by union leaderships, etc.

Q 29 § 3.

10 Different Kinds of Normative Grammar

For schools. For so-called educated people. The difference is due in reality to the reader's or pupil's different level of intellectual development and to the different technique needed to teach or increase the organic knowledge of the national language for those children who cannot be taught without a certain peremptory and authoritarian rigidity ('You have to say it this way') and for the 'others' who need rather to be 'persuaded' to make them freely accept a given solution as the best (shown to be the best for attaining the goal which is proposed and shared, when it is shared). Furthermore, one must not forget that in the traditional study of normative grammar, other elements of the general teaching programme, such as certain elements of formal logic, have been inserted. One might debate whether this insertion is or is not opportune, whether the study of formal logic is justified or not (it seems to be, and it also seems justifiable to attach it to the study of grammar, rather than to arithmetic, etc., because of its natural resemblance and because together with grammar the study of formal logic is made relatively more lively and easier), but the question itself must not be evaded.

Q 29 § 4.

11 Historical and Normative Grammars

Taking normative grammar to be a political act and taking this starting-point as the only one from which one can 'scientifically' justify its existence and the enormous amount of patience needed to learn it (all the effort required to form hundreds of thousands of recruits, of the most disparate origins and mental preparation, into a homogeneous army capable of moving and acting in a disciplined and united manner, all the 'practical and theoretical lessons' on the regulations, etc.), one needs to posit its relationship to historical grammar. The failure to define this relationship explains many inconsistencies of normative grammars, including that of Trabalza-Allodoli.[19] We are dealing with two distinct and in part different things, like history and politics, but they cannot be considered independently, any more than politics and history. Besides, since the study of languages as a cultural phenomenon grew out of political needs (more or less conscious and consciously expressed), the needs of normative grammar have exerted an influence on historical grammar and on its 'legislative conceptions' (or at least this traditional element has reinforced, during the last century, the application of the positivist-naturalist method to the study of the history of languages conceived as the 'science of language'). It appears from Trabalza's grammar and from Schiaffini's damning review of it (*Nuova Antologia*, 16 September 1934), that not even the so-called 'idealists' have understood the innovation which the doctrines of Bartoli have brought to the science of language. The 'idealist' current has found its most complete expression in Bertoni: it involves a return to old rhetorical conceptions, to words which are 'beautiful' and 'ugly' in and by themselves, conceptions which have been glossed over with a new pseudo-scientific language. What these people are really looking for is an extrinsic justification of normative grammar, after having 'demonstrated', in an equally extrinsic fashion, its theoretical and also practical 'uselessness'.

Trabalza's essay on 'The History of Grammar'[20] could be a useful source on the interferences between historical grammar (or better, the history of language) and normative grammar, on the history of the problem, etc.

Q 29 § 5.

12 Grammar and Technique

Does grammar involve the same question as 'technique' in general? Is grammar only the technical aspect of language? At all events, are the idealists (especially the Gentilians) justified in

[19] C. Trabalza and E. Allodoli, *La grammatica degl'Italiani*, Florence 1935 (fourth edition).

[20] C. Trabalza, *Storia della grammatica italiana*, Milan 1908.

their arguments about the uselessness of grammar and its exclusion from the schools? If one speaks (expresses oneself with words) in a manner which is historically determined by nations and linguistic areas, can one dispense with teaching this 'historically determined manner'? Granted that traditional normative grammar was inadequate, is this a good reason for teaching no grammar at all, for not being in the least concerned with speeding up the process of learning the particular way of speaking of a certain linguistic area, and rather leaving 'the language to be learnt through living it', or some other expression of this sort used by Gentile or his followers? All in all, this is a 'liberalism' of the most bizarre and eccentric stripe. Differences between Croce and Gentile. As usual, Gentile bases himself on Croce, exaggerating some of the latter's theoretical tenets to the point of absurdity. Croce maintains that grammar does not pertain to any of the theoretical activities of the spirit elaborated by him, but ends up justifying in the 'practical' sphere many activities denied at the theoretical level. At first, Gentile also excludes from practice what he denies theoretically, only to find a theoretical justification for the most outdated and technically unjustified practical manifestations.

Does a technique have to be learnt 'systematically'? In practice, the technique of the village artisan has been set against that of Ford. Think of the variety of ways in which 'industrial technique' is learnt: artisanally, during factory work itself, watching how others work (and hence wasting more time and energy and learning only partially); in professional schools (where the whole trade is systematically learnt, even though some of the notions one learns will be applied very rarely in one's lifetime, if ever); by combining various methods, with the Taylor-Ford system which created a new kind of qualification and a skill limited to certain factories, or even to specific machines and stages of the production process.

Normative grammar, which by abstraction only can be considered as divorced from the living language, tends to make one learn the entire organism of the language in question and to create a spiritual attitude that enables one always to find one's way around the linguistic environment (see note on the study of Latin in the classical curriculum).[21] If grammar is excluded from

---

[21] See 'In search of the educational principle' in SPN, pp. 33–43, especially pp. 37–39.

education and is not 'written', it cannot thereby be excluded from 'real life', as I have already pointed out elsewhere.[22] The only thing excluded is the unitarily organized intervention in the process of learning the language. In practice the national-popular mass is excluded from learning the educated language, since the highest level of the ruling class, which traditionally speaks standard Italian, passes it on from generation to generation, through a slow process that begins with the first stutterings of the child under the guidance of its parents, and continues through conversation (with its 'this is how one says it', 'it must be said like this', etc.) for the rest of one's life. In reality, one is 'always' studying grammar (by imitating the model one admires, etc.). In Gentile's attitude there is much more politics than one thinks and a great deal of unconscious reactionary thought, as has in any case already been noted at other times and on other occasions. There is all the reactionary thought of the old liberal view, a 'laissez faire, laissez passer' which is not justified, as it was in Rousseau (and Gentile is more like Rousseau than he thinks) by opposition to the paralysis of Jesuit education,[23] but which has become an abstract, 'ahistorical' ideology.

Q 29 § 6.

13 The So-called 'Question of the Language'

It seems evident that Dante's *De vulgari eloquentia* should be considered essentially as an act of national-cultural politics (in the sense that 'nations' had at that time and in Dante),[24] just as what is called the 'question of the language' has always been an aspect of the political struggle and becomes interesting to study from this point of view. It was a reaction of the intellectuals to the break-up of the political unity that existed in Italy under the name of the 'balance of the Italian states', to the break-up and disintegration of the political and economic classes that had been gradually formed after the year 1000 with the communes. It

[22] See V 8.

[23] In Rousseau's *Émile* (1762) the child is schooled by nature (direct observation, etc.) rather than artificially socialized, and is kept away from religious dogmas till the age of fifteen.

[24] For Gramsci's views on Dante's politics, see footnote 16 on p. 160. On the linguistic ideas of the *De vulgari eloquentia*, see footnote 3 above.

represents the attempt, which to a considerable extent can be said to have succeeded, to conserve and indeed to strengthen a unified intellectual class, whose existence was to have no small significance in the eighteenth and nineteenth centuries (in the Risorgimento). Dante's treatise also has no small significance for the time in which it was written: not only in fact, but by elevating fact to theory, the Italian intellectuals of the most thriving period of the communes 'broke' with Latin and justified the vernacular by raising it up against Latinizing 'mandarinism', in the same period in which the vernacular had such great artistic expressions. That Dante's endeavour had an enormous innovative importance is seen later with the return of Latin as the language of educated people (and here one can insert the question of the double face of Humanism and the Renaissance, which were essentially reactionary from the national-popular point of view and progressive as an expression of the cultural development of the Italian and European intellectual groups).

Q 29 § 7.

14 Observations on Folklore: Giovanni Crocioni

Crocioni (in his volume *Problemi fondamentali del folclore*, Zanichelli, Bologna, 1928) criticizes as confused and inaccurate the division of folklore material proposed by Pitré in the introduction to *Bibliografia delle tradizioni popolari* (1897).[25] He suggests his own division into four sections: art, literature, science and the morality of the people. But even this division is criticized as imprecise, badly defined and too broad: Raffaele Ciampini (in *La Fiera Letteraria*, 30 December 1928) asks: 'Is it scientific? Where do superstitions fit in, for example? And what is the meaning of a morality of the people? How can it be studied scientifically? And why not speak of a religion of the people as well?'

One can say that until now folklore has been studied primarily as a 'picturesque' element. (Actually, until now only scholarly material has been collected. The science of folklore mostly consists of methodological studies on how to collect, select and classify such material, i.e. of the investigation of the practical precautions and empirical principles necessary for profitably

---

[25] Giuseppe Pitré (1841–1916) was a specialist in Sicilian and Italian folklore. He produced the 25-volume *Biblioteca delle tradizioni popolari siciliani*.

carrying out a particular aspect of scholarship. To say this is not to disregard the importance and historical significance of some of the major scholars of folklore.) Folklore should instead be studied as a 'conception of the world and life' implicit to a large extent in determinate (in time and space) strata of society and in opposition (also for the most part implicit, mechanical and objective) to 'official' conceptions of the world (or in a broader sense, the conceptions of the cultured parts of historically determinate societies) that have succeeded one another in the historical process. (Hence the strict relationship between folklore and 'common sense', which is philosophical folklore.)[26] This conception of the world is not elaborated and systematic because, by definition, the people (the sum total of the instrumental and subaltern classes of every form of society that has so far existed) cannot possess conceptions which are elaborated, systematic and politically organized and centralized in their albeit contradictory development. It is, rather, many-sided – not only because it includes different and juxtaposed elements, but also because it is stratified, from the more crude to the less crude – if, indeed, one should not speak of a confused agglomerate of fragments of all the conceptions of the world and of life that have succeeded one another in history. In fact, it is only in folklore that one finds surviving evidence, adulterated and mutilated, of the majority of these conceptions.

Philosophy and modern science are also constantly contributing new elements to 'modern folklore' in that certain opinions and scientific notions, removed from their context and more or less distorted, constantly fall within the popular domain and are 'inserted' into the mosaic of tradition. (*La scoperta de l'America* by C. Pascarella shows how notions about Christopher Columbus and about a whole set of scientific opinions, put about by school textbooks and the 'Popular Universities', can be strangely assimilated.)[27] Folklore can be understood only as a

---

[26] On philosophy and common sense, see SPN, pp. 323–28.

[27] 'La scoperta de l'America' ('The Discovery of America', 1894) by Cesare Pascarella (1858–1940) is a humorous account in linked Roman dialect sonnets of Columbus's voyage. It ends with a praise of great Italians and their flair for discoveries. Gramsci deals elsewhere with the poem in relation to 'the naïve and fanatical admiration for intelligence as such, for intelligent men as such, which corresponds to the cultural nationalism of the Italians, perhaps the only form of popular chauvinism in Italy . . . Pascarella is the bard of this nationalism, and his burlesque tone is the one most suited to such an epic' (Q 9 § 141).

reflection of the conditions of cultural life of the people, although certain conceptions specific to folklore remain even after these conditions have been (or seem to be) modified or have given way to bizarre combinations.

Certainly, there is a 'religion of the people', especially in Catholic and Orthodox countries, which is very different from that of the intellectuals (the religious ones) and particularly from that organically set up by the ecclesiastical hierarchy. One could claim, though, that all religions, even the most refined and sophisticated, are 'folklore' in relation to modern thought. But there is the essential difference that religions, in the first place Catholicism, are 'elaborated and set up' by the intellectuals (as above) and the ecclesiastical hierarchy. Therefore, they present special problems. (One should see if such an elaboration and set-up may not be necessary to keep folklore scattered and many-sided: the conditions of the Church before and after the Reformation and the Council of Trent and the different historico-cultural development of the Reformed and Orthodox countries after the Reformation and Trent are highly significant elements.) Thus it is true that there is a 'morality of the people', understood as a determinate (in space and time) set of principles for practical conduct and of customs that derive from them or have produced them. Like superstition, this morality is closely tied to real religious beliefs. Imperatives exist that are much stronger, more tenacious and more effective than those of official 'morality'. In this sphere, too, one must distinguish various strata: the fossilized ones which reflect conditions of past life and are therefore conservative and reactionary, and those which consist of a series of innovations, often creative and progressive, determined spontaneously by forms and conditions of life which are in the process of developing and which are in contradiction to or simply different from the morality of the governing strata.

According to Ciampini, Crocioni is quite right in maintaining that folklore should be taught in the institutions where future teachers are trained, but he then denies that it is possible to raise the question of the usefulness of folklore. There is undoubtedly a confusion in this between the 'science of folklore' or 'knowledge of folklore', and 'folklore' or 'the existence of folklore'. Ciampini here really seems to mean 'the existence of folklore' so that the teacher should not have to struggle against the Ptolemaic conception, which is characteristic of folklore. For Ciampini folklore (?) is an end in itself or is only useful in offering to a people the elements for a deeper knowledge of itself (here folklore must mean the 'knowledge and science of folklore'). To study superstitions in order to uproot them would be, for Ciampini, as if folklore were to kill itself, while science is nothing but disinterested knowledge, an end in itself! But then why teach folklore in teacher training institutions? To enlarge the disinterested culture of school-teachers? To show them what they must not destroy?

As is apparent, Ciampini's ideas are very muddled and even internally inconsistent since in other contexts he himself recognizes that the state is not agnostic but has its own conception of life and has the duty of spreading it by educating the national masses. But this formative activity of the state, which is expressed particularly in the education system, as well as in political activity generally, does not work upon and fill up a blank slate. In reality, the state competes with and contradicts other explicit and implicit conceptions, and folklore is not among the least significant and tenacious of these; hence it must be 'overcome'. For the teacher, then, to know 'folklore' means to know what other conceptions of the world and of life are actually active in the intellectual and moral formation of young people, in order to uproot them and replace them with conceptions which are deemed to be superior. Folklore was already under systematic bombardment, from the elementary schools to . . . the chairs of agriculture. The teaching of folklore to teachers should reinforce this systematic process even further.

It is clear that, in order to achieve the desired end, the spirit of folklore studies should be changed, as well as deepened and extended. Folklore must not be considered an eccentricity, an oddity or a picturesque element, but as something which is very serious and is to be taken seriously. Only in this way will the teaching of folklore be more efficient and really bring about the birth of a new culture among the broad popular masses, so that the separation between modern culture and popular culture of folklore will disappear. An activity of this kind, thoroughly carried out, would correspond on the intellectual plane to what the Reformation was in Protestant countries.

Q 27 § 1.

15 Observations on Folklore: 'Natural Law' and Folklore

Even today there is a certain amount of not very outstanding criticism, for the most part journalistic and superficial, of so-called natural law. (See some of the lucubrations of Maurizio Maraviglia and the sarcastic remarks and rather stale and conventional jokes of the newspapers and reviews.)[28] What is the real significance of this practice?

To understand it one must, it seems to me, distinguish some of the forms in which 'natural law' has traditionally been manifested.

1) The Catholic form, against which the present polemicists lack the courage to take a clear-cut position, although the concept of 'natural law' is an essential and integral part of Catholic social and political doctrine.[29] It would be interesting to recall the close relationship existing between the Catholic religion, as it has always been understood by the broad masses, and the 'immortal principles of 1789'. Those in the Catholic hierarchy themselves admit this relationship when they assert that the French Revolution was a 'heresy' or that a new heresy sprang from it. In other words, they recognize that a scission occurred in the fundamental mentality and conception of the world and of life.[30] Besides, it is only like this that the religious history of the French Revolution can be explained. Otherwise, it would be impossible to account for the mass support of a population that was

[28] The references are to Maurizio Maraviglia's article in *Scuola e Cultura: Annali della istruzione media* September–October 1932, p. 223 ff and to the comments on it by A. Messineo in *La Civiltà Cattolica* LXXXIV (1933) 1, pp. 324–36. Messineo writes: 'Every new conception in philosophy always starts from a critique of the ones preceding it in order to expose their weak sides. According to M. Maraviglia, the Achilles' heel of previous philosophies, founded on natural law and rational exigencies, is their attempt to resolve contrast by appealing to nature or to pure reason. They ought to have appealed instead to history; and it is to history that Maraviglia appeals.' Maraviglia (1878–1955) had been a leading Nationalist.

[29] The theory of natural law, developed from Aristotle and the Stoics, attempted to base civil law on an underlying law of nature. The medieval Catholic jurists (St Thomas Aquinas, Duns Scotus) argued that a *lex naturalis* pre-existed the state and determined its laws: this natural law derived ultimately from God and human (conventional) law should therefore not be at variance with it.

[30] The concept of 'scission' derives from Sorel who, following Renan, had linked together primitive Christianity, the Reformation and the French Revolution as instances of 'myths' producing a popular scission or cleavage from the ruling order. For the equation between religious heresy and revolution, compare Engels's remarks at the end of *Ludwig Feuerbach* on the English bourgeois revolution. See also VI 13 and footnote 2 on p. 390.

undoubtedly still profoundly religious and Catholic for the new ideas and revolutionary policies of the Jacobins against the clergy. It can therefore be said that conceptually it is not the principles of the French Revolution which surpass religion, since they belong to the same mental sphere, but the principles which are historically superior (in that they express new and higher needs) to those of the French Revolution: those based on the actual reality of force and struggle.

2) The form manifested by various groups of intellectuals of different juridico-political tendencies. This is the form upon which the scientific controversy over 'natural law' has so far been conducted. In this respect the question has been fundamentally resolved by Croce, who recognized that one was dealing here with political and journalistic currents whose significance and importance lay in the fact that they expressed real needs in the dogmatic and systematic form of the so-called science of law (see Croce's essay).[31] In opposition to this tendency is the 'apparent' polemic of the present practitioners of the science of law. The latter are actually more uncritical and anti-historical than the theorists of natural law because they do not distinguish between the real content of 'natural law' (concrete demands of a socio-economico-political character), the form in which it is theorized, and the mental justifications which natural law gives of the real content. In other words, they are blindfolded mules of the most narrow-minded conservatism (which also refers to past things 'historically' surmounted and swept away).

3) The aim of the controversy is in fact to curb the influence that the popular currents of 'natural law' may (and in fact do) have, particularly on young intellectuals. These popular currents are the ensemble of opinions and beliefs concerning one's 'own' rights which circulate uninterruptedly among the popular masses and are continuously renewed under the pressure of real living conditions and the spontaneous comparison between the ways in which the various social strata live. Religion has a great deal of

[31] Natural law theory was developed by pre-Enlightenment and Enlightenment thinkers in terms of a rational law of nature. Gramsci's reference here is probably to the chapter in Croce's *Elementi di politica* which criticizes Rousseau's *Social Contract* for basing its concept of freedom through association not on real life but on a suprahistorical idea, a 'mechanical model'. Croce argued that the school of natural law which Rousseau represented nevertheless had 'great political importance in those centuries when the last vestiges of the Middle Ages and the privilege of the nobility and clergy were put to rout and modern society was constituted'. (*Etica e politica*, cit., p. 257).

influence on these currents: religion in every sense of the word, as it is really felt and put into effect or as it is organized and arranged by the hierarchy, which cannot renounce the concept of popular law. Through uncontrollable and capillary intellectual meatuses, however, these currents have also been influenced by a number of concepts put out by the lay exponents of natural law; and, through the most varied and bizarre contaminations, certain programmes and propositions of 'historicism' also continue to become 'natural law'. There is, then, a mass of 'juridical' popular opinions that assume the form of 'natural law' and these are juridical 'folklore'. The considerable importance of such a current has been demonstrated by the organization of the 'courts of assizes' and by an entire series of arbitral magistracies and courts of conciliation covering every field of individual and group relationships. It is the task of these courts to base their decisions on the 'law' as it is understood by the people, overseen by positive or official law. Nor should one think that the importance of this question has disappeared with the abolition of people's juries, since in no way can a magistrate set opinion aside. On the contrary, it is likely that the question will re-emerge in another form and to a much greater degree than in the past. This will doubtless raise dangers and a new set of problems to resolve.

Q 27 § 2.

16 Folklore: ['Contemporary Pre-history']

Raffaele Corso calls the set of facts of folklore a 'contemporary pre-history', which is simply a game with words to define a complex phenomenon that eludes compact definitions. One can recall in this respect the relationship between the so-called 'minor arts' and the so-called 'major arts', between the activity of creators of art and that of the artisans (of luxury objects, or at least those without immediate utility). The minor arts have always been tied to the major arts and have been dependent upon them. Thus folklore has always been tied to the culture of the dominant class and, in its own way, has drawn from it the motifs which have then become inserted into combinations with the previous traditions. Besides, there is nothing more contradictory and fragmentary than folklore.

In any case, this is a very relative and highly questionable 'prehistory' and there could be nothing vainer than to try to find the different stratifications in a single area of folklore. But even a comparison between different areas, although it is the only methodologically rational approach, cannot allow inflexible conclusions but only probable conjectures, since it is hard to write a history of the influences absorbed by each area, and one is often comparing heterogeneous entities. Folklore, at least in part, is much more unstable and fluctuating than language and dialects, and this can also be said of the relationship between the culture of the educated class and literary language. The language is modified, at its sense level, much less than the cultural content, and only in semantics, naturally, can an adhesion be registered between sense form and intellectual content.

Q9 § 15.

17 Folklore: [Popular Songs]

A division or distinction of popular songs formulated by Ermolao Rubieri:[32] 1) songs composed by the people and for the people; 2) those composed for the people but not by the people; 3) those written neither by the people nor for the people, but which the people adopt because they conform to their way of thinking and feeling.

It seems to me that all popular songs can and must be reduced to this third category, since what distinguishes a popular song within the context of a nation and its culture is neither its artistic aspect nor its historical origin, but the way in which it conceives the world and life, in contrast with official society. From this follow other criteria of research into folklore: the people themselves are not a homogeneous cultural collectivity but present numerous and variously combined cultural stratifications which, in their pure form, cannot always be identified within specific historical popular collectivities. Of course, when one historically 'isolates' these collectivities to a greater or lesser degree, such an identification is at least partially possible.

Q5 § 156.

---

[32] This information on Rubieri's classification was drawn from an article by G.S. Gargàno, 'Definizioni e valutazioni della poesia popolare', *Il Marzocco* XXXIV (1929) 18.

VI
PEOPLE, NATION AND CULTURE

Introduction

'National-popular', with its variants ('people-nation', etc.), is a recurrent term in the Prison Notebooks and one whose meaning has been a subject of dispute. In Italy, particularly in the 1950s, it tended to become diluted into a cultural slogan and was more or less collapsed into 'neo-realism' or 'social realism' in the arts, while in the 1960s it was used by new left intellectuals as a sort of courtroom exhibit with which to accuse Gramsci of 'populism', 'idealism' and 'intellectualism' and of having renounced an international perspective of struggle. In reality, not much of this stands up against Gramsci's texts themselves and the accusations of populism and intellectualism actually identify the concept with two of the things he employs it to attack.

The term 'national-popular' operates at a number of levels in Gramsci's writing. Politically, it emerged out of his rethinking of Communist strategy for Italy in 1924–26, the period of his leadership of the Party, when the revolutionary moment had passed and the fascists were in power. He attempted to identify the specific *national* features that had permitted this solution of the crisis in Italy and in whose context the struggle for a revolutionary transformation had to be waged. The relative smallness of the industrial proletariat and its geographical confinement mostly to the north-west of the peninsula made it necessary, on his reckoning, to construct a hegemonic alliance of the proletariat with the peasantry and petty-bourgeois intellectuals in order to prise apart the defensive alliance between northern industrialists and southern landowners, cemented by petty-bourgeois consent, that constituted the backbone of fascist power. In the Prison Notebooks this strategy of alliances begins to be called 'national-popular' as the notion of hegemony is extended from simple class domination to the securing of active consent in the form of a 'collective will'. 'Any formation of a national-popular collective will is impossible, unless the great mass of peasant farmers bursts *simultaneously* into political life', Gramsci writes in a note drafted in 1932. 'All history from 1815 onwards shows the effort of the traditional classes to prevent the formation of a collective will of this kind, and to maintain "economic-corporate" power in an international system of passive equilibrium' (SPN, p. 132). Building this collective will involved the struggle to win support among groups at present under the sway of other hegemonic ideologies and beliefs, most notably Catholicism. In order to do this, the revolutionary class itself had to overcome a narrowly 'economic-corporate' self-interest and form expansive, universalizing alliances with other subaltern social groups who felt their interests to coincide with those of the new hegemonic class.

The term 'national-popular' also becomes in the Notebooks a key analytical and descriptive tool which Gramsci uses to examine long-term trends in Italian history that have their critical phase in the Risorgimento. In his reading of nineteenth-century history (see the 'Notes on Italian History' in SPN, pp. 52ff), the Italian *national* movement had failed precisely to be a *popular* movement, to generalize its struggle beyond the radical bourgeoisie around the Action Party and win the support of the peasantry by carrying out agrarian reforms. The Action Party was overtaken by the Moderates around Cavour, who were able to construct a class alliance between the bourgeoisie and the southern landowners. The Risorgimento had played itself out as a 'reform-revolution' or 'passive revolution' by these classes from above, whose contradictions and whose inability to contain popular pressure after the First World War had led to the successive 'reform-revolution' of fascism. Already in 1919 Gramsci had assessed the bourgeoisie's failure to establish itself in Italy as a 'national' class in the Jacobin sense: 'Historically the bourgeois class is already dead . . . Today the "national" class is the proletariat' (ON, p. 278). In the Notebooks this is reformulated in terms of proletarian hegemony: 'The Italian people are the people with the greatest "national" interest in a modern form of cosmopolitanism [i.e. socialist internationalism]. Not only the worker but also the peasant, especially the southern peasant.' (p. 247 below).

Culturally, too, 'national-popular' points to a lack, a chronic absence in Italy, the product of centuries of 'cosmopolitan' rule by the Roman Empire and the Papacy and the cultural dominance of cosmopolitan traditional intellectuals. The purely 'cultural' appearance of many of Gramsci's notes on the national-popular should not be allowed to obscure the fact that the same political and historical preoccupations are at work in them. The cultural aspects of the national-popular question are not simply 'reflections', cultural 'doubles' of its political aspects but indicate that the question is organically rooted deep in Italian history with ramifications at many levels – the lack of a common vernacular language in the past, the absence of a genuine Romantic movement in the nineteenth century, the non-popularity of Italian literature and so on. They also indicate that the ideological terrain of civil society is precisely where a widespread national-popular movement has to be constructed. A guiding motif of Gramsci's analysis of Italian history is the separation between intellectuals and the people. In his discussion of the Renaissance (VI 9) he traces this separation back to the fourteenth and fifteenth centuries when a literary and philosophical élite became detached from the bourgeoisie. The latter had acquired political domination in the period of the communes (twelfth to fourteenth centuries) but had been unable to consolidate it because it had failed to go beyond its economic-corporate limits and become hegemonic as a class. Whereas in the northern European countries the Renaissance was linked to the development of secular and scientific ideologies and to the emergence of mass religious movements from below (the Protestant Reformation), in Italy itself it led to the involutionary Counter-Reformation and the ideological triumph of the Catholic intellectual hierarchy. The Italian nation had in this way been more a rhetorical or a 'legal' entity than a felt cultural reality, existing at most for the intellectual and ruling élites but not for the people. It was therefore necessary to break the grip of these élites, which meant also breaking with their intellectualistic way of posing questions of national culture in terms of a merely ideal or high-cultural 'nation'. The nineteenth-century culture of France, which had undergone both a bourgeois revolution and a much earlier process of cultural and linguistic unification, provides a constant pole of comparison with Gramsci's analysis of Italy. Trends in American culture too indicated the extent to which the European intellectuals as a whole had become insulated from modern economic development and had lost their critical function in relation to the bourgeoisie.

1 Connection of Problems

Controversies arising in the period of the formation of the Italian nation and of the struggle for political and territorial unity which have obsessed and continue to obsess at least some Italian intellectuals. Some of these problems, such as that of the language, are very old and date back to the early formation of an Italian cultural unity. They sprang from the comparison between the general conditions of Italy and those of other countries, especially France, or from the reflection of conditions peculiar to Italy such as the fact that the peninsula was the seat of Imperial Rome and became the seat of the major centre of Christianity. The sum of these problems reflects the laborious emergence of a modern Italian nation, impeded by a balance of internal and international forces.

The intellectual and leading classes in Italian society have never been aware of the fact that there is a connection between these problems, one of co-ordination and subordination. Nobody has ever presented these problems as a coherent and connected whole, but each of them has periodically reappeared, according to immediate and not always clearly expressed polemical interests, with no desire to look deeper. Therefore, they have always been treated in an abstractly cultural and intellectualistic form, without a precise historical perspective and hence without a coherent and concrete socio-political solution to them ever emerging.

The statement that there has never been an awareness of the organic unity of these problems needs to be understood properly. It may well be that nobody has had the courage to pose the question exhaustively because it was feared that vital dangers for the unified life of the nation would immediately result from such a rigorously critical and consequential formulation. This timidity on the part of many Italian intellectuals, which is characteristic of our national life, needs to be explained in its turn. It seems undeniable, though, that none of these problems can be resolved individually (in that they are still current and alive today). It follows that a critical and dispassionate treatment of these questions (the unity of the language; the relationship between art and life; the question of the novel and the popular novel; the question of an intellectual and moral reformation, i.e. a popular revolution having the same function as the Protestant

Reformation in Germanic countries and as the French Revolution; the question of the 'popularity' of the Risorgimento, which was supposedly achieved with the 1915–18 war and with successive upheavals, whence the inflationary use of the terms revolution and revolutionary) can provide the most useful approach for reconstructing the fundamental characteristics of Italian cultural life, and the needs they point to and for which they demand solutions.

Here is the 'catalogue' of the most important questions to be examined and analysed: 1) 'Why is Italian literature not popular in Italy?' (to use a phrase of Ruggero Bonghi);[1] 2) is there an Italian theatre – a controversy begun by Ferdinando Martini, which should be connected with the other question concerning the greater or lesser vitality of theatre in dialect and in standard Italian?[2] 3) the question of the national language as set forth by Alessandro Manzoni;[3] 4) whether there has been an Italian romanticism? 5) is it necessary in Italy to provoke a religious reformation like the Protestant one? In other words, was the absence of broad and profound religious struggles (due to the Papacy being in Italy when the political innovations which produced modern states fermented) a cause of progress or of regression? 6) were Humanism and the Renaissance progressive or regressive? 7) the unpopularity of the Risorgimento or the indifference of the masses towards the struggle for independence and national unity; 8) the political non-involvement of the Italian people, expressed in the phases 'rebellionism', 'subversivism'

---

[1] In *Perché la letteratura italiana non sia popolare in Italia* (1856), Ruggero Bonghi (1826–95) diagnosed why Italian books had a comparatively small readership: the conservative attitude of Italian writers to their literary and linguistic tradition made them hard to read and unpopular, and this forced readers to turn to French and English novels. Bonghi's prescriptions for a cure worked on the assumption (influenced by Manzoni's views on the Italian language) that a reform 'from above' by writers could change spoken language-use, supplemented by educational reform in the teaching of language and literature. He also held that a simpler and more natural language would follow inevitably from the adoption by writers of clearer and more logical ways of thinking.

[2] Ferdinando Martini (1841–1928) attributed the disunity of Italian theatre to the cultural fragmentation of the peninsula persisting after the unification. Gramsci had been familiar with this critic's ideas since his days as a theatre reviewer (see LVN, p. 230). Martini called for state intervention in the Italian theatres and exhorted dramatists to go back to the imitation of life, like their precursor Goldoni. On the question of dialect theatre, see VI 30.

[3] See I 3.

and a primitive and elementary 'anti-statism';[4] 9) the non-existence of a popular literature in a strict sense (serial novels, adventure stories, scientific novels and detective stories) and the persistent 'popularity' of this type of novel translated from foreign languages, especially from French; the non-existence of a children's literature. In Italy the nationally produced popular novel is either anticlerical or consists of the biographies of brigands. Italy, though, is pre-eminent in opera, which in a certain sense is the popular novel set to music.[5]

One of the reasons why such problems have not been given explicit and critical attention can be discovered in the rhetorical prejudice (originating in literature) according to which the Italian nation has always existed, from ancient Rome to the present day. This and other totems and intellectual conceits, although politically 'useful' in the period of national struggle as a means of stirring up and concentrating energies, are critically inept and become, ultimately, a weakness because they do not permit a correct appreciation of the effort of those generations who really fought to establish modern Italy and because they lead to a sort of fatalism and passive expectation of a future which is supposedly predetermined completely by the past. At other times, these problems are badly posed because of the influence of aesthetic concepts deriving from Croce, particularly those concerning so-called 'moralism' in art, the view that 'content' is extrinsic to art, and that the history of culture is not to be confused with the history of art, etc.[6] There is no concrete understanding of the fact that art is always tied to a definite culture or civilization and that by fighting to reform culture one comes to modify the 'content' of art and works to create a new art, not from the outside (by professing a didactic, moralistic or prescriptive art) but from deep within, because man is totally altered when his feelings, his conceptions and the relationships of which man is the necessary expression are themselves altered.

[4] See the note 'Subversive' in SPN, pp. 272–75. Gramsci defines subversivism as an embryonic, negative class-awareness expressed in generic hatred for the 'signori' and the state.

[5] On opera as popular art see VI 2; IX 22, 23, 24.

[6] For these Crocean concepts, see the introduction to Section II. The reference to 'moralism' here is almost certainly to Croce's *separation* of art from moral acts and his rejection of theories of moral and didactic art (as made in his 1902 and 1913 aesthetics) rather than to his later view (1928) that 'the basis of all poetry is the moral consciousness'.

'Futurism', especially the most intelligent form expressed by the Florentine reviews *Lacerba* and *La Voce* with their 'romanticism' or popular *Sturm and Drang*, is connected to the fact that some of these questions have been poorly formulated and left unresolved. The latest manifestation is the 'Super-country' trend.[7] But the Futurism of Marinetti, that of Papini, and the Super-country movement have all collided, as well as with everything else, with this obstacle: the lack of character and firmness in their stage-managers and the carnival-like and clownish tendency of arid and sceptical petty-bourgeois intellectuals.

Regional literature, too, has been essentially folkloric and picturesque. The 'regional' people was seen 'paternalistically' from the outside, with the disenchanted cosmopolitan spirit of tourists in search of strong and original raw sensations. The deeply rooted 'apolitical' nature of Italian writers, coated with a verbose national rhetoric, has been really harmful to them. From this point of view Pascoli and Enrico Corradini, with their avowed and militant nationalism, were more congenial in that they at least sought to resolve the traditional literary dualism existing between nation and people, although they fell into other forms of rhetoric and oratory.[8]

Q 21 § 1.

---

[7] On the Super-country (*strapaese*) movement, see footnote 61 on p. 329 and VIII 15 and 16. See also 'Super-city and Super-country' in SPN, pp. 287–89.

[8] Enrico Corradini (1865–1931), rightist intellectual, author of politically tendentious novels and plays; Giovanni Pascoli (1855–1912), major poet who evolved from socialism to social-nationalism. Corradini founded the first major reactionary nationalist review, *Il Regno*, in 1903 and edited from 1918–20 *L'Idea Nazionale*, organ of the Italian Nationalist Association (ANI). He called for colonialist war in Libya in a key speech of 1910. Its title – 'Proletarian classes: socialism; proletarian nations: nationalism' – encapsulates Corradini's appropriation of the concept of class struggle to nationalist militaristic ends. Italy was a 'proletarian nation' which needed to struggle for colonial space against the plutocratic nations. This struggle would transcend and neutralize class conflict within Italy's frontiers. The idea was echoed in Pascoli's article 'La grande Proletaria si è mossa' (The great proletarian nation has stirred) published in November 1911 after the war in Libya had broken out. Pascoli saw the war as unifying the distinct Italian regions into a single nation which, by seizing a colony, would rise from its underdog position, provide employment and a home for its hitherto dispersed emigrant workforce and complete the historical mission of the Risorgimento. Corradini adhered to fascism in 1922 and in 1923 the ANI merged into the PNF. He became a senator and in 1928 a minister of state. See also VIII 18 on Corradini and VI 17 on Pascoli.

2 Popular Literature. Content and Form

In the criticism of art the bringing together of these two terms can take on many meanings. To grant that content and form are the same thing does not mean that we cannot distinguish between them. We could say that the person who insists on 'content' is actually fighting for a specific culture, a specific conception of the world, in opposition to other cultures and world views. We could also say that, historically, the so-called contentists have so far been 'more democratic' than their Parnassian adversaries.[9] In other words, they wanted a literature that was not for 'intellectuals'.

Can one speak of a priority of content over form? One can in this sense: that the work of art is a process and that changes of content are also changes of form. It is 'easier', though, to talk about content than about form because content can be logically 'summarized'. When one says that content precedes form, one simply means that in the process of elaboration successive attempts are presented under the name of content and that is all. The first content that was unsatisfactory was also form and, in reality, when one arrives at a satisfying 'form', the content has also changed. It is true that often those who go on about form, at the expense of content, are saying precisely nothing. They lump words up against each other that don't always hold together even grammatically (Ungaretti, for example), and by technique and form they mean the vacuous jargon of a mindless coterie.

This, too, should be placed among the questions of Italian national history referred to in another note,[10] and it assumes various forms: there is a stylistic difference between writings directed to the public and others – for example between letters and works of literature. The difference is often so great that one seems to be dealing with two different writers. Sobriety, simplicity and immediacy predominate in memoirs, in letters (with certain exceptions, such as D'Annunzio, who play-acts to himself in front of the mirror) and, generally, in all writings meant for a very small public or for oneself. In other writings pompousness, stylistic hypocrisy and the oratorical style predominate. This 'disease' is so widespread that the people have caught it. In fact, for them 'to write' means to get up on stilts, to dress up, to 'feign' a redundant

[9] For the topical content of this discussion of content and form, see II 5 ('"Contentism" and "calligraphism"') and the introduction to Section II.

[10] See p. 200 above.

style, etc., and in any case to express oneself in an unusual way. Since the people are not literary-minded and the only literature that they know are the libretti of nineteenth-century operas, it happens that members of the popular classes behave 'operatically'. And therefore 'content' and 'form' have a 'historical' meaning, besides an 'aesthetic' one. 'Historical' form means a specific language, just as 'content' indicates a specific way of thinking that is not only historical but also 'sober', expressive but not flamboyant, passionate but without the passions being overdone in the manner of Othello or the opera – in short, without a theatrical mask. This phenomenon, I believe, only occurs here in Italy (at least as a mass phenomenon since there are individual instances everywhere). But one should be careful about this. Ours is a country in which Arcadian conventions have followed Baroque ones – still theatrical though, and still conventional. It must be said that in recent years things have greatly improved. The last illness to attack the Italian people has been D'Annunzio. Newspapers, because of their peculiar requirements, have had the great merit of 'rationalizing' prose. At the same time, they have impoverished and stunted it and this, too, is harmful. Unfortunately, though, among the people there are still 'baroque stylists', by conversion, alongside the 'anti-academic Futurists'. On the other hand, here one must treat the question historically in order to explain the past and not be taken up with a purely topical struggle against present evils, even though these evils have not completely disappeared and recur notably on certain particular occasions – e.g. solemn speeches, especially funeral and patriotic orations and inscriptions.

One could say that it is a question of 'taste', but this would be mistaken. Taste is 'individual' or a matter for small groups. Here it is a matter of large masses and it is inevitably a question of culture. 'Sober' taste is individual, the other one is not; the national taste, that is, the national culture, is operatic.

Nor should it be said that there is no need to bother about this question. On the contrary, the formation of a lively, expressive and at the same time sober and measured prose must be set as a cultural goal. In this instance, too, form and expression are identical and to emphasise 'form' is only a practical way to work on content, to deflate the traditional rhetoric that ruins every form of culture, even (alas) 'anti-rhetorical' culture.

The question as to whether there ever was an Italian

romanticism[11] can be answered in several ways, depending on what one means by 'romanticism'. Certainly many definitions have been given to the term, but we are only concerned with one of them, and not with the narrowly 'literary' aspect of the problem. Among its other meanings romanticism has assumed that of a special relationship or bond between intellectuals and the people, the nation. In other words, it is a particular reflection of 'democracy' (in the broad sense) in literature (in the broad sense, so that at this level Catholicism could have been 'democratic', while 'liberalism' might not). It is in this sense that the problem interests us in relation to Italy, and it connects with the other problems we have listed: whether there has ever been an Italian theatre, the question of the language, why our literature has never been popular, etc. Therefore, in the endless literature on romanticism one must isolate this aspect and study it theoretically and practically as a historical fact, as a general tendency that can give rise to a current movement, a current problem to resolve. In this sense, romanticism precedes, accompanies, sanctions and develops that entire European movement which took its name from the French Revolution. Romanticism is the literary aspect, the aspect of feeling of this movement; it is more a question of feeling than of literature, since the literary aspect was only a part of the expression of a current of feeling which pervaded all of life and only a minuscule portion of this life managed to find its expression in literature.

Our research is thus into the history of culture and not literary history; or rather it is into literary history as a part or an aspect of a broader history of culture. And in this specific sense romanticism has never existed in Italy. Its manifestations have been at best minimal, very sporadic and in any case of a purely literary nature. (In this regard, remember the theories of Thierry and their reflection in Manzoni, theories which are one of the most important features of the aspect of romanticism we are referring to.)[12]

One should also see why in Italy interest in the pre-Roman populations, or Gioberti's discussion of the 'Pelasgians',[13]

---

[11] See the list of questions on p. 200 above.

[12] On Thierry and Manzoni, see VII 4 and footnote 6 on p. 293.

[13] The Pelasgians were supposed in Antiquity to have been the original inhabitants of Greece, before the Hellenes, and to have settled also in Italy. Gioberti followed a tradition of Risorgimento historiography in reconstructing the descent of the Italians from the

assumed an abstract and intellectual tone, in no way related to people living in the present, although Thierry and similar political historians were interested in such a relationship.

We have said that the word 'democracy' must not be used only in the 'lay' or 'secularist' sense, but can also be used in its 'Catholic' and, if you like, reactionary sense. What matters is that a bond is being sought with the people, the nation, and that one considers necessary not a servile unity resulting from passive obedience, but an active unity, a life-unity, whatever the content of this life may be. It is precisely this living unity, irrespective of content, which has been missing in Italy, or there has not been enough of it to make it an historical fact. Hence the meaning of the question 'has there been an Italian romanticism?'

Q 14 § 72.

3 Concept of 'National-Popular'

A note in *Critica Fascista* of 1 August 1930 complains that two major daily newspapers, one in Rome and the other in Naples, have begun serial publication of these novels: *The Count of Monte-Cristo* and *Joseph Balsamo* by Alexandre Dumas and *A Mother's Calvary* by Paul Fontenay. *Critica* writes:

> The nineteenth century in France was undoubtedly a golden period for the serial novel; but those newspapers which reprint novels of a century ago (as if taste, interest and literary experience had not changed at all from then until now) must have a very poor idea of their readers. Furthermore, why not take account of the fact that, despite opinions to the contrary, a modern Italian novel exists? And to think that these people are ready to shed tears of ink over the sad fate of our national literature.

Critica is confusing different categories of problems: that of the non-circulation of so-called artistic literature among the people; and that of the non-existence in Italy of a 'popular' literature, which means that the newspapers are 'forced' to take in supplies abroad. Of course, in theory nothing prevents the possible existence of an artistic popular literature. The most obvious example is the 'popular' success, even today, of the great Russian novelists. But in fact neither a popular artistic literature nor a local production of 'popular' literature exists because 'writers'

Pelasgians via the Etruscans, as evidence of the antiquity of Italian civilization (*Del primato morale e civile degli italiani*, Brussels 1843, Volume 2, pp. 53–54).

and 'people' do not have the same conception of the world. In other words the feelings of the people are not lived by the writers as their own, nor do the writers have a 'national educative' function: they have not and do not set themselves the problem of elaborating popular feelings after having relived them and made them their own. Nor does *Critica* set itself these problems and it is unable to draw the 'realistic' conclusions from the fact that if people like the novels of a hundred years ago, it means that their taste and ideology are precisely those of a hundred years ago. Newspapers are politico-financial bodies, and they do not propose to put out *belles-lettres* in their own columns if these *belles-lettres* increase the return of unsold issues. The serial novel is a way of circulating newspapers among the popular classes – remember the example of *Il Lavoro* of Genoa, under the editorship of Giovanni Ansaldo, which reprinted all the French serial literature, while at the same time trying to give the most refined cultural tone to the other parts of the newspaper – and this means political and financial success. Hence the newspaper looks for that novel, that type of novel, which the people are 'certain' to enjoy and which will assure a permanent and 'continuous' clientele. The man of the people buys only one newspaper, when he buys one. The choice is not even personal, but is often that of the family as a group. The women have a large say in the choice and insist on the 'nice interesting novel'. (This does not mean that the men do not read the novel too, but it is the women who are particularly interested in it and in items of local news.) This always meant that purely political papers or papers of pure opinion never had a large circulation (except in periods of intense political struggle). They were bought by young people, men and women, without too many family worries, who were keenly interested in the fortunes of their political opinions, and by a small number of families highly compact in their ideas. In general, those who read the newspapers do not share the opinion of the newspaper they buy or are minimally influenced by it. From the point of view of journalistic technique, then, one should study the case of *Il Secolo* and *Il Lavoro* which used to publish up to three serial novels in order to gain a large and steady circulation. (One does not consider that for many readers the 'serial novel' has the same importance as quality 'literature' has for educated people. It used to be a kind of 'social obligation' for the porters, the courtyard and the people upstairs to know the 'novel' that the

Stampa was publishing. Every instalment led to 'conversations' sparkling with the logical and psychological intuitions of the 'most distinguished' presences. It can be claimed that the readers of serial novels enthuse about their authors with far more sincerity and a much livelier human interest than was shown in so-called cultured drawing rooms for the novels of D'Annunzio or is shown there now for the works of Pirandello.)

But the most interesting problem is this: if the Italian newspapers of 1930 want to increase (or maintain) their circulation, why must they publish serial novels of a hundred years ago (or modern ones of the same kind)? Why is there no 'national' literature of this type in Italy, even though it must be profitable? One should note that in many languages, 'national' and 'popular' are either synonymous or nearly so (they are in Russian, in German, where *völkisch* has an even more intimate meaning of race, and in the Slavonic languages in general; in France the meaning of 'national' already includes a more politically elaborated notion of 'popular' because it is related to the concept of 'sovereignty': national sovereignty and popular sovereignty have, or had, the same value).[14] In Italy the term 'national' has an ideologically very restricted meaning, and does not in any case coincide with 'popular' because in Italy the intellectuals are distant from the people, i.e. from the 'nation'. They are tied instead to a caste tradition that has never been broken by a strong popular or national political movement from below. This tradition is abstract and 'bookish', and the typical modern intellectual feels closer to Annibal Caro or Ippolito Pindemonte than to an Apulian or Sicilian peasant.[15] The current term 'national' is connected in Italy to this intellectual and bookish tradition. Hence the foolish and ultimately dangerous facility of calling 'anti-national' whoever does not have this archaeological and moth-eaten conception of the

---

[14] The linking of these two concepts in French political thought can be traced from Rousseau's concept of the sovereignty of the general will, inalienable and thus not delegable to representatives, through the 1789 Declaration of the Rights of Man ('sovereignty resides essentially in the nation') and the unimplemented Jacobin constitution of 1793 ('sovereignty resides in the people'). They re-emerged among the republicans in 1848.

[15] Compare Gramsci's similarly phrased remark on the ecclesiastical intellectuals in SPN, p. 8. Annibal Caro (1507–66) poet and dramatist, one of whose more florid compositions sparked off a protracted debate on Italian poetic language. Ippolito Pindemonte (1753–1828) minor poet, dedicatee and addressee of Foscolo's 'Dei sepolcri' (see VI 20).

country's interests.

One should also see Umberto Fracchia's articles in the June 1930 issue of *L'Italia Letteraria* and Ugo Ojetti's 'Letter to Umberto Fracchia on Criticism' in the August 1930 number of *Pègaso*.[16] Fracchia's complaints are very similar to those of *Critica Fascista*. The so-called 'artistic' 'national' literature is not popular in Italy. Whose fault is it? That of the public, which does not read? That of the critics, who are not able to present and extol literary 'values' to the public? That of the newspapers, which publish the old *Count of Monte-Cristo* instead of serializing the 'modern Italian novel'? But why does the public not read in Italy, when in other countries it does? Besides, is it true that in Italy nobody reads? Would it not be more accurate to state the problem in this way: why does the Italian public read foreign literature, popular and non-popular, instead of reading its own? Has not Fracchia himself published ultimatums to the editors who publish (and thus must sell, relatively speaking) foreign works, threatening them with governmental measures? And has the government not tried to intervene, at least partly, in the person of Michele Bianchi, Undersecretary of Internal Affairs?[17]

What is the meaning of the fact that the Italian people prefer to read foreign writers? It means that they *undergo* the moral and intellectual hegemony of foreign intellectuals, that they feel more closely related to foreign intellectuals than to 'domestic' ones, that there is no national intellectual and moral bloc, either hierarchical or, still less, egalitarian. The intellectuals do not come from the people, even if by accident some of them have origins among the people. They do not feel tied to them (rhetoric apart), they do not know and sense their needs, aspirations and feelings. In relation to the people, they are something detached, without foundation, a caste and not an articulation with organic functions of the people themselves.

The question must be extended to the entire national-popular culture and not restricted just to narrative fiction. The same things must be said about the theatre, about scientific literature in general (the sciences of nature, history, etc.). Why do no writers like Flammarion emerge in Italy?[18] Why has no

[16]   Ojetti's letter is dealt with in VI 22.

[17]   See footnote 79 on p. 253.

[18]   Camille Flammarion (1842–1925), author of popular books on science.

popularized scientific literature arisen as in France and other countries? These foreign books are read and sought after in translation and are often very successful. All this means that the entire 'educated class', with its intellectual activity, is detached from the people-nation, not because the latter has not shown and does not show itself to be interested in this activity at all levels, from the lowest (dreadful serial novels) to the highest – indeed it seeks out foreign books for this purpose – but because in relation to the people-nation the indigenous intellectual element is more foreign than the foreigners. The question has not just arisen now. It has been posed since the foundation of the Italian state, and its previous existence is a document for explaining the delay in forming the peninsula into a national political unit: see Ruggero Bonghi's book on the unpopularity of Italian literature. The question of the language posed by Manzoni also reflects this problem, that of the moral and intellectual unity of the nation and the state, sought in the unity of the language. The unity of the language, though, is one of the external means, and not an exclusively necessary one, of national unity. Anyway, it is an effect and not a cause.[19] See F. Martini's writings on the theatre: there is an entire literature on the theatre which is still developing.

A national-popular literature, narrative and other kinds, has always been lacking in Italy and still is. (In poetry there have been no figures like Béranger or the French *chansonnier* in general.)[20] Still, there have been individual popular writers who have been successful. Guerrazzi, for instance, was successful and his books are still published and circulated. People once read Carolina Invernizio and perhaps still do, even though she is inferior to the Ponsons and the Montépins. People also read Francesco Mastriani.[21] (G. Papini wrote an article on Invernizio in *Il Resto*

[19] On the question of the language, see V 1 and 13, and the summary of Manzoni's views in I 3.

[20] Pierre-Jean Béranger (1780–1857), light verse writer from a poor Parisian background, immensely popular for his satiric treatments of Restoration society.

[21] Carolina Invernizio (1858–1916) wrote over a hundred novels which had a wide popular readership. Most of her work was published in instalments in *La Gazzetta di Torino* and *L'Opinione Nazionale*. Papini's article, mentioned in this paragraph, appeared shortly after her death in 1916 and was reprinted in the volume *Stroncature*. Francesco Mastriani (1819–91) prolific pioneer 'social' novelist whose work, serialized in the Neapolitan press, was influenced by the philanthropic socialism of Eugène Sue (e.g. *I misteri di Napoli* 1875). On Ponson du Terrail and Xavier de Montépin see footnote 10 on p. 353.

del Carlino, during the war, in 1916 or so: check if the article is included in a collection. He had something interesting to say on this old trooper of popular literature, observing precisely that she got herself read by ordinary people. Perhaps the date of the article and other data can be found in the bibliography of Papini in Palmieri's essay, or some other source.)

In the absence of their own 'modern' literature, certain strata of the *menu peuple* have satisfied their intellectual and artistic needs (which do exist, albeit in a plain and elementary form) in a variety of ways: the circulation of medieval romances of chivalry – the *Reali di Francia, Guerino detto il Meschino*, etc. – especially in southern Italy and the mountains;[22] the *Maggi* in Tuscany (the subjects represented by the *Maggi* are taken from books, tales and especially popular legends like Pia dei Tolomei; there are various publications on the *Maggi* and their repertoire).[23]

The lay forces have failed in their historical task as educators and elaborators of the intellect and the moral awareness of the people-nation. They have been incapable of satisfying the intellectual needs of the people precisely because they have failed to represent a lay culture, because they have not known how to elaborate a modern 'humanism' able to reach right to the simplest and most uneducated classes, as was necessary from the national point of view, and because they have been tied to an antiquated world, narrow, abstract, too individualistic or caste-like. French popular literature, on the other hand, which is the most widespread in Italy, does represent this modern humanism, this in its own way modern secularism, to a greater or lesser degree, and in a more or less attractive way. Guerrazzi, Mastriani and our few other popular writers were also representations of it. Yet if the lay forces have failed, the Catholics have not had any more success. One should not be deceived by the moderately high circulation of certain Catholic books. This is due to the vast and powerful organization of the Church, not to an inner force of expansion. The books are given away at the innumerable ceremonies and are read for chastisement, on command or out of

---

[22] See IX 6.

[23] *Maggi* are traditional May Day festivals in central Italy where peasants act out stories of popular biblical, chivalric or historical figures in a sequence of songs interspersed with refrains on the fiddle. The story of Pia dei Tolomei, murdered by her husband, was famous from Dante's *Purgatorio* V, 130–36.

desperation.[24]

It is a striking fact that in the field of adventure literature the Catholics have only managed to produce mediocrities: and yet they possess an excellent source in the travels of the missionaries and their eventful and often risky lives. Yet even when the geographical adventure novel was in its heyday, the Catholic version of this literature was mediocre and in no way comparable to its French, English and German secular counterparts. The most remarkable book is the story of Cardinal Massaja's life in Abyssinia. This apart there has been an invasion of books by Ugo Mioni (formerly a Jesuit priest) which are utterly sub-standard. In scientific popular literature, too, the Catholics offer very little, despite their great astronomers, like Father Secchi (a Jesuit), and the fact that astronomy is the science which interests the people most. This Catholic literature oozes with Jesuitic apologetics, like a goat with musk, and is nauseating in its mean narrow-mindedness. The inadequacy of Catholic intellectuals and the limited success of their literature are one of the most eloquent indications of the profound split that exists between religion and the people. The people are reduced to an extreme state of indifference and lack of a lively spiritual life. Religion has remained at the level of superstition, but it has not been replaced by a new humanistic and secular morality, because of the impotence of the lay intellectuals. (Religion has neither been replaced, nor internally transformed and nationalized as it has in other countries – like Jesuitism itself in America. Popular Italy is still in the conditions created immediately after the Counter-Reformation. At best, religion has been combined with pagan folklore and has remained at this stage.)

Q21 § 5.

4 Study of the Moral and Intellectual Tendencies and Interests Prevalent in Literary Circles

Toward what form of activity are Italian literary circles 'sympathetic'? Why are they not interested in economic activity, in work as individual and group production? If a work of art deals

---

[24] Compare the note on 'Catholic art' below (VIII 23). See also X 1.

with an economic subject, it is the aspect of the hero's 'leadership', 'domination' or 'control' over the producers that interests them. Or, their interest is in production or work in general, as a generic element of life and national strength, and therefore provokes flights of oratory. The life of the peasantry occupies a large space in literature, but here, too, not as work and toil but as 'folklore'. The peasants are treated as picturesque representatives of curious and bizarre customs and feelings. For this reason the 'peasant woman' is given even more space, with her sexual problems dealt with in their most external and romantic aspect and because the woman, through her beauty, can easily rise to the higher social classes.

The work of the clerk is an inexhaustible source of comedy: in every clerk one sees Oronzo E. Marginati of the old *Travaso*.[25] The intellectual's work is either given little space or is presented in its 'heroic' or 'superhuman' form, with the comical result that mediocre writers represent 'geniuses' of their own size. As is well known, an intelligent man can pretend to be a fool, but a fool cannot pretend to be intelligent.

Of course, one cannot force one or more generations of writers to be sympathetic towards this or that aspect of life, but the fact that one or more generations of writers have certain intellectual and moral interests, and not others, has some significance. It indicates that a particular cultural trend is prevalent among intellectuals. Even Italian *verismo* is distinct from the realistic currents of other countries. It either confines itself to describing the 'bestiality' of so-called human nature (a 'verismo' in the debased sense), or it turns its attention to provincial and regional life, to what the real Italy was in contrast to the official 'modern' Italy. It does not offer valuable portrayals of work and effort. The major preoccupation of intellectuals of the verist movement was not (as in France) that of establishing contact with the popular masses who had already been 'nationalized' into a unity, but that of providing the elements from which it emerged that the real Italy was still not unified. Furthermore, there is a difference between the *verismo* of northern writers and that of southern ones (for example, Verga, in whom there was a strong nationalist feeling, as is evident from the attitude he assumed in 1920

---

[25] Oronzo E. Marginati, the 'protesting citizen', was a character created by the humorist Luigi Lucatelli (1877–1915) in the Rome magazine *Il Travaso delle Idee*.

towards the autonomist 'Sicilia Nuova' movement).[26]

But it is not only that writers consider productive activity unworthy of epic treatment, even though such activity represents the whole life of the active part of the population: when they do deal with it, their attitude is that of Father Bresciani.

(It is worth looking at Luigi Russo's writings on Verga and Giuseppe Cesare Abba.)[27] Giuseppe Cesare Abba can be cited as an example of an Italian 'national-popular' writer, although he is not a 'people's' writer and does not belong to any current that, for party or sectarian reasons, is critical of the position of the ruling class. One should analyse not only those of Abba's writings that have poetic value, but also the others, like the one addressed to the soldiers which was awarded a prize by the military and governmental authorities and for a while circulated among the troops. One should also read Papini's essay published in *Lacerba* after the events of June 1914.[28]

Alfredo Oriani's position also needs to be clarified, although it is too abstract, oratorical and deformed by his titanic stance as a misunderstood genius.[29] There are some interesting things in the work of Piero Jahier (remember Jahier's attraction to

---

[26] On *verismo* and Verga see also footnotes 2 and 41 on p. 92 and p. 116 above. The reference here can be explained by an earlier note, Q 5 § 157: 'Verga was never a socialist nor a democrat but a "Crispian" in a broad sense [in the Risorgimento Francesco Crispi abandoned his Sicilian autonomism for a policy of national unity] . . . In Sicily the intellectuals are divided into two general classes: Crispian unitarists and democratic separatists . . . In 1920 a certain Enrico Messineo founded (or wanted to found?) a newspaper called *La Sicilia Nuova* "which aimed to fight for Sicilian autonomy". He invited Verga to contribute and Verga wrote back "I am first and foremost an Italian and therefore not an autonomist."'

[27] Luigi Russo, *Giovanni Verga* (Naples 1919) and the preface to G.C. Abba, *Da Quarto al Volturno* (Florence 1925). Abba took part in the 1860 expedition of Garibaldi's Thousand, keeping a diary which he was later to rework into various texts, notably the three published versions of his *Noterelle* (all in diary form), the last of which (1891) has the main title *Da Quarto al Volturno*. This was (and is) a popular set text in Italian state schools. Gramsci also refers later in this note to Russo's 1921 study of the Neapolitan dialect writer Salvatore Di Giacomo (1860–1934). On Russo see footnote 32 below.

[28] Papini's article 'I fatti di giugno' (*Lacerba* II (1914) 12, pp. 177–84) dealt with 'Red Week' (7–14 June 1914), the spontaneous protests and general strike sparked off by the massacre of anti-war demonstrators (three dead, fifteen injured) by troops in Ancona. Papini identified the cause of the repression and strike in economic instability and lack of confidence in the government and legislature. Gramsci in 1921 had referred to Red Week as 'the first, magnificent intervention of the mass of the people in politics, to directly oppose the arbitrary actions of the authorities and to give effective expression to the sovereign will of the people, which no longer found any voice in the Chamber of Representatives' (SPW I, p. 372).

[29] See VI 21 below.

Proudhon),[30] which is also in a popular-military vein, although disagreeably flavoured by the writer's biblical and Claudellian style which tends to make it less effective and even irritating because it masks a snobbish form of rhetoric. To judge by its programme, all of the literature of the 'Super-country' movement ought to be 'national-popular' but it is so precisely according to a programme and this has made it a thoroughly second-rate cultural phenomenon. Longanesi must also have written a manual for recruits, which shows that such meagre national-popular tendencies as there are arise from military preoccupations perhaps more than anything else.[31]

Concern for the national-popular element in formulating the critical-aesthetic and moral-cultural problem appears to be considerable in Luigi Russo (whose small volume *I Narratori* should be read), as a consequence of his 'return' to the experiences of De Sanctis after his move to Crocism.[32]

It should be noted that Brescianism is basically a form of anti-state and anti-national individualism even when and although it may mask itself under a frenetic nationalism and statism. 'State' means above all the conscious control of large national masses. Consequently, an emotional and ideological 'contact' with these masses and, to a certain extent, a sympathetic understanding of their needs and requirements is necessary. Now the absence of a national-popular literature, due to the lack of a concerned interest in these needs and requirements, has left the literary 'market' open to the influence of intellectuals from other countries. 'National-popular' writers at home, they become national-popular in Italy too because the needs which they satisfy are the same in this country. Thus, through the French popular-historical novel the Italian people became passionately interested in French monarchical and revolutionary traditions (and, as the

---

[30] On Jahier and Proudhon see VIII 17.

[31] Leo Longanesi, leading light of the Super-country movement (see VIII 15 and 16). Gramsci is probably referring here to his *Vademecum del perfetto fascista*.

[32] Luigi Russo (1892–1961), literary critic, began as a follower of Croce but, through work on De Sanctis and the Neapolitan liberal intelligentsia, came to attenuate Croce's division between poetry and history and recouped the 'progressive' and popular qualities of writers like Verga and Abba. Gramsci detected the importance of this 'national-popular' drift in Russo and the latter's research was probably his principal source of information on the ideas of the later De Sanctis. Russo remained a liberal antifascist under the regime. He edited the review *Leonardo* from 1925 to 1929. After the war he founded the review *Belfagor* and joined the PCI.

latest book gazettes demonstrate, their interest continues). They know the popular figure of Henri IV better than that of Garibaldi, the Revolution of 1789 better than the Risorgimento and the invectives of Victor Hugo against Napoleon III better than the invectives of Italian patriots against Metternich. Culturally speaking, they are interested in a past that is more French than Italian. They use French metaphors and cultural references in their language and thought.

For the national-popular slant that De Sanctis gave to his critical activity, one should see Luigi Russo's *Francesco De Sanctis e la cultura napoletana, 1860–1885* (1928) and De Sanctis's essay 'Science and Life'. Perhaps one can say that De Sanctis strongly felt the 'Renaissance-Reformation' contrast, that is, the contrast between life and science in the Italian tradition that weakened the national and state structure, and that he sought to react against it. This is why at a certain point he breaks away from speculative idealism and embraces positivism and 'verismo' (his sympathies for Zola, like Russo's for Verga and Di Giacomo). Russo seems to make this point in his book:

> The secret of De Sanctis's effectiveness is to be sought in his democratic spirituality, which makes him suspicious and hostile to all absolutist and privileged movements and theories, and in his compelling tendency to see scholarship as part of a broader activity (both spiritual and practical) as formulated in the famous lecture 'Science and Life'.[33]

The anti-democratic attitude of Brescianist writers has no politically noteworthy or coherent significance. It is the form of opposition to any national-popular movement and is determined by the economic-corporate caste spirit, of medieval and feudal origin.

Q23 § 8.

5 The Study of the Historical Formation of the Italian Intellectuals

This leads one back to the times of the Roman Empire when Italy, by having Rome in her territory, became the crucible of the

---

[33] The words here are those of Giulio Marzot paraphrasing Russo's book. On 'Science and Life' see introduction to Section II and II 1.

educated classes of all the imperial territories. The ruling class became increasingly imperial and decreasingly Latin. It became cosmopolitan: even the emperors were not Latin.

There is, therefore, a unitary line in the development of the Italian intellectual classes (operating on Italian territory), but this line of development is far from national. This fact leads to an internal imbalance in the composition of the population living in Italy.

The problem of what the intellectuals are can be shown in all of its complexity through this study.

Q3 § 88.

6 Humanism and Renaissance [i]

What does it mean that the Renaissance discovered 'man', that it made him the centre of the universe, etc.? Does it mean that before the Renaissance 'man' was not the centre of the universe? One could say that the Renaissance created a new culture or civilization, in opposition to the preceding ones or as a development of them, but one must 'limit' or 'specify' the nature of this culture. Is it really true that before the Renaissance 'man' was nothing and then became everything or is it that a process of cultural formation was developed in which man tended to become everything? It seems that we must say that before the Renaissance the transcendent formed the basis of medieval culture; but were those who represented this culture 'nothing' or was not perhaps that culture their way of being 'everything'? If the Renaissance was a great cultural revolution, it is not because everybody began to think that he was 'everything' instead of 'nothing'. It is because this way of thinking became widespread, became universal leaven. Man was not 'discovered', rather a new form of culture was initiated, a new effort to create a new type of man in the dominant classes.

Q17 § 1.

7 Humanism and Renaissance [ii]

From a review (in *Nuova Antologia*, 1 August 1933) by Arminio Janner of Ernst Walser's *Gesammelte Studien zur Geistesgeschichte der Renaissance* (Benno Schwabe, Basel, 1932). According to Janner, our idea of the Renaissance is determined above all by two fundamental works: *The Civilization of the Renaissance in Italy* by Jacob Burckhardt and *The History of Italian Literature* by De Sanctis. Burckhardt's book was interpreted differently in Italy and abroad. Published in 1860, it was known throughout Europe and influenced Nietzsche's ideas on the superman, giving rise thereby to a whole body of literature, especially in the northern countries, on artists and *condottieri* of the Renaissance. This literature proclaimed the right to the beautiful and heroic life, to the free expansion of the personality without regard for moral restraints. Thus the Renaissance is epitomized by Sigismondo Malatesta, Cesare Borgia, Leo X, and Aretino, with Machiavelli as its theoretician and, alone and to one side, Michelangelo. In Italy D'Annunzio represents this interpretation of the Renaissance. Burckhardt's book (translated by Valbusa in 1877) had a different influence in Italy. The Italian translation gave more emphasis to the anti-papal tendencies which Burckhardt saw in the Renaissance and which coincided with the political and cultural tendencies of the Risorgimento. The other element which Burckhardt highlighted in the Renaissance, that of individualism and the formation of the modern mind, was also seen in Italy as an opposition to the medieval world represented by the papacy. In Italy the admiration for a life of pure beauty and energy was less noticed. Less attention was paid to the *condottieri*, adventurers, and immoralists. (These observations seem to be worth taking into account: there is an interpretation of the Renaissance and of modern life that is attributed to Italy – as if it had originated in Italy and were based on its history – but it is only the interpretation of a German book on Italy, etc.).

De Sanctis accentuates the dark colours of political and moral corruption in the Renaissance: despite all the merits that can be acknowledged in the Renaissance, it undid Italy and conveyed it in servitude into foreign hands.

Thus Burckhardt sees the Renaissance as the starting point of a new progressive epoch of European civilization, the cradle of modern man. De Sanctis sees it from the point of view of Italian history, and for Italy the Renaissance was the start of a regression. Burckhardt and De Sanctis do, however, coincide in the details of their analyses of the Renaissance, and agree that its characteristic elements are the formation of the new mentality and the breaking of all the medieval ties of religion, authority, homeland and family. (These observations of Janner's on Burckhardt and De Sanctis should be looked over again.) According to Janner, 'in the last ten or fifteen years, however, a countercurrent of scholars, mostly Catholics, has begun to contest the validity of these aspects of the Renaissance' (highlighted by Burckhardt and De Sanctis) 'and is attempting to emphasize others which are for the most part opposed to them. In Italy Olgiati, Zabughin and Toffanin; in the German speaking countries Pastor, with the early volumes of *The History of the Popes*, and Walser.' Of Walser's there is a study on the religious beliefs of Pulci ('Lebens und Glaubensprobleme aus dem Zeitalter der Renaissance' in *Die Neueren Sprachen*, Beiheft n. 10). Continuing the work of Volpi and others, he analyses Pulci's brand of heresy and the retraction he was forced to make later on.[34] He reveals its origins (Averroism and the Judaic mystic sects) 'most convincingly' and shows that in Pulci it is not only a question of breaking with orthodox religious sentiments but also of a new faith of his (interwoven with magic and spiritualism) which later became an open and tolerant attitude to all faiths. (It should be seen whether spiritualism and magic are not necessarily the form that the naturalism and the materialism of that epoch had to take, i.e. the reaction to Catholic transcendence or the first form of primitive and crude immanence.) In the volume reviewed by Janner, it seems that there are three studies of particular interest in that they illustrate the new interpretation: 'Christianity and Antiquity as understood in the early Italian Renaissance', 'Studies on the thought of the Renaissance', and 'Human and artistic problems of the Italian Renaissance'.

According to Walser, Burckhardt's assertion that the Renaissance was pagan, critical, anti-papal and irreligious is imprecise. The attitude to the Church of Humanists of the first generation like Petrarch, Boccaccio and Salutati was much the same as that of the medieval scholars. The fifteenth-century Humanists – Poggio, Valla, Beccadelli – were more critical and independent, but when faced with the revealed truth, they too

---

[34] Luigi Pulci (1432–84), Florentine poet. Attacked for his lack of orthodoxy (he had practised magic arts and satirized pilgrims), around 1479 he produced a recantation in the form of a verse credo and wrote some conventional Christian beliefs into the mouth of a character in his *Morgante* (XXV 233–44). These aspects of Pulci's life had been dealt with by G. Volpi in *Giornale storico della letteratura italiana* XXII (1893) 1–64 and in Walser's study of 1926 cited here.

remained silent and accepted it. On this point Walser agrees with Toffanin who, in his book *Che cosa fu l'umanesimo*, says that Humanism, with its cult of Latinity and Romanity, was much more orthodox than the erudite vernacular literature of the thirteenth and fourteenth centuries. (This claim can be accepted if one distinguishes within the movement of the Renaissance the break which occurred between Humanism and the national life which had gradually formed after the year 1000, if one considers Humanism as a progressive process for the educated 'cosmopolitan' classes but regressive from the point of view of Italian history.)

. (The Renaissance can be considered as the cultural expression of a historical process in which a new intellectual class of European importance is formed. This class divided into two branches: one carried out a cosmopolitan function, linked to the papacy and reactionary in character; the other was formed abroad by political and religious exiles and had a progressive – cosmopolitan – function in the various countries in which it took up residence where it then took part in the organization of the modern states performing a technical role in the armed forces, in politics, in engineering, etc.)

Q 17 § 3.

8 Humanism and Renaissance [iii]

Walser, who lived for a long time in Italy, observes that a knowledge of the psychology of modern Italians is useful, within certain limits, for understanding the character of the Italian Renaissance. This seems to me a very acute observation, especially as regards the attitude towards religion. It raises the question of the nature of the religious spirit in modern Italy, and whether it may be compared, not so much with the religious spirit of the Protestants, but with that of other Catholic countries, especially France. That the religiosity of the Italians is very superficial is undeniable, as is the fact that it is of a strictly political nature, one of international hegemony. Connected with this form of religiosity is Gioberti's *Primato* which in turn helped to solidify and give a shape to what already existed in a diffuse state.[35] It should not be forgotten that from the sixteenth century

[35] On Gioberti's *Primato*, see footnote 69 below.

onwards Italy contributed to world history especially because it was the seat of the papacy, and that Italian Catholicism was felt not only as a surrogate for the spirit of the nation and the state but also as a worldwide hegemonic institution, as an imperialistic spirit. It is therefore correct to point out that the anti-papal spirit is a form of struggle against privileged groups. In Italy the religious groups undeniably had a much more radical political and economic function (position) than in other countries, where the national formation limited the ecclesiastical function. The anti-papalism of the lay intellectuals and the anticlerical *facetiae* are also a form of combat between lay and religious intellectuals, given the prevailing position the latter enjoyed.

If the scepticism and the paganism of the intellectuals are to a large extent mere superficial appearances which are compatible with a degree of religious spirit, the licentious manifestations of the people (see the book by Domenico Guerri on *Correnti popolari nel Rinascimento*), the floats and songs of the carnival, which seem more serious to Walser, can be explained in the same way.

Like the Italians of today, those of the Renaissance, Walser says, were able 'to develop separately and simultaneously the two factors of human understanding, the rational and the mystical, and in such a way that rationalism, pushed to the limits of absolute scepticism, is reconnected, by an invisible bond inconceivable to the Nordic man, with the most primitive mysticism, the blindest fatalism and with fetishism and crass superstition.' These are apparently the most important corrections that Walser makes to Burckhardt's and De Sanctis's conception of the Renaissance. Janner writes that Walser fails to distinguish Humanism from the Renaissance, and that although without Humanism the Renaissance might not have happened, the latter nevertheless surpassed Humanism in its importance and its consequences.

This distinction too needs to be more subtle and profound. A more correct opinion seems to be that the Renaissance is a very significant movement which begins after 1000, of which Humanism and the Renaissance (in the strict sense) are two conclusive moments, which have Italy as their principal seat, while the more general historical process is European and not just Italian. (Humanism and the Renaissance, as the literary expression of this European historical movement, had their main seat in Italy. But the progressive movement after 1000 – although the Italian communes played so large a part in it – deteriorated precisely in Italy and precisely with Humanism and the Renaissance, which were regressive in Italy. In the rest of Europe, however, the general movement culminated in the formation of national states and then in the world expansion of Spain, France, England and Portugal. What corresponded in Italy to the national states of these countries was the organization – begun by Pope Alexander VI – of the papacy as an absolute state, an organization which broke up the rest of Italy.) Machiavelli represents in Italy the realization that there can be no real Renaissance without the foundation of a national state. As a man, though, he is the theoretician of what is happening outside Italy, not of Italian events.

Q17§8.

9 The Renaissance

See the article by Vittorio Rossi, 'Il Rinascimento', *Nuova Antologia*, 16 November 1929, pp. 137–50. Very interesting and comprehensive in its brevity. Rossi notes, correctly, that the re-emergence of studies dealing with classical literature was a fact of secondary importance, an indication, a symptom, and not the most striking aspect of the deep essence of the age which merits the name of Renaissance. 'The central and fundamental fact, the one from which all others germinate, was the birth and maturation of a new spiritual world which appeared then on the stage *not only of Italian but of European* history, as a result of the vigorous and coherent creativity unleashed in every field of human activity after the year 1000.' After 1000, a reaction set in against the feudal regime 'which stamped its impress on the whole of life' (through the landed aristocracy and the clergy). In the two or three centuries that followed, the economic, political and cultural order of society underwent a profound transformation. Agriculture was reinvigorated; industry and commerce were revived, extended and organized. The bourgeoisie arose, the new ruling class (this requires clarification and Rossi does not clarify), eager with political passion (where? in all of Europe or only in Italy and Flanders?) and bound in powerful financial corporations; with a growing spirit of autonomy, the communal city-states were established.

(This point, too, needs to be clarified. One should establish the meaning that 'state' had in the city-state. It was a limited 'corporate' meaning, which prevented it from developing beyond intermediate feudalism, i.e. that which followed absolute feudalism – without a third estate, so to speak – which lasted until the year 1000 and which was replaced by absolute monarchy in the fifteenth century, until the French Revolution. In the Netherlands and only in the Netherlands was there an organic passage from the commune or city-state to a regime that was no longer feudal. In Italy the communes were unable to get out of the corporate phase. Feudal anarchy took over in forms appropriate to the new situation and then there was foreign domination. Compare this with some of the notes on the 'Italian Intellectuals'. For the entire development of European society after 1000 to which Rossi refers, Henri Pirenne's book on the origin of the cities should be kept in mind.)[36]

Reform movements of the Church; new religious orders arose to revive the apostolic life. (Were these movements positive or negative symptoms of the new world then developing? They certainly appeared as a reaction to the new economic society, although the demand for Church reform was progressive. It is also true, however, that they indicate a greater interest in the people on the part of the principal religious personalities, in other words the most prominent intellectuals of the age. But they too, at least in Italy, were either suffocated or domesticated by the Church, while in other parts of Europe they continued to be the leaven which would give rise to the Reformation. Speaking of the cultural tendencies after 1000, one should not forget the Arab contribution through Spain – see the articles by Ezio Levi in *Il Marzocco* and *Leonardo* – and, as well as the Arabs, the Spanish Jews.) 'In the philosophical and theological schools of France there were fierce discussions, which were a sign of the new religious spirit as well as of the growing demands of reason.' (Were not these disputations caused by the Averroist doctrines that were conquering the European world, in other words by the pressure of Arab culture?) 'The struggle for investitures broke out, caused by the reawakened sense of the imperial Roman spirit' (what does this mean? by the reawakened sense of the state which wanted to absorb all the activities of its citizens, as in the

---

[36] Henri Pirenne, *Les villes du Moyen Age*, Brussels 1927.

Roman Empire?) 'and by the awareness of current spiritual, political, and economic interests. This struggle stirred up the whole world of the secular princes, the clergy, and the anonymous mass of monks, bourgeois, peasants, and artisans.' Heresies (but smothered with fire and the sword).

'Chivalry, while sanctioning and consecrating the possession of moral virtues in the individual, nourished a love of human culture and practised a certain refinement of manners.' (But in what sense can chivalry be linked with the Renaissance after 1000?) Rossi does not distinguish the contradictory movements because he does not take into account the different forms of feudalism and the local autonomies that existed within it. On the other hand, chivalry cannot be overlooked as an element of the Renaissance proper around 1500, although the *Orlando Furioso*, with its mixture of sympathy, irony, and caricature, is already a lament for its passing and *The Courtier* is its philistine, scholastic, and pedantic phase.)[37] The Crusades, the wars of the Christian kings against the Moors in Spain, the wars of the Capetians against England, and those of the Italian communes against the Swabian emperors in which the sense of national units matures or emerges (this is an exaggeration). It is strange to see a proposition like the following in a scholar of Rossi's stature: 'In the effort those men made to renew themselves and build the conditions for a new life, they felt the stirring of the deep ferments of their history. And in the Roman world, so rich in experiences of free and full human spirituality, they found congenial souls.' This seems to me nothing but a string of vague and meaningless statements: 1) because there was always a continuity between the Roman world and the period after 1000 (middle-Latin period); 2) because 'congenial souls' is a meaningless metaphor and in any case the phenomenon occurred in the fifteenth and sixteenth centuries and not in this first phase; 3) because there was nothing Roman in the Italian Renaissance other than the literary veneer, since the very thing that was specific to Roman civilization – unity of the state and thus of the territory – was lacking.

Latin culture flourished in the schools of France in the twelfth century with a magnificent growth of grammatical and rhetorical

---

37 On Ariosto's *Orlando Furioso* see footnote 50 below. Castiglione's *Il libro del Cortegiano* (*Book of the Courtier*), published in 1528, was the most widely diffused Renaissance handbook on noble behaviour.

studies and of solemn and balanced prose and poetic compositions, to which there corresponded in Italy a later and more modest production by Venetian poets and scholars, and by the *dictatores*. This culture was a phase of middle-Latin, it was a purely feudal product in the primitive sense of the period before 1000. This also applies to juridical studies, which were revived because of the need to give a legal framework to the new and complex political and social relations. These studies, it is true, drew on Roman law, but they rapidly degenerated into the most meticulous enumeration of cases, precisely because 'pure' Roman law could not regulate the new complex relations. In fact, these cases of the glossarists and post-glossarists led to the formation of local systems of jurisprudence where the right of the strongest (either the noble or the bourgeois) prevailed and which were the 'only law' that existed. The principles of Roman law were forgotten or subordinated to the interpretive gloss which was in turn interpreted, with a final product where nothing Roman was left other than the pure and simple principle of property.

Scholasticism 'rethought and reordered the truths intuited by Christianity within the forms of ancient philosophy' (which, let it be noted, had re-entered the circle of European civilization not because of the 'stirrings' of the deep ferments of history but because it had been put back there by the Arabs and the Jews).

Romanesque architecture. Rossi is quite correct in stating that all these manifestations from 1000 to 1300 were not the fruit of a calculated will to imitate but the spontaneous manifestation of a creative energy that sprang from the depths and put those men in a position to feel and revive antiquity. The last of these propositions is, however, mistaken because in reality those men enabled themselves to feel and live the *present* intensely, whereas later a stratum of intellectuals was formed which appreciated and revived antiquity and increasingly separated itself from the life of the people, because the bourgeoisie in Italy declined or was downgraded until the end of the eighteenth century.

It is also strange that Rossi is unaware of the contradictions he falls into by claiming: 'Nevertheless, if "Renaissance" really means, as I have no doubt it does, the whole multiform explosion of human activity from the eleventh to the sixteenth centuries, then its most conspicuous sign is not the revival of Latin culture, but the rise of vernacular literature, which throws into relief one of the most remarkable products of that energy: the breaking up of medieval unity into differentiated national entities.' Rossi has a realistic and historicist conception of the Renaissance but he is unable to abandon completely the old rhetorical and literary conception: his contradictions and his tendency to go by the book spring from this. The rise of the vernacular marked a break with. antiquity and the fact that this phenomenon was accompanied by a rebirth of literary Latin requires explanation. Rossi is quite right to say that 'the use a people makes of one language rather than another for disinterested intellectual ends is not an individual or collective whim, but the spontaneous act of a peculiar inner life, springing out in the only form that is suited to it.' In other words, every language is an integral conception of the world and not simply a piece of clothing than can fit indifferently as form over any content. Well then? Does not this mean that two conceptions of the world were in conflict: a bourgeois-popular one expressing itself in the vernacular and an aristocratic-feudal one expressing itself in Latin and harking back to Roman antiquity? And is not the Renaissance characterized by this conflict rather than by the serene creation of a triumphant culture? Rossi is unable to explain the fact that this return to antiquity was purely a political-instrumental element and could not by itself have created a culture, and thus that the Renaissance naturally had to resolve itself into the Counter Reformation, in other words into the defeat of the bourgeoisie who had arisen with the communes and in the triumph of the Roman spirit – but in the form of papal power over the consciences of the people and an attempted return to the Holy Roman Empire: a farce after the tragedy.

In France, the literature in *langue d'oc* and *langue d'oïl* flourished between the end of the first and the beginning of the second century after 1000, when the country was in ferment due to the great political, economic, religious and cultural facts mentioned earlier.[38] 'And if in Italy the advent of the vernacular as a literary language was delayed by over a century, this is because here the great movement, which established a new national civilization on the ruins of medieval universalism, was more varied and everywhere autochthonous and spontaneous, because of the

[38] 'Langue d'oc' and 'langue d'oïl' were the vernaculars of southern and northern France, named after their respective words for 'yes'.

variety of the age-old history of our cities. Italy lacked the disciplining force of a monarchy and powerful lords. Therefore, the formation of that new world of the spirit, the most striking aspect of which was the new vernacular literature, was much more gradual and laborious.' Another bundle of contradictions: in reality the innovatory movement after 1000 was more violent in Italy than in France, and the class which led that movement in Italy gained economic power sooner and more powerfully than it did in France, managing to overturn the domination of its enemies; this did not occur in France. French history developed differently from Italian history: this is Rossi's truism, and yet he is unable to point to the real differences of development and he locates them in a greater or less spontaneity and autochthony – things which are very difficult, if not impossible, to prove. Besides, even in France the movement was not a unitary one; because there was quite a difference between North and South, expressed in a great epic literature in the North and an absence of epic in the South. Evidence of the origin of the historical differentiation between Italy and France can be found in the Strasbourg oath (about 841),[39] namely in the fact that the people participated actively in history (the people-army) by becoming guarantors of the observance of treaties between the descendants of Charlemagne. The people-army gives its guarantee by 'swearing in the vernacular,' they introduce their language into their nation's history, assuming a political function of the first order, presenting themselves as a collective will, as an element of a national democracy. This 'demagogic' appeal of the Carolingians to the people in their foreign policy is very important for understanding the development of French history and the monarchy's function in it as a national factor. In Italy the first vernacular documents are individual oaths for establishing ownership over certain monastery lands or they have an anti-popular character ('Traite, traite, fili de putte').[40] This is a long way away from the spontaneous and the autochthonous. The protective shell of monarchy, the true continuation of the unified Roman state, allowed the French bourgeoisie more room to

---

[39] On the Strasbourg oaths see footnote 2 on p. 168.

[40] 'Fili dele pute, traite' ('Pull, sons of bitches'): one of the vernacular inscriptions on a late 11th century fresco in the Basilica of St Clement in Rome. A pagan patrician is depicted ordering three servants with these words to drag the bound saint along the ground.

develop than the complete economic autonomy reached by the
Italian bourgeoisie, since the latter were incapable of going
beyond a narrow-minded corporatism or of creating their own
integral state civilization. (One should see how the Italian
communes, in claiming the feudal rights of the Count over the
surrounding territory of his *comitatus* and after incorporating
them became a feudal element, with power being exercised by a
corporative *comitatus* instead of by the Count.)

Rossi notes that 'the form of commune of the so-called pre-
Humanism of the thirteenth and fourteenth centuries *coincided
with and indicated the same inner activity of our people*' as literature
in the vernacular, and that this pre-Humanism and vernacular
literature were followed by the philological Humanism of the late
fourteenth and fifteenth centuries. He then concludes: 'These
are three facts which, if considered in a purely extrinsic (!) way by
contemporaries and descendants, might seem antithetical, and
yet which mark, in the cultural order, stages in the development
of the Italian spirit which are progressive and to which, in the
political order, the commune (to which the vernacular literature
and certain forms of pre-Humanism correspond) and the
Signory (whose literary correlative is philological Humanism) are
wholly analogous.' Thus everything is in its place, under the
generic gloss of the 'Italian spirit'.

With Boniface VIII, the last of the great medieval popes, and
with Henry VII, the epic battles between the two highest
authorities on earth came to an end. Decline in the political
influence of the Church: Avignon 'servitude' and schism. The
Empire dies as a municipal political authority (sterile attempts by
Lewis the Bavarian and Charles IV).[41] 'Life lay in the young and
industrious bourgeoisie of the communes who gradually
consolidated their power over external enemies and the common
people and who, as they followed their course in history, were
about to generate, or had already generated, national signories.'
What national signories? The origin of the signories in Italy is
quite different than in other countries. In Italy they derived from
the inability of the bourgeoisie to maintain a corporate regime, to

[41] Boniface VIII, pope from 1294 to 1303, attempted to reassert the temporal supremacy
of the papacy. Rival Popes in Rome and Avignon emerged in 1378 (the Great Schism).
Henry VII of Luxembourg, German emperor, led a campaign to Italy in 1310–13, aiming
to revive imperial claims south of the Alps. The attempt was repeated by Lewis the
Bavarian in 1327–29. His successor Charles IV made two brief visits to Italy (1354–55 and
1368–69), during the second of which he effectively abandoned imperial ambitions there.

govern the common people with pure violence. In France, however, the origin of absolutism lay in the struggle between bourgeoisie and feudal classes, yet there the bourgeoisie were united to the common people and the peasants (within certain limits, naturally). Can one speak of a 'national signory' in Italy? What did 'nation' mean at that time?

Rossi continues: 'In the face of these great events, the idea – which seemed to be incarnated in the universal perpetuity of the Empire, the Church and Roman law and which still held good for Dante – of a universal continuation into the Middle Ages of universal Roman life, gave way to the *idea that a great revolution* had taken place in recent centuries and *that a new historical era had begun*. There arose the sense of an abyss separating the new from the old civilization. The legacy of Rome was no longer felt as an immanent force in everyday life. But the Italians began to turn their attention to antiquity as if it were their own past, one of admirable force, freshness and beauty, to which they had to return in their thoughts through meditation and study for the purpose of humane education, like children returning to their father after a long absence, not like old people looking back on their youth with regret.' This is a real historical novel. Where can one find '*the idea that a great revolution had taken place*'? Rossi expands bookish anecdotes, the Humanist's contempt for medieval Latin and the refined gentleman's haughtiness towards medieval 'barbarity', into historical facts. Antonio Labriola is right to maintain in his *Da un secolo all'altro* that only with the French Revolution is a break with the past, with all of the past, experienced, and that this feeling has its ultimate expression in the attempt to renew the computation of dates with the Republican calendar.[42] If what Rossi claims were really true, the passage from the Renaissance to the Counter-Reformation would not have been so smooth.

Rossi is unable to free himself from the rhetorical conception of the Renaissance and is therefore unable to weigh the fact that there are two currents, one progressive and the other regressive, and that in the final analysis the latter triumphed after the general phenomenon had reached its full splendour in the sixteenth century (not as a national and political fact, though, but as a

[42] Antonio Labriola, *Saggi intorno alla concezione materialistica della storia* IV. *Da un secolo all'altro*, Bologna 1925, pp. 45–46.

prevalently if not exclusively cultural fact). As such, it was the phenomenon of an aristocracy removed from the people-nation. Meanwhile, the people were preparing the reaction against this splendid parasitism in the form of the Protestant Reformation, in Savonarolism with its 'burning of vanities', through such popular banditry as that of Re Marcone in Calabria and through other movements that would be interesting to record and analyse, at least as indirect symptoms. Machiavelli's political thought was also a reaction to the Renaissance, a reminder of the political and national need to return to the people as the absolute monarchies of France and Spain had done. Another symptom was the popularity of Cesare Borgia in Romagna in as much as he put down the petty signori and condottieri.

According to Rossi, there is already in Dante a *virtual* 'awareness of the ideal separation that had occurred in the centuries between antiquity and the new epoch'. But this then became *actual* in the political order in the person of Cola di Rienzo, 'the heir of Dante's thought who wanted to vindicate the Roman spirit, and therefore the Italian spirit, of the Empire' (why 'therefore'? Cola di Rienzo was really only concerned about the people of Rome, materially speaking) 'and to draw all the Italian peoples together with the sacred bond of Empire into a unified nation. As for popular culture, Petrarch greets Cola as "our Camillus, our Brutus, our Romulus" and he calls up antiquity through patient study while his poet's soul assimilates and relives it.'[43] (The historical novel still. What was the result of Cola di Rienzo's efforts? Absolutely nothing. And how can you make history with wishes and pious desires? And those Camilluses, Brutuses and Romuluses grouped together by Petrarch, do they not smack of pure rhetoric?)

Rossi is unable to separate middle-Latin from humanistic or philological Latin, as he calls it. He does not want to understand that in reality these are two languages, because they express two conceptions of the world which are in a sense antithetical to each other, although limited to the category of the intellectuals. Nor does he want to understand that pre-Humanism (Petrarch) is still

---

[43] Cola di Rienzo led a republican coup and revolution in Rome from May to December 1347. He was a self-educated plebeian who romanticized his popular revolt as a return to the institutions of classical Rome. Petrarch wrote a letter of exhortation to Cola and the Roman people in which he idealized them in similar terms as restoring classical Roman liberty against the tyranny of the rival noble factions.

different from Humanism because 'quantity has become quality'. One might say that Petrarch is typical of this passage: as a vernacular writer, he is a poet of the bourgeoisie, but as a writer of Latin, as an 'orator' and political figure, he is already an intellectual of the anti-bourgeois reaction (signories, papacy). This also explains the sixteenth-century phenomenon of 'Petrarchism' and its insincerity. It was a purely literary phenomenon because the feelings which had given rise to the poetry of the *dolce stil novo* and of Petrarch himself no longer dominated public life, just as the bourgeoisie of the communes no longer dominated, since it was driven back into its warehouses and decaying manufactures. Politically, an aristocracy made up mostly of *parvenus* dominated, gathered as it was round the courts of the lords and protected by mercenary troops: it produced the culture of the sixteenth century and helped the various arts, but it was politically limited and ended up under foreign domination.

Thus, Rossi cannot see the class origins of the passage from Sicily to Bologna and Tuscany of the earliest vernacular poetry.[44] He places the 'imperial and ecclesiastical pre-Humanism (in his sense) of Pier delle Vigne and Master Berardo of Naples, so cordially hated by Petrarch' and 'still rooted in the sense of an imperial continuation of antiquity' (i.e. it is still middle-Latin, like the 'pre-Humanism' of the communes as represented by the Veronese and Paduan philologists and poets and the Bolognese grammarians and the rhetoricians) together with the Sicilian school of poetry. He says that both phenomena would have been sterile because they were both tied 'to an already eclipsed political and intellectual world'. The Sicilian school was not sterile because Bologna and Tuscany animated 'its empty technical frame with the new democratic cultural spirit'. But is this interpretation correct? In Sicily the mercantile bourgeoisie developed under the monarchical shell. With Frederick II it found itself involved in the question of the Holy Roman Empire

---

[44] The first refined poetry in the Italian vernacular was that of the 'Sicilian school' – made up mostly of notaries and other court functionaries attached to the Emperor Frederick II (1197–1250). They included Giacomo da Lentini, (reputedly) Frederick himself and, in north-central Italy, Frederick's natural son Enzo (Heinz) who was captured by the Bolognese in 1249 and kept prisoner in Bologna until his death in 1272. Enzo is thought to have been instrumental in introducing the Sicilian manner into central Italian poetry, from where it influenced Dante and his circle in Tuscany. Frederick's court chancellor Pier della Vigna (c. 1190 – c. 1249) also wrote vernacular verse but was more important as a writer of imperial letters in Latin. Dante places him in Hell as a suicide. Berardo da Napoli (c. 1230–93) was a papal notary and diplomat, also a stylist of epistolary Latin.

of the Germanic nation. Frederick was an absolute monarch in Sicily and in the South, but he was also the medieval emperor. The Sicilian bourgeoisie, like its French counterpart, developed more rapidly from the cultural point of view than Tuscany. Frederick himself and his sons wrote poetry in the vernacular and in this respect they participated in the new thrust of human activities after 1000. But not just in this respect: in reality, the Tuscan and Bolognese bourgeoisie were ideologically more backward than Frederick II, the medieval emperor. Paradoxes of history. But one must not falsify history, as Rossi does, by inverting the terms for the sake of a general thesis. Frederick II failed, but his attempt was quite different from that of Cola di Rienzo and he was a quite different man. Bologna and Tuscany welcomed the 'empty Sicilian technical frame' with a very different historical understanding than that of Rossi. They realized that this was 'something of theirs', while they did not understand that Enzo too was theirs. Although he carried the flag of the universal Empire, they made him die in prison.

Unlike the imperial and ecclesiastical 'pre-Humanism,' Rossi finds that 'in the scabrous and at times bizarre Latinity of the pre-Humanism which flourished in the shadows of the signories of the communes, there were hatching (!) the reaction to medieval universalism and indistinct aspirations to national forms of style' (what does this mean? that the vernacular was disguised under Latin forms?) 'As a result, the new scholars of the classical world would see in this Latinity the seeds of that Roman imperialism which Cola had dreamed of as the centre of national unification and which they felt and desired to be a form of Italian cultural domination over the rest of the world. The nationalization (!) of Humanism, which in the sixteenth century was to occur throughout the civilized countries of Europe, was born precisely from the universal empire of a culture – our own – which, although it germinated from the study of antiquity, took root and spread as a vernacular literature too and thus as an Italian national literature.' (This is the rhetorical conception of the Renaissance at its fullest extent. If the Humanists looked towards a cultural domination of Italy over the world, this was at most the beginning of this 'rhetoric' as a national form. The interpretation of the 'cosmopolitan function of the Italian intellectuals' enters the picture here. This function is a far cry from a national 'cultural domination'. It attests rather, to the very absence of a national character in the culture.)

The word *humanista* first appeared in the second half of the fifteenth century and in Italian in the third decade of the sixteenth. The word *humanism* is even more recent. At the end of the fourteenth century, the first Humanists called their studies *studia humanitatis*, that is, 'studies intended for the integral improvement of the human spirit, and thus the only kind truly worthy of man. For them, culture was not only knowledge, it was also life, doctrine, morality and beauty (. . .), all mirrored in the unity of the living literary work.' Caught in his contradictions, which are determined by his mechanically unitary conception of the history of the Renaissance, Rossi resorts to images to explain how humanistic Latin gradually declined until the vernacular triumphed in every domain of literature 'and Italian Humanism finally had a language of its own, while Latin descended into the tomb'. (Not completely, though, for the Church and the sciences used it until the eighteenth century. This demonstrates the nature of the social current that had always sustained its continuing use. Latin was expelled from the secular camp only by the modern bourgeoisie, leaving the various reactionaries to lament its passing.) 'Humanism is not Latinism; it is the affirmation of full humanity, and the humanity of the Italian Humanists was, in its historical aspect, Italian. It could thus only be expressed in the vernacular, which the Humanists too spoke in everyday life and which, despite all their classicizing, boldly forced open the gates of their Latin. By withdrawing themselves from life, they were able to dream their dream, and firmly convinced that no literature worthy of the name could exist if not in Latin, they rejected the new language. A different historical reality generated both them and their dream, and within it they lived their lives, men born almost a millenium and a half after the great Roman orator.' What does all this mean? Why this distinction between Latin-dream and vernacular-historical reality? And why was Latin not a historical reality? Rossi cannot explain this bilingualism of the intellectuals. He does not want to admit that for the Humanists the vernacular was like a dialect, that is, it did not have a national character, and that as a result the Humanists were continuators of the universalism of the Middle Ages – in other forms of course – and not a national element. They were a 'cosmopolitan caste', for whom Italy perhaps represented what the region represents in the modern nation, but nothing more and nothing better than this. They were apolitical and anational.

'The classicism of the Humanists no longer had religious morality as its end; instead, it aimed at the integral education of the human spirit. Above all it rehabilitated the human spirit as the creator of life and history.' Quite right: this is the most interesting aspect of Humanism. But does it contradict what I said earlier about the non-national and thus regressive spirit – for Italy – of Humanism? I don't think so. In fact this – the most original and promising content of Humanism – was not developed in Italy, where Humanism assumed the aspect of a restoration. Yet, like every restoration, it assimilated and developed, better than the revolutionary class it had politically suffocated, the ideological principles of the defeated class, which had not been able to go beyond its own corporate limits and create the superstructures of an integral society. Except that this development was 'abstract', it remained the patrimony of an intellectual caste and had no contact with the people-nation. When the reactionary movement in Italy, to which Humanism had been a necessary prelude, developed into the Counter-Reformation, the new ideology was also suffocated, and the Humanists (with a few exceptions) produced retractions before the stake (see the chapter on Erasmus published by La Nuova Italia from De Ruggiero's book *Rinascimento, riforma e controriforma*).

The ideological content of the Renaissance was developed outside Italy, in Germany and France, in political and philosophical forms. In Italy, though, the modern State and modern philosophy were imported because our intellectuals were cosmopolitan and anational as in the Middle Ages – in different forms, but in the same general relations.

There are other interesting elements in Rossi's article, but they concern specific aspects. It will be necessary to study Rossi's book on the Quattrocento (Vallardi), Toffanin's *Cosa fu l'umanesimo* (Sansoni), De Ruggiero's book cited above, as well as the classical works on the Renaissance published by foreign scholars (Burckhardt, Voigt, Symonds, etc.).[45]

Q5 § 123.

[45] Vittorio Rossi, *Il Quattrocento* (Milan, n.d.; 2nd ed, 1931); Giuseppe Toffanin, *Che cosa fu l'umanesimo*, (Florence 1929); J. Burckhardt, *Die Kultur der Renaissance in Italien* (1860); Georg Voigt, *Die Wiederbelebung des klassischen Altertums* (Berlin 1859); J.A. Symonds, *Renaissance in Italy* (1875).

10 The Sixteenth Century

The manner of judging sixteenth-century literature according to particular stereotyped canons has given rise in Italy to curious opinions and limitations in the practice of criticism. These are significant for judging the abstract character of the national-popular reality of our intellectuals. This situation is now slowly changing but the old manner is reacting. In 1928 Emilio Lovarini published a comedy in five acts entitled *La Venexiana, commedia di ignoto cinquecentesco* which was recognized to be a very fine work of art (cf. Benedetto Croce, *La Critica*, 20 March 1930). Ireneo Sanesi (author of the volume *La Commedia* in the Literary Genres collection published by Vallardi), in an article entitled 'La Venexiana' in *Nuova Antologia* of 1 October 1929, states what for him is the critical problem raised by the comedy: the unknown author of *La Venexiana* is caught in the past, a reactionary, a conservative because he represents the type of comedy born from the medieval novella, the realistic and lively type of comedy (even though written in Latin) which takes its subject matter from the ordinary real life of the bourgeoisie or the common citizenry, whose characters are drawn from this same reality, with actions that are simple, clear and linear, and whose greatest source of interest is precisely their sobriety and sparkle – whereas, in Sanesi's opinion, those writers of erudite theare on the classical model, who brought back on stage the ancient types and motifs dear to Plautus and Terence, are revolutionary. For Sanesi, the writers of the new historical class are reactionaries and the courtly writers are revolutionaries. Amazing!

What has happened to *La Venexiana* shortly after what had happened to the comedies of Ruzzante is interesting.[46] The latter were translated into an archaic-like French from sixteenth-century Paduan dialect by Alfred Mortier. Ruzzante had been discovered by Maurice Sand (son of George Sand) who proclaimed him to be greater not only than Ariosto (as a comic dramatist) and Bibbiena, but even than Machiavelli, and a precursor of Molière and of modern French naturalism. Adolfo Orvieto also wrote about *La Venexiana* (*Il Marzocco*, 30 September 1928), saying that it seems to be 'the product of a dramatic

---

[46] Ruzzante: stage name of Angelo Beolco (1496?–1542) most of whose plays dealing with peasant life were written in the dialect of Padua.

imagination of our times' and he made reference to Becque.[47]

It is interesting to note this double vein in the sixteenth century: one truly national-popular (in the dialects, but in Latin too) and tied to the preceding tradition of the novella and an expression of the bourgeoisie; the other learned, courtly and non-national but exalted by the rhetoricians.

Q5 § 104.

11 Non-National-Popular Character of Italian Literature

Croce's volume *Poesia popolare e poesia d'arte. Studi sulla poesia italiana dal Tre al Cinquecento* (1933) should be studied under this heading. His concept of 'popular' is different from the one used in these notes. For Croce it is a question of a psychological attitude, so that the relationship between popular poetry and artistic poetry is like that between good sense and critical thinking, between natural awareness and skilled awareness, between candid innocence and knowing and scrupulous goodness.[48] But from a reading of some of the essays in the book, which first appeared in *La Critica*, it seems we can deduce the following: while from the fourteenth century to the sixteenth popular poetry is remarkably important even in this sense, since it is still tied to a certain energetic resistance on the part of those social forces which arose with the reawakening of the reform movement occurring after the year 1000 and culminating in the communes, after the sixteenth century these forces have degenerated utterly and popular poetry declines until we reach its current forms in which popular interest is satisfied by such literature as *Il Guerin Meschino*.[49] After the sixteenth century, in other words, the separation between intellectuals and the people, which underlies these notes and which has been of such

---

[47] Henry Becque (1837–99), early naturalist dramatist, author of *Les Corbeaux* (1876) and *La Parisienne* (1885).

[48] See Croce, *Poesia popolare e poesia d'arte* 4th ed. (Bari, 1957) pp. 5–6: 'Now popular poetry is, in the aesthetic sphere, analogous to good sense in the intellecrtual sphere and candour or innocence in the moral sphere. It expresses stirrings of the soul which do not contain within themselves, as immediate precedents, great labourings of thought or passion; it depicts simple feelings in correspondingly simple forms.'

[49] See IX 6.

importance for modern Italian political and cultural history, becomes radical.

Q 15 § 42.

12 Philosophical Novels, Utopias, etc.

The Counter-Reformation and utopias: the desire to rebuild European civilization according to a rational plan. Another origin and perhaps the more common one: a way of expounding a heterodox, non-conformist philosophy, especially before the French Revolution. Utopias were thus, by this argument, the source of the fashion for attributing to foreign peoples the institutions desired in one's own country or for criticizing the presumed institutions of a foreign people in order to criticize those of one's own country. The practice of extolling primitive peoples, savages (the noble savage) presumed to be closer to nature also probably derived from utopias. (This is repeated in the exaltation of the idealized 'peasant' by populist movements.) All of this literature has been of no small importance in the history of the spread of social-political opinions among given masses and, therefore, in the history of culture.

One could observe that this 'fictionalized' political literature reacts against 'chivalric' literature in decline (*Don Quixote, Orlando Furioso*, Thomas More's *Utopia, City of the Sun*).[50] Therefore it marks the transition from the exaltation of a feudal social type to the exaltation of the popular masses in general, with all of their elementary needs (food, clothing, protection, reproduction) which one tries to satisfy rationally. Studies of these writings neglect the deep marks which must have been left, often for generations, by the great famines and plagues that decimated and exhausted generations of the popular masses. These elementary disasters along with phenomena of religious morbidity, of resigned passivity, also aroused 'elementary' critical feelings and hence pressures towards a certain activity, pressures which were expressed precisely in this utopian literature, even several generations after the disasters occurred.

Q 6 § 157.

[50] Ariosto's *Orlando Furioso* (1516, 1532) and Cervantes' *Don Quixote* (1605, 1615) are both, to different degrees, late parodistic variants of romances of chivalry. More's *Utopia* (1516) and Tommaso Campanella's *Città del sole* (1602) give detailed descriptions of the workings of ideal states on a more or less collectivist basis.

13 Indirect Sources:[51] 'Utopias' and So-called 'Philosophical Novels'

1) These have been studied for the history of the development of political criticism, but one of their most interesting aspects to consider is their unwitting reflection of the most elementary and profound aspirations of even the lowest subaltern social groups, albeit through the minds of intellectuals preoccupied with other concerns. The quantity of this type of publication is enormous, if one also includes those books with no literary and artistic importance, that is, if one starts with the attitude that this is a social phenomenon. The first problem arises from this: does the (relatively) mass publication of such literature coincide with definite historical periods, with the symptoms of deep socio-political upheavals? Can one say that it is like a collection of indefinite and generic *cahiers de doléance*[52] of a particular type? At the same time one must also observe that a part of this literature expresses the interests of dominant or dispossessed groups and has a reactionary and backward character. It would be interesting to compile a list of these books, 'utopias' proper, so-called philosophical novels, books that attribute to distant and little-known, but real, countries specific customs and institutions that one wants to contrast with those of one's own country. More's *Utopia*, Bacon's *New Atlantis*, Fénelon's *The Island of Delights* and *Salento* (but also his *Adventures of Telemachus*), Swift's *Gulliver's Travels*, etc. In Italy one should remember the reactionary fragments of Federico De Roberto and Vittorio Imbriani (*Naufragazia*, fragment of an unpublished novel with a foreword by Gino Doria in *Nuova Antologia*, 1 August 1934).[53]

2) In his article on 'Federico Cesi linceo' in *Nuova Antologia* of 1 August 1930, Giuseppe Gabrieli states that there is a historico-

---

[51] I.e. for the 'history of the subaltern social groups' – the general title of the notebook (Q 25) in which this note was included.

[52] Statements of grievances drawn up by the three estates in France before the Revolution of 1789.

[53] De Roberto's posthumous fragments were parts of the unfinished novels *L'ebbrezza* and *L'arcipelago della fortuna* (published in *La Fiera Letteraria* IV (1928) nos. 3, 4 and 27). The chapter from the latter is an allegorical satire on parliamentarism. De Roberto was a brilliant but uneven novelist who identified with Italian imperialism (in 1911) and fascism (in 1923) prior to his death in 1927. Vittorio Imbriani (1840–86) had shifted from Garibaldism to monarchism after the Unification.

ideological connection between the Counter-Reformation (which, according to Gabrieli, set against individualism, sharpened by Humanism and given free rein by Protestantism, the Roman (!) spirit of collegiality, discipline, corporation and hierarchy, for the reconstruction (!) of society), the Academies (like that of the Lincei set up by Cesi[54] which fostered the collegial work of scientists, quite different from that of the university centres which had remained medieval in their methods and forms) and the ideas and audacities of the great theories, the palingenetic reforms and the utopian reconstructions of human coexistence (*City of the Sun, New Atlantis*, etc.)

This connection is too strained, unilateral, mechanical and superficial. It can more justifiably be maintained that the most famous utopias were born in Protestant countries, and that even in the countries of the Counter-Reformation, utopias are rather an expression (the only possible one and in certain forms) of the 'modern' spirit, which is essentially contrary to the Counter-Reformation. (All of Campanella's work is a document of this 'underhand' effort to cut away at the Counter-Reformation from within; besides, like all restorations, the latter was not a homogeneous bloc, but a substantial, if not a formal, combination between the old and the new.) Utopias are created by individual intellectuals who in formal terms go back to the Socratic rationalism of Plato's *Republic*, and in terms of substance reflect, greatly misshapen, the conditions of instability and rebellion latent in the popular masses of the age. They are basically the political manifestos of intellectuals who want to create the optimum state. One should also take into account the scientific discoveries of the time and scientistic rationalism, which was first expressed precisely in the period of the Counter-Reformation. In its own way, Machiavelli's *Prince* was also a utopia (cf. in this

[54] Federico Cesi was a co-founder of the Accademia dei Lincei (Rome, 1603), Italy's first and most prestigious scientific academy. It was suppressed and merged with the Accademia d'Italia in 1939, reviving in 1944.

[55] This view of Campanella as essentially opposed to the Counter-Reformation reflects a 'deist' and 'freethinking' image of Campanella put forward by Luigi Amabile and by Croce (*Materialismo storico*, Chapter VII). This interpretation has since been challenged, and the many pro-papal and theocratic elements in Campanella's work have been reassessed. The fact remains that Gramsci is using here the Amabile-Croce view of Campanella as heretic to support the historical nexus heresy-Protestantism-bourgeois revolution (see V 15) against the move in fascist ideology to recoup the nexus 'Roman spirit' – Counter-Reformation-restoration which is evident in Gabrieli's article (compare VIII 7 on Curzio Malaparte).

connection some notes in another notebook).[56] One can say that Humanism itself, that is, a certain form of individualism, was suitable terrain for the rise of utopias and politico-philosophical constructions. With the Counter-Reformation the Church definitively cut itself off from the 'humble' masses in order to serve the 'powerful'. Through utopias individual intellectuals attempted to solve a series of problems of vital importance to the humble masses, that is, they tried to find a link between intellectuals and people. They must, therefore, be considered the historical forerunners of the Jacobins and the French Revolution, the event that put an end to the Counter-Reformation and spread the heresy of liberalism, much more effective against the Church than the Protestant heresy.[57]

3) Ezio Chiòrboli's article on Anton Francesco Doni in *Nuova Antologia* of 1 May 1928: an interesting profile of this publicist, very popular in his time (the sixteenth century), witty, caustic, modern.[58] Doni dealt with an infinite number of problems of all kinds, anticipating many scientific innovations. His inclinations were towards what today would be called (vulgar) materialism: he mentions the importance of the facial angle and the specific signs of criminality two centuries before Camper (Petrus, Dutch, 1722–1789), and, two and a half centuries before Lavater (Johann Kaspar, Swiss, born Zurich, 1741–1801) and Gall (Franz Joseph, German, 1758–1828), he spoke about the functions of the intellect and the parts of the brain delegated to them. He wrote a utopia, *Mondo pazzo o savio* – 'an imaginative social reconstruction painted with many of the iridescences and anxieties which torment contemporary socialism' – which he may have taken from More's *Utopia*. He knew More's book and he himself published it in Lando's Italian translation. 'Yet the invention is no longer the same, just as it is no longer the same as that of Plato in the *Republic* nor of any other writer, even obscure or unknown; for he made it, changed it, reshaped it in his own way, so that he has now given life to another that is truly his, and which he is so taken by that it comes out in the *Marmi* and here and there in various works and opuscules in this or that

---

56   See especially Q 13 § 1 (SPN, p. 125).

57   On the French Revolution as a heresy, see V 15.

58   Anton Francesco Doni (1513–74). The *Mondo pazzo o savio* is one of a series of satirical dialogues, the *Mondi* (1552–53), contrasting real and ideal worlds.

detail or in this or that feeling.' For a bibliography on Doni see the edition of *I Marmi* edited by Chiòrboli in the Laterza series 'Scrittori d'Italia' and the Doni anthology published by Treves, 'Le più belle pagine'.

4) Shakespeare's *Tempest* (the opposition between Caliban and Prospero; the utopian nature of Caliban's speeches). See the article 'Pensiero e soggetti economici in Shakespeare' by Achille Loria in *Nuova Antologia* of 1 August 1928. This can be used as an initial selection of the socio-political passages in Shakespeare and as an indirect document of the way the common people of the day thought. With regard to *The Tempest*, see Renan's *Caliban* and *L'Eau de Jouvence.*[59]

Q 25 § 7.

14 Moments of Intensely Collective and Unitary Life in the National Development of the Italian People

Within the context of the development of national life from 1800 onwards, examine all the moments in which the Italian people has been assigned the resolution of an at least potentially common task, when a collective (in depth and breadth) and unified action or movement could thus have occurred. In the various historical phases, these moments may have been different in nature and of differing national-popular importance. What is important in this investigation is the potential character (and therefore the extent to which this potentiality has been translated into action) of the collective and unitary dimension, namely its territorial extent (the region answers to this requirement, if not indeed the province) and its mass intensity (the greater or lesser number of participants, the greater or lesser positive and even actively negative repercussion the movement has had in the various strata of the population).

The nature and character of these moments may have been various: wars, revolutions, plebiscites, general elections of particular importance. Wars: 1848–49, 1859, 1860, 1866, 1870, in Africa (Eritrea and Libya), the world war. Revolutions: 1820–21, 1831, 1848–49, 1860, the Sicilian fasci, 1898, 1904, 1914,

---

[59] These two *Drames philosophiques* by Renan, sequels to Shakespeare's *Tempest*, are mentioned in Loria's article cited here.

1919–20, 1924–25. Plebiscites for the formation of the Kingdom; 1859–60, 1866, 1870.[60] General elections: with differing extension of suffrage. Typical elections: the one that brought the Left to power in 1876, the one following the widening of the suffrage after 1880, the one after 1898. The election of 1913 is the first with distinct popular characteristics because of the very large participation of the peasants. That of 1919 is the most important of all because of the proportional and provincial character of the vote, which forced the parties to group themselves and because throughout the territory, for the first time the same parties stood with (roughly) the same programmes. To a much greater and more organic extent than in 1913 (when the uninominal college limited the possibilities and falsified the mass political positions because of the constricting delimitation of the colleges), in 1919 throughout the territory, in a single day, the most active segment of the Italian population raised the same questions and sought to resolve them in its historical-political consciousness. The significance of the elections of 1919 lies in the sum of the 'unifying elements', both positive and negative, that came together within them. The war had been a unifying element of the first order in that it had made the large masses aware of the importance that the construction of the governmental apparatus has also for the destiny of each single individual, as well as having posed a series of concrete problems, both general·and specific, which reflected the national-popular unity.[61] One can state that for the people the elections of 1919

---

[60] Liberal and carbonarist risings in the Kingdom of the Two Sicilies (1820), Piedmont (1821), Modena and Emilia (1831). Revolutions in Italian states and war against Austrians (1848–49). War of French against Austrians and annexation of Lombardy to Piedmont (1859). Annexation of central Italian states and Kingdom of Two Sicilies by Piedmont and insurrectionary movements before and after Garibaldi's campaign (1860). War against Austria with Prussian support to annex Venetia (1866). Annexation of Rome after withdrawal of French garrison during Franco-Prussian war (1870). Ratification of union of these territories with Italy by plebiscite. Socialist agitations of Sicilian *fasci* (1893–94). Ethiopian war culminating in Italian defeat at Adowa (1896). Brutally crushed working-class agitation in several major cities – Milan, Florence, Bari, Palermo, Naples, etc. – (1898). The first general strike (1904). War with Turkey in Libya (1911–12). Red Week (1914: see footnote 28 above). Post-war agitation of the Red Years (1919–20) culminating in the occupation of the factories. Disturbances during the Matteotti crisis (summer-autumn 1924) leading to Muśsolini's introduction of the 'exceptional laws' in January 1925.

[61] See Gramsci's articles on the 1919 elections (ON, pp. 307–16; SPW, I pp. 127–29) stressing their revolutionary function because of the mass adhesion to the socialist

had the character of a constituent assembly, although they did not
have it for 'any one' party of the time. (The elections of 1913 also
had this character, as anyone can recall who witnessed the
elections in the regional centres where the transformation of the
electoral body was greater and as was demonstrated by the high
percentage of voters. There was a widespread mystical conviction
that everything would be different after the vote, that it was a real
social palingenesis: at least in Sardinia.) In this contradiction and
separation between the people and the parties lay the historical
drama of 1919. It was understood immediately only by a few of
the shrewder and more intelligent ruling groups (who had more
to fear for their future). It should be noted that the traditional
party of the constituent assembly in Italy, the Republicans,
showed the minimum of historical sensitivity and political ability
and allowed the ruling groups of the right to impose their
programme and line (an abstract and retrospective defence of
intervention in the war). In their way the people were looking to
the future (over the question of intervention too). Here lies the
implicit character of a constituent assembly that the people gave
to the elections of 1919. The parties were looking to the past (only
to the past) concretely and to the future 'abstractly', 'generically',
in terms of 'have faith in your party', rather than in terms of a
constructive historical-political conception. Among the other
differences between 1913 and 1919, one should recall the active
participation of the Catholics, who had their own men, their own
party and their own programme.[62] In 1913 also, the Catholics had
participated in the elections, but through the Gentiloni pact and
in a devious way that falsified the significance of the alliance and
the influence of the traditional political forces.[63] For 1919 one
should remember the speech delivered by Giolitti which had a
(retrospectively) constituent slant and the attitude of the
Giolittians to the Catholics as emerges from Luigi Ambrosini's

programme. After the elections, the expanded parliamentary PSI should struggle to
establish 'the sufficient and necessary conditions in which the class of producers can build
the apparatus of its social power' (ON, p. 313).

[62] i.e. the Popular Party (PPI): see footnote 42 on p. 412.

[63] The Gentiloni pact was a deal made in the run-up to the 1913 general election, before
the papal *non-expedit* preventing the formation of a Catholic party was lifted. Ottorino
Gentiloni of the Catholic Electoral Union promised Catholic votes to those liberal
candidates who agreed to support Catholic policies (defence of Catholic private
education, opposition to divorce, etc.). Over 200 deputies were elected through the pact.

articles in *La Stampa*.[64] The Giolittians were in reality the winners of the elections in the sense that they placed the stamp of a constituent assembly without a constituent assembly on the elections themselves and succeeded in drawing attention from the future to the past.

Q 19 § 19.

15 Popular Aspects of the Risorgimento: Volunteers and Popular Intervention

Gioventù Fascista of 24 May publishes the following message by Italo Balbo (reported in the *Corriere della Sera* of 21 May 1932):

> The original creations of Italian history and civilization, from the day in which the country reawoke from centuries of lethargy until today, are due to youth volunteer action. Garibaldi's holy rabble, the heroic interventionism of 1915, the Black Shirts of the Fascist Revolution have brought unity and power to Italy, they have turned a scattered people into a nation. Those generations now embarking on life under the banner of the Lictor have the task of giving the name of Rome to the new century.

The assertion that modern Italy has been characterized by volunteer action is correct (one can add the *arditi* in the war), but it needs to be pointed out that volunteerism, for all its undeniable historical merit, has been a surrogate for popular intervention.[65] In this respect it has been a solution of compromise with the passivity of the national masses. Volunteerism-passivity, they go together more than one thinks. The solution through volunteer action is an authoritarian one, a solution from above, formally legitimized with the consent of the 'best', as the expression has it. But the 'best' are not enough to build a lasting history; it requires the broadest and most numerous national-popular energies.

Q 19 § 11.

---

[64] In a speech at Dronero on 12 October 1919, Giolitti criticized the powers of the executive to act above Parliament in foreign affairs, as exemplified by the Treaty of London, negotiated secretly by Salandra and Sonnino, which committed Italy to intervention on the Allied side in the war.

[65] On volunteer action see SPN, pp. 202–5. The 'arditi' were volunteer commando squads in the Italian army. The term was also used by the 'arditi del popolo', formed to control the fascist squads in the summer of 1921.

16 Interpretations of the Risorgimento [i]

All the intense activity of interpreting Italy's past and the series of ideological constructions and historical fictions that have derived from it is predominantly linked to the 'claim' of finding a national unity, at least *de facto*, over the whole period from Rome to the present (and often even before Rome, as in the case of Gioberti's 'Pelasgians' and other more recent examples).[66] How did this claim originate, how was it maintained and why does it survive even today? Is it a sign of strength or of weakness? Is it the reflection of new self-confident social formations which seek (and create) for themselves titles of nobility in the past? Or is it instead the reflection of a sinister 'will to believe', an element of ideological fanaticism (and fanaticization) whose purpose is precisely to 'patch up' structural weaknesses and prevent a feared collapse? The latter seems to me the correct interpretation, together with the fact of the excessive importance (in relation to the economic formations) of the intellectuals, i.e. of the petty bourgeoisie, in comparison with the economically backward and politically powerless classes. In reality national unity is felt to be something precarious because 'wild' forces, imprecisely known and elementarily destructive, are agitating at its base. The iron dictatorship of the intellectuals and of certain urban groups with landed property maintains its compactness only by overexciting its militant element with this myth of historical fatalism, stronger than any deficiency and any political and military ineptitude. It is on this terrain that an organic adhesion of the national-popular masses to the state is replaced by a selection of 'volunteers' of the 'nation' abstractly conceived. Nobody has realized that precisely the problem posed by Machiavelli when he proclaimed the necessity of replacing the untrustworthy, temporary mercenaries by a national militia cannot be resolved until 'volunteerism' has been superseded by mass 'national-popular' action, since volunteerism is an intermediate, equivocal solution, as dangerous as the phenomenon of mercenaries.

Q 19 § 5 (excerpt).

[66] See footnote 13 above.

17 Interpretations of the Risorgimento [ii]

Must the political movement that led to national unification and to the formation of the Italian state necessarily end up in nationalism and militaristic imperialism? One can argue that this outlet is anachronistic and antihistorical (i.e. artificial and short lived). It is in reality contrary to all the Italian traditions, first Roman, then Catholic. These traditions are cosmopolitan. That the political movement should react against tradition and give rise to an intellectualistic nationalism can be explained, but one is not dealing with an organic-popular reaction. Besides, even in the Risorgimento Mazzini and Gioberti sought to graft the nationalist movement on to the cosmopolitan tradition, to create the myth of a mission of Italy reborn into a new European and international Cosmopolis. But this is a rhetorical and verbal myth, founded on the past and not on present conditions already formed or in the process of development. (Such myths have always stirred the whole of Italian history, even the most recent, which extends from Quintino Sella to Enrico Corradini and D'Annunzio.)[67] Because an event took place in the past this does not mean that it must be reproduced in the present and the future. The conditions for military expansion in the present and the future do not exist and do not seem to be in the process of formation. Modern expansion is of a finance-capitalist kind. At present in Italy the element 'man' is either 'man-capital' or 'man-labour'. Italian expansion can only be that of 'man-labour' and the intellectual who represents 'man-labour' is not the traditional intellectual, swollen with rhetoric and literary memories of the past. Traditional Italian cosmopolitanism should become a modern type of cosmopolitanism, one that can assure the best conditions for the development of Italian 'man-labour' in whatever part of the world he happens to be. Not the citizen of the world as *civis romanus* or as Catholic, but as producer of civilization. One can therefore maintain that the Italian tradition is continued dialectically in the working people and their intellectuals, not in the traditional citizen and the traditional

---

[67] Quintino Sella (1827–84) was Finance Minister in 1864–66 and Prime Minister in 1869–73. Gramsci records in Q 2 § 42: 'In reply to Theodor Mommsen who asked with what idea Italy was going to Rome, Quintino Sella said: *that of science.*' Corradini (see footnote 8 above) conceived of the classical Roman past as the mythical foundation of the present; D'Annunzio (see footnote 38 on p. 54) promoted the cult of the glorious Renaissance spirit, aristocratism, the superman and national destiny.

intellectual. The Italian people are the people with the greatest 'national' interest in a modern form of cosmopolitanism. Not only the worker but also the peasant, especially the southern peasant. It is in the tradition of the Italian people and Italian history to collaborate in rebuilding the world in an economically unified way not in order to dominate it hegemonically and appropriate the fruit of others' labour but to exist and develop precisely as the Italian people. It can be shown that Caesar is at the source of this tradition. Nationalism of the French stamp is an anachronistic excrescence in Italian history, proper to people who have their heads turned backwards like the damned in Dante. The 'mission' of the Italian people lies in the recovery of Roman and medieval cosmopolitanism, but in its most modern and advanced form. Even indeed a proletarian nation, as Pascoli wanted; proletarian as a nation because it has been the reserve army of foreign capitalism, because together with the Slavic peoples it has given skilled workers to the entire world.[68] For this very reason, it must joint the modern front struggling to reorganize also the non-Italian world, which it has helped to create with its labour.

Q 19 § 5 (excerpt).

18 Gioberti and Jacobinism[69]

Gioberti's attitude to Jacobinism before and after 1848. After 1848, in the *Rinnovamento*, not only does Gioberti not mention the panic which 1793 had spread during the first half of the century, but indeed he shows clearly that he has sympathy for the Jacobins (he justifies the extermination of the Girondins and the fight on two fronts by the Jacobins: against the foreign invaders and against the reactionaries at home, even though he makes a

[68] On Pascoli and the 'proletarian nation' see footnote 8 above.

[69] Vincenzo Gioberti (1808–1852), liberal Catholic philosopher who worked mostly in exile in Paris and Brussels (from 1833–48 and from 1849–52). *Il primato morale e civile degli italiani* (1843) employed various historiographical myths of Italy's origin and development to theorize a return of the European peoples to Catholicism under the spiritual dominance of the Papacy, and suggested a linking of the Italian states in a confederation under the Pope and excluding Austria. After the revolutions of 1848–49 when, as head of the Sardinian (Piedmont) government, Gioberti witnessed the failure of this 'neo-Guelph' strategy, he returned to exile and wrote *Il rinnovamento civile d'Italia* (1851), which abandoned the federalist solution for a unitarist one, whereby the states would unify under the initiative and hegemony of Piedmont (i.e. the solution of Cavour in 1859–60).

very restrained reference to the Jacobins' methods which could have been gentler, etc.). This post-1848 attitude of Gioberti's to French Jacobinism should be noted as a cultural fact of great importance: it was justified by the excesses of the reaction after 1848, which led to a better understanding and justification of the wild energy of French Jacobinism.

But in addition to this passage one should note that in the *Rinnovamento* Gioberti shows himself to be a genuine Jacobin, at least in theory and in the given situation in Italy. The elements of this Jacobinism can be broadly summed up thus: 1) In the affirmation of the political and military hegemony of Piedmont which ought, as a region, to be what Paris was for France: this point is most interesting and should be studied in the pre-1848 Gioberti too. Gioberti felt the lack in Italy of a popular centre to the movement of national revolution as Paris was for France. His understanding of this shows his political realism. Before 1848, Piedmont and Rome had to be the centres of propulsion, the first for politics-armed forces, the second for ideology-religion. After 1848, Rome no longer has the same importance, indeed Gioberti says that the movement must be against the Papacy. 2) Gioberti, albeit vaguely, has the concept of the Jacobin 'national-popular', of political hegemony, namely the alliance between bourgeoisie-intellectuals (*ingegno*) and the people. This holds for economics (and Gioberti's economic ideas are vague but interesting) and for literature (culture), where his ideas are clearer and more concrete since not so much hangs in the balance. In the *Rinnovamento* (part II, the chapter 'On Writers') he says:

> . . . A literature cannot be national unless it is popular; for, although its creation is the work of a few, its use and enjoyment must be universal. In addition, since it must express common ideas and feelings and bring to the surface those senses which lie hidden and confused in the heart of the multitudes, its practitioners must not only aim for the good of the people but must also depict their spirit, such that this becomes not only the end but in a way also the beginning of civil literature. And this can be seen from the fact that this literature does not rise to the height of its perfection and efficacy unless it is incorporated and becomes in a sense one with the nation, etc.

At any rate, the fact that the absence of an 'Italian Jacobinism' was felt is apparent from Gioberti. And Gioberti should be studied in this light. Futhermore, it should be noted how

Gioberti, in both the *Primato* and the *Rinnovamento*, shows himself to be a *strategist* of the national movement and not just a tactician. His realism leads him to make compromises, but always in the sphere of the general strategic plan. Gioberti's weakness, as a statesman, can be traced to the fact that he was always an exile. He thus did not know the men he had to manipulate and lead and he had no loyal friends (i.e. a party). The more he was a strategist the more he needed to base himself on real forces. He did not know these forces and could not dominate and direct them. (For the concept of national-popular literature, Gioberti and his tempered romanticism should be studied.) Gioberti should also be studied in order to analyse what other notes refer to as the 'historical node of 1848-49'[70] and the Risorgimento in general, but I feel the most important cultural point is this one of 'Gioberti as Jacobin' – a theoretical Jacobin, naturally, since in practice he was unable to apply his theories.

Q 17 § 9.

19 Formation and Spread of the New Bourgeoisie in Italy

I have noted elsewhere that one could make a 'molecular' study of the Italian writings of the Middle Ages to understand the process of intellectual formation of the bourgeoisie, whose historical development was to culminate in the communes and then break up and dissolve. The same could be done for the period 1750–1850, when one has the new bourgeois formation which culminates in the Risorgimento. Here too Groethuysen's model (*Origines de l'esprit bourgeois en France*: I. *L'Eglise et la Bourgeoisie*, Paris, 1927) could be of use, extended of course with those themes that are specific to Italian social history. The conceptions of the world, of the state and of life against which the bourgeois spirit had to struggle in Italy are not like those that existed in France.

Foscolo and Manzoni can, in a certain sense, be made typical for Italy. Foscolo extols the literary and artistic glories of the past (see the *Sepolcri* and the *Discorsi civili*). His is essentially a 'rhetorical' conception (although one should note that in his time this

---

[70] See Q 19 § 22, 49, 51 and Q 8 § 33 and 93.

rhetoric had a live practical effectiveness and was therefore 'realistic').[71] In Manzoni we find new and more strictly bourgeois (technically speaking) elements. Manzoni glorifies commerce and debases poetry (rhetoric). Leters to Fauriel. In the *Opere inedite* there are passages where Manzoni censures the one-sidedness of poets who despise the traders' 'thirst for gold' and refuse to acknowledge the audacity of navigators while they speak of themselves as superhuman. In a letter to Fauriel[72] he writes: 'Think what would make the world more uneasy, to find itself without bankers or without poets; which of these two professions is more useful, not for the comfort, but for the *culture* of humanity?' (See Carlo Franelli, 'Il Manzoni e l'idea dello scrittore' in *Critica Fascista*, 15 December 1931). Franelli observes:

> He puts works of history and political economy higher than a rather (?!) light literature. In the letter to his friend Fauriel, he makes very explicit statements about the quality of Italian culture of the time. As for the poets, he finds their traditional megalomania offensive. He notes that today they are losing all of that esteem which they enjoyed in the past. He repeatedly recalls that he was fond of poetry in his 'youth'.

Q8 § 3.

20 Ugo Foscolo and Italian Literary Rhetoric

The *Sepolcri* must be considered the major 'source' of the rhetorical cultural tradition that sees in monuments a stimulus for exalting national glories. The 'nation' is not the people, or the past that continues in the 'people', but the set of material things that recall the past. This is a strange distortion which was explicable in the early nineteenth century, when it was a case of awakening latent energies and rousing the young, but which is a 'distortion' precisely because it has become a purely decorative,

---

[71] Ugo Foscolo (1778–1827), patriotic writer, went into exile in 1816 after the restoration of Austrian rule in Lombardy-Venetia. He based his concept of the Italian nation both on historical precedent (an 'epoch of liberty' from 1070 to 1530 had preceded the 'epoch of servitude' to the foreign yoke) and on the collective memory of past national glories, kept alive by the tombs of illustrious Italians like Machiavelli, Michelangelo, Galileo etc. celebrated in the poem 'Dei Sepolcri' (On Tombs), 1807.

[72] This letter – of 2 June 1832 – is in fact to Marco Coen, not Claude Fauriel. On Manzoni see Section VII below.

external and rhetorical motif. (The inspiration of tombs in
Foscolo is not the same as in so-called sepulchral poetry: it is a
'political' inspiration, as he himself writes in his letter to
Guillon.)[73]

Q5 § 32.

21 Alfredo Oriani[74]

He should be studied as the most honest and enthusiastic
proponent of Italy's national-popular greatness among the Italian
intellectuals of the old generation. However his position is not
critical-reconstructive; hence all the reasons for his failure.
Whom did this work really address? Not the ruling classes, from
whom he nevertheless hoped for recognition and honours,
despite his corrosive diatribes. Not the republicans, although his
recriminatory attitude is similar. *La lotta politica* seems like the
manifesto for a grand democratic national-popular movement,
but Oriani is too steeped in idealist philosophy of the type that
developed in the Restoration period to be able to speak to the
people as a leader and an equal at the same time or to make the
people join in a criticism of themselves and their own weaknesses
without making them lose faith in their own strength and their
own future. Oriani's weakness lies in the purely intellectual
character of his criticisms, which make him doctrinaire and
abstract. But there is a quite healthy movement in his thought
which is worth further study. His recent return to fame is more
a ceremonial embalmment than a resuscitation of his living
thought.

Q8 § 165.

---

[73] Foscolo wrote of 'Dei Sepolcri', in reply to his critic Guillon: 'The author considers
tombs in a political light; he aims to inspire political emulation in Italians with his examples
of the nations which honour the memory of the tombs of great men: thus he has had to
"travel further than Young, Hervey and Gray", and preach the resurrection not of bodies
but of virtues' (*Opere*, Volume VI, Florence 1972, p. 518). This Risorgimento myth re-
emerged in fascism as the tradition of illustrious precursors of the national destiny.

[74] Alfredo Oriani (1852–1909) novelist and dramatist, wrote a panoramic history of Italy
in terms of 'idea-forces', *La lotta politica in Italia* (1892). He saw the Unification as an
awkward compromise between the national ideal (Mazzini), military force (Garibaldi) and
political pragmatism (Cavour), and from this he derived Italy's weaknesses in the 1890s.
Art was divorced from the national consciousness. The diplomatic straitjacket imposed by
the Triple Alliance was holding Italy back from completing its national mission. On
Oriani, see also Q 19 § 5 and Q 6 § 69. After being practically disregarded for nearly
twenty years the *Lotta politica* was exhumed by *La Voce* as a clarion call of the new
nationalism. In 1924 Oriani received an official posthumous blessing as a precursor of
fascism and Mussolini began editing his complete works.

22 Italian National Culture

In his 'Letter to Umberto Fracchia on criticism' (*Pègaso*, August 1930), Ugo Ojetti[75] makes two notable observations. 1) He recalls that Thibaudet divides criticism into three classes: that of the professional critics, that of the authors themselves and that of the *honnêtes gens*, the 'enlightened' public who, ultimately, are the real stock exchange of literary values, since in France there is a large public ready to follow all of the vicissitudes of literature.[76] In Italy, according to Ojetti, there is no criticism by the public (an enlightened *moyen* public, like the one in France, is lacking or is too small): 'there is no belief, or if you prefer illusion, that he [the writer] creates a work of national importance, or indeed of historical importance in the case of the best writers; because, as you [Fracchia] say, "every year and every day that passes has its literature all the same; so it has always been and so it will always be. It is absurd to wait or to prognosticate or to invoke for tomorrow the reality of today. Each century, each portion of a century, has always exalted its own works. In fact, if anything, each has been led to exaggerate their importance, greatness, value and endurance." True, but not in Italy.' (Ojetti is discussing Fracchia's open letter to Senator Gioacchino Volpe, published in *L'Italia Letteraria* on 22 June 1930, which refers to an address of Volpe's given at the Academy during an award ceremony. Volpe said, among other things, 'No great paintings, historical works or novels are being produced. One who looks closely, though, will see in current literature latent forces, the desire to rise higher, and a few good and promising achievements.')[77]

2) Ojetti's other observation is this: 'The slight popularity of our past literature, of our classics. It is true: in English and

---

[75] Ugo Ojetti (1871–1946), a dominant figure in Italian literary culture during the 1920s and 30s. Editor of the *Corriere della Sera* in 1926–27, founder of the reviews *Pègaso* (1922) and *Pan* (1923), author of the anecdotal essays *Cose viste* (in the *Corriere* 1921–43 and collected in book form at various intervals), Ojetti was the quintessential bourgeois *littérateur*, cornerstone of the conservative cultural edifice of fascism and despised by younger writers.

[76] Albert Thibaudet (1874–1936), major French critic in the first part of this century. The reference is to his *Physiologie de la critique* (1930), based on a subdivision into 'la critique des honnêtes gens, la critique des professionels et la critique des artistes'.

[77] Gioacchino Volpe (1876–1971), historian who specialized in medieval Italy, parliamentary deputy 1924–29, then senator. He was also a historical apologist for fascism, producing *L'Italia in cammino* (Italy on the march) (1927) and *Storia del movimento fascista* (1939).

French criticism one often reads comparisons between living and classical authors, etc.'

This observation is fundamental for a historical judgement of present Italian culture. The past does not live in the present, it is not an essential part of the present; in the history of our national culture there is no continuity or unity. The affirmation of continuity and unity is only rhetorical or amounts to mere evocative propaganda. It is a practical act which aims to create artificially that which does not exist. It is not an actualized reality. (There did seem to be some continuity and unity from the Risorgimento to Carducci and Pascoli, who could refer back as far as Latin literature. With D'Annunzio and his successors, though, this was broken off.) The past, literature included, is not an element of life, only of a bookish and scholastic culture. This means then that national feeling is recent, if indeed we should not say that it is still only being formed, re-affirming that in Italy literature has never been a national fact, but a 'cosmopolitan' one.

Some typical passages can be extracted from Fracchia's open letter to Senator Volpe: 'Just a little more courage, conviction (!), faith (!) would be enough to transform the tight-lipped praise that Your Excellency has offered to the literature of today into open and explicit praise; to say that the literature of today has not only latent but also uncovered and visible (!) forces which wait only (!) to be seen (!) and recognized by those who ignore them', etc. Volpe had given a 'straight' paraphrase of Giusti's humorous verses: 'Heroes, heroes, what are you up to? – We're straining after the future' and Fracchia moans and groans that these strainings are not appreciated for what they are.[78]

Fracchia has often threatened publishers who print too many translations with legislative corporative measures to protect Italian writers (one may recall the ordinance introduced by Undersecretary of the Interior Bianchi, which had to be 'interpreted' and *de facto* revoked and which was connected with a press campaign of Fracchia's).[79] But to return to Fracchia's

---

[78] 'Eroi, eroi, che fate voi?'/'Ponziamo il poi': opening lines of Giusti's 'Il poeta e gli eroi di poltrona' (The poet and the arm-chair heroes) (1844), a satirical jibe at the Risorgimento moderates Gioberti and Cesare Balbo for their apparently placid postponement of the task of national unification.

[79] The reference here is probably to a circular sent out by Bianchi in August 1929 to remove 'certain over-excessive impediments placed on some publishers and booksellers by the authorities of Public Security against the sale of works by Russian authors like

argument, quoted above: every century, every fraction of a century, not only has its own literature, but also exalts it; so much so that literary histories have had to revalue many highly praised works which are now recognized as worthless. In general terms Fracchia's point is correct, but we must deduce from it that the present period of literature is incapable of interpreting its time, that it is removed from the real life of the nation. So that works are not even exalted for 'practical reasons', works which will perhaps later be considered artistically null once their 'practical' function has ended. Is it true, though, that there are no widely read books? There are, but they are foreign, and they would be read even more if they were translated, like the books of Remarque, etc.[80] In reality, the present is without a literature that meets its most elementary and profound needs because current literature, apart from rare exceptions, is not tied to national-popular life, but to restricted groups that act as if the life of the nation were in their hands.

Fracchia complains about criticism, which only looks at the great masterpieces, which is rarefied in the perfection of aesthetic theories, etc. But if books were examined from the standpoint of the history of culture he would still complain, and all the more because the ideological and cultural content of current literature is practically nil. What is more, it is contradictory and quietly jesuitical.

It is not even true (as Ojetti writes in his letters to Fracchia) that in Italy a 'criticism by the public' does not exist. It exists, but in its own way, because the public reads a great deal and, thus, chooses among what is available. Why does this public still prefer Alexandre Dumas and Carolina Invernizio and avidly read its way through detective novels? Besides, this criticism of the Italian public has an organization of its own, represented by the publishers and the editors of daily newspapers and popular periodicals. It is expressed in the choice of serials to publish, in the translation of foreign books, not only current but also old, very old, ones and in the repertories of theatrical companies. Nor is

Gorky, Gogol, Dostoyevsky, Tolstoy, Turgenev and also Jack London. . . .' (note in *L'Italia Letteraria*, I (1929) 21). The publication of foreign works and translations increased under the regime. 818 were published in 1935 as against 443 in 1932, and a total of 2849 translated books came out in 1932–36.

[80] Remarque's anti-militarist *All Quiet on the Western Front*, banned by the fascist censors, was widely read in Italy in a French translation published in 1929.

this a case of total exoticism since the public's choice in music includes Verdi, Puccini and Mascagni, who naturally do not have counterparts in literature. Furthermore, foreign audiences often prefer Verdi, Puccini and Mascagni to their own national and contemporary musicians.

This fact is the most peremptory confirmation that in Italy writers are separated from the public and that the public seeks 'its' literature abroad because it feels that this literature is more 'its own' than the so-called national literature. In this fact lies an essential problem of national life. If it is true that each century or fraction of a century has its own literature, it is not always true that this literature is produced in the same national community. Every people has its own literature, but this can come to it from another people, in other words the people in question can be subordinated to the intellectual and moral hegemony of other peoples. This is often the most strident paradox for many monopolistic tendencies of a nationalistic and repressive character: while they make magnificent hegemonic plans, they fail to realize that they are the object of foreign hegemonies, just as while they make imperialistic plans, they are in fact the object of other imperialisms. On the other hand, it may be that the central political leadership understands the real situation perfectly and is trying to overcome it. It is clear, though, that in this case the literary men are not helping the central political leadership in their efforts to achieve their goal, and their empty brains obstinately persist in exalting the nation so as not to feel the oppressive weight of the hegemony on which they depend.

Q 23 § 57.

23 French and Italian Historical Culture

The works of French historians and French culture in general have been able to develop and become 'national-popular' because of the very complexity and variety of French political history in the last 150 years. The dynastic tendency has dissolved through the succession of three dynasties that were radically antagonistic towards each other – the legitimist, the liberal-conservative, the military-plebiscitary – and through the succession of republican governments also strongly different from each other – the Jacobin, the radical socialist, and the present one.[81] A unilinear national 'hagiography' is impossible: any attempt of this sort appears immediately sectarian, false, utopian, and anti-national because one is forced to cut out or undervalue unforgettable pages of national history (see Maurras' current line and Bainville's miserable history of France).[82] That is why the permanent element of these political variations, the people-nation, has become the protagonist of French history. Hence a type of political and cultural nationalism that goes beyond the bounds of the strictly nationalist parties and impregnates the whole culture. Hence also a close and dependent relationship between people-nation and intellectuals.

There is nothing of the sort in Italy, where one must search the past by torchlight to discover national feeling, and move with the aid of distinctions, interpretations, and discreet silences. If one praises Ferrucci, one must explain Maramaldo; if one extols Florence, then one must justify Clement VII and the papacy; if one praises Milan and the League, then one must explain Como and the cities favourable to Frederick Barbarossa; if one exalts Venice, then one must explain Julius II, etc.[83] The preconception that Italy has always been a nation complicates its entire history and requires anti-historical intellectual acrobatics. Consequently, in the history of the nineteenth century, there could not have been national unity, since the permanent element, the people-nation, was missing. On the one hand, the dynastic element had to prevail given the support it received from the state apparatus, and the divergent political currents could not have had a shared minimum objective. History was political propaganda, it aimed to create national unity – that is, the nation – from the

---

[81] References, respectively, to the Bourbons (1815–30), Louis-Philippe (1830–48) and Napoleon III (1851–70), and to the three French republics of 1792–1804, 1848–52 and 1870–1940.

[82] Charles Maurras (1868–1952), French reactionary, co-edited with Léon Daudet the nationalist-monarchist *Action Française*. Jacques Bainville (1879–1936), popularizing historian and a leading contributor to *Action Française*; his *Histoire de France* was published in 1924.

[83] Francesco Ferrucci (1489–1530) was the hero of the resistance of the last Florentine republic against combined papal and imperial forces in the 1528–30 siege. Fabrizio Maramaldo was the Neapolitan mercenary who killed him and Clement VII was Pope at the time. The Lombard League was an association of cities in Lombardy formed in 1167 to resist encroachments on their communal liberties and powers by the Holy Roman Emperor: Frederick I Barbarossa was Emperor from 1155–90. Pope Julius II repossessed the portions of the Papal States appropriated by Venice after joining the anti-Venetian League of Cambrai in 1509.

outside and against tradition, by basing itself on literature. It was a *wish*, not a must based on already existing conditions. Due to this position of theirs, the intellectuals had to distinguish themselves from the people, place themselves outside, create or reinforce among themselves a spirit of caste and have a deep *distrust* of the people, feeling them to be foreign, fearing them, because, in reality, the people were something unknown, a mysterious hydra with innumerable heads.

It seemed to me that some conditions existed in the present for overcoming this state of affairs, but they have not been exploited properly. Rhetoric has once again got the upper hand (the uncertainty in interpreting Caporetto offers an example of this present state of things, as does the polemic over the Risorgimento and, lately, over the Concordat). But one must not deny that many steps forward have been taken in every sense: to do so would be to fall into an opposite rhetoric. On the contrary, many intellectual movements, especially before the war, attempted to renew the culture, strip away its rhetoric and bring it nearer to the people, in other words nationalize it. (The two tendencies could be called nation-people and nation-rhetoric.)

(On this last subject see Volpe's *L'Italia in cammino*, which contains many factual inaccuracies and distortions and claims that a new rhetoric is being born; Croce's *Storia d'Italia*, which contains defects of the other kind, but not less dangerous, because history is dissolved into conceptual abstractions; also Prezzolini's books on Italian culture.)[84]

Q3 § 82.

24 Balzac

(Cf. some other notes: references to the admiration for Balzac by the founders of the philosophy of praxis; recently published letter

---

[84] Gioacchino Volpe, *L'Italia in cammino, l'ultimo cinquantennio* (Milan, 1927), a history of Italy since the Unification which, in Volpe's words, sought the seeds of the present régime in the past, stressing the moments of national expansion and nationalist fervour (Crispi's bellicose foreign policy, the Libyan war, Great War interventionism). Benedetto Croce, *Storia d'Italia dal 1871 al 1915* (Bari, 1928): Croce's historical vindication of post-Unification liberalism and the Giolitti system as well as of the renewal of Italian culture which accompanied it. Giuseppe Prezzolini's *La cultura italiana* appeared in two editions: Florence 1923 and (revised) Milan 1930.

by Engels where this admiration is critically justified.)[85] See Paul
Bourget's article 'Les idées politiques et sociales de Balzac' in *Les
Nouvelles Littéraires* of 8 August 1931. Bourget begins by noting
that today Balzac's ideas are being given increasingly more
importance: 'The traditionalist' – i.e. reactionary – 'school that
we see growing each day writes his name alongside those of
Bonald, Le Play and of Taine himself.' It was not so in the past.
Sainte-Beuve, in an article in the *Lundis* dedicated to Balzac after
his death, does not even mention his social and political ideas.
Although he admired Balzac the novelist, Taine denied him any
doctrinal importance. Even the Catholic critic, Caro, around the
beginning of the Second Empire, thought Balzac's ideas trifling.
Flaubert writes that the political and social ideas of Balzac are not
worth discussing, 'He was a Catholic, a legitimist, a property
owner,' says Flaubert, 'a splendid fellow, but second-rate.' And
Zola: 'There is nothing stranger than his support of absolute
power, when his talent is essentially democratic and he has
written the most revolutionary work.' Etc.

Bourget's article is understandable. The idea is to find in
Balzac the origin of the positivist but reactionary novel, to find
science in the service of reaction (as in Maurras), which is anyway
the true destiny of the positivism established by Comte.

Balzac and science. See the 'General Preface' to *The Human
Comedy* where Balzac writes that the naturalist will have the
eternal honour of having shown that

> the animal is a principle which derives its external form, or, to speak
> more precisely, its divergent forms, from the media in which it is called
> upon to develop itself. The species of zoology are the reslts of these
> differences. . . . Deeply imbued with this system . . . I observed that
> in this respect social life resembled nature. Does not society mould
> the human being according to the sphere in which he is called upon
> to act into as many different sorts of men as there are varieties in
> zoology? The differences which exist between the soldier, the
> artisan, the public functionary, the advocate, the man of leisure [oisif]
> (!!), the scientific man, the statesman, the merchant, the sailor, the
> poet, the poor man (!!), the priest are as considerable as, though more

[85] Gramsci's references are back to Q 8 § 209 and 230. Engels's letter to Margaret
Harkness, drafted in English in April 1888, was first published (in German) in *Die
Linkskurve*, vol. IV, no. 3, March 1932, under the title 'Ein unveröffentlichter Brief
Friedrich Engels über Balzac'. Gramsci's source of information about the letter and its
contents is not known. He refers to it in Q 8 § 230 as having been 'published just recently
(perhaps in 1931)'.

difficult to seize than, those which distinguish the wolf, the lion, the ass, the raven, the shark, the seal, the sheep.[86]

It is not surprising that Balzac wrote these things and maybe took them seriously and imagined he was building a complete social system on these metaphors. Nor does it in the least diminish the greatness of Balzac the artist. What is remarkable is that today Bourget and, as he puts it, the 'traditionalist school' should base themselves on these thin 'scientific' fantasies to build socio-political systems without the justification of the artistic activity.

Starting from these premises, Balzac sets himself the problem of 'making these social species as perfect as possible', of harmonizing them. But since the 'species' are created by the environment, it will be necessary to 'conserve' and organize the given environment in order to maintain and perfect the given species. It seems Flaubert was not mistaken in writing that Balzac's social ideas are not worth discussing. Bourget's article only shows how fossilized the French traditionalist school is.

Yet although Balzac's entire construction is useless as a 'practical programme' – i.e. from the standpoint of Bourget's examination – there are interesting elements in it for reconstructing Balzac's poetic world, his conception of the world insofar as it is artistically expressed, his 'realism' which, although it has reactionary ideological origins (restoration, monarchism, etc.) is not thereby any the less realism in action. The admiration that the founders of the philosophy of praxis had for Balzac is understandable: Balzac perceived clearly that man is the complex of the social conditions in which he has developed and lives, and that in order to 'change' man one has to change this complex of conditions. That Balzac is 'politically and socially' a reactionary is only apparent from the extra-artistic part of his writings (digressions, prefaces, etc.). That this 'complex of conditions' or 'environment' is in its turn understood 'naturalistically' is true as well; in fact Balzac precedes a definite current in French literature.

Q 14 § 41.

---

[86] *The Cat and Battledore and Other Tales* by Honoré de Balzac, translated by Philip Kent, London 1879 (translation slightly modified).

25 Julien Benda

His article 'Comment un écrivain sert-il l'universel?' in *Les Nouvelles Littéraires* of 2 November 1929, is a corollary of his book *La Trahison des clercs*.[87] He refers to a recent work, *Esprit und Geist* by Wechssler, which tries to demonstrate the national character of thought and to explain that the German *Geist* is quite different from the French *Esprit*. He invites the Germans not to forget this particularity of their genius, yet he considers himself to be working for the unification of peoples by virtue of an idea of André Gide's according to which the more one is particular the better one serves the general interest. Benda recalls the manifesto of 54 French writers published in *Le Figaro* of 29 July 1919 'Manifeste du parti de l'intelligence', where it says: 'Is it not by nationalizing itself that a literature takes on a more universal meaning, a more humanly general interest?' For Benda it is correct that the universal is better served the more one is particular. But it is one thing to *be* particular and another to *preach* particularism. Here lies the equivocation of nationalism, which on the basis of this equivocation often lays claim to being the true universalism, the true pacifism. National, in other words, is different from nationalist. Goethe was a German 'national', Stendhal a French 'national', but neither of them was a nationalist. An idea is not effective if it is not expressed in some way, artistically, that is, particularly. But is a spirit particular in as much as it is national? Nationality is a primary particularity, but the great writer is further particularized among his fellow countrymen and this second 'particularity' is not the extension of the first. Renan, as Renan, is by no means a *necessary* consequence of the French spirit. Through his relation to it he is an original event, arbitrary and (as Bergson says) *unpredictable*. And yet, Renan remains French, just as man, while being man, remains animal. But his value, as is true of man, lies precisely in his difference from the group from which he was born.

---

[87] In *La Trahison des Clercs* (The Betrayal of the Intellectuals) Benda (1867–1956) accused the intellectuals of abandoning their traditional function as guardians of abstract speculation and values by descending 'to the market place', using their minds to justify 'realistic political passions' and identifying with concrete political movements: socialism, nationalism, fascism. It should be noted that Gramsci's text here (including the contrast between 'national' and 'nationalist') is almost wholly a translation and paraphrase of Benda's cited article. His own words are those interpolated in the brackets in the third and fifth paragraphs, and the interlinear gloss 'great intellectuals' over Benda's word 'masters' (*maîtres*) in the second paragraph.

It is precisely this that the nationalists do not want. For them the value of the masters (great intellectuals) consists in their likeness to the spirit of their group, in their loyalty, in their punctual expression of this spirit (which is, moreover, defined as the spirit of the masters (great intellectuals) so one always ends up being right).

Why do so many modern writers care so much for the 'national soul' which they say they represent? It is useful for one who is without personality to decree that the important thing is to be a nationalist. Max Nordau writes about someone who exclaimed, 'You say that I am nothing. Well, I am something. I'm a contemporary!' Likewise, many claim to be French writers to the bone. (In this way a hierarchy and a *de facto* organization are set up and this is the nub of the whole question: Benda, like Croce, examines the question of the intellectuals abstracting from the class situation of the intellectuals themselves and from their function, which has become more defined with the mass circulation of books and the periodical press.)[88] But if this position is explicable in the mediocre writers, how can one explain it in the great personalities? (Perhaps the explanation co-ordinates the two: the great personalities govern the mediocre ones and certain practical prejudices are necessarily involved which are not detrimental to their works.) Wagner (cf. Nietzsche's *Ecce Homo*) knew what he was doing when he stated that his art was the expression of the German genius, thereby inviting a whole race to applaud itself in his works. But for many Benda finds an explanation in the belief that the spirit is good to the extent that it adopts a certain *collective* manner of thinking and bad to the extent that it seeks to differentiate itelf. When Barrès wrote, 'It is the role of the masters to justify the habits and prejudices peculiar to France, so as to prepare our children in the best way possible, to take their place in the national procession,' he meant precisely that his duty and that of the French thinkers worthy of the name was also to join this procession.

This tendency has had disastrous effects in literature (insincerity). In politics: this trend towards national

---

[88] The same comparison between Benda and Croce recurs in Q 10 II § 41 and 47. In the second of these notes Gramsci adds: 'In reality, despite certain appearances, the agreement between Croce and Benda is only superficial or regards only certain particular aspects of the question. In Croce there is an organic construction of thought, a doctrine on the state, on religion and on the function of the intellectuals in the life of the state which is absent in Benda, who is essentially a "journalist".'

distinctiveness has brought it about that war, instead of being simply political, has become a war of national souls, characterized by depth of passion and ferocity.

Benda concludes with the observation that all of this intense activity to maintain the nationalization of the spirit means that the European spirit is being born, and that it is at the heart of this European spirit that the artist must differentiate himself if he wishes to serve the universal. (Indeed, the war has demonstrated that these nationalist attitudes were not accidental or due to intellectual causes – logical errors, etc. They were and are connected to a determinate historical period in which only the union of all the national elements can be a condition of victory. If the intellectual struggle is conducted without a real struggle aimed at overturning this situation, it is sterile. It is true that the European spirit is being born, and not only the European one, but it is precisely this which exacerbates the national character of the intellectuals, especially the highest stratum.)

Q3 § 2.

26 Emmanuel Berl

He has written a book, *Mort de la pensée bourgeoise*, that seems to have made something of a stir.[89] In 1929 he delivered a talk at Zola's house in Médan on the occasion of the annual pilgrimage (I believe), of the 'friends of Zola' (democrats, 'Jeunesses laïques et républicaines', etc.). 'After the death of Zola and Jaurès, no one is any longer able to speak to the people about the people, and our "literature of the aesthetes" is dying because of its egocentrism.' Zola in literature and Jaurès in politics were the last representatives of the people.[90] Pierre Hamp deals with the

[89] Berl's book (1929), which Gramsci did not have available in prison, starts as a polemical rejoinder to Benda's thesis on the intellectuals and ends by pleading for a literature more open to political reality. The error of the intellectuals was not, for Berl, that they had become 'contaminated' with politics but rather that by assuming political 'forms' they had distanced or intellectualized political truth, either by accepting a bourgeois conformism which kept them 'in retard of the age' or by embracing an anarchic revolutionism (e.g. surrealism). The same contrast between 'conformism' and the 'revolutionary' Zola discussed here appears also in Berl's book. Gramsci's source here was *Les Nouvelles Littéraires* of 12 October 1929, which contained the text of Berl's speech.

[90] Jean Jaurès (1859–1914), French reformist socialist leader, founded *L'Humanité* and wrote the four volumes on the French Revolution in the *Histoire socialiste*. He was assassinated in a Paris café just before the outbreak of the First World War. Zola had died in 1902.

people, but his books are read by the literati. The peole read V.
Margueritte, but he does not deal with the people.[91] The only
French book that continues Zola is Barbusse's *Le Feu*, because
the war had rekindled a degree of fraternity in France.[92] Today
the popular novel (what does he mean by the popular novel?) is
increasingly separated from literature proper, which has become
a literature of the aesthetes. Separated from the people, literature
wastes away – the proletariat excluded from the spiritual life (!)
loses its dignity (n'est plus fondé en dignité). (It is true that
literature is turning away from the people and is becoming a caste
phenomenon, but this leads to a greater dignity of the people.
Traditional 'fraternity' was nothing but the expression of the
French literary bohemians, a certain moment of French culture
around '48 and extending to '70. It had a certain revival in Zola).
'And around us we sense the growth of this famine amongst the
people who question us without our being able to answer them,
who throng around us without our being able to satisfy them, who
demand a justification of their pain without our being able to give
one. One might say that the gigantic factories create a zone of
silence from which the worker can no longer escape and which
the intellectual can no longer enter. So separated that the
intellectual who comes from a working-class background can no
longer find access to it.' 'The difficulty of fidelity, Jean Gúehenno
writes. Perhaps the impossibility of fidelity. The scholarship-boy
does not at all build, as one was hoping he would, a bridge
between the proletariat and the bourgeoisie. One more bourgeois
and that's fine. But his brothers cease to recognize him. They no
longer see in him one of themselves. Since the people have nothing
to do with the way in which the intellectuals express themselves,
they must either set themselves against the intellectuals and set
up a sort of nationality with their own peculiar language, or have
no language at all and sink into a sort of barbarism.' It is the fault
of the intellectuals, who have become conformist while Zola was
a revolutionary (!); their style refined and precious, writers of
intimate journals while Zola was epic. But the world has changed
too. Zola knew a people that today no longer exists, or at least it
no longer has the same importance. High capitalism – the

---

[91] Pierre Hamp (1876–1962), novelist who dealt with the processes of industry. Victor
Margueritte (1867–1942), novelist who repudiated Zola's naturalist theories.

[92] Barbusse's novel about life in the trenches was published in 1916 (in English in 1917
as *Under Fire*, Dent, London). See also VIII 11 below.

Taylorized worker – has replaced the old composition of the people which was not yet clearly distinguished from the petty bourgeoisie and which appears in Zola, as in Proudhon, Victor Hugo, Sand and Eugène Sue. Zola describes the rise of industry. But if the writer's task is now more difficult, it should not therefore be neglected. Thus the return to Zola, the return to the people. 'With Zola, then, or with nothing, fraternity or death. This is our motto. This our drama. And this our law.'

Q 3 § 4.

27 The Public and Italian Literature

In an article published in *Il Lavoro* and then reprinted in extracts in *La Fiera Letteraria* of 28 October 1928, Leo Ferrero writes:

> For one reason or another, it can be said that Italian writers no longer have a public. A public means a group of people who not only buy books but above all admire men. A literature can only flourish in a climate of admiration and admiration is not, as one might think, the reward but the stimulus for work. The public that admires, that really admires, with feeling, joyfully, the public that has the felicity to admire, is a literature's greatest encouragement (nothing is more harmful than conventional admiration). But sadly it is clear from many signs that the Italian public is abandoning its writers.

Ferrero's 'admiration' is nothing but a metaphor and a 'collective name' to indicate the complex system of relations, the form of contact between a nation and its writers. Today, this contact is lacking: our literature is not national because it is not popular. A paradox of the present. Furthermore, there is no hierarchy in the literary world, there is no eminent personality able to exercise a cultural hegemony.

The question of why and how a literature is popular. 'Beauty' is not enough. There must be a specific moral and intellectual content which is the elaborated and finished expression of the deepest aspirations of a given public, of the nation-people in a certain phase of its historical development. Literature must be at one and the same time a current element of civilization and a work of art. Otherwise, instead of artistic literature there will be a preference for serial literature, in its way a current element of culture, a degraded culture maybe, but one that is energetically felt.

Q 21 § 4.

28 On Italian Literature: [G.A. Borgese][93]

See Borgese's essay 'Il senso della letteratura italiana', in *Nuova Antologia*, 1 January 1930.

> An epithet, a motto, cannot sum up the spirit of an epoch or a people but at times it is useful as a reference or a prop to memory. It is often said of French literature that it has grace or logical clarity. One could say: a chivalric loyalty of analysis. For English literature we might say: a lyricism of intimacy; for German: the audacity of liberty; for Russian: the courage of truth. The words we can use for Italian literature are precisely those we have made use of for these visual memories: majesty, magnificence, grandeur.

In short, Borgese finds that the character of Italian literature is 'theological-absolute-metaphysical-antiromantic'. Perhaps this hierophantic language of his could be translated into the plainly phrased opinion that Italian literature is separated from the real development of the Italian people. It belongs to a caste, it does not feel the drama of history, in other words, it is not national-popular.

He deals with Bonghi's book:[94]

> The author and his friends soon realized, but too late to correct a title which quickly became much too famous, that the little book should have been called: Why Italian prose is not popular in Italy. It is precisely this that is relatively weak in Italian literature: prose or better still prose understood as a literary genre and verbal rhythm, what we could call the *sense of the prosaic*, the interest in, curiosity of observing and patient love for historical and contingent life as it moves under our eyes, for the world in its becoming, for the dramatic and progressive fulfilment of the divine.

[93] Giuseppe Antonio Borgese (1882–1952), critic and writer, broke with his former mentor Croce around 1910 by siding with D'Annunzio, aestheticism and the classic-heroic-spiritual tradition. In the late 1920s he became a chief spokesman for 'contentism'. Politically, Borgese started as a reactionary nationalist, writing in 1904–6 on Corradini's *Regno* and editing his own review, *Hermes*. In 1931 he emigrated to the USA after repudiating fascism, and wrote tracts denouncing its barbarity and theorizing a utopian universal republic.

[94] See footnote 1 above.

There is an interesting passage just before this on De Sanctis with a comical reproach: 'He saw Italian literature living for over six centuries and asked it to be born.' In fact, De Sanctis wanted 'literature' to renew itself because the Italian people had been renewed, because the separation between literature and life had disappeared. It is interesting to note that De Sanctis is a progressive even today in comparison with the many Borgeses of current criticism. 'Its limited popularity (Italian literature), the singular, almost aristocratic and remote kind of fortune that befell it for so long is not explained only (!) by its inferiority. It is more completely (!) explained by its heights (! – heights mixed with inferiority!), by the rarefied air in which it grew. Non-popularity is like saying non-divulgation, a consequence of the premiss: *odi profanum vulgus et arceo*. Anything but common and profane, this literature was born sacred, with a poem which its poet himself called sacred (sacred because it speaks about God, but what subject is more popular than God? And in the *Divine Comedy* the author speaks not only of God but also of devils and their 'strange bagpipe'),[95] etc., etc. The political fate that took from Italy its liberty and its material strength also made it into what in the terms of the Bible, of Leviticus, would be called a people of priests.' The essay concludes, and just as well, that the character of Italian literature can, indeed must change, but this jars with the essay as a whole.

Q6 § 44.

29 [The Italians and the Novel]

It will be worth looking at a lecture on 'The Italians and the Novel' delivered by Angelo Gatti and published in part in *L'Italia Letteraria* of 9 April 1933. An interesting point seems to be that dealing with the relations between moralists and novelists in France and Italy. The French type of moralist is quite different from the Italian, who is more 'political'. The Italian studies how to 'dominate', how to be stronger, more skilled, more cunning. The French type studies how to 'direct' and thus how to 'understand' in order to influence and obtain an 'active and spontaneous consent'. The *Ricordi politici e civili* of Guicciardini

[95] *Inferno* XXII, 10: at the end of the previous canto a devil has been described as trumpeting through his arse.

are of this kind. Thus the great abundance in Italy of books like *Galateo*, concerned with the external stance of the upper classes.[96] There are no books like those of the great French moralists (or of a lesser order as in Gasparo Gozzi),[97] with their refined and capillary analyses. There is this difference in the novel which in Italy is more external, narrow-minded, without a national-popular or universal human content.

Q 15 § 14.

30 Luigi Capuana[98]

Extract from an article by Luigi Tonelli, 'Il carattere e l'opera di Luigi Capuana' (*Nuova Antologia*, 1 May 1928):

> *Re Bracalone* is a fairytale novel: the twentieth century is created by magic for a few days during a period of 'once upon a time', but after having a bitter experience of it the king destroys it, preferring to return to primitive times. For us the novel also has an ideological interest since Capuana, in a period of internationalist socialistic infatuation (!), had the courage (!) to lambaste (!) 'the idiotic sentimentalities of universal peace and disarmament and the no less idiotic sentimentalities of economic equality and community of goods', and to express the urgent need 'to curtail the agitation that has already created a state within the state, an irresponsible government', and to assert the necessity of a national consciousness: 'We are lacking in national dignity; we must create this dignity and push it to excess. It is the only case where excess of a thing does not spoil it'.

Tonelli is a fool, but Capuana is not joking either with his stock phrases of the provincial Crispian journalist. And one should see what value his ideology of 'once upon a time' had then, with its exaltation of a paternalism which was anachronistic and anything but national for the Italy of the period.

Capuana's dialect plays and his views on the language of the theatre need to be remembered for the question of the language

---

[96] A treatise on good conduct and good speaking by Giovanni Della Casa (1503–56).

[97] Gasparo Gozzi (1713–86). His *Sermoni* in blank verse included satirical pieces on contemporary men of letters. In Gramsci's time he had been revived by Falqui and *La Ronda* as a model of good prose (*Lettere diverse*, 1750) and moderate conservatism.

[98] On Capuana, see footnote 2 on p. 92.

in Italian literature. Some of his plays (like *Giacinta, Malia, Il cavalier Pedagna*) were written originally in Italian and then turned into dialect. Only the dialect versions were successful. Tonelli, who understands nothing, says that Capuana was led to using dialect in the theatre 'not only by his belief that "one has to pass through theatre in the dialects if one really wants to arrive at an Italian national theatre" . . . , but also, and above all, by the particular character of his dramatic creations. These are quintessentially (!) dialectal, and they find their most natural and straightforward expression in dialect.' But what does 'quintessentially dialectal creations' mean? The fact is used to explain the fact: i.e. it is not explained. (It should be remembered that Capuana corresponded with a working-class 'kept' woman of his in dialect; in other words he realized that if he used Italian he would not have been properly and 'sympathetically' understood by the people, whose culture was not national but regional, or Sicilian-national. How, in conditions like these, one could pass from a dialect theatre to a national one is an argument by enigmas that demonstrates a limited understanding of the problems of national culture.)

One should examine why in the theatre of Pirandello certain play are written in Italian and others in dialect. In Pirandello such a study is particularly interesting since Pirandello has also acquired a cosmopolitan cultural physiognomy and has become Italian and national in that he has completely lost his provincialism and has been Europeanized. Language has still not acquired a mass 'historicity'; it has not yet become a national fact. In literary Italian Pirandello's *Liolà* has little value, although *Il fu Mattia Pascal*, from which it is drawn, can still be read with pleasure.[99] In the Italian text the author does not succeed in getting in tune with the public, he lacks the perspective of the historicity of the language when the characters wish to be concretely Italian before an Italian public. In reality there are many 'popular' languages in Italy and they are the regional dialects that are usually spoken in private conversation in which the most common and diffused feelings and emotions are expressed. The literary language is still largely a cosmopolitan language, a type of 'Esperanto', limited to the expression of partial notions and feelings.

[99] The plot of *Liolà* reworks an episode in Chapter 4 of Pirandello's novel *Il fu Mattia Pascal* (1904). Compare I 25 and III 3 for the other points here.

When the literary language is said to be very rich in expressive means, something equivocal and ambiguous is being asserted. the 'possible' richness of expression recorded in the dictionary or lying inert in 'authors' is being confused with individual richness that can be used on an individual basis. The latter, though, is the only real and concrete richness, and it is through it that one can measure the degree of national linguistic unity that is given by the living spoken language of the people, the degree of nationalization of the linguistic patrimony. In theatrical dialogue the importance of such an element is evident. From the stage the dialogue must create living images, expressed with all their historical concreteess. But all too often it evokes bookish images and feelings mutilated by a lack of understanding of the language and its nuances. The language of domestic scenes comes across to the listener like a recollection of words read in books or in newspapers or looked up in the dictionary – a bit like someone who has learnt French from books without a teacher listening to a play being performed in French. Speech is ossified and lacks the articulation of nuances; its exact meaning, which is given to it by the whole period, is not understood. One has the feeling of being clumsy, or of other people being clumsy. Notice how many errors of pronunciation the man of the people makes in spoken Italian: 'profúgo', 'roséo' and so on. This means that such words have been read rather than heard; they have not been heard many times over and thus not been placed in various perspectives (various grammatical periods) each of which has lit up one facet of the many-sided figure which is a word. (Syntactic errors are even more significant.)

Q 23 § 39.

31 Tendencies in Italian Culture: Giovanni Cena[100]

On Cena there is a very interesting article by Arrigo Cajumi, 'Lo strano caso di Giovanni Cena' (*L'Italia Letteraria*, 24 November 1929). [. . .]

---

[100] Giovanni Cena (1870–1917), writer from a poor family, worked on *Nuova Antologia* in Rome and became involved with his lover, the writer Sibilla Aleramo, in a philanthropic project of setting up schools and medical facilities for the illiterate seasonal workers of the Agro Romano.

One or two extracts from the article:

'Born in 1870, died in 1917, Giovanni Cena strikes us as a representative figure of the intellectual movement that the best of our bourgeoisie carried out when following the new ideas coming from France and Russia. His was personally a bitterer and more energetic contribution, due to his proletarian (! – or peasant?) origins and the years of poverty he suffered. A self-educated man, he miraculously escaped from the brutalizing experience of his father's job and his native town. Unconsciously Cena joined that trend which in France – continuing a tradition (!) deriving (!) from Proudhon on (!) through Vallès and the Communards to Zola's *Quatre évangiles*, the Dreyfus affair, the Popular Universities of Daniel Halévy and which today continues in Gúehenno (!) (rather in Pierre Dominique and others) – was defined as going to the people.' (Cajumi transports into the past a contemporary slogan, that of the populists. After the French Revolution and up to Zola, there was never a split between the people and the writers in France. The symbolist reaction dug a ditch between people and writers, between writers and life. Anatole France is the most fully-realized example of a bookish, caste writer.) 'Cena came from the people, hence the orginality (!) of his position. But the environment of struggle was still the same, that in which the socialism of someone like Prampolini took shape. It was the second generation petty bourgeoisie after the unification of Italy (the first has been masterfully chronicled by Augusto Monti in *Sansoussi*), alien to the politics of the dominant conservative classes, more connected in literature to De Amicis or Stecchetti than to Carducci, and far removed from D'Annunzio. This new generation preferred to form itself on Tolstoy, seen more as a thinker than as an artist. It discovered Wagner and believed vaguely in the symbolists and in social poetry (symbolists and social poetry?) and in perpetual peace. It insulted those in government for their lack of idealism and did not reawaken from its dreams even with the gunshots of 1914 (all this is a little affected and stretched). . . . Having grown up amidst incredible privations, he was capable of being amphibious, neither bourgeois, nor man of the people: "When I think of how I got through an academic education and took exams I often set myself completely on edge. And when, in thinking about it, I feel that I can *forgive*, then I truly have the sense of being victorious." "I feel deeply that only the outlet of literature and faith in its power to liberate and elevate have saved me from becoming a Ravachol".'

In the first draft of *Gli ammonitori* Cena had the suicidal character throw himself under a real car, but in the final version he cut out the scene:[101] 'A student of social phenomena, a stranger to Croce, Missiroli, Jaurès and Oriani as well as to the real exigencies of the northern proletariat which he, a peasant, could not feel. Coming from Turin, he was hostile towards the newspaper that represented the liberal, indeed social-democratic, bourgeoisie. No trace of syndicalism, Sorel is not mentioned. Modernism did not concern him.' This passage shows how superficial Cajumi's political knowledge is. Cena is by turns a man of the people, a proletarian, a peasant. *La Stampa* is a social-democratic newspaper; indeed, there is a social-democratic bourgeoisie in Turin. In this Cajumi imitates certain Sicilian politicians who founded social-democratic or even labour parties, and he falls into the trap of many ridiculous journalists who have cooked the word social-democracy in every sauce. Cajumi forgets that in Turin before the war *La Stampa* was to the right of the *Gazzetta del Popolo*, a moderate democratic newspaper. Also, the combination Croce-Missiroli-Jaurès-Oriani for social studies is delightful.

In the article 'What is to be done?' Cena wanted to merge the nationalists with philo-socialists like himself. Ultimately, however, was not all this petty bourgeois socialism of the De Amicis type an embryo of nation-based socialism, or national-socialism, which sought to assert itself in so many ways in Italy and which found a propitious soil after the war?

Q 6 § 42 (excerpt).

32 Gino Saviotti

Many men of letters have written and continue to write about the anti-popular or at least non-popular-national character of Italian literature. But in these writings the subject is not confronted in its real terms and the actual conclusions are often staggering. Gino Saviotti for example, who willingly writes against the

---

[101] *Gli ammonitori* (1904) documents the positivist and philanthropic socialism of the period. The protagonist resolves in the end to kill himself and rejoin the flux of living matter.

literature of the literati, is quoted in *L'Italia Letteraria* of 24 August 1930 (the passage is from an article published in *Ambrosiano* of 15 August): 'Worthy Parini, it is clear why you raised up Italian poetry in your day. You gave it the seriousness it lacked. You transfused into its arid veins your good popular blood. May you be thanked today a hundred and thirty-one years after your death. We could do with another man like yourself now in our so-called poetry.'[102] In 1934 a literary prize (part of the Viareggio prize) has been given to Saviotti for a novel [*Mezzo matto*] which portrays the effort of a man of the people to become an 'artist' (he tries in other words to become a 'professional artist', to be no longer 'one of the people' but to raise himself to the rank of the professional intellectuals). This is essentially an 'anti-popular' subject in which caste is exalted as a model of 'superior' life: the oldest and stalest part of the Italian tradition.

Q 23 § 44.

33 Popular Literature: [Giuseppe Ungaretti]

That a part of current poetry is 'pure baroque'[103] is spontaneously confessed by some of its orthodox critics. For example, in his essay on Ungaretti (quoted in the March 1934 issue of *Leonardo*), Aldo Capasso writes: 'The *wonderstruck* aura could not take form if the poet were less laconic.' The *wonderstruck aura* recalls the famous definition: 'of poetry the end is wonder'. We might note, however, that the classical baroque, sadly, was and is popular (it is well-known that the man of the people likes the acrobatics of images in poetry), while the current baroque style is popular among pure intellectuals.

Ungaretti has written[104] that his comrades in the trenches, who

---

[102] Giuseppe Parini (1729–99) son of a small silk dealer, worked as a tutor to Milanese noble families. He associated with Milan Enlightenment circles, wrote an unfinished verse satire (*Il giorno*) against the aristocracy and a cycle of odes which contrasted virtuous rural life with corrupt social practices.

[103] 'Baroque' here translates 'secentismo', a pejorative critical term for the formalistic poetry written in the seventeenth century (Seicento) by Giambattista Marino (1569–1625) and his followers, whose poetic is roughly summed up by the line from Marino quoted by Gramsci in this paragraph: 'È del poeta il fin la meraviglia'. Croce made the terms 'secentismo' and 'barocco' interchangeable, criticizing the baroque as a hedonistic capricious 'ugly in art' (*Storia dell'età barocca in Italia*).

[104] Ungaretti's letter was published in *L'Italia Letteraria* IV (1932) 15. Gramsci reproduces the text of the letter in VIII 21, below.

were 'common people', liked his poems, and it may be true: a particular kind of liking to do with the feeling that 'difficult' (incomprehensible) poetry must be good and its author a great man precisely because he is detached from the people and is incomprehensible. This is also the case with Futurism and is part of the people's cult of the intellectuals (who are in fact admired and despised at the same time).

Q 17 § 44.

34 [The 'People' and the 'Public']

The people (oh!), the public (oh!). The political adventurists ask with the scowl of those who know what's what, 'The people! But what is this people? Who knows them? Who has ever defined them?' And in the meantime they do nothing but devise endless tricks to win the electoral majority (from '24 to '29 how many communiqués have there been in Italy to announce new alterations of the electoral law? How many plans for new electoral laws presented and withdrawn? The catalogue in itself would be interesting).[105] The pure literati say the same thing: 'Calling on the people to decide is a vice carried over from Romanticism. What is the public? Who is it? Where is this omniscient head, this exquisite taste, this absolute probity, this pearl?' (G. Ungaretti, *Il Resto del Carlino*, 23 October 1929). In the meantime, however, they ask for some form of protection against translations from foreign languages and when they sell a thousand copies of a book they have the bells rung in their home town. The 'people', though, has provided the title for many important newspapers, precisely those that today ask 'What is this people?' in the very newspapers that are named after the people.

Q 3 § 7.

35 [Intellectuals and Literature]

It is noteworthy that in Italy there is a purely bookish concept of culture: the literary journals deal with books or the people who

---

[105] In July 1924 Mussolini passed a 'trick law' whereby a relative majority of votes (25 per cent) for the national list could be transformed into an absolute majority of seats in Parliament. A subsequent fascist law of March 1928 provided for 400 deputies elected by a single national college with candidates chosen by the Grand Council from the nominations of the employers' and workers' unions.

write them. Articles containing impressions of collective life, of ways of thinking, 'signs of the times' or changes occurring in people's behaviour are nowhere to be found. Difference between Italian literature and other literatures. In Italy there are no writers of memoirs and biographies and autobiographies are rare. There is a lack of interest in living man, in life as it is lived. (Is Ugo Ojetti's *Cose viste* really that great masterpiece which everyone began talking about after Ojetti became editor of the *Corriere della Sera*, that literary organ which pays writers more and makes them more famous? In *Cose viste* the author speaks mostly about writers, at least in those parts that I read years ago. This could be checked.) This is another sign of the separation between Italian intellectuals and the national-popular reality.

In 1920 Prezzolini made this observation about intellectuals (*Mi pare . . .* , p. 16):

> The Italian intellectual has the presumption to act the parasite. He considers himself like the bird made for a golden cage, who must be served mash and millet seed. The disdain that still exists for everything that resembles work, the affectation always surrounding the romantic notion that one must wait for inspiration from heaven (like the Pythia waiting to be possessed)[106] are fairly fetid symptoms of inner decay. The intellectuals should realize that the good old days for these uninteresting masquerades are over. Within a few years one will not be allowed to be afflicted with literature or to remain useless.

Intellectuals conceive of literature as a 'profession' unto itself that should 'pay' even when nothing is immediately produced and that should give them the right to a pension. Who, though, is to decide that such and such a writer is really a 'literary figure' and that society can support him while waiting for his 'masterpiece'? The literary man claims the right to be 'idle' (*otium et non negotium*), to travel, to day-dream, without worrying about money. This way of thinking is linked to court patronage, but the patronage is badly interpreted because the great literary men of the Renaissance also did some other type of work besides writing (even Ariosto, *littérateur par excellence*, had administrative and political duties): thus, a false and mistaken image of the Renaissance man of letters. Today, the literary man is a professor or journalist or a simple man of letters (in the sense that he tends to become one,

---

[106] The Pythia was the priestess of Apollo at Delphi who delivered the oracles when possessed by the god.

if he is a public official, etc.).

We might say that literature is a social function but that literary men, taken individually, are not necessary for this. This may seem paradoxical, but it is true in the sense that, while other professions are collective and their social function is distributed among individuals, this does not occur in literature. The question is one of 'apprenticeship', but can one speak of artistic or literary 'apprenticeship'? The intellectual function cannot be separated from productive work in general, not even in the case of artists unless they have effectively proved to be 'artistically' productive. Nor will this be harmful to 'art'. Perhaps it will even prove helpful. It will only harm the artistic bohemia and there is nothing wrong with that. Far from it.

Q6 § 29.

36 Consent of the Nation or of the 'Elect'

What ought to interest an artist more, the recognition of his work by the 'nation' or by the 'elect'? Yet can there be a separation between the 'elect' and the 'nation'? The fact that the question has been and continues to be put in these terms in itself shows a historically determined separation between intellectuals and the nation. Who are these 'elect' anyway? Every writer or artist has his 'elect', intellectuals being in fact fragmented groups and sects of the 'elect', fragmented because of their non-adherence to the nation-people and because of the fact that the felt 'content' of art, its cultural world, is detached from the deep currents of national-popular life which itself remains scattered and without expression. Every intellectual movement becomes or returns to being national if a 'going to the people' has taken place, if there has been a phase of 'Reformation' and not just a phase of 'Renaissance' and if these two phases 'Reformation-Renaissance' follow one another organically instead of coinciding with distinct historical phases (as was the case in Italy where, from the viewpoint of popular participation in public life, there was a historical hiatus between the commune movement – reformation – and the movement of the Renaissance). Even if one had to begin by writing serial novels and operatic rhymes, without a period of going to the people there can be no 'Renaissance' and no national literature.

Q8 § 145.

37 [The Bureaucrats]

Article by Orazio Pedrazzi in *L'Italia Letteraria* of 4 August 1929, 'Le tradizioni antiletterarie della burocrazia italiana'. Pedrazzi fails to make certain necessary distinctions. It is not true that the Italian bureaucracy is so 'anti-literary' as Pedrazzi asserts, while it is true that the bureaucracy (meaning the upper bureaucracy) does not write about its own activity. The two things are different. In fact, I believe that the bureaucracy has its own literary mania but it is for 'good style', 'art' and so on. Perhaps one could discover that the great mass of literary trash is due to the bureaucrats. On the other hand, it is true that in Italy there is not (as in France and elsewhere) any literature of value produced by state (military and civil) employees which deals with the activity of diplomatic personnel abroad, or of officers etc. at the front. What there is is mostly 'apologetic'. 'In France, in England, generals and admirals write for their people. In our country they write only for their superiors.' In other words, the bureaucracy does not have a national character, but a caste one.

Q5 § 38.

38 [Enrico Thovez]

In dealing with this question, but especially in drawing up the history of the attitude of a whole set of literary men and critics who recognized the falsity of the tradition, its distance from historical reality and the false ring of the rhetoric embedded in it, one should not forget Enrico Thovez and his book *Il pastore, il gregge, la zampogna*.[107] Thovez's reaction was not correct, but in this instance what matters is that he reacted, that he at least felt something was wrong.

His distinction between poetry of form and poetry of content was theoretically false. The so-called poetry of form is characterized by its indifference to content, by its moral indifference, but this too is 'content', the 'moral and historical

---

[107] Enrico Thovez (1869–1925) poet and critic. *Il pastore, il gregge, la zampogna* (1910) criticized the recent impoverishment of the Italian lyric, firstly in Carducci (eulogized by Croce) and his followers for their deviation into rhetoric and a cold flat public content, then in D'Annunzio for the superficial dazzle of his forms unsupported by real feeling. For Thovez the model of lyric verse was provided by Leopardi, who had also been the subject of an influential study by De Sanctis.

void of the writer'. Thovez was, to a large extent, latching on to De Sanctis, in his role as an 'innovator of culture' in Italy, and he should be considered along with *La Voce* as one of the forces that was working, admittedly in a chaotic way, for a moral and intellectual reformation during the period before the war.

One should also look at the disputes Thovez's attitude provoked. In the article 'Enrico Thovez, poeta e il problema della formazione artistica' by Alfonso Ricolfi in *Nuova Antologia* of 16 August 1929, there are a few useful suggestions, but too few. One should also find Prezzolini's article 'Thovez il precursore'.

Q5 § 94.

39 Antonio Fradeletto[108]

A former radical Freemason later converted to Catholicism. He was a journalist in the rhetorical and sentimental vein, an orator for great occasions. He represented a type of old Italian culture that seems to be disappearing in its primitive form, because the type has become universal and diluted. Writers dealing with artistic, literary and 'patriotic' subjects. The type consisted precisely in the patriotism being not a widespread and deeply rooted sentiment, the mood of a national class, an accepted fact, but an 'oratorical speciality' of a number of 'personalities' (look at Cian, for example),[109] a professional qualification, so to speak. (Do not confuse it with the nationalists, although Corradini belonged to this type and differed in this respect from Coppola and also from Federzoni. Nor did D'Annunzio ever fit perfectly into this category. What is striking is that it would be very difficult to explain to a foreigner, especially a Frenchman, what this type consisted of, connected as it was to the specific development of Italian culture and the formation of the nation. No comparison is

[108] Fradeletto (1858–1930) public orator, Radical Party deputy from 1900 to 1919, Senator from 1920. In 1915 Gramsci had published in *Avanti!* a denunciation of Fradeletto's twisting of Venetian history to nationalistic ends: see CT, pp. 40–45 (PV, pp. 18–23). See also CT, p. 54 (SM, p. 6) and CT, p. 158 (PV, p. 28).

[109] Vittorio Cian (1862–1951), professor of Italian literature at Turin 1913–35 and Nationalist parliamentary Deputy. Gramsci had attacked him in 1916–17 for his attempts to exclude non-nationals from applying to university chairs and for having proposed at the time of the Libyan war a boycott of teachers opposed to Italian imperialism (see CT, pp. 81–82, 85–86, 421–22).

possible, for example, with Barrès or Péguy.)[110]

Q 23 § 48.

40 Americanism: [Babbitt][111]

See Carlo Linati's article 'Babbitt compra il mondo' in *Nuova Antologia*, 16 October 1929. A mediocre article, but for that very reason significant as an expression of an average opinion. It can serve to establish what the more intelligent of the petty bourgeoisie think of Americanism. The article is a variation on Edgard Ansel Mowrer's book *This American World*, which Linati judges 'truly acute, rich with ideas and written with a pleasing concision between the classical and the brutal, by a writer who clearly lacks neither a spirit of observation nor a sense of historical nuances nor variety of culture.' Mowrer reconstructs the cultural history of the United States up to the breaking of the umbilical cord with Europe and the advent of Americanism.

It would be interesting to analyse the reasons why *Babbitt* was such a great success in Europe. It is not a great book: it is constructed schematically and its mechanism is also too apparent. It is of cultural more than artistic importance: the criticism of manners prevails over art. That there exists in America a realistic literary current that starts out as a criticism of manners is a very important cultural fact. It means that there is an increase in self-criticism, that a new American civilization is being born that is aware of its strengths and its weaknesses. The intellectuals are breaking loose from the dominant class in order to unite themselves to it more intimately, to be a real superstructure and not only an inorganic and indistinct element of the structure-corporation.

European intellectuals have already partially lost this function. They no longer represent the cultural self-consciousness, the

[110] On Corradini see note 8 above. Francesco Coppola (1878–1957) and Luigi Federzoni (1878–1967) were leading nationalists, the latter a subsequent lynchpin of the nationalist-fascist alliance. On D'Annunzio see footnote 38 on p. 54. Maurice Barrès (1862–1923) was a prominent right wing nationalist. Charles Péguy (1873–1914), a former socialist, turned to nationalism and was killed in action at the beginning of the war.

[110] *Babbitt*, Sinclair Lewis's satirical novel about a middle-American real estate man, was first published in 1922. This and the following note are thematically linked to Gramsci's 'Americanism and Fordism' notes – see SPN, pp. 277–318, particularly the last note in that section.

self-criticism of the dominant class. Once again they have become the immediate agents of the dominant class, or else they have completely broken loose from it by making up a caste in themselves, without roots in national-popular life. They laugh at Babbitt and are amused at his mediocrity, his naïve stupidity, his automatic way of thinking and his standardized mentality. They do not even ask the question: are there Babbitts in Europe? The point is that in Europe the standardized petty bourgeois exists but his standardization, instead of being national (and of a great nation like the United States), is regional and local. The European Babbitts belong to a historical gradation inferior to that of the American Babbitt: they are a national weakness, whereas the American one is a national strength. They are more picturesque, but also more stupid and ridiculous. Their conformism is based on a rotten and debiltating superstition, whereas Babbitt's is naïve and spontaneous and based on an energetic and progressive superstition.

For Linati, Babbitt is 'the prototype of the modern American industrialist'. In fact, Babbitt is a petty bourgeois and his most typical mania is that of being friends with 'modern industrialists', being their equal, and showing off their moral and social 'superiority'. The modern industrialist is a model to be emulated, the social type to which one must conform, while for the European Babbitt the model and type are given by the canon of the cathedral, the petty nobleman from the provinces and the section head at the ministry. This uncritical attitude of European intellectuals is worth noting: in the preface to his book on the United States, Siegfried compares the artisan of a Parisian luxury goods industry to the Taylorized American worker, as if the former were a common type of worker.[112] In general, European intellectuals think that Babbitt is a purely American type and are delighted with old Europe. This anti-Americanism is comical before it is stupid.

Q 5 § 105.

41 Americanism: Babbitt Again

The European petty bourgeois laughs at Babbitt and therefore laughs at America which is supposedly populated by 120 million

[112] André Siegfried, *Les États-Unis d'aujourd'hui*, Colin, Paris, 1928.

Babbitts. The petty bourgeois cannot get outside of himself or understand himself, just as the imbecile is incapable of understanding that he is an imbecile (without demonstrating thereby that he is intelligent). The real imbecile is the one who doesn't know he is one, and the philistine who doesn't know he is one is the real petty bourgeois. The European petty bourgeois laughs at the philistinism of Americans but is not aware of his own. He does not know that he is the European Babbitt, inferior to the Babbitt of Lewis's novel in that he tries to escape and not to be Babbitt. The European Babbitt does not struggle with his philistinism but basks in it, believing that the croaking he makes like a frog stuck in the quagmire is a nightingale's song. In spite of everything, Babbitt is the philistine of a country in motion; the European petty bourgeois is the philistine of conservative countries that are rotting in the stagnant swamp of commonplaces about the great tradition and great culture. The European philistine believes that he discovered America with Christopher Columbus and that Babbitt is a puppet intended for the amusement of those like him, weighed down with millennia of history. Meanwhile, no European writer has been able to depict the European Babbitt for us and show that he is capable of self-criticism: in fact, the only imbecile and philistine is precisely the one who isn't aware of it.

Q 6 § 49.

42 Notes on American Culture

In 'Strange Interlude' (*Corriere della Sera*, 15 March 1932), G.A. Borgese divides the population of the United States into four strata: the financial class, the political class, the Intelligentsia, the Common Man. Compared to the first two, the Intelligentsia is extremely small: a few tens of thousands, concentrated especially in the East, among which are a few thousand writers. 'One should not judge by numbers alone. It is intellectually among the best equipped in the world. Someone who belongs to this class compares it to what the Encyclopaedists were in eighteenth-century France. For the moment, to one who likes to stick to the facts, it appears to be a brain without limbs, a soul without locomotive power; its influence over the public realm is almost nil.' He notes that after the crisis, the financial class which at first controlled the political class has in recent months 'undergone' the latter's assistance and virtual control. 'Congress is supporting the banks and the stock market; the Capitol in Washington is propping up Wall Street. This is undermining the old equilibrium of the American state, but without the rise of a new order.' Since in reality the financial class and the political class are the same in America, or two aspects of the same thing, this can only mean that a real differentiation has taken place, that the economic-corporate phase of American history is in crisis and America is about to enter a new phase. This will be evident only if the traditional parties (Republican and Democratic) enter into crisis and a major new party is created that can organize the Common Man on a permanent basis. The seeds of such a development were already there (the progressive party), but the economic-corporate structure has so far always reacted effectively against them.

The observation that the American Intelligentsia has a historical position like that of the French Encyclopaedists of the eighteenth century is very acute and can be developed.

Q 8 § 89.

43 The English and Religion

From an article entitled 'L'opera della grazia in una recente conversione dall'anglicanismo' in *La Civiltà Cattolica* (4 January 1930), I take the following quotation from Vernon Johnson's book *One Lord, One Faith* (Sheed and Ward, 1929; Johnson is the recent convert referred to): 'To the average Englishman the question of any authority in his religion hardly ever occurs. He accepts that aspect of the Church of England's teaching in which he has been brought up either Anglo-Catholic, Broad, or Evangelical, and follows it until it either fails to satisfy his needs or else comes into conflict with his own personal views about God and religion. He then, being essentially honest and sincere and not desiring to profess more than he really believes, discards all that he cannot accept and evolves a personal religion of his own.'

The writer in *La Civiltà Cattolica* continues, perhaps paraphrasing: 'He (the average Englishman) considers religion as an exclusively private affair between God and the soul; and with this attitude, he is extremely cautious, diffident and unwilling to accept the intervention of any authority. Hence there is a growing number of people whose minds are becoming increasingly open to doubt: whether the Gospels are really to be believed, whether the Christian religion is obligatory for all the world and whether one can know for certain what the doctrine of Christ actually was. Consequently, they hesitate to admit that Jesus Christ is truly God.' And again: ' . . . The greatest of all (the difficulties for the return of the English to the Roman Church): the love of independence in every Englishman. He does not accept any interference, still less in religion and least of all by a foreigner. The instinct that national independence and religious independence are inseparable is innate and deeply rooted. He maintains that England will never accept a Church governed by Italians.'[113]

Q6 § 22.

44 Intellectuals: Notes on English Culture [i]

In an article in *Il Marzocco*, 'Libri nuovi e nuove tendenze nella cultura inglese', 17 April 1932, Guido Ferrando analyses the organic changes that are now taking place in modern English culture, and that are most conspicuous in publishing and in the overall organization of the university departments of the United Kingdom. 'In England there is an increasing swing towards a technical and scientific form of culture to the detriment of humanistic culture. In England, until the last century, one could almost say until the World War, the best schools set as their highest educational goal the formation of gentlemen. As everybody knows, the word "gentleman" does not correspond to the Italian "gentiluomo"; and it cannot be translated accurately into our language. It indicates a person who has not only good manners but who possesses a sense of balance, a sure mastery of himself, a moral discipline that permits him to subordinate voluntarily his own selfish interest to the wider interests of the society in which he lives. The gentleman, therefore is a cultured person in the noblest sense of the word, if by culture we mean not simply a wealth of intellectual knowledge but also the ability to fulfil one's duty and understand one's fellow man by respecting

[113] Vernon Johnson, *One Lord, One Faith*, London 1929. The quotation is from p. 49 and the sections paraphrased are on p. 51 and pp. 22–23.

every principle, every opinion, every faith that is sincerely professed. It is clear, then, that English education aimed not so much at cultivating the mind, at enriching it with a wide knowledge, as at developing character, at preparing an aristocratic class whose moral superiority was instinctively recognized and accepted by the lower classes. Higher or university education was reserved (also because of its high cost) for the few, for the sons of the great noble or wealthy families, without thereby entirely excluding the poorer people, provided they were clever enough to win a scholarship. The others, the great majority, had to be content with an undoubtedly good but primarily technical and professional education that prepared them for those subordinate offices which they would later be called to assume in industry, commerce, and public administration.'

Until a few decades ago, there were in England only three large and comprehensive universities, Oxford, Cambridge and London, and one minor one at Durham. To enter Oxford and Cambridge one must come from the so-called public schools which are everything except public. The most famous of these schools, Eton, was founded in 1440 by Henry VI to receive 'seventy poor and indigent scholars'. Today, it has become the most aristocratic school in England, with over a thousand students. There are still the seventy inside places which are assigned through competition to the best scholars and which give them the right to free tuition and board. The others are external and cost huge sums. 'The seventy collegians . . . are those who will later specialize in a particular discipline at university and will become the future professors and scientists. The other thousand, who generally study less, receive above all a moral education and will become, through the official blessing of the university, the ruling class, destined to occupy the highest places in the army, the navy, in political life and in public administration. This conception of education, which has until now prevailed in England, has a humanistic base.' In most of the public schools and in the universities of Oxford and Cambridge, which have maintained the medieval and Renaissance traditions, 'knowledge of the major Greek and Latin authors is considered not only useful but indispensable for the formation of a gentleman, a politician. It serves to give him that sense of balance and harmony, that sophistication of taste, which are an integrating element of real culture.' Scientific education is now gaining the upper hand. 'Culture is being democratized and fatally levelled.' In the last thirty or forty years, new universities have sprung up in the great industrial centres such as Manchester, Liverpool, Birmingham, Sheffield, Leeds and Bristol. Wales wanted its own university and founded it at Bangor, with branches at Cardiff, Swansea and Aberystwyth. After the war and in recent years, still more universities have been created at Hull, Newcastle, Southampton, Exeter and Reading and two others are planned for Nottingham and Leicester. In all of these centres, the trend is to give a prevalently technical character to culture in order to meet the demands of the large numbers of scholars. The most popular disciplines, besides the applied sciences, like physics and chemistry, are the professional disciplines, medicine, engineering, political economy, sociology, and so on. 'Oxford and Cambridge have also had to make concessions and give increasing importance to the sciences.' Furthermore, they have established extension courses.

The movement towards this new culture is very widespread: there are now evening schools and private institutions for adults that offer a hybrid, but essentially technical and practical education. In the meantime, a whole popular scientific literature has sprung up. Finally, admiration for science is such that even youths of the educated and aristocratic classes consider classical studies a pointless waste of time. The phenomenon is worldwide. But England had held out longer than other countries and now it is turning towards a dominantly technical form of culture. 'The type of the perfect gentleman no longer has a *raison d'être*. It represented the ideal English education when Great Britain, ruler of the seas and mistress of the great markets of the world, could allow herself the luxury of a politics of splendid isolation and a culture that had an undoubtedly aristocratic note. Today, things have changed.' The loss of its naval and economic supremacy; its very culture is menaced by America. Along with American culture, American books are entering the market and are increasingly a competitive threat to English books. English publishers, especially those with branch offices in America, have had to adopt American advertising and distribution methods. 'In England, books have a remarkable formative and educative effectiveness because they are read more and have a wider circulation than in Italy. They more faithfully reflect the intellectual life of the nation than ours do.' This intellectual life is now undergoing a change.

Of the volumes published in the first quarter of 1932 (which have increased numerically in comparison with the same period in 1931), the novel holds first place. Second place is no longer held by children's books but by school books and educational publications in general, and there is a marked increase in historical and biographical works and in technical, scientific and above all popular books.

From the volumes sent to the International Book Fair at Florence, 'we see that recent books of a cultural character are more technical than educational. They tend to discuss scientific questions and aspects of social life or to provide practical knowledge rather than to form character.'

Q4 § 93.

45 Intellectuals: Notes on English Culture [ii]

There is an article by Guido Ferrando in *Il Marzocco* of 4 October 1931, entitled 'Educazione e colonie' from which I take a few points. Ferrando attended 'The British Commonwealth Education Conference', at which were present hundreds of teachers of all levels, from the elementary school to the university, and coming from every part of the Empire; from Canada, India, South Africa, Australia, Kenya and New Zealand. The conference took place in London towards the end of July, and its purpose was to discuss the various aspects of the education problem 'in a changing Empire'. Several renowned educators from the United States were present. One of the fundamental themes of the congress was that of 'inter-racial understanding', how to promote and develop a better understanding between the various races, especially between the European colonizers and the African and Asian colonized.

It was interesting to see with what frankness and dialectical acumen the Indian delegates reproved the English for not understanding the Indian soul. Such incomprehension is revealed, for example, in that sense almost of disgust, in that attitude of contemptuous superiority which the majority of the British people still have today towards the

Indians. Even during the war this sense led the English officers to leave the table and the room when an Indian officer entered.

Among the many themes discussed was that of language. The problem was to decide if it was opportune to teach even the semi-savage population of Africa to read English instead of their native language, if it was better to maintain a bilingual approach or to aim at making the indigenous language disappear through the educational process. Ormsby Gore, former Under Secretary of State for the Colonies, argued that it was a mistake to attempt to denaturalize the African tribes and said he was in favour of an education that would seek to give the Africans a sense of their own dignity as a people and the ability to be self-governing. During the discussion which followed Ormsby Gore's speech, 'I was struck by the short statement of an African, I think he was a Zulu, who made a point of saying that his co-nationals, so to speak, had no wish to become Europeans. One could feel in his words a touch of nationalism, a faint sense of racial pride.'

'We do not want to be English': echoing this cry that issued spontaneously from among the representatives of the natives of the British colonies of Africa and Asia was the other cry of the representative of the Dominions: 'We do not feel English.' Australians and Canadians, citizens of New Zealand and South Africa all agreed in declaring their spiritual as well as political independence. Prof. Cillie, Dean of the Faculty of Letters in a South African university, had pointedly observed that traditionalist and conservative England was living in the past, while they, the South Africans, were living in the future.

Q9§87.

VII

MANZONI

Introduction

Gramsci's student research into Manzoni's proposals for reforming the Italian language had focused on their limitations in terms of real national linguistic change. His view here of Manzoni's novel, *The Betrothed*, which had been consciously popularizing both in its language and its subject matter, as non-national-popular is in effect the literary counterpart of that judgement, and it makes a significant contrast with Lukács's positive view of the novel as '*the* tragedy of the Italian people as a whole' (*The Historical Novel*, written 1936/7: p. 70 of the English edition, London 1962). Gramsci's approach to the novel is linked to his analysis of the caste tradition of the Italian intellectuals, the reformist nature of the Risorgimento, Catholicism and 'Brescianism' (see Section VIII). Manzoni provides him with a symptomatic illustration of all these things.

Although baptized a Catholic, Alessandro Manzoni (1785–1873) had been an agnostic liberal before his conversion in Paris in 1810. He was then influenced by Jansenism, a religious movement which by the early nineteenth century had become politically ambiguous since its conception of grace as restricted to the few was apparently in conflict with its overt links with French Revolution liberalism. The Papacy opposed it for its espousal of the revolutionary Civil Constitution of the Clergy, which subjected Church to State, and the Jesuits treated it as a heresy. Manzoni coupled his liberalism after 1810 with an evangelical kind of Catholicism, directed at social reform and based strongly on a vindication of the poor and the meek, yet he also wrote a defence of Catholic morality against Sismondi's anti-clerical interpretation of Italian history and a discourse in which he ascribed a historically progressive role to the medieval Papacy. His novel, written and recast in several versions from 1821, is set in Counter-Reformation Lombardy of the seventeenth century. In it, a pastorally protective Catholic hierarchy guides the people through error and religious doubt. Gramsci reads in the novel the contradictions in Manzoni's liberal Catholicism, with its

paternalist and populist elements, and examines how they relate
to Manzoni's interest as a historical novelist in the tribulations of
his popular protagonists, in reconstructing an unwritten history
of the 'humble' classes.

The first note in this section establishes Gramsci's guidelines
for analysing Manzoni's novel. Although he distinguishes
between propaganda and art, he makes it clear that his
concentration on the cultural significance of *The
Betrothed* tends to displace an aesthetic judgement. The cultural
problem turns on the paradox of why a novel with a 'popular'
content and language is not read and appreciated by the people,
as Gramsci claims is the case. His assessment of the limitations
of Manzoni's linguistic reform are partly relevant to this question,
but his answer here draws specifically on the point made earlier
(see II 14) that the writer's attitude must be treated as an essential
component of a literary work's content. This leads him into
looking at what can be seen of Manzoni's attitude to his subject
matter in the text of the novel, the way it uses an élitist irony,
whose nuances are only perceptible to cultured readers, in
treating the popular characters (peasant, artisan, servant, village
priest) and the way the functions of noble and popular characters
are related to each other in the narrative. These observations are
linked in turn to those on the contradictions in Manzoni's
Catholicism and progressivism, again apparent in the text.
Gramsci is not 'criticizing' Manzoni for having the outlook he
had or for being insufficiently progressive (see his remarks on
Tolstoy's and Shaw's criticism of Shakespeare), but is rather
exposing the historical and cultural conditions of which
Manzoni's work is symptomatic. Criticism, in a narrowly literary
sense, is not Gramsci's declared intention here, but rather 'a
study of cultural history'.

1 The 'Popularity' of Tolstoy and Manzoni

In *Il Marzocco* of 11 November 1928 there is an article by Adolfo
Faggi entitled 'Fede e dramma' ('Faith and drama'), which
contains elements for setting up a comparison between Tolstoy's
conception of the world and that of Manzoni – despite Faggi's
arbitrary claim that *'The Betrothed* corresponds perfectly to his

(Tolstoy's) concept of religious art', set forth in his critical study on Shakespeare:

> Art in general and dramatic art in particular was always religious, its scope was to explain to men their relationship with God according to the understanding that the most eminent men of every age had constructed of it, those men therefore who were destined to guide others. . . . Then there was a deviation in art by which it was enslaved to the function of a pastime and an amusement, a deviation that also occurred in Christian art.[1]

Faggi notes that in *War and Peace* the two characters with the greatest religious importance are Platon Karatayev and Pierre Bezukhov. The first is a man of the people, and his naïve and instinctive thought has a great deal of influence on Pierre Bezukhov's view of life.[2]

It is characteristic of Tolstoy that the naïve and instinctive wisdom of the people, even when uttered casually, enlightens and brings about a crisis in the educated man. That is the most notable trait of Tolstoy's religion which interprets the gospel 'democratically', according to its initial and original spirit. Manzoni, by contrast, has undergone the Counter-Reformation. His Christianity wavers between a Jansenistic aristocratic stance and a populist jesuitical paternalism. For Faggi, in *The Betrothed* 'it is the superior souls, like Fra Cristoforo and Cardinal Borromeo, who act on the inferior ones and are always able to find the right word to enlighten and guide them'. There is no substantial link between this observation and Tolstoy's definition of religious art, which refers to the general conception and not to the particular modes of expression. The conceptions of the world are necessarily elaborated by eminent minds, but 'reality' is expressed by the 'humble' people, by the simple in spirit.

Furthermore, it should be noted that in *The Betrothed* there is not one common person who is not teased and laughed at: including Don Abbondio, Fra Galdino, the tailor, Gervasio, Agnese, Perpetua, Renzo and even Lucia. They are depicted as wretched and narrow people without an inner life. Only the

[1] Gramsci would appear to be quoting Faggi's paraphrase of Tolstoy here. For Tolstoy's text in English, see pp. 68–69 of *Tolstoy on Shakespeare*, Christchurch, 1907 (including Tolstoy's 'Shakespeare and Drama', Ernest Crosby's 'Shakespeare and the Working Classes', and extracts from letters by George Bernard Shaw to V. Tchertkoff).

[2] Karatayev is the old Russian soldier who appears in Book 4 (Part 1, Chapter 12) and is later executed by French prison guards (Part 3, Chapter 14).

nobles have an inner life: Fra Cristoforo, Borromeo, the Unnamed and Don Rodrigo. According to Don Abbondio, Perpetua had said more or less the same thing as Borromeo says later on. But in this case it is a matter of doing what is practical, and anyway the incident is a source of comedy.[3] Likewise for the fact that Renzo's opinion on the value of Lucia's vow of virginity coincides externally with the opinion of Fra Cristoforo. The importance that Lucia's words have in troubling the conscience of the Unnamed and in contributing to his moral crisis is not enlightening and dazzling as is the contribution of the people, the course of moral and religious life, in Tolstoi.[4] It is mechanical and 'syllogistic'. In fact there are considerable traces of Brescianism in Manzoni too.

Note that, before Parini, it was the Jesuits who 'brought out' the qualities of the people 'paternalistically': see C.A. Vianello, *La giovinezza del Parini, Verri e Beccaria* (Milan 1933), where he refers to the Jesuit father Pozzi 'who long before Parini stood up to defend and exalt – in front of the assembly of the highest patriciate of Milan – the "plebeians" or, as one would say now, the proletariat' (see *La Civiltà Cattolica*, 4 August 1934, p. 272).[5]

In another article – 'Tolstoi e Shakespeare' – published in *Il Marzocco* of 9 September 1928, Faggi examines Tolstoy's pamphlet on Shakespeare: *Shakespeare, eine kritische Studie*, Hanover, 1906. The small volume also contains an article by Ernest Crosby on 'Shakespeare and the Working Classes' and a short letter by Bernard Shaw on Shakespeare's philosophy. Tolstoy seeks to demolish Shakespeare from the point of view of his own Christian ideology; his criticism is not artistic, but moral

---

[3] In Chapter 1, Perpetua (Don Abbondio's housekeeper) says 'My advice'd be: as everyone says our archbishop's a holy man, and a man with guts too, who's not afraid of anyone, and just loves backing one of his parish priests and squashing one of those bullies, I'd say, write him a nice letter and tell him all about. . .' (*The Betrothed*, translated by Archibald Colquhoun, London 1951, p. 15). In Chapter 26, Cardinal Borromeo reproves Don Abbondio: '"Why did you not think of informing your bishop of the obstacles put by an infamous violence to the exercise of your office?" – Perpetua's advice! – thought Don Abbondio irritably' (ibid. p. 337).

[4] See *The Betrothed* Chapter 21 (p. 310): 'All of a sudden the words which he had heard repeated again and again a few hours before came back into his mind: – God forgives so much, for one deed of mercy! – And they no longer came back to him in those accents of humble supplication in which they had been uttered, but in a tone full of authority, which induced at the same time a far-away hope'.

[5] On Parini see footnote 102 on p. 272.

and religious. Crosby's article, which was Tolstoy's starting point, shows that there is hardly a word of sympathy for the people and the working classes in all of Shakespeare's work, contrary to the opinion of many renowned Englishmen. In line with the tendencies of his time, Shakespeare openly sides with the upper classes of society: his plays are essentially aristocratic. Almost every time that he puts bourgeois or common people on to the stage, he presents them in a scornful or repugnant manner and makes them the matter or subject of laughter. (Compare what I said about Manzoni, who has a similar tendency, although its signs are attenuated.)

Shaw's letter is directed against Shakespeare the 'thinker', not against Shakespeare the 'artist'. According to Shaw, in literature one *must* give pride of place to those authors who have gone beyond the morality of their time and perceived the new demands of the future. Shakespeare was not 'morally' superior to his time, etc.

These notes should avoid any moralistic tendentiousness like Tolstoy's and also any tendentiousness of 'hindsight' like Shaw's. This is a study of cultural history, not artistic criticism in the strict sense. The aim is to show that it is the authors being studied who introduce an extrinsic moral content, that they make propaganda and not art, and that the conception of the world implicit in their works is narrow and impoverished, not national-popular but that of a closed caste. The study of the beauty of a work is made subordinate to the study of why it is 'read', 'popular', 'sought after', or, in the opposite case, why it does not touch the people and arouse their interest, showing up the lack of unity in the cultural life of the nation.

Q 23 § 51.

2 Attitude to the People in 'The Betrothed'

The 'aristocratic' character of Manzoni's Catholicism is apparent from the jocular 'sympathy' shown towards the figures of the common people (which does not appear in Tolstoy): Fra Galdino (compared with Fra Cristoforo), the tailor, Renzo, Agnese, Perpetua and also Lucia.

On Zottoli's book see Filippo Crispolti, 'Nuove indagini sul

Manzoni', in *Pègaso*, August 1931. Crispolti's article is interesting in its own right for understanding the attitude of Jesuitic Christianity toward 'the humble'. Yet I feel that Crispolti's criticism of Zottoli is right, although Crispolti argues 'jesuitically'. He says of Manzoni, 'The *people* in themselves have all his sympathy, but he never stoops to flatter them; in fact, he sees them rather with the same severe gaze with which he sees *the majority* of those who do not belong to the people'.

But the point is not that of wanting Manzoni to 'flatter the people'; the question is one of his psychological attitude towards individual characters who belong to the people. It is clearly a caste attitude, even in its religious Catholic form. For Manzoni the people do not have any 'inner life', any deep moral personality. They are 'animals' and Manzoni is 'benevolent' towards them, with exactly that benevolence of a Catholic society for the protection of animals. In a sense, Manzoni reminds one of the epigram about Paul Bourget: for Bourget a woman must have an income of 100,000 francs before she can have an inner life. Manzoni (and Bourget) are in this respect unmitigatedly Catholic. There is nothing in them of Tolstoy's 'popular spirit', of the evangelical spirit of primitive Christianity. Manzoni's attitude to the people is the attitude of the Catholic Church to the people: one of indulgent benevolence, not shared humanity. Crispolti, in the sentence quoted, unconsciously confesses this 'partiality' (or 'partisanship') of Manzoni's. Manzoni sees *all* of the people with 'a severe gaze', while he sees with a severe gaze *'the majority* of those who do not belong to the people': he finds 'magnanimity', 'noble thoughts' and 'great feelings' only in some of the upper class and in none of the people, who as a whole are basely animal-like.

As Crispolti rightly says, the fact that the 'humble' play a leading role in Manzoni's novel is not greatly significant. Manzoni puts the 'people' into his novel, both as principal characters (Renzo, Lucia, Perpetua, Fra Galdino, etc.) and as the masses (the Milan riots, the country people, the tailor, etc.), yet his attitude towards the people is not 'national-popular' but aristocratic.

One should bear Crispolti's article in mind when studying Zottoli's book. It can be shown that 'Catholicism', even in superior and non-'jesuitical' men like Manzoni (Manzoni certainly had a Jansenist and anti-Jesuit vein in him), did not help towards creating the 'people-nation' in Italy, not even in the Romantic period. On the contrary, it was an anti-national-popular and solely high-cultural element. Crispolti refers only to the fact that for a certain time Manzoni accepted Thierry's idea (for France) of racial conflict in the midst of the people (Longobards and Romans, like Franks and Gauls in France) as the struggle between the humble and the powerful.[6]

(Zottoli tries to reply to Crispolti in *Pègaso* of September 1931.)

Q7 § 50.

3 'The Humble'

This expression, 'the humble', is characteristic for defining the traditional attitude of Italian intellectuals towards the people and hence the meaning of 'literature for the humble'. We are not dealing with the relationship contained in Dostoyevsky's expression 'the humiliated and offended'.[7] There is a strong national-popular feeling in Dostoyevsky, an awareness that the intellectuals have a mission towards the people. The people may be 'objectively' made up of 'the humble' but they must be freed from this 'humility', transformed and regenerated. For the Italian intellectual the expression 'the humble' indicates a relationship of paternal and divine protection, the 'self-sufficient' sense of his undiscussed superiority. It is like the relationship between two races, one considered superior and the other inferior, like the relationship between adult and child in the old schools or, worse still, like that of a 'society for the protection of animals' or like

[6] Augustin Thierry (1795–1856), French liberal historian, developed a view of history as a series of conflicts between occupying and occupied races where the occupiers became a national ruling class (e.g. Normans over Saxons in England, Franks over Gauls in France). Manzoni was influenced by Thierry's interest in the historical role of the masses, ignored by traditional chroniclers. The eighth-century Longobard occupation and oppression of the indigenous Romans is the subject of his play *Adelchi* (1821). As Gramsci notes in VII 4 below, Marx indicated his debt to Thierry and other French bourgeois historians of the Restoration period in elaborating the concept of class struggle. See Marx's letter to Engels of 27 July 1854 (reproduced in Karl Marx and Frederick Engels, *Collected Works*, Vol. 39, p. 472), to Weydermeyer of 5 March 1852 (*Collected Works* Vol. 39, p. 60) and Engels's letter to Starkenburg of 25 July 1894. See also Engels's reference to Thierry in *Ludwig Feuerbach*, Chapter 4.

[7] A reference to the title of Dostoyevsky's novel *Unizhennye i oskorblennye*, known in English as *The Insulted and Injured* and in Italian as *Umiliati e offesi*.

that between the Salvation Army and the cannibals of Papua.

Q21 § 3.

4 Manzoni and 'The Humble'

Manzoni's 'democratic' attitude towards the humble (in *The Betrothed*) – in that it is of 'Christian' origin and should be connected to the interest in historical studies that Manzoni derived from Thierry and from his theories about racial conflict (conquerors and conquered) becoming class conflict. Zottoli's book, *Umili e potenti nella poetica di A. Manzoni*, should be looked at for these relations between Manzoni's attitude and Thierry's theories.

In Manzoni the theories of Thierry become complicated or at least take on new aspects in the discussion on the 'historical novel' inasmuch as it depicts people of the 'subaltern classes' who 'have no history': there are no traces of their history in the historical documents of the past. (This point can be linked up with the notes on 'History of the Subaltern Classes', where reference can be made to Thierry's doctrines, which were in any case very important for the origins of the historiography of the philosophy of praxis.)[8]

Q14 § 39.

5 Popular Literature: Manzoni

In *Il Marzocco* of 1 November 1931 Adolfo Faggi makes a few observations on the maxim 'Vox populi vox Dei' in *The Betrothed*. The maxim is quoted twice in the novel (according to Faggi): once in the final chapter where Don Abbondio uses it about the Marquis who succeeds Don Rodrigo: 'And then you don't want to hear me call you a fine man. I say so and I want to say so; in spite of you I want to say so. And even if I was silent, it wouldn't be any avail for that's what everyone says; and *vox populi, vox Dei.*'[9] Faggi points out that this solemn proverb is used rather

---

[8] Since 1930 Gramsci had been writing a series of notes with this heading. They were regrouped and expanded in special notebook Q 25 (1934), to which he gave the general title 'On the margins of history: history of the subaltern social groups'.

[9] *The Betrothed*, p. 567.

effusively by Don Abbondio, while he is in that happy frame of mind caused by Don Rodrigo's death. It has no particular importance or meaning. The other time the maxim occurs is in Chapter 31 referring to the plague: 'Many doctors, too, echoing the voice of the people (was it the voice of God, also in this case?), derided the ominous predictions and threatening warnings of the few. . . .'[10] Here the proverb is given in Italian and in brackets, with an ironic tone. In *Gli sposi promessi* (Book IV, Chapter 3, Lesca edition),[11] Manzoni writes at length about the ideas that men have generally held to be true at one time or another. He concludes that, although the ideas current among the people during the plague of Milan may be considered ridiculous today, we cannot know if today's ideas will not be considered ridiculous tomorrow. This long argument of the first draft is summed up in the definitive text in a brief question: 'Was it the voice of God, also in this case?'

Faggi distinguishes those times when, for Manzoni, the voice of the people is not *in certain cases* the voice of God from others in which it may be. He argues that it is not the voice of God 'in the case of ideas or, better, specific notions that can only be determined by science and its continual progress; but in the case of those general principles and feelings naturally common to all men which the ancients included under the well-known expression of the *conscientia generis humani*.' Faggi, however, does not put the question very accurately. It cannot be answered without referring to Manzoni's religion, his Catholicism. Thus, for example, he cites Perpetua's famous advice to Don Abbondio, which coincides with the opinion of Cardinal Borromeo. In this case, though, we are not dealing with a moral or religious question, but with a suggestion of practical prudence dictated by the most banal common sense. The fact that Cardinal Borromeo finds himself in agreement with Perpetua is not as important as Faggi thinks. It seems to me that it is related to the time and the fact that the ecclesiastical authorities had political power and influence. It is natural for Perpetua to think that Don Abbondio

[10] Ibid. p. 453.

[11] Manzoni's novel exists in three versions: a first draft (1821–23) and two published editions (1827 and 1840). An integral text of the first draft (now known as *Fermo e Lucia*) was first edited in 1915 by Giuseppe Lesca with the title *Gli sposi promessi*. The 1840 edition represents Manzoni's definitive reworking of the text into Florentine, in line with his ideas on standardizing the Italian language.

should turn to the Archbishop of Milan (it only serves to show how Don Abbondio had lost his head at that point and that Perpetua had more *'esprit de corps'* than he), just as it is natural that Federico Borromeo should speak the way he does. In this case the voice of God is irrelevant. Nor does the other case have much significance: Renzo does not believe in the effectiveness of Lucia's vow of chastity and over this he is in agreement with Fra Cristoforo. Here, too, it is a question of 'casuistry' and not of morality.[12] Faggi says that 'Manzoni wanted to write a novel of the humble people', but the significance of this is more complex than Faggi apparently thinks. There is a disjunction of feeling between Manzoni and the 'humble' people. For Manzoni they are a 'problem of historiography', a theoretical problem that he believes he can solve with the historical novel and the 'verisimilitude' of the historical novel. Hence the 'humble' people are often presented as popular 'caricatures', with good-natured irony, but irony none the less. Manzoni is too Catholic to think that the voice of the people is the voice of God: between the people and God there is the Church. Tolstoy can believe that God is incarnate in the people, but not Manzoni.

Of course, this attitude of Manzoni's is felt by the people and therefore *The Betrothed* has never been popular among them. Emotionally, the people felt that Manzoni was distant from them and felt his novel to be like a book of devotion, not a popular epic.

Q 14 § 45.

6 [Irony]

In *Il Marzocco* of 18 September 1932, Tullia Franzi writes about the argument between Manzoni and the English translator of *The Betrothed*, the Anglican pastor Charles Swan, over the expression near the end of Chapter 7 used to indicate Shakespeare: 'Between the first conception of a terrible undertaking and its execution (as a barbarian who was not without intelligence has

---

[12] In Chapter 21 the abducted Lucia vows to remain chaste if the Virgin Mary will rescue her from danger. Renzo (her betrothed) argues that the Virgin helps those in trouble but does not take revenge for the broken promises of her devotees (Chapter 27), that Lucia made the vow when she did not know what she was saying and that the Virgin would not want promises that would harm one's neighbour (Chapter 36). Padre Cristoforo says (Chapter 36) that Lucia's vow contradicted her previous pledge to marry Renzo and he exercises his authority as God's minister to annul the vow.

said) the interval is a dream full of phantasms and fears.'[13] Swan wrote to Manzoni: '"A barbarian who was not without intelligence" is a phrase, calculated to draw upon you the anathema of every admirer of our bard.' Although Swan was acquainted with Voltaire's writings against Shakespeare, he missed Manzoni's irony which was in fact aimed precisely at Voltaire (who defined Shakespeare as 'a savage with sparks of genius').[14] Swan published as a preface to his translation the letter in which Manzoni explains to him the meaning of his ironic expression. Franzi, however, recalls that in other English translations Manzoni's expression is either omitted or blunted ('a foreign writer writes. . . ', etc.). The same occurs in other foreign language translations. This proves that this irony, which must be explained in order to be understood and savoured, is ultimately an irony in the 'jargon' of a literary coterie. It seems to me that this fact is much more widespread than it might appear and makes it not only difficult to translate from Italian but also often difficult to understand an Italian in conversation. The 'finesse' seemingly required in such conversations is not a matter of normal intelligence, but of having to know the intellectual minutiae and attitudes of a 'jargon' peculiar to literati or indeed to specific groups of literati. (Notice in Tullia Franzi's article a surprising 'feminine' metaphor: 'Manzoni received this letter with the feeling of a man who, ill-treated and beaten by his wife out of jealous suspicion, rejoices in her anger and blesses those blows as proof of her love.' A man who rejoices in being beaten by his wife is certainly an original form of contemporary feminism.)[15]

Q 15 § 37.

---

[13] *Julius Caesar* II, i, 63–65: 'Between the acting of a dreadful thing / And the first motion, all the interim is/Like a phantasma, or a hideous dream'.

[14] 'La vérité, qu'on ne peut déguiser devant vous, m'ordonne de vous avouer que ce Shakespeare, si sauvage, si bas, si éffrené, et si absurde, avait des étincelles de génie.' (Letter of 1776 to Académie Française).

[15] The metaphor of the beaten husband is in fact Manzoni's, in the opening sentence of the letter to Swan; Franzi is paraphrasing.

VIII
FATHER BRESCIANI'S PROGENY

Introduction

Gramsci's coinage 'Brescianism' comes from the name of a nineteenth-century reactionary historical novelist, the Jesuit father Antonio Bresciani (1798–1862). A novel by Bresciani about Italy in 1848, *L'Ebreo di Verona* ('The Jew of Verona'), had been the subject of a scathing critical essay by Francesco De Sanctis in 1855. Exposing the author's mastery of the 'art of simulation and dissimulation', De Sanctis showed how Bresciani had presented the 1848 revolution as if it were entirely the work of fanatical conspirators and secret societies, while at the same time expropriating revolutionary language to the cause of reaction, presenting Catholicism as the 'true liberty' and calling the liberals 'libertines'. He also drew attention to the laboriously wordy elegance and fixation on form in Bresciani's style. On 10 November 1917, Gramsci printed an extract from De Sanctis's essay in *Il Grido del Popolo* (reprinted in SC pp. 327–28), giving it the title 'Reaction and Revolution'. His point was to draw a parallel between Bresciani's reaction to 1848 and that of the bourgeois press to the Bolshevik revolution. He returned to the analogy several times in 1920: '*La Stampa* [in 1917–18] adopted the same stance towards the workers' revolution as the Jesuits towards the liberal revolution' (SM p. 491). 'Every historical period of struggle and profound social transformation has its Jesuits; this seems to be a law of human development. The liberals and Mazzinians had Father Antonio Bresciani; the communists have the renegades from socialism who have installed themselves in the editorial offices of the bourgeois press' (ON p. 349). In the Prison Notebooks, he extends the comparison to the anti-socialist reaction in Italy after the Red Years 1919–20. This reaction has brought fascism to power and 'Brescianism' has become the 'pre-eminent and unofficial "school" of fiction' under the regime: 'Regardless of the name they assume, restorations, especially those of the present epoch, are universally repressive: "Father Bresciani" and Brescianist literature predominate. The psychology behind such an intellectual expression is based on panic, on a cosmic fear of unintelligible demoniac forces which can only be controlled by a universally repressive force.' (II 13).

The opening note in this section implicitly dates the emergence of latter-day Brescianism from the same post-war crisis by assigning to its 'prehistory' a number of novels published before then. It also divides Brescianism into clerical, lay and 'intermediate' variants. A high proportion of Gramsci's notes on Brescianism in fact deal with Catholic writers, whom he calls 'technically' Brescianist or Catholic or Jesuit. In Italian, the words 'Jesuit' and 'jesuitical' carry a strong figurative flavour of 'underhand' or 'two-faced'. Gramsci overlays the literal and figurative senses. His discussion here is related to analyses of the Catholic Church elsewhere in the notebooks. The Jesuits began life as the shock-troops of the Counter-Reformation and it was then, according to Gramsci, that the Church reversed its earlier process of absorbing mass heretical movements into its ranks and started propping itself up with state coercion to re-establish its undermined ideological leadership. 'The Society of Jesus is the last of the great religious orders. Its origins were reactionary and authoritarian, and its character repressive and "diplomatic".' (SPN p. 332). After 1848 the Jesuits, recently restored to legality, reacted against the liberal trend in Catholicism (neo-Guelphism) and again dominated a repressive phase to maintain hegemony. February 1929, the month in which Gramsci started work on the notebooks, saw a crucial change in Church-State relations with the Concordat between the fascist state and the Vatican. After having liquidated the mass Catholic Popular Party (PPI) with Vatican and Jesuit backing between 1923 and 1926, Mussolini used the Concordat to try and secure the support of the Catholic peasant masses and intellectuals in return for a partitioning of hegemony with the Church in civil society. Gramsci noted that, since by the Concordat the Catholics now held the monopoly of secondary as well as elementary education in Italy, they had acquired an ideological monopoly over the proletariat, peasantry and petty bourgeoisie who would not go on to higher education (where lay intellectuals were still dominant). 'The entry *en masse* of the Catholics into the life of the state after the Concordat . . . has made much more difficult the task of "transformism" of the new forces of democratic origin' (i.e. the intellectuals of the subaltern classes) (Q 10 II § 14). At the same time, the Concordat had fused into a 'moral unity' the two main ideological branches of the dominant class, the Catholic and lay intellectuals.

Gramsci's survey of the Jesuit aspect of Brescianism is thus part of a contemporary analysis of recent alignments of Italian intellectuals since February 1929. Giovanni Papini, former iconoclast of *La Voce* and flirter with Futurism, a convert to Catholicism in 1919 after a spiritual crisis, has become an 'apprentice Jesuit'. Ugo Ojetti, an ex-liberal conservative who became one of the most prestigious figures in bourgeois literary culture under fascism, writes a fawning letter to Father Rosa, the editor of Bresciani's old Jesuit periodical *La Civiltà Cattolica*, to opt himself into the new intellectual alliance with the Catholics. At the same time, the non-Jesuit Curzio Malaparte exalts fascism as a restoration of the Counter-Reformation Latin spirit against the canker of northern modernity. At this level, it is not of primary importance to Gramsci whether these writers are 'technically' Jesuit or not. They are all Brescianists because they have renounced their 'historical task' of promoting an intellectual and moral reformation, of 'satisfying the intellectual needs of the people', of elaborating a modern 'humanism' (see VI 3).

The 'post-history' of the review *La Voce* plays an important part in Brescianism. The campaign for a moral and intellectual renewal that Gramsci saw in the early *Voce* had collapsed with the First World War. Now some of the review's leading lights – Papini, Prezzolini, Soffici – were reincarnated as the 'progeny' of Father Bresciani and their pre-war ideologies (nationalism, interventionism, populism, Futurism) had come into line with various articulations of fascist ideology. At the same time the 'pure' literary preoccupations of the writers of *La Ronda* (Cardarelli, Bacchelli) had solidified into the stance of 'high-priestly' detachment from political reality that constitutes another component of Brescianism.

In the Notebooks as a whole, Gramsci uses the heading 'Father Bresciani's progeny' over a wide range of notes on literature and at times rather loosely. At its most generic, 'Brescianism' appears to be a simple polemical and 'journalistic' label, the counterpart in literary culture of Gramsci's similar pejorative term 'Lorianism' (from Achille Loria) in social-scientific thought. In its more restricted senses it is still multi-faceted: Brescianism includes the political element of reaction and the aping of revolution, the Catholic-Jesuit element, the stylistic element of casuistry and 'false elegance' or formalism, the ideologies of apolitical detachment, nostalgia and populism. In fact these facets of the concept accurately represent the incoherent and contradictory nature of fascist ideology: the old combative spirit of the squads alongside the traditionalist conservatism of the regime; Europeanism alongside provincialism; urbanism alongside ruralism; modernity alongside Roman antiquity. Gramsci's term is at once broad enough to contain these various stratifications of fascist culture and unitary enough to reduce them to a common denominator which exposes their real roots.

1 Father Bresciani's Progeny

The examination of a conspicuous part of Italian narrative literature, especially of the last decades. The prehistory of modern (post-war) Brescianism can be identified in a number of writers such as Antonio Beltramelli with books like *Gli uomini rossi, Il cavalier Mostardo*, etc.;[1] and 'Polifilo' (Luca Beltrami), with his various stories about 'the folk of Casate Olona', etc.[2] The literature, fairly abundant and widespread in certain milieux, which has a more technically 'sacristan' quality; it is little known in the lay cultural milieu and is not at all studied. Its tendentious and propagandistic character is openly admitted: these are the 'good publications'. In between literature of the vestry and lay Brescianism there is a literary trend that has developed considerably in recent years (the Florentine Catholic group led by Giovanni Papini):[3] a typical example are the novels of Giuseppe Molteni. One of these, *Gli atei*, reflects the monstrous

---

[1] Antonio Beltramelli (1879–30) was a republican from Romagna. Attracted to the anticlerical and anarchoid fascism of 1919, he published in 1923 a bestselling monograph on Mussolini, *L'uomo nuovo*. In 1929 he was nominated to the Accademia d'Italia. The 'reds' in *Gli uomini rossi* (1904) are republicans involved in local political struggles with the Catholics. *Il cavalier Mostardo* (1922) is a sequel where the enemies have become the socialists of the Workers' League who attack 'sacred' sharecropping.

[2] Luca Beltrami (1854–1933), professor of architecture at Milan and from 1900 to 1920 a joint owner of the *Corriere della Sera*. He serialized his populist and paternalistic stories of small-town life in the imaginary Lombard town of Casate Olona under the pseudonym 'Polifilo'. They were collected in 1909 in the volume *Casate Olona 1859–1909*. See also VIII 8 below.

[3] Papini – an active Catholic since 1920 – was a co-founder of the Catholic intellectuals' review *Frontespizio* (Florence 1929–40) which had emerged after the Concordat. On Papini see footnote 23 on p. 46 above and VIII 5 below.

scandal of Father Riva and Sister Fumagalli in an even more monstrously aberrant way.[4] Molteni goes so far as to assert that precisely because Father Riva was obliged to be celibate and chaste he must be pitied (he raped and infected some thirty little girls offered to him by Sister Fumagalli to keep him 'faithful'). He believes that the vulgar adultery of an atheist lawyer can be treated as morally equivalent to this sort of massacre. Molteni was well known in the Catholic literary world. He was literary critic and columnist for a whole series of clerical dailies and periodicals, including *L'Italia* and *Vita e Pensiero*.

Brescianism assumes some importance among the literary 'laity' of the post-war period and is increasingly becoming the pre-eminent and unofficial 'school' of fiction.

Ugo Ojetti and his novel *Mio figlio ferroviere*.[5] The general characteristics of Ojetti's work and his various 'ideological' attitudes. Writings on Ojetti by Giovanni Ansaldo, who incidentally resembles Ojetti more than was apparent in the past.[6] Ojetti's most characteristic piece is his open letter to Father Enrico Rosa which was published in *Pégaso* and reprinted in *La Civiltà Cattolica* with a commentary by Rosa.[7] After the conciliation between Church and state was announced, Ojetti was not only convinced that all the work of Italian intellectuals would now be controlled along strict Catholic and clerical lines, but he had already adjusted himself to this idea and addressed Father Rosa in a style which unctuously flattered the cultural merits of the Society of Jesus in order to beg for a 'fair' artistic freedom. Nor can it be said in the light of subsequent events (Head of the Government's speech to the Chamber)[8] which was worse: Ojetti's abject prostration, or the comic self-assurance of

---

[4] In 1909, Don Giovanni Riva was sentenced to 16 years for sexually abusing children in a girls' convent college. A nun, Maria Giuseppina Fumagalli, was given 10 months for abetting him. Molteni's novel, published in 1910, alludes to the case through the character of Don Gino Amati.

[5] On Ojetti, see footnote 75 on p. 252 above and VIII 3 below. *Mio figlio ferroviere* (1922) is narrated by a doctor whose son 'drops out' to become a railway worker and branch leader of a socialist union, only to lose his convictions and return to his bourgeois family. The narrator divides the generations after the First World War into maddened and drunken 'saints' who want revolution and healthy sceptics who resign themselves in the hope of a restoration of order.

[6] On Ansaldo see VIII 10 below. His articles mildly ridiculing Ojetti had appeared in *La Rivoluzione Liberale* in 1924–25.

[7] Ojetti's letter is quoted in VIII 3 below.

Father Rosa, who in any case gave a character lesson to Ojetti – in the Jesuit manner of course. Ojetti is representative in many respects; but the man's intellectual cowardice exceeds any normal measure.

Alfredo Panzini: already part of the prehistory of Brescianism with, for example, some passages from *La lanterna di Diogene* (the episode of the 'livid blade' is a gem of comic idiocy),[9] then *Il padrone sono me, Il mondo è rotondo* and almost all of his books from the war onwards. In his *Vita di Cavour* there is even a reference to Father Bresciani, truly amazing if it were not symptomatic.[10] All of the pseudo-historical literature of Panzini should be re-examined from the viewpoint of lay Brescianism. The Croce-Panzini episode, reported in *La Critica*, is a case of personal as well as literary jesuitism.[11]

Of Salvatore Gotta one could say what Carducci wrote of Rapisardi: *'Oremus* at the altar and flatulences in the sacristy';[12] his whole literary output is Brescianist.

[8] Mussolini's speech to the Chamber of Deputies on 13 May 1929 aimed to reassure the fascist laity who feared the Concordat had conceded too much to the Church. 'In the state', he told them, 'the Church is neither sovereign nor free' . . . 'We have not resuscitated the temporal power of the Popes, we have buried it.' The speech shattered the initial optimism of Pius XI over the agreement.

[9] The reference is to a passage in Panzini's novel where the schoolteacher-narrator meets an anarchist worker who wields a barber's razor (the 'livid blade') to cut a cigar. His instinct is 'to seize his wrist like a claw and make him drop the horrible weapon. . . but I ran the risk of making my stomach a cushion for that pin'. (*La lanterna di Diogene*, Milan 1918, pp. 112–13). Gramsci elsewhere suggested an explanation for Panzini's obsession with knives: 'Maybe he was present by chance at some disturbance in Romagna and he must have seen a pair of eyes staring grimly at him: hence the "livid blades" that run him through the heart etc.' (Q 23 § 32). Alfredo Panzini (1863–1939) taught in secondary schools until 1928 and was nominated to the Accademia d'Italia in 1929. Gramsci comments critically on his *Guida alla grammatica italiana* in V 8 above. See also VIII 4 below.

[10] Panzini's *Vita di Cavour* was serialized in *L'Italia Letteraria*. Gramsci devoted a separate note to it (Q 23 § 32) where he quotes the passage referred to here: 'And whoever wants to see how the Carbonarist sect could take on the appearance of Beelzebub should read the novel *L'Ebreo di Verona* by Antonio Bresciani. He will enjoy it immensely because, despite what the moderns say, that Jesuit father was a powerful writer'.

[11] Panzini had made a sarcastic remark in his *Dizionario Moderno* about Croce's introduction of the obscure new word 'allotria' into Italian. Reviewing the dictionary in *La Critica* XXIII (1925) 6, p.375, Croce claimed that this permanently jocular manner of Panzini's masked his essential stupidity.

[12] Giosue Carducci, 'Rapisardiana' in *Opere* IV, Bologna 1890, p.381: 'the kyrie of the high altar ends with the flatulences of the chorus'. Mario Rapisardi (1844–1912) was an anti-clerical poet who feuded with Carducci. Gramsci had read Gotta's novel *La donna mia* (1924) during his Milan imprisonment.

Margherita Sarfatti and her novel *Il Palazzone*.[13] Goffredo Bellonci's review in *L'Italia Letteraria* of 23 June 1929 says: 'How absolutely true the virgin's shyness as she stands chastely in front of the marriage bed while at the same time feeling that it is "kindly and welcoming for future jousting".' This chaste virgin who feels with the technical language of writers of licentious tales is priceless: the virgin Fiorella must also have had a foreboding of 'many a ride' and 'times in the saddle'. An idle digression could be made on this business of jousts: remember the legend of Dante and the prostitute included in Papini's collection (published by Carabba) on how a man can talk about 'jousting' but not a woman;[14] and remember what the Catholic Chesterton says in *The New Jerusalem* about the battle of the sexes and how the point of view of the key cannot be the same as the point of view of the lock. (It is worth noting how Bellonci, who is quite happy to flirt with 'precious' – and cheap – erudition to make a name for himself among the hack journalists in Rome, can find it 'true' that a virgin thinks in terms of 'jousting'.)

Mario Sobrero and the novel *Pietro e Paolo* can be added to the general picture of Brescianism, to balance it out.[15]

Francesco Perri and his novel *Emigranti*. Isn't this Perri the same person as the Paolo Albatrelli of *I conquistatori*?[16] At any rate, *I conquistatori* should also be taken into account. The most characteristic trait of *Emigranti* is its crudeness, but it is not the crudeness of the naïve beginner, in which case it might be unelaborated material with the possibility of being worked out further. It is an opaque, material crudeness, that of a pretentious

---

[13] Margherita Sarfatti (1883–1961), journalist on *Il Popolo d'Italia* and the fascist review *Gerarchia*, and leading theorist of the 'Novecento' movement in the visual arts. Her biography of Mussolini, *Dux* (1926), was one of the best-selling books in Italy until the late 1930s. She was forced to leave the country after the anti-semitic legislation of 1938.

[14] *La leggenda di Dante. Motti, facezie e tradizioni dei secoli XIV–XIX*, introduction by Giovanni Papini, Lanciano 1911, pp. 89–91. The anecdote refers to the sex act with metaphors of horse-riding and card-playing.

[15] Sobrero's novel (Milan 1924) includes a caricature of Gramsci in the *Ordine Nuovo* period in the character of Raimondo Rocchi, editor of 'L'Età nuova'.

[16] The first edition of Perri's novel *I conquistatori* (1925) appeared under the pseudonym Paolo Albatrelli. *Emigranti* (1928) tells the story of a fictitious Calabrian village, Pandore, where the peasants are incited by the mayor and the schoolteacher to occupy the land, applying the old antifeudal laws introduced in 1808 under the Napoleonic rule of Joachim Murat. The attempt is suppressed by the *carabinieri* and many of the younger generation later emigrate to the USA.

dotard, not a primitive. According to Perri, his novel is 'verist' and he is the originator of a kind of neo-realism. But can there be a non-historicist *verismo* today? Nineteenth-century *verismo* itself was basically a continuation of the old historical novel within the context of modern historicism. There are no chronological references in *Emigranti* and it is clear why. There are two generalized references: one to the phenomenon of southern emigration which has had a certain historical development; the other to the attempts to invade the aristocratic landholdings 'usurped' from the people, attempts which also belong to very specific periods. The phenomenon of emigration has created an ideology (the myth of America) which has become opposed to the old ideology to which were linked the sporadic but endemic attempts to invade the land before the war. The movement of 1919–20, which was simultaneous and widespread, is completely different and has an implicit organization in the southern ex-soldiers' movements. In *Emigranti* all of these historical distinctions, essential for understanding and depicting the life of the peasant, are wiped out, and the confused whole is reflected in a rough and brutal way, without being worked through artistically. It is evident that Perri has no direct knowledge of the Calabrian peasant environment. Instead of a personal psychological and emotional experience of it, he knows it through old regionalist clichés. (If he is Albatrelli, one must take into account his political origins, which are hidden under pseudonyms so that he does not, in 1924, lose his job in the Milanese city or provincial administration.) The (attempted) occupation at Pandore is inspired by 'intellectuals' on a juridical basis (the anti-feudal laws of Joachim Murat, no less). It ends in nothing, as if the event (although described in the text as a mass exodus) had not even touched the habitual way of life of a patriarchal village. Mere phrase-making. Likewise the emigration. This village of Pandore, with the family of Rocco Bléfari, is (to use the words of another Calabrian with a personality tempered like steel, Leonida Répaci) a lightning-rod for every misfortune. Emphasis on the errors the peasants make in speaking, which is typical of Brescianism, if not of literary imbecility in general.[17] The pitiful 'character sketches' (Galeoto,

---

[17] In the text of Perri's novel the peasants' grammatical errors and malapropisms are printed in italics.

etc.) are without wit or humour. The absence of the historical dimension is 'deliberate' in order to lump together pell-mell all the generic folklore motifs that in reality have very distinct temporal and spatial characteristics.

Leonida Répaci: the need to take apart the revolting mechanisms of *L'ultimo cireneo*; see also *I fratelli Rupe* who are apparently the Répaci brothers and who someone has compared to the Cairoli family.[18]

Umberto Fracchia: see in particular *Angela*. (In the general picture, Ojetti, Beltramelli and Panzini occupy the foreground; in them the jesuitical-rhetorical character is more striking. They also have a more important place assigned to them in the most recent criticism.

Q23 § 9.

2 Two Generations

The old generation of intellectuals has failed, but it had its youth (Papini, Prezzolini, Soffici, etc.). The present generation does not even have this age of brilliant promises (Titta Rosa, Angioletti, Malaparte, etc.)[19] Their youthful dazzle was dim from the start.

Q23 § 10.

3 Ugo Ojetti and the Jesuits

U. Ojetti's 'Letter to Rev. Father Enrico Rosa' was published in *Pégaso* of March 1929 and reprinted in *La Civiltà Cattolica* on 6 April 1929 with a long note by Father Rosa himself. Ojetti's letter is refinedly jesuitical. It begins like this: 'Reverend Father, since 11 February[20] the throng of converts to a Catholicism of

---

[18] On Répaci and these novels see VIII 9 below. The Cairoli were a family of clowns.

[19] On these three figures, see VIII 13 below; on Malaparte, see also VIII 7.

[20] The Concordat (Lateran pacts) between the Italian State and the Catholic Church was signed on 11 February 1929. The pacts consisted of a treaty between Italy and the Vatican, a financial deal and a concordat, which gave the Church complete control of marriage and extended compulsory religious education from primary to secondary schools. Father Enrico Rosa (1870–1938) was editor of the Jesuit periodical *La Civiltà Cattolica* from 1915 to 1931. The Jesuits had been vociferously pro-fascist since 1923.

convenience and fashion is such that you will permit a Roman who belongs, as they once used to say, to a papal family, who was baptized in Santa Maria in Via and received his religious education in Sant'Ignazio di Roma itself and from you Jesuits, to spend half an hour with you, to take a rest from the great hubbub, considering a man like you, upright and judicious, who was yesterday what he is today and what he will be tomorrow.' Further on, recalling his first Jesuit teachers: 'And those were difficult times, when outside the word "Jesuit" meant underhand power or dark iniquity, while inside, on the top floor of the Collegio Romano, beneath the roof' (where the Jesuit school of religion was at which Ojetti was educated), 'all was order, trust, cheerful benevolence and, even in politics, tolerance with never a word against Italy and never, as unfortunately occurred in the state schools, base homage to the real or imagined supremacy of this or that foreign culture over ours.'

He also remembers being 'an old subscriber to *La Civiltà Cattolica*' and 'a faithful reader of the articles that you publish there'. Therefore, 'I, a writer, address myself to you, a writer, and declare to you my matter of conscience'. It is all here: the papal family, baptism in the Jesuit church, a Jesuit education, the cultural idyll of these schools, the Jesuits alone or almost alone representing the national culture, the reading of *La Civiltà Cattolica*, Father Rosa as Ojetti's old spiritual guide, Ojetti's present recourse to his guide for a matter of conscience. Ojetti, then, is not a Catholic of today, a Catholic of 11 February, out of convenience or fashion; he is a traditional Jesuit, his life an 'example' to be used in sermons, etc. Ojetti was never 'made in Paris'. He has never dabbled in scepticism and agnosticism. He has never been a Voltairean. He has never considered Catholicism as being at best just an emotional subject-matter of the figurative arts. Therefore, 11 February found him prepared to accept the Conciliation with 'cheerful benevolence'. Nor does he think (God forbid) that it may be an *instrumentum regni*, because he himself has felt 'how powerful religious fervour is in the minds of adolescents and how, once kindled, its warmth pervades all other feelings, from love of one's country and family to devotion to one's leaders, giving to the moral formation of character a divine sanction and reward'. Is not this, all in all, the biography, even the autobiography of Ojetti? And yet: 'And poetry? And art? And critical judgements? And moral judgements? Will you all go back to obeying the Jesuits?' a sprite asks Ojetti in the person of 'a French poet, who really is a poet'. Not for nothing did Ojetti attend a Jesuit school, and he has found a supremely jesuitical solution to these questions, except for one thing: that he has divulged it and made it public. Ojetti needs to improve the 'moral formation' of his character further with divine reward and sanction: these are things one does without telling. Here, then, is Ojetti's solution: 'The Church, without relaxing its dogmas, is capable of being indulgent towards the times and it demonstrated this well in the Renaissance' (but after the Renaissance there was the Counter-Reformation, whose champions and representatives were precisely the Jesuits). 'Pius XI, a humanist, knows how much air poetry needs in order to breathe. For many years now in Italy, without waiting for the Conciliation, lay culture and religious culture have been collaborating cordially in science and history . . . Conciliation is not confusion. The papacy will condemn as is its right; the Italian government will permit as is its duty. And you, if you think it opportune, will explain in *La Civiltà Cattolica* the reasons for the condemnation and will defend the arguments of faith. And we here, without anger, will defend the arguments of art, if they really are our convictions, because it may be, as has often occurred from Dante to Manzoni, from Raphael to Canova, that faith and beauty will seem also to us to be two sides of the same face, two rays of the same light. And sometimes we shall want to enjoy a polite discussion. For example, is or is not Baudelaire a Catholic poet? . . . The fact is that today the practical and historical conflict is resolved. But the other conflict – between the absolute and the relative, between spirit and body, the eternal contrast present in the conscience of each of us, which caused B. Croce and G. Gentile, non-Catholics, to oppose Modernism (?) and be content (?) to see it defeated because (?) it would have been a bad (?) conciliation, making underhand equivocation into sacred doctrine – the conflict which is innermost and eternal (and if it is eternal, how can it be reconciled?) is not and cannot be resolved. And the help that religion can and does give daily to everyone to resolve this

[21] Catholic modernism was a movement which attempted to reconcile the truths of religion with the methods of modern scientific thought (textual scholarship, evolutionary history). It emerged around 1890 under the liberalizing pontificate of Leo XIII and was suppressed by his successor Pius X.

conflict, it gave to us Catholics even earlier.' (How can one be. Catholic with this 'eternal contrast'? At the most one can be a Jesuit!) 'It is our own shortcomings that are to blame if, in spite of such help we have not yet managed to resolve it once and for all (!?). But you know it is precisely from the continual resurgence, renewal and rekindling of this eternal conflict, that art and poetry burst forth and shine.' Truly an amazing document of jesuitism and moral baseness. Ojetti can create a new superjesuitical sect: a jesuitical aestheticist modernism!

Father Rosa's reply is less interesting because jesuitically more anodyne. Rosa is very careful not to scrutinize too closely the Catholicism of Ojetti and the new converts. It is too soon: it is good that Ojetti and company are proclaiming themselves Catholic and fawning on the Jesuits; perhaps no more will in fact be asked of them. Rosa puts it well: 'a convenience or fashion which, nevertheless, – let us admit it between ourselves confidentially and in passing – is perhaps a lesser evil and therefore a definite good compared with that previous fashion or convenience of a futile anticlericalism and close-fisted materialism by which many ... kept a distance from the profession of the faith which they still nourished in the bottom of their "naturally Christian" souls.'

Q5 § 66.

4 Panzini

Another note has pointed out how F. Palazzi, reviewing Panzini's book *I giorni del sole e del grano*, observes that Panzini's attitude towards the peasant is more that of the slave-owner than that of the disinterested and candid georgic.[22] But this observation can be extended to others besides Panzini, who is only the type or the mask of an age. But Palazzi also makes other observations that are closely connected with Panzini (and related to a number of Panzini's obsessions, his 'pavid' obsessions, such as that with the 'livid blade').

[22] The note (Q 23 § 12) reads: 'In *L'Italia che scrive* of June 1929, Fernando Palazzi, reviewing Panzini's *I giorni del sole e del grano*, notes: ". . . above all he deals with and worries about rural life as would a landowner who wants to assure himself of the working abilities of the labouring animals he owns and who, on seeing a cultivated field, immediately starts wondering if the harvest will be as he hopes". Panzini the slave-owner, in a word.'

In *L 'Italia che scrive* of June 1929, Palazzi writes:

When [Panzini] perfunctorily sings the praises of a frugal meal eaten on the grass, you will notice, if you look closely, that his mouth is grimacing in disgust and that deep down he is wondering how on earth one can live off onions and a Spartan brown broth when God has put truffles under the ground and oysters on the sea bed. . . 'Once,' he confesses, 'I was even brought to tears.' But those tears did not spring from his eyes, as did Leo Tolstoy's, because of the poverty in front of them, because they glimpsed some humble faces or because of a deep sympathy for the lowly and the afflicted who are not absent among the coarse workers of the fields. Oh, no! He cries because in hearing recalled certain forgotten words for household goods, he remembers when his mother called them by these names. He sees himself as a child again and thinks of the ineluctable brevity of life, of the swiftness of death which hangs over us. 'Archpriest, I beg you: only a little earth over the coffin.' Panzini cries, in other words, because he pities himself. He cries for himself, for his approaching death and not for others. He passes near the soul of the peasant without seeing it. He sees external appearances, hears what barely comes from his mouth, and wonders whether property for the peasant may not by chance be synonymous with 'theft'.

Q 23 § 50.

5 Giovanni Papini [i]

In 1912–1913, when Giovanni Papini wanted to make the stomachs of the Italian philistines crawl, he published in *Lacerba* the article 'Gesù peccatore', a sophisticated collection of anecdotes and forced conjectures taken from the apocryphal Evangelists. Because of this article it looked as though legal action was going to be brought against him, which scared him no end. He had put forward as plausible and probable the hypothesis that Jesus and John had homosexual relations with each other.[23] In his article 'Cristo romano', in the volume *Gli operai della vigna*, he used the same critical procedures and the same intellectual 'vigour' to maintain that Caesar is a precursor of Christ, whom providence arranged to be born in Rome to prepare the terrain for Christianity.[24] In a third period it is likely that Papini, utilizing

[23] 'Gesù peccatore', *Lacerba* I (1913) 11, pp. 110–12. Papini referred to *John* XIII, 23, to support his argument.

[24] Papini, *Gli operai della vigna*, Florence 1929, pp. 13–58.

the brilliant critical insights characteristic of Achille Loria, will reach the conclusion that Christianity and homosexuality are necessarily related.

Q 23 § 16.

[ii]

Note how the writers of *La Civiltà Cattolica* treat him as their darling. They fondle him, pet him and defend him against every accusation of unorthodoxy.[25] Phrases contained in Papini's book *Sant'Agostino* which reveal the tendency towards baroque writing (the Jesuits were conspicuous representatives of the literary baroque): 'When he was struggling to escape from the cellars of pride to breathe the divine air of the absolute', 'to ascend from the dunghill to the stars', etc. Papini has really been converted not to Christianity but to Jesuitism (besides, Jesuitism, with its veneration of the Pope and its organization of an absolute spiritual empire can be said to be the latest phase of Catholic Christianity).

Q 23 § 37.

[iii]

In March 1932 Papini published an article in *Nuova Antologia* (against Croce) and one on A. Gide's *Oedipus* in the *Corriere della Sera*.[26] So far I have read only the latter. It is patched up, prolix, pompous and empty. In March new members must be nominated to the Academy of Italy to fill the vacant seats. The two articles are evidently Giovanni Papini's dissertation and mini-dissertation for the degree.[27]

Q8 § 98.

[iv] Papini as a Jesuit Apprentice

The article by Papini in *Nuova Antologia* of I March 1932 ('Il Croce e la Croce') seems to me to demonstrate that even as a

---

[25] *La Civiltà Cattolica* of 19 July 1930 contained a review of recent publications about St Augustine in which Papini's *Sant'Agostino* was highly praised.

[26] *Corriere della Sera*, 10 March 1932.

[27] Papini was not in fact nominated to the Accademia d'Italia until 1935. He took office on 12 April 1937.

Jesuit Papini will never be more than a modest apprentice.[28] He is an old jackass who wants to go on being a young one, despite the weight of his years and infirmities, and who toddles and capers about basely.

To me the characteristic quality of this article is its insincerity. Look how Papini begins the article with his usual mechanical and stereotyped jests against Croce, and how towards the end, acting the part of the paschal lamb, he announces unctuously that in his collected works all the 'playful' parts of his writings on Croce will be expurgated and only the 'theoretical' discussion will appear. It is clear that the article was written straight off and that in the course of writing it Papini's attitude changed. He forgot, however, to harmonize the barking of the first pages with the bleating of the last. The self-satisfied man of letters, pleased with his clever remarks which he believes have hit the mark, still carries it over the pseudo-Catholic, but also over the Jesuit (poor old Jesuit) and he did not want to sacrifice what was already written. But the whole piece looks clumsy, forced, mechanically constructed, like one cherry pulling another along. This is especially true of the second part where the hypocrisy is repugnantly transparent. It seems to me, though, that Papini is obsessed with Croce. Croce acts as his conscience, like the 'bloody hands' of Lady Macbeth, and Papini reacts to this obsession in turn by acting defiant, trying to joke and tease, or by whimpering miserably. Either way is a pitiful spectacle. The very title of the article is indicative: the fact that Papini makes a pun out of the word 'croce' is evidence of the literary quality of his Catholicism.

Q 8 § 105.

[v]

Papini's style is affected by Catholicism. He no longer says 'seven' but 'as many as there are deadly sins': 'Not that Italian translations of Goethe's masterpiece had been lacking: Manacorda has taken into account, either complete or, abridged,

---

[28] The article ('Croce and the cross') criticized Croce's *Storia d'Europa nel secolo XIX* (1932) for emphasizing liberal forces excessively over Catholic ones in nineteenth-century history. Papini digressed at the end into an autobiographical justification of his conversion to Catholicism and offered the 'hope, not unaccompanied by a prayer' that Croce too would come in time to espouse the true religion.

as many as there are deadly sins' ('Il Faust svelato' in *Corriere della Sera* of 26 April 1932).[29]

Q8 § 160.

[vi]

In *L'Italia Letteraria* of 20 August 1933, Luigi Volpicelli writes the following about Papini (in passing, in an essay on 'Problems of Contemporary Literature', published in several instalments):

> At the age of fifty it is not enough – I hope Papini will pardon my frankness – it is not enough to say that the writer must be a teacher. One should at least be able to say: here, you panders, is real art, master art. But to limit oneself to proposing, at the age of fifty or thereabouts, the writer as teacher when teacher he has never been, is no good even as a *mea culpa*. But this is just what he always does! Papini has tried all trades only to cast dirt on them all: the philosopher, to conclude that philosophy is a kind of gangrene of the cerebellum; the Catholic, to scatter ash around the universe with an appropriate dictionary; the literary man, to decree in the end that we do not know what to do with literature. This does not detract from the fact that Papini has won a small place in the history of literature in the chapter on the 'polemicists'. But polemic is the same as oratory. It is pure and empty form, the mere love of words, techniques and gestures, a congenital and spiritual calligraphism: all in all, the furthest thing possible from the writer as teacher.

Papini has always been a 'polemicist' in the sense used by Volpicelli, and he still is today, since we do not know whether in the expression 'Catholic polemicist' it is the noun or the adjective that interests Papini the more. With his 'Catholicism' Papini would have liked to demonstrate that he is not a pure 'polemicist', a pure 'calligrapher', a tightrope-walker of the word and technique, but he has failed. Volpicelli is wrong not to make clear that a polemicist is the polemicist of a conception of the world, even if it is the world of Pulcinella, but Papini is the 'pure' polemicist, the professional boxer of the word at random. Volpicelli ought to have arrived at the explicit statement that Catholicism for Papini is a clown's costume, not the 'skin' formed

---

[29] Guido Manacorda (1879–1965) an ardently political and pro-fascist Catholic, was a contributor to *Frontespizio* (see footnote 3 above).

by his 'renewed' blood.

Q 17 § 13.

[vii]

See the paper 'Carducci, alma sdegnosa' delivered by Papini at Forlì for the inauguration of 'Poetry Week of Romagna' and published in *Nuova Antologia* of 1 September 1933. The falsity, the histrionic insincerity of this lecture is enough to pop one's eyes.

It would be interesting, not only for Papini, to investigate the aversion for Rome that was fashionable in Italy in the Futurist and *Voce* movements until 1919. See Papini's remarks against Rome and Benedetto Croce;[30] out of this hated pair for Papini (in 1913), Benedetto Croce has remained hateful. Compare this openly trivial attitude towards Croce in the lecture on Carducci with the unctuously jesuitical and petty-Christian attitude of the essay 'Il Croce e la Croce'.

Q 17 § 16.

[viii]

Papini lacks rectitude: moral dilettantism. In the first period of his literary career this was not a striking deficiency because Papini based his authority on himself. He was 'his own party'. He was entertaining, he could not be taken seriously, except by a few philistines (remember the discussion with Annibale Pastore).[31]

Today Papini has become a part of a broad movement from which he draws his authority. Consequently, his activity has become degenerate in the worst sense, that of a hired gun, the mercenary killer. It is one thing if a child breaks windows for the sake of amusement or out of mischief, even if it is faked; it is another if he breaks windows on behalf of the glaziers.[32]

Q 17 § 24.

[30] See I 10 on this speech.

[31] Annibale Pastore taught philosophy at Turin when Gramsci was a student. Gramsci's first published article, 'Per la verità' (written 1913, in CT, pp. 3–5 and PV, pp. 3–5) dealt with Papini: 'he thinks he is still twenty years old ... his diatribes now seem to many people impotence trying to appear as strength'.

[32] Probably a recollection of Papini's 'Rome speech' of 1913 (see I 10): 'I have always enjoyed breaking other people's windows and balls'.

6 Giuseppe Prezzolini [i][33]

His book *Il Codice della Vita italiana* (La Voce, Florence, 1921) ends the first and original period of Prezzolini's activity, of the moralist writer always campaigning for the renewal and modernization of Italian culture. Immediately afterwards, Prezzolini 'goes into a crisis', with most curious highs and lows, until he joins the herd of the traditional current and takes to praising what he had once attacked.

A moment of this crisis is represented by the letter written in 1923 to Piero Gobetti entitled 'Per una società degli Apoti', reprinted in the volume *Mi pare. . .* Prezzolini feels that his position as 'spectator' is 'a bit, just a bit (!), cowardly'. 'Should it not be our duty to join in? Is there not something irritating (!), unpleasant (!), melancholy (!), in the sight of these youths who (almost all of them) remain outside the conflict, watching the combatants and asking only how the blows are delivered and why?' He finds a very convenient solution: 'Given the divisive disagreements that are now in evidence and given the pangs with which the world of tomorrow is getting ready, our task, our usefulness for the present can only be that to which we have already committed ourselves: we must make ideas clear, enhance values and save, above the sphere of conflict, an ideal inheritance so that it can return and bear fruit in the future.' The way in which he sees the situation is amazing: 'The time which we are now going through is so credulous (!), fanatic, partisan, that a critical ferment, an element of thought (!), a group of people who look beyond their own interests cannot but do good. Do we not see many of the best blinded? Today everything is accepted by the masses (!).' (And during the Libyan war was it not the same? Yet, at the time Prezzolini did not restrict himself to proposing a society of 'Apoti'.) 'False documents, crude legends, primitive superstitions are received without scrutiny, with closed eyes, and are put forward as a material and spiritual remedy. And how many leaders openly propose the enslavement of the spirit as the

[33] Giuseppe Prezzolini (1882–1982), a key impresario of Italian 'militant culture' in the first quarter of this century. A close friend of Papini's, he co-edited with him *Leonardo* and the nationalist *Il Regno* and edited *La Voce* from 1908 to 1914. An interventionist and war volunteer, he collaborated on *Il Popolo d'Italia* and became a theoretical mediator between Sorelian syndicalism and early fascism, remaining personally close to Mussolini until the consolidation of the regime. In 1925 he left Italy, living first in Paris and then from 1930 in New York, where he took up a chair of Italian at Columbia University.

remedy for the weary, the refuge for the hopeless, the panacea for the politicians, the tranquillizer for the exasperated. We could call ourselves the congregation of the Apoti, of "those who won't swallow it",[34] since not only the habit of swallowing it but also the general will to swallow it is now manifest and widespread.' There follows a singular example of jesuitical sophistry: 'What is needed is a minority, fit for the purpose, that will sacrifice itself if necessary and renounce the many occasions of worldly success, that will also sacrifice the desire for sacrifice and heroism (!), not so much to go against the current as to establish a firm point from which the movement will recover in the future,' etc., etc.' Differences between Prezzolini and Gobetti. See whether there was a reply to the letter and what it said.[35]

Q 23 § 31.

[ii]

The article in which Prezzolini defends *La Voce* and 'claims by full right a place for it in the preparation of contemporary Italy' is cited in *La Fiera Letteraria* of 24 February 1928 and therefore must have been published in *Il Lavoro Fascista* a few days earlier (in the ten days between 14 and 24 February). The article was provoked by a series of short articles in *La Tribuna* against Papini. In his study 'Su questa letteratura' (published in the first number of *Pégaso*) traces of the old 'protestantism' of *La Voce* were discovered. The *Tribuna* writer, an ex-nationalist of the early *Idea Nazionale*, had not yet managed to forget his old grudges against *La Voce*, while Prezzolini did not have the courage to uphold his earlier position.[36] On this subject Prezzolini also published a

---

[34] The name 'Apoti' (Greek for 'non-drinkers') is a play on this idiom.

[35] Gobetti had in fact appended a reply to Prezzolini's letter when it was first published in *La Rivoluzione Liberale* in September 1922. The reply and a subsequent article on Prezzolini's proposal are reproduced in Piero Gobetti, *Scritti politici*, ed. P. Spriano, Turin 1969, pp. 409–15. The second of these pieces is the more significant and marks, at the time of the march on Rome, Gobetti's shifting of the proposal into a clear antifascist key: 'Faced with a fascism which, by abolishing freedom of elections and the press, would suffocate the seeds of our action, we will do well to form not the Congregation of Apoti but the company of death'. Gobetti (1901–26) believed in an alliance between liberal-democratic intellectuals, the proletariat and the peasantry. *La Rivoluzione Liberale*, an important early platform for anti-fascist intellectuals, was suppressed in 1925 and Gobetti died in exile shortly afterwards. For Gramsci's views of 1926 on his political orientation see SPW II pp. 460–62. Gramsci had been in Moscow when Prezzolini's letter appeared in the review and probably first came across it in the collection *Mi pare. . .* of 1925.

letter in *Il Davide*, which came out irregularly in Turin in 1925 and 1926 and was edited by Gorgerino. Remember also his book on Italian culture of 1923 and his volume on fascism (in French).[37] If Prezzolini had civil courage, he would be able to recall that his *Voce* certainly had a great influence on some socialists and was an element of revisionism. He, Papini and many others of the *Voce* circle contributed in the early years to *Il Popolo d'Italia*.[38]

Q 1 § 90.

[iii]

Prezzolini's article 'Monti, Pellico, Manzoni, Foscolo, veduti da viaggiatori americani' published in *Pégaso* (edited by Ojetti) of May 1932. Prezzolini quotes a passage from the American art critic H.Y. Tuckerman (*The Italian Sketch-book*, 1848, p. 123): 'Some of the young liberals in Italy are most disenchanted because one of them who was about to become a martyr of their cause, has turned to devotion, and they are sorry that he is using his pen to write Catholic hymns and religious odes.' He comments: 'The *vexation* that the most fervid were feeling for not having found in Pellico an instrument for a *petty* political polemic is depicted in these "observations"'[39] Why it should be a question of narrow-minded vexation and why, before 1848, the polemic against the Austrian and clerical persecutions should be 'petty' is a 'profane' mystery of the Brescianist mentality.

Q 23 § 24.

[36] On *La Tribuna* and *L'Idea Nazionale*, see footnote 5 on p. 391. Shortly after *L'Idea Nazionale* was founded in March 1911, *La Voce* launched a campaign of opposition to the projected war in Libya, for which the nationalist paper was the most vociferous mouthpiece.

[37] Prezzolini's letter appeared in the April 1926 issue of *Il Davide*. The books referred to are *La cultura italiana*, Florence 1923 and *Le Fascisme* translated by Georges Bourgin, Paris 1925. (An English translation of the latter was published by Methuen in 1926.)

[38] *Il Popolo d'Italia* was the pro-war paper founded by Mussolini in 1914 after he broke with the Socialist Party.

[39] Silvio Pellico (1789–1854), liberal arrested in 1820 for Carbonarist activities, wrote an account of his incarceration by the Austrians which was highly influential in rousing Italian nationalist feeling before 1848. The work (*Le mie prigioni*, 1832) also records how Pellico found increasing refuge in the consolations of religious faith. After his release in 1830 he renounced political activity, produced some devotional verse, then gave up writing.

7 Curzio Malaparte [i][40]

His real name is Kurt Erich Suckert, Italianized around 1924 to Malaparte through a pun on the Buonapartes (cf. his review *La Conquista dello Stato*). After the war he at first flaunted his foreign name. He belonged to Guglielmo Lucidi's organization which imitated Henri Barbusse's *Clarté* group in France and the English Union of Democratic Control.[41] In the collection of Lucidi's review entitled *Rassegna* (or *Rivista*) *Internazionale*, he published a book on the war, *La rivolta dei santi maledetti*. The book praised the supposedly defeatist attitude of the Italian soldiers at Caporetto; it was corrected in a Brescianist way in the subsequent edition to invert its meaning and then withdrawn from the market.[42] Suckert is, above all, an unrestrained social climber, excessively vain, and a chameleon-like snob. For the sake of success Suckert was capable of any villainy. His books on *Italia barbara* and his exaltation of the 'Counter-Reformation': nothing serious or less than superficial.[43]

---

[40] Curzio Malaparte (1898–1957) born of a German father and an Italian mother, initially a republican, interventionist and war volunteer, he joined the PNF in September 1922. Editor of *La Stampa* from 1929–31 and co-editor with Angioletti of *L'Italia Letteraria* from 1928–32, he became a principal ideologue and polemicist of the Super-country movement (see footnote 61 below). His tenacious adherence to the 'revolutionary' fascism of the squads left him marginalized by the regime from the mid-1920s. After trips to the Soviet Union and France and the publication of his scandalous *Technique du coup d'état* (1931), Malaparte was stripped of his party card and sent into internal exile. After the Liberation, he flaunted suspect anti-fascist credentials and sought entry into the PCI.

[41] Democratic internationalist organizations: Lucidi was in the Rome leadership of the Associazione del Controllo Popolare (founded Milan 1916). In May 1920 this became the Unione Italiana del Controllo Popolare, affiliated to the Union of Democratic Control in London, to Barbusse's Clarté group in France and to the Geneva Central Committee 'for the renewal of international relations'. Its organ, the monthly *Rassegna Internazionale*, began publication in April 1919.

[42] *La rivolta dei santi maledetti*, (originally published in 1921) interpreted the retreat of Italian soldiers at Caporetto in 1917 as a revolutionary mutiny: theirs was the revolt, Malaparte claimed, of a 'resigned' and 'martyred' masses against the militarism of their political leaders and generals. Reissued in an amended edition of 1923, the central political thesis of the book was altered from an internationalist and pro-Bolshevik to a nationalist and pro-fascist one. Some of the changes were noted by Piero Gobetti in an article of January 1924 (now in *Scritti politici*, cit., pp. 564–69): '"The national idea has, fortunately, not yet had time to settle" wrote C. Erich Suckert in 1920; and now Curzio has maliciously corrected to "unfortunately"'. The changes were also criticized by Ottavio Pastore in *L'Unità* of 13 March 1924. Malaparte challenged Pastore to a duel.

[43] *Italia barbara* (1925) and *L'arcitaliano* (1928) developed the argument outlined in the revised edition of *La rivolta* that Italy had been witnessing since 1922 a restorative revolution: 'I believe that the Italian revolutionary phenomenon is, or should be, anti-

As for the exhibition of his foreign name (which at a certain point came into conflict with his sham racism and popularism, so he replaced it with a pseudonym where Kurt (Corrado) was latinized to Curzio), it is indicative of a fairly widespread tendency among certain Italian intellectuals of the 'moralist' or moralizing type. They were led to believe that people abroad were more honest, more able, more intelligent than in Italy. This 'xenomania' took on tedious and sometimes repugnant forms in spineless characters like Graziadei,[44] but it was more widespread than is believed and brought about revolting snobbish poses. Remember the brief conversation in Rome with Giuseppe Prezzolini in 1924 and his disconsolate exclamation: 'I should have procured English citizenship for my children when there was time!' or something similar. It seems this state of mind was not peculiar only to certain groups of Italian intellectuals but has also appeared during certain periods of moral degradation in other countries. At any rate, it is a remarkable sign of the absence of the national-popular spirit, as well as a sign of stupidity. An entire people is confused with a few corrupt strata, especially of the petty bourgeoisie (and these gentlemen themselves in fact belong essentially to these strata), which in basically agricultural countries, civilly backward and poor, is very widespread and can be compared to the Lumpenproletariat of the industrial cities. The camorra and the mafia are nothing other than a similar form of criminality that lives parasitically off the big proprietors and the peasantry. The moralizers fall into the most simple-minded pessimism because their preachings do not change a thing. Characters like Prezzolini, instead of deducing their own organic

modern, anti-European. I believe that fascism is the latest aspect of the Counter-Reformation, because it tends towards a restoration of the natural, historical civilization proper to the Italian spirit, which is of its nature ancient, classical and *unsuited to modernity*. . .' (2nd edn., Rome 1923, p. 276).

[44] In Q 7 § 30 Gramsci writes of Antonio Graziadei: '. . . note his grumbling-pessimistic view of the "Italians" en bloc, all characterless, spineless, civilly inferior beings etc., etc., a stupid and banal defeatist view, a form of anti-rhetoric. . .' Graziadei (1873–1953) joined the Italian Communist Party at the Livorno split, wrote the theses on the agrarian question for the 1922 Rome Congress and became one of the main leaders of the Right after the congress. At the Fourth World Congress, he was the principal spokesman for the minority in the Italian party, arguing for a full acceptance of the united front policy. Co-opted into the Central Committee after the wave of arrests of Communist leaders in early 1923, he was violently attacked by Zinoviev at the Fifth World Congress for his revision of Marxism – the 'critical revisionism' put forward in his *Prezzo e sovraprezzo nell'economia capitalistica* (Turin 1923). He remained on the extreme right of the party until his expulsion in 1928.

ineptitude, find it more convenient to conclude that the people as a whole are inferior. Therefore there is nothing left to do but resign oneself: 'Long live France and long live Germany, so long as full bellies have we!' These men, even though they sometimes display a nationalism of the most extreme kind, should be marked out by the police among those capable of spying against their own country.

Q 23 § 14.

(ii)

See Malaparte's article 'Analisi cinica dell'Europa' in *L'Italia Letteraria* of 3 January 1932. At the end of 1931, in the École de la Paix in Paris, ex-president Herriot gave a lecture on the best way to organize peace in Europe. Malaparte then spoke opposing Herriot: 'Since you too are in some respects (*sic*) a revolutionary, I said, among other things, to Herriot,' Malaparte writes in his article, 'I think you can understand that the problem of peace should be considered not only from the viewpoint of academic pacifism, but also from a revolutionary point of view. Only the patriotic spirit and the revolutionary spirit (if it is true, as it is true, for example, in fascism, that the one does not exclude the other) can suggest the means by which peace can be secured in Europe. "I am not a revolutionary" Herriot replied, "I am simply a Cartesian. But you, dear Malaparte, are just a patriot."'

Thus, for Malaparte, Herriot too is a revolutionary, at least in a certain sense, and it thus becomes even harder to understand what 'revolutionary' means both for Malaparte and in general. If in the common parlance of certain political groups 'revolutionary' was increasingly taking on the meaning of 'activist', 'interventionist', 'volunteer', 'dynamic', it is hard to see how Herriot can qualify as one. Hence Herriot's witty reply that he was a 'Cartesian'. One may assume that for Malaparte 'revolutionary' has become a compliment as 'gentleman' or 'true gentleman' once was. This too is Brescianism: after 1848 the Jesuits called themselves 'real liberals' and called the liberals 'libertines' and demagogues.

Q 23 § 22.

8 Luca Beltrami (Polifilo)[45]

To find the Brescianist writings of Beltrami (*I popolari di Casate Olona*), see the *Bibliografia degli scritti di Luca Beltrami*, which covers March 1881 to March 1930. It is edited by Fortunato Pintor, honorary librarian of the Senate, with a preface by Guido Mazzoni. From a note published in *Il Marzocco* of 11 May 1930, it appears that Beltrami's writings about the hypothetical 'Casate Olona' number as many as thirty-five. Beltrami has annotated this bibliography. About 'Casate Olona' *Il Marzocco* writes:

> The bibliography of the thirty-five writings about the hypothetical 'Casate Olona' has given him the idea of bringing together his statements, proposals and polemics of a politico-social nature. These, out of tune with a parliamentary democratic regime, must be considered in a sense an anticipation of which someone other than Beltrami could have boasted of being a foreseeing precursor (!?).

Beltrami was a moderate conservative and it is not clear that his role as 'precursor' is accepted with enthusiasm. His writings, besides, are of an alarming intellectual vulgarity.

Q 23 § 42.

9 Leonida Répaci [i][46]

In his 'autobiographical' story 'Crepuscolo' (*Fiera Letteraria*, 3 March 1929), he writes:

> In that period I already marshalled within me, strengthening them every day on the deepest roots of instinct, those fine qualities that would later, in the years to come, make me a magnetic centre for misfortune: love of the loser, the downtrodden and the humble, the

---

[45] On Beltrami see footnote 2 above.

[46] Leonida Répaci (b. 1898), Calabrian writer, published his first novel *L'ultimo Cireneo* in 1923 and made his literary reputation with a long cycle of semi-autobiographical novels about the 'Rock brothers' and their turbulent and calamitous life. He trained in Turin as a lawyer, joined the PSI and acted on the workers' defence committee during the 1920 occupation of the factories. He met Gramsci and collaborated on *L'Ordine Nuovo*, subsequently joining the Communists and writing a literary column for *L'Unità*. In 1926, released after a police frame-up in Calabria where he was accused of murdering a local fascist, he resigned from the PCd'I and withdrew completely from political life, justifying his resignation, in a letter to *L'Unità* on 5 May 1926, 'because of the necessities of life, which was, unfortunately, to be lived every day, because of that modicum of peace I owe to my troubled spirit and above all because of a promise I made my mother by her deathbed'.

spurning of danger for the just cause, an independence of character that reveals rectitude, a wild pride that remains bold even in the face of destruction. . .

How many fine qualities Leonida Répaci has lost since then! It appears, though, that right from a very tender age, Répaci would have walked over his mother's body to win literary praise from the *Corriere della Sera.*

Q 23 § 13.

[ii]

The first volume of a so-called 'cyclical' novel by Leonida Répaci, *The Rock Brothers* (*I fratelli Rupe*, Milan, Ceschina, 1932, 15 lire) has been published. The novel as a whole is meant to represent the development of Italian life in the first thirty years of the century, as seen from Calabria (Répaci presents the plan of the work in his preface). Apart from the moral oafishness of the title, one might ask whether Calabria has had a representative national function and in general whether the Italian provinces have had a progressive or any other function, in leading a movement of any kind in the country, in selecting the leaders, in refreshing the closed, rarefied or corrupt environment of the big urban centres of the national life. In reality the provinces (particularly in the South) were, as regards leaders, much more corrupt than the centre (in the South the popular masses demanded northern leaders for their economic institutes) and those who went from the provinces to the towns brought, only too often, a new kind of corruption in the form of chicanery and a passion for underhand intrigues. A characteristic example of this were, precisely, the Répaci brothers, who emigrated from Palmi to Turin and Milan. The Rock brothers are, of course, the Répaci brothers: but, leaving aside Mariano, where is the rocky character of the others, of Ciccio and Leonida? What prevails is the 'mud and curd cheese' character, with the moral oafishness of claiming to be 'rock', no less. It should be note that 'Répaci, Leonida' lacks any kind of inventive – not to mention creative – imagination. He merely has this mediocre tendency to amplify mechanically (by aggregation, inflation and 'syncretism') the string of low-key 'dramatic events' which characterize the anecdotal history of most Italian petty-bourgeois families (particularly in the South) at the beginning of this century, which have characterized the Répaci family, too, and which Leonida in his transcription has exalted to mythic status. This process of mechanical augmentation could be demonstrated by analysis. Anyway, this mythology of the Répaci family is an odd one, lacking in serious human feeling and a sense of modesty, lacking in dignity and decorum, let alone moral grandeur. The immodesty of a cheap tart is what characterizes Leonida in relation to his family. *L'ultimo cireneo*, with the nauseating scenes of the obscene tormented writhings of his brother Ciccio, who has become impotent not from war wounds but from physiological causes perhaps of syphilitic origin (Ciccio did not make it to the front, and his military feats are those of Leonida, who was a courageous and daring man before he went soft with all this literary vanity), shows what stuff Leonida's humanity is made of (there's an impotent character in the *Rock Brothers* too). Leonida could be said to be capable of feeling sorry that there has not been any incest in his family: otherwise he could write a novel about it and say that the 'Rock' brothers have experienced every tragedy, even that of Phaedra and Oedipus.

Q 23 § 26.

10 Giovanni Ansaldo[47]

A place to one side in the section on 'Father Bresciani's progeny' must also include Giovanni Ansaldo. Recall his political-literary dilettantism that caused him to advocate, in a certain period, the need to 'be few in number', to constitute an 'aristocracy'. His attitude was one of banal snobbery more than an expression of any firm ethico-political conviction; a procedure of 'distinct' dubious salon literature. Thus Ansaldo became the 'Black Star' of *Il Lavoro*, a five-pointed star not to be confused with the one in *I Problemi del Lavoro* which is used to indicate Franz Weiss and has six points. (That Ansaldo is proud of his five points is

---

[47] Giovanni Ansaldo edited the Genoa newspaper *Il Lavoro* and wrote for Gobetti's *Rivoluzione Liberale*. When Gobetti published the southernist Guido Dorso's *La rivoluzione meridionale* in 1925, Ansaldo reviewed it in *Il Lavoro* and argued that Dorso's call for an overthrow of the southern ruling class, as well as Gramsci's idea ('Some Aspects of the Southern Question') of a southern revolution to break the landowning bloc, ran the risk of a Bourbon reaction in the south which would destroy national unity. On Ansaldo, see also Q 19 § 24, Q 1 § 44, Q 3 § 40 and Q 15 § 52.

apparent from the Genoa section in the *Almanacco delle Muse* of 1931. The *Almanacco delle Muse* was published by the Alleanza del Libro). For Ansaldo, everything becomes cultural and literary elegance: erudition, precision, castor oil, truncheon, knife; morality is not moral seriousness, but elegance, a flower in the buttonhole. This attitude too is jesuitical, a form of the cult of one's own particularity in the sphere of the intelligence, an outer form like a whited sepulchre. Besides, how can one forget that it is precisely the Jesuits who have always been masters of (jesuitical) 'elegance' in language and style.

Q23 § 23.

11 War Literature

What resonance has the 'Brescianist' trend had in war literature? The war forced the different social strata to come closer together, to get to know each other, to appreciate each other mutually, in a shared suffering and a shared resistance to exceptional conditions which made them more sincere and closer to humanity in the 'biological' sense. What did men of letters learn from the war? What in general was learnt from the war by those classes from which most writers and intellectuals usually come? There are two lines of research that may be followed:

1) There is the question of the social stratum and this has in many ways already been explored by Adolfo Omodeo in the series of chapters *Momenti della vita di guerra. Dai diari e dalle lettere dei caduti* which came out in *La Critica* and were then collected in a book.[48] Omodeo's collection presents material already selected according to a tendency which can also be called national-popular because he implicitly aims to show that by 1915 there was already a strong national-popular consciousness. This consciousness, formed by the liberal-democratic tradition, found an expressive outlet in the torment of war. Omodeo thus wants to show the absurdity of any claim about rebirth along these lines during the postwar period. Whether or not Omodeo succeeds in carrying out his task as a critic is another question. He has too narrow and mediocre a conception of what is national-popular,

[48] Published in twelve parts in *La Critica* from January 1929 to November 1933 and in volume form by Laterza in 1934.

and the cultural origins of his view are easy to trace. He is a descendant of the moderate tradition, with an added democratic or, better, a folk tone, who is unable to free himself from deep 'Bourbon' streaks. For Omodeo the question of a national-popular consciousness is not presented as that of a deep-seated bond of democratic solidarity between directing intellectuals and popular masses but as that of the intimacy of single and individual consciousnesses which have attained a certain level of noble national disinterestedness and a spirit of sacrifice. We are still at the level of exalting moral 'voluntarism' and still with the idea of élites which run their course in isolation and do not set themselves the problem of being organically tied to the large national masses.

2) War literature properly speaking, that which comes from 'professional' writers aiming for publication, has had varied success in Italy. Immediately after the armistice it was very limited and of little value; it looked for its source of inspiration in Barbusse's *Le Feu*.[49] It is very interesting to study Mussolini's *Diario di guerra* to discover traces of the truly national-popular political ideas which had been present, years earlier, in the movement whose culminating expressions were the trial over the massacre of Roccagorga and the events of June 1914.[50] Then there was a second wave of war literature that coincided with a parallel European movement created after the international success of Remarque's book and with the prevalent aim of stemming the pacifist mentality that Remarque represented.[51] This literature is generally mediocre both as art and as culture,

[49] See footnote 92 on p. 263.

[50] On 6 January 1913, troops opened fire on the villagers of Roccagorga who were demonstrating to have sanitation introduced. Seven people were killed. Mussolini, at that time editor of *Avanti!*, opened a campaign urging violent retaliation ('No violence is more legitimate than that which comes from below as a human reaction to the criminal politics of massacre') and stressing the need for co-ordination between the actions of southern peasantry and northern proletariat. *Avanti!* was put on trial for the campaign but acquitted after arranging for survivors of the massacre to testify in its defence. On Red Week in June 1914 see footnote 28 on p. 214. Mussolini's war diary appeared in instalments in *Il Popolo d'Italia* from 1915–17. It exalted the war as a fusion of classes, a 'people's war': 'I have noted with pleasure, with joy, that the most cordial *camaraderie* resigns between officers and soldiers. The life of continual risk binds souls together.' (*Il mio diario di guerra (1915–1917)* in Mussolini, *Opera Omnia*, ed. E. and E. Susmel, Florence 1961, Vol. 34, p. 14.)

[51] Remarque, *All Quiet on the Western Front (Im Westen nichts Neues*, Berlin 1929).

as the practical creation of 'masses of feelings and emotions' to impose on the people. Much of this literature belongs perfectly to this 'Brescianist' type. A characteristic example is Curzio Malaparte's book *La rivolta dei santi maledetti* already mentioned.

One should look at the contribution made to this literature by the group of writers usually called 'Vociani', and who were already working before 1914 with discordant harmony to elaborate a modern national-popular consciousness. The best books have been written by the 'minor' members of this group, for example those of Giani Stuparich.[52] Ardengo Soffici's books are deeply repugnant, because of a new form of rhetoric, even worse than the traditional kind.[53] A review of war literature under the heading of Brescianism is necessary.

Q 23 § 25.

12 The Academy of Ten

See Curzio Malaparte's article 'Una specie di accademia' in *La Fiera Letteraria* of 3 June 1928. *Il Lavoro d'Italia* supposedly paid 150,000 lire for the novel *Lo Zar non è morto* written co-operatively by the Ten.

> For the 'Novel of the Ten' the members of the Confederation, the large majority of them workers, have had to shell out no less than 150,000 lire. Why? For the surprising reason that there are ten authors and that among the Ten are not only the president and the general secretary of *Il Raduno*, but also the national secretary and two members of the directorate of the Authors' and Writers' Union. . . What a paradise, the intellectual unionism of Giacomo di Giacomo.[54]

[52] Giani Stuparich (1891–1961) fled in 1915 from his native Trieste – then in Austria-Hungary – to fight on the Italian side for annexation of the unredeemed territories (Trieste and the Trentino). In *Colloqui con mio fratello* (1925) and *Guerra del '15* (1931) he charts the erosion of his initial war optimism through his experience of the trenches, the suicide of his brother and his two years as a prisoner.

[53] On Soffici see footnote 28 on p. 48 and VIII 19 below. His war books are *Kobilek*. *Giornale di battaglia* (1918) and *La ritirata del Friuli* (1919). The former projects an image of the resigned peasant soldier estranged from the national cause. The latter (like Malaparte's *Rivolta*) lays the blame for the defeatism of Caporetto on the ruling classes.

[54] Giacomo Di Giacomo had pioneered the movement for intellectuals' trade unions, setting up in 1922 a National Union of Intellectual Labour: 'The fascist intellectual workers aim to offer the proletariat the contribution of their culture, education and directive ability and, in return, ask from them discipline, love of work and spontaneous

Malaparte continues:

> *If those leaders* we have mentioned *were Fascists*, whether of old or recent date, we would have chosen *another way* to denounce the squandering and the *camorras*. We would have appealed to the Secretary of the Fascist Party. But since we were dealing with people without party cards, some of them politically none too clean and with bad connections, others who have slipped into the Unions at lunchtime, we have preferred to get the matter over with *without scandal* (!), with these few words spoken in public.

This piece is priceless. In the article there is also a heated attack on Bodrero, then Under-Secretary of Public Education, and on Fedele, the Minister. In *La Fiera Letteraria* of 17 June, Malaparte published a second article, 'Coda di un Accademia', in which he impassively turns the screws on Bodrero and Fedele. (Fedele had sent a letter about the Salgari question, which was the 'star turn' of the 'Writer's Union' and had everyone laughing.)[55]

Q3 § 9.

13 'La Fiera Letteraria'

This magazine, subsequently *L'Italia Letteraria*, has always been a shambles, but is becoming more and more of one.[56] It has two editors, but it is as if it did not have any, as if a secretary examined the incoming mail and drew by lot the article to be published. What is curious is that the two editors, Malaparte and Angioletti, do not write for their journal but prefer other showcases. The editorial columns must be written by Titta Rosa and Enrico Falqui and of the two the more comical is the latter, who compiles

co-operation with the efforts aimed at raising them morally and intellectually'. Mussolini successively remodelled the structure of the intellectual unions, first through a law of April 1926 instituting a National Confederation of Fascist Unions which decentralized and weakened the earlier united union front, then (in November 1928) by subordinating the unions completely to the party and state. From 1928, the intellectual categories were forcibly collected into a Confederation of Fascist Unions of Professional Workers and Artists counting over 100,000 members, of which Di Giacomo was president.

[55] Emilio Salgari (1862–1911) was the author of popular adventure novels, notably the stories of the Malayan pirate Sandokan. *Il Raduno*, organ of the Artists' and Writers' Union, had hailed Salgari on the sixteenth anniversary of his death as 'our true leader' and 'one of the greatest Italian artists' and had argued that his influence had replaced that of the democrat Jules Verne (*Il Raduno* 1, 31 December 1927). Cf. Q3 § 36.

[56] On this periodical see footnote 13 on p. 96.

the 'press review' jumping to the left and to the right, without a compass and without ideas. Titta Rosa pontificates more and puffs himself up like a disillusioned supreme pontiff even when he writes rubbish. Angioletti appears rather reluctant to hurl himself on the high seas. He does not have the effrontery of Malaparte. It is interesting to note that *L'Italia Letteraria* does not risk giving its own opinions but waits until the big shots have spoken first. That is what happened for Moravia's *Gli indifferenti* but, even more serious, for Nino Savarese's *Malagigi*, a really witty book that was reviewed only when it was shortlisted for a literary prize, while it had not been noted when in the pages of *Nuova Antologia*.[57] The contradictions of this group of scribblers are truly amusing, but it is not worth pointing them out. They remind one of the Bandar Log of *The Jungle Book*: 'Now we're going to ... we're going to do some splendid things?!' etc., etc.[58]

Q1 § 102.

14 Bontempelli's Novecentismo

The manifesto written by Bontempelli for the review *'900* is nothing but a reworking of Giuseppe Prezzolini's article 'Viva l'artificio!' published in 1915 and republished in his collection *Mi pare...* (Delta Editions: Fiume, 1925).[59] Bontempelli has done

[57] *Gli indifferenti* (*The Time of Indifference*), Alberto Moravia's first novel, was published in 1929. Nino Savarese's *Malagigi* had been serialized in *Nuova Antologia* in August–September 1928. *L'Italia Letteraria* only reviewed it in December 1929.

[58] Gramsci in 1921 had drawn an analogy between the Bandar Log, the lawless Monkey-People in Kipling's *Jungle Book*, and the Italian petty bourgeoisie, first interventionists in the war, then backers of fascism, 'desperately seeking to maintain a position of historical initiative ... aping the working class and coming out on to the streets'. The Bandar Log 'believed they were better than all the other jungle people, that they had a monopoly on intelligence, historical intuition, revolutionary spirit, governing know-how, etc.' ('The Monkey-People' SPW I, p. 373).

[59] Massimo Bontempelli (1878–1960) founded the review *'900* in 1926 ('900 or 'Novecento' means '20th century': in Bontempelli's programme the century was born with the fascist revolution which coincided with a new third epoch of art, following the successive demises of classicism and romanticism: 'The nineteenth century ends in 1915. The twentieth begins in 1922'). Bontempelli's 'manifesto' consisted of the editorials of the first four issues of *'900* which theorized a rejection of romantic lyricism and subjectivity, a setting up of 'virile ugliness' against 'feminine beauty', an attempt to 'fuse' art with the people and catch up with the gains of the European avant-gardes while remaining wholly 'Roman'. Until 1928 the review was published in French with the title *Cahiers d'Italie et d'Europe*: James Joyce and other foreign writers were on its editorial board. It folded in 1929.

nothing but work out and water down a series of points contained in Prezzolini's article by making them mechanical. The play *Nostra Dea* of 1925 is a mechanical extension of what Prezzolini says on page 56 of *Mi pare*. . . . It should be pointed out that Prezzolini's article is very clumsy and pedantic: it records the author's efforts, after his experience with *Lacerba*, to become 'lighter and more vivacious'. What could be expressed in an epigram is chewed and slobbered on with many tedious grimaces. Bontempelli imitates and multiplies this clumsiness. In Prezzolini an epigram becomes an article and in Bontempelli a volume.

Q 23 § 29.

15 'Novecentismo' and 'Super-country'

The Baroque and Arcadia adapted to modern times.[60] That familiar figure, Malaparte, who had been editor of Bontempelli's *'900*, became shortly afterwards the 'leader' of the Super-country group and the hornet jabbing at Bontempelli.[61]

Q 23 § 30.

---

[60] 'Arcadia' was the name of a late seventeenth and early eighteenth-century Italian literary movement which emerged in reaction to the stylistic extravagances of baroque poetry by imitating the classics – notably through pastorals.

[61] After breaking with *'900*, Malaparte collaborated briefly on *Il Selvaggio* (The Savage), a review originally set up in 1924 in the wake of the Matteotti murder as the organ of the fascists of the Val d'Elsa in Tuscany. In the words of Mino Maccari, who edited it in Florence from 1927, 'We call ourselves Savages to distinguish us from those domesticated fascists whom we consider to be the bubonic plague of the PNF'. The 'savages of fascism' were 'the *squadristi*, the enthusiasts, the intransigents, the passionate apostles, committed to defending the idea at all costs'. From 1927 *Il Selvaggio* became the chief organ of the 'Super-country' (*strapaese*) movement, pitted against the intellectual isolationism of the ex-*Ronda* group, the officialist bourgeois culture of Ojetti and – most vociferously – against the 'Super-city' (*stracittà*) line of Bontempelli and *'900* (the labels 'Super-country' and 'Super-city' were both coined by Malaparte). According to *Il Selvaggio's* programme of 1927, 'Super-country has been created to defend with drawn sword the rural and village character of the Italian people, [to be] a bulwark against the invasions of foreign fashions and ideas and of modernist civilization'. The review attacked the writers of Super-city as 'the perfect incarnation of the petty-bourgeois ideal of the fashionable *littérateur*, always up with the latest happenings in Paris, London or New York'. Malaparte subsequently joined another vehicle of Super-country, Leo Longanesi's *L'Italiano*. Super-country was increasingly pushed to the margins of fascist culture thereafter. Its final demise came in 1934.

16 Super-city and Super-country

See Massimo Bontempelli's open letter to G.B. Angioletti in
L'Italia Letteraria of 16 November 1930 with the latter's marginal
note ('Il Novecentismo è vivo o morto?'). Bontempelli wrote this
letter immediately after he was nominated to the Academy, and
every word oozes with the author's satisfaction at being able to
say that he made his enemies 'bite the dust'. Malaparte and the
band of *L'Italiano*. This polemic between Super-country and
Super-city was, according to Bontempelli, motivated by obscure
and ignoble sentiments. This can be accepted by one who takes
into consideration Malaparte's behaviour as a social climber
throughout the postwar period. It was the battle of a small group
of 'orthodox' writers who saw themselves smitten by the 'disloyal
competition' of the writers who formerly worked for *Il Mondo*,
like Bontempelli and Alvaro, and who wanted to give a cultural
ideological-artistic content to their resistance.

Q6 § 27.

17 Jahier, Raimondi and Proudhon[62]

Giuseppe Raimondi's article 'Rione Bolognina' in *La Fiera
Letteraria* of 17 June 1928; its epigraph is this motto by Proudhon:
'La pauvreté est bonne et nous devons la considérer comme le
principe de notre allégresse.' ('Poverty is good and we should
consider it the basis of our gaiety') This article is a kind of
'ideological-autobiographical' manifesto and culminates in these
words:

> Like every worker and every son of a worker, I have always had a clear
> sense of the division of social classes. I will remain, unfortunately
> (*sic*), among those who work. On the other hand, there are those I
> can respect, those to whom I can also feel sincerely grateful (!); but
> something prevents me from weeping (!) with them and I cannot
> bring myself to embrace them spontaneously (!). Either they make
> me feel uneasy (!), or I despise them. (A nice way to present a
> superior form of working-class dignity!) It is in the suburbs that
> revolutions have always been made. The people are nowhere so

[62] Piero Jahier (1884–1966), one of the young writers associated with *La Voce*, war
volunteer in the Alpine corps, published *Ragazzo* and *Con me e con gli alpini* (both 1919).
Giuseppe Raimondi (b. 1898) writer and former editorial secretary of *La Ronda* (see
introduction to this Section).

young, so uprooted from any tradition, so ready to follow a sudden wave of collective passion as in the suburbs, which are no longer the city and are not yet the country. . . From here a new civilization will eventually be born and a new history which will have that sense of revolt and secular rehabilitation proper to the people whose worthiness only the morality of the modern age has brought to recognition. One will speak of it as today one speaks of the Italian Risorgimento and American Independence. The worker has simple tastes: he educates himself by reading the weekly instalments of the Discoveries of Science and the History of the Crusades. His mentality will always remain that of the suburban clubs and the Popular Universities, a little atheistic and Garibaldian. . . Leave them their defects, spare them your ironies. The people are unable to joke. Their modesty is real, like their confidence in the future.

(Very oleographic, but pretty much in the manner of the worser Proudhon, including the axiomatic and peremptory tone.)

In *L'Italia Letteraria* of 21 July 1929, Raimondi speaks of his respectful friendship for Piero Jahier and of their conversations:

. . . he talked about Proudhon, his greatness and his modesty, the influence his ideas have had in the modern world, the importance these ideas have assumed in a world based on socially organized labour, a world where the consciousness of men is increasingly evolving and perfecting itself in the name of labour and its interests. Proudhon has made a human living myth of these poor (!) interests. My own admiration for Proudhon is more one of feeling and instinct, a kind of affection and an inherited respect, which were transmitted to me at birth. Jahier's admiration is wholly intellectual, derived from his studies, and therefore (!) very deep.

This Giuseppe Raimondi was a fairish *poseur* with his 'inherited admiration'; he had found one of the countless ways of distinguishing oneself from among the literary youth of today. For some years now, though, no more has been heard of him. (From Bologna, he collaborated with Leo Longanesi on *L'Italiano*; was then violently and scornfully challenged by Longanesi; member of *Ronda* group.)

Q 23 § 34.

18 [Enrico Corradini][63]

Corradini's *Carlotta Corday* was reprinted in 1928 in the Barbèra drama collection. In 1907 or 1908, when it was written, it was disastrously received and was withdrawn from the stage. Corradini published the play with a preface (also reprinted in the Barbèra edition) in which he blamed the disaster on an article in *Avanti!* asserting that he had wanted to defame the French Revolution. Corradini's preface also sounds interesting, from the theoretical point of view, for the compilation of this section on Brescianism, because it seems he makes a distinction between 'little politics' and 'big politics' in the 'theses' contained in works of art. Naturally, for Corradini, since his is 'big politics', the accusation of 'playing at politics' in the artistic field could not be raised against him. But this is not the issue: in works of art one must see if extra-artistic elements intrude, whether of high or low quality; if, in other words, this is 'art' or oratory with a practical aim. All Corradini's work is of the latter type: not art and even bad politics, i.e. simple ideological rhetoric.

Q 5 § 27.

19 Ardengo Soffici

Lineal descent of *Lemmonio Boreo* from Romain Rolland's *Jean-Christophe*. Why was *Lemmonio Boreo* broken off? The Quixotic aspect of *Lemmonio Boreo* is external and factitious. In fact it lacks epic-lyric substance: it is a rosary of insignificant events, not an organism.[64]

Could a book like *Jean-Christophe* be written in Italy? On

---

[63] On Corradini see footnote 8 on p. 202.

[64] Gramsci's early interest in *Jean-Christophe* is attested in ON, pp. 453–54 and SC p. 194. According to Prezzolini, Rolland's novel made a great impression on the group of *La Voce*, which included Soffici. *Lemmonio Boreo* (1911) is the first volume of an unfinished novel in which the eponymous hero returns to Tuscany after ten years abroad, absorbs himself in books and newspapers which give him the measure of the intellectual and moral degeneracy of the country and embarks on a campaign of correction, attempting with the aid of a proletarian 'strong man' and a petty-bourgeois intellectual to restore justice to the people. In one of the central episodes the trio joins with a group of anarchists and they violently disrupt a socialist rally. (The passage is translated in Adrian Lyttleton (ed.) *Italian Fascisms*, London 1973). Piero Gobetti wrote in 1922 that *Lemmonio Boreo* had become 'the *Iliad* of fascism' and Malaparte in 1923 called Soffici one of the 'prophets of fascism'.

consideration, *Jean-Christophe* ends an entire period of French popular literature (from *Les Misérables* to *Jean-Christophe*). Its content goes beyond that of the preceding period: from democracy to syndicalism. *Jean-Christophe* is an attempt at a 'syndicalist' novel, but a failure. Rolland was anything but anti-democratic, even if he strongly felt the moral and intellectual influences of the syndicalist atmosphere.

From the national-popular point of view, what was the attitude of Soffici? A Quixotic superficiality without reconstructive elements, an aestheticist and superficial criticism.

Q 7 § 105.

20 Cardarelli and 'La Ronda'

A note by Luigi Russo on Cardarelli in *La Nuova Italia* of October 1930.[65] Russo sees in Cardarelli the (modern-fossil) type of what Vito Fornari of Naples was in comparison with De Sanctis: the Crusca Dictionary, Counter-Reformation, Academy, reaction, etc. On *La Ronda* and its references to practical life in 1919–21 see Lorenzo Montano, *Il Perdigiorno* [The Loafer], Edizione dell'Italiano, Bologna, 1928 (includes Montano's topical observations published by *La Ronda*).

Q 5 § 154.

21 A Sphinx Without Riddles

In the *Ambrosiano* of 8 March 1932 Marco Ramperti had published an article called 'La corte di Salomone' [Solomon's court] where among other things he wrote:

This morning I woke up with a word-puzzle of four lines in my head, over which I had stayed up for the last seven hours of solitude, naturally without being able to make sense of it. Dense shadow! Endless mystery! Once awake, I realized, however, that in my

---

[65] Luigi Russo, 'Parere su De Sanctis', *La Nuova Italia* I (1930) 10, pp. 432–33. Vito Fornari (1821–1900) was a Catholic intellectual dominant in Neapolitan culture in the decade following the 1849 reaction, when De Sanctis was in exile. He offered *Dell'arte del dire*, a codification of classical rhetoric and puristic poetic theory, as an antidote to De Sanctis' 'subversive' teachings. The poet Vincenzo Cardarelli (1887–1959) was editor of *La Ronda* (see introduction to this Section).

feverish fatigue I had mistaken 'Solomon's court' for *L'Italia Letteraria*, the enigmatic word-puzzle for a composition by the poet Ungaretti. . .

Ungaretti has replied to these witticisms of Ramperti's with a letter, published in *L'Italia Letteraria* of 10 April, which seems to me a 'sign of the times'.[66] One can see from it what 'demands' Ungaretti puts to 'his country' in order to be compensated for his national and worldwide merits (Ungaretti is nothing but a buffoon of mediocre intelligence):

> Dear Angioletti, on returning after a tiring journey to earn a meagre crust for my young ones, I found the latest numbers of the *Ambrosiano* and *La Stampa* in which a certain Signor Ramperti believes he has offended me. I could reply to him that the peasants, my brothers, understood my poetry in the trenches; my Duce, who chose to honour it with a preface, understands it; simple and learned people of good faith will always understand it. I could tell him that for the last fifteen years everything new that has been done both in and outside Italy bears in poetry the imprint of my dreams and my expressive torment; and that honest critics, Italian and foreign, willingly recognize it: besides, I have never asked for anyone's praise. I could tell him that an intensely hard life like mine, proudly Italian and fascist, would always deserve, in the presence of foreigners and my fellow countrymen, at least the right not to see its difficulties further increased by Italian and fascist newspapers. I should tell him that if there is anything enigmatic in the year X[67] (I live off articles in total uncertainty about tomorrow, at over forty years of age!), it is only the obstinate malice towards me of persons of. . . wit. With affection, Giuseppe Ungaretti.

This letter is a masterpiece of literary hypocrisy and presumptuous fatuity.

Q9 § 2.

22 Portrait of the Italian Peasant

See, in Pitré's *Fiabe e leggende popolari* [Fables and popular legends] (p. 207),[68] a popular Sicilian tale to which (according

[66] On Ungaretti see footnote 15 on p. 97.

[67] i.e. 1932 in the fascist calendar.

[68] On Pitré see footnote 25 on p. 188.

to Domenico Bulferetti in *La Fiera Letteraria* of 29 January 1928)
there corresponds a woodcut of old Venetian prints in which one
sees God impart from heaven these orders: to the Pope: 'Pray';
to the Emperor: 'Protect'; to the peasant: 'Toil'.

The spirit of these popular tales depicts the conception of
himself and of his position in the world that the peasant has
resignedly absorbed from religion.

Q6 § 48.

23 'Catholic Art'

In his article 'Domande su un'arte cattolica', published in
L'Avvenire d'Italia and reprinted in *La Fiera Letteraria* of 15
January 1928, Edoardo Fenu reproaches 'almost all Catholic
writers' for their apologetic tone.

> The defence (!) of the faith must derive from the facts, from the
> critical (!) and natural process of the narrative: it must be, as in
> Manzoni, the 'juice' of the art itself. It is obvious (!) that a genuinely
> Catholic writer (!) will never go beating his head against the opaque
> walls (!) of heresy, whether moral or religious. A Catholic, by the very
> fact (!) of being one, is already invested (! from without?) with that
> deep and simple spirit which, instilled into the text of a story or a
> poem, will make his (!) a calm, straightforward art, in no sense
> pedantic. Hence (!) it is utterly pointless to linger over every page in
> order to show us that the writer has a path he wants us to follow, a
> light to guide us. Catholic art must (!) learn to become that path itself,
> that light, without getting lost in the mire (only snails get lost in
> mires) of pointless reproaches and idle warnings, (In literature) . . .
> if you take away a handful of names, Papini, Giuliotti[69] and to an
> extent Manacorda, the balance is pretty much on the debit side.
> Schools? . . . *ne verbum quidem*. Writers? Yes, if we wish to be
> generous we could pull out a few names, but with what an effort!
> Unless you are going to classify Gotta as a Catholic or give Gennari
> the title of novelist, or show your appreciation for that endless horde
> of perfumed and overdressed authors and authoresses for 'young
> ladies'

This article of Fenu's contains many contradictions,
improprieties and much naïve silliness. But the implicit

[69] Domenico Giuliotti (1877–1956) was, with Papini and Manacorda, one of the
Frontespizio group (see footnote 3 above); he advocated an intolerant form of Catholicism.

conclusion is correct: Catholicism is sterile for art, there are and can be no 'simple and sincere souls' who are educated writers and refined and disciplined artists. Catholicism has become a very difficult thing for intellectuals. Even in its innermost being, it cannot be without a meticulous and pedantic apologetic. This is an old state of affairs now: it goes back to the Council of Trent and the Counter-Reformation. From then onwards writing has become particularly dangerous, especially writing about religious matters and feelings. Since then the Church has used a double standard to measure orthodoxy. It has become at one and the same time very easy and very difficult to be a 'Catholic'. It is very easy for the people, who are asked only to 'believe' in general and to show respect for practices of cult: no real and effective struggle against superstition, against moral and intellectual deviations, so long as they are not 'theorized'. In reality, a Catholic peasant can be intellectually Protestant, Orthodox or idolatrous without being aware of it: it is sufficient for him to say he is 'Catholic'. Not much is asked of the intellectuals either, if they limit themselves to the external practices of cult. They are not even asked to believe, but only not to give a bad example by neglecting the 'sacraments', especially the more visible ones over which popular control falls: baptism, matrimony, funerals (the Viaticum, etc.) On the other hand, it is extremely difficult to be an active 'Catholic' intellectual and 'Catholic' artist (especially a novelist or a poet). This is because one is required to be equipped with a great number of notions on encyclicals, counter-encyclicals, briefs, apostolic letters and so on, and deviations from the orthodox ecclesiastical line have been so many and so subtle in history that to fall into heresy or semi-heresy or a quarter heresy is extremely easy. Genuine religious feeling has been dried up: one has to be doctrinaire to write 'orthodoxly'. Therefore, religion is no longer a feeling native to art; it is a motive, a starting point. Catholic literature can have its Father Brescianis and Ugo Mionis, but it can no longer have a Saint Francis, a Passavanti, a Thomas à Kempis. It can be 'soldiering', propaganda, agitation but it can no longer be a naïve and uncontested outpouring of faith. It is challenged, even in the hearts of those who are sincerely Catholic. The example of Manzoni can serve as evidence: how many articles on Manzoni has *La Civiltà Cattolica* published in the eighty-four years of its life and how many on Dante? The most orthodox Catholics are in fact suspicious of Manzoni and speak of him as little as they can. They certainly do not analyse him as they do Dante and a few others.

Q 23 § 18.

24 'Technically' Catholic Writers

There is a notable scarcity of Catholic writers in Italy, a scarcity explained by the fact that religion is detached from militant life in all its expressions. I refer to 'writers' who have a degree of intellectual dignity and produce works of art, drama, poetry, novels. I have already [Q 23 § 19] mentioned Gallarati Scotti in pointing out a characteristic trait of *Storie dell'Amor Sacro e dell'Amor Profano* [Tales of Sacred and Profane Love], which has its artistic dignity but stinks of modernism. Paolo Arcari (better known as a writer of political and literary essays, besides being the former editor of the liberal review *L'Azione Liberale* of Milan, but who has also written a few novels). Luciano Gennari (who writes in French). It is not possible to compare the artistic activity of the French Catholics (and their literary stature) with that of the Italians. Crispolti has written a propaganda novel, *Un duello*. Actually, Italian Catholicism is sterile in the literary field as in the other fields of culture (see Missiroli's *Date a Cesare*. . . [Render unto Caesar].[70] Maria Di Borio (remember the typical episode of Di Borio during the lecture by the Hindu Arcandamaya on the value of religions).[71] The Florentine group of *Frontespizio*, led by Papini, is active in producing an extremist Catholic literature, which is proof of the indifference of the intellectuals for the religious world view.

Q 23 § 35.

---

[70] Mario Missiroli, *Date a Cesare (La politica religiosa di Mussolini con documenti inediti)*, Rome 1929. Missiroli's books highlights in particular the poverty of religious studies in Italy, but it also deals negatively with other aspects of Italian Catholic culture, e.g. on pp. 391–99. On Missiroli see footnote 20 on p. 395.

[71] Gramsci had written critically about the Catholic writer Di Borio in 1916 (SM, pp. 183–85, CT, pp. 408–9). The anecdotal reference here has not been traced.

25 Bruno Cicognani[72]

His novel *Villa Beatrice, Storia di una donna* published in 1931 in *Pégaso*. Cicognani belongs to the group of Florentine Catholic writers: Papini, Enrico Pea, Domenico Giuliotti.

Can *Villa Beatrice* be called the novel of the neo-scholastic philosophy of Father Gemelli, the novel of Catholic 'materialism', a novel of the 'experimental psychology' so dear to the neo-scholastics and the Jesuits? Comparison between psychoanalytic novels and Cicognani's. It is difficult to say in what way Catholic doctrine and religiosity contribute to the construction of the novel (its characters and its actions). In the conclusion the priest's intervention is external, we are simply told of Beatrice's religious awakening, and the changes in the protagonist could also have been explained by physiological reasons alone. Beatrice's whole personality, if one can call it personality, is described in meticulous detail like a phenomenon of natural history. It is not represented artistically: Cicognani 'writes well', in the vulgar sense of the word, in the sense that he would write 'well' a book on how to play chess. Beatrice is 'described' as the personification and type of emotional coldness. Why is she 'incapable' of loving and of entering into an emotional relationship with anyone (even her father and mother) except in an extreme and stereotypical way? Is it that her genital organs are physiologically imperfect, that she suffers physiologically in intercourse and would not be able to give birth? But this internal imperfection (and why did nature not make her physically ugly, undesirable, and so forth? Contradiction of nature!) is due to the fact that she has a weak heart. Cicognani believes that the new being which inherits an organic illness begins to prepare itself against the future attack of its illness right from the fertilization of the ovum. Thus, the ovum Beatrice, born with a weak heart, develops an imperfect sexual organ which will make her detest love and all expressions of affection. All this theory is Cicognani's, it is the general framework of the novel. Naturally, Beatrice is not aware that her psychic existence is thus predetermined. She acts the way she does not because she thinks she is like this, but because that is how she is independently of her consciousness. In reality, her consciousness is not represented, it is not a motor that explains the action. Beatrice

[72] Bruno Cicognani (1879–1969), positivist Catholic novelist.

is an 'anatomical specimen', not a woman.

Cicognani does not avoid the contradictions, because it seems that at times Beatrice suffers from being compelled to be cold, as if this suffering were not itself a 'passion' that could precipitate her cardiac illness. It appears, therefore, that only sexual intercourse and conception with childbirth are dangerous 'by nature', but then nature should have provided otherwise for the 'safeguard' of Beatrice's ovaries. She should have been made 'sterile' or, better, 'physiologically' incapable of sexual intercourse. Ugo Ojetti has extolled all this muddle as Cicognani's attainment of 'artistic classicity'.[73]

Cicognani's way of thinking could be incoherent and he could still have written a good novel, but this is not the case.

Q6 § 201.

26 Alessandro Luzio

Article by A. Luzio, 'La morte di Ugo Bassi e di Anita Garibaldi', in *Il Corriere della Sera* of 25 March 1932, in which he attempts to rehabilitate Father Bresciani.[74]

The works of Bresciani 'after all cannot, <u>as for their content,</u> be liquidated by a <u>summary</u> judgement'. Luzio puts De Sanctis's essay together with an epigram of Manzoni (who, when asked if he knew *L'Ebreo di Verona*, is said to have replied, according to the diary of Margherita di Collegno: 'I have read the first two sentences; they are like two sentries who say, "Go no further"') and then calls the judgments 'summary'. Is there not something jesuitical in this cunning trick?

And again: 'The tone with which he, as spokesman of the reaction that followed upon the events of 1848–49, represented and judged the champions of national aspirations is <u>certainly</u> not agreeable: but in <u>more than one</u> of his short stories, and, <u>especially</u> in 'Don Juan or the Secret Benefactor' (Vols. XXVI–XXVII of *La Civiltà Cattolica*), hints of human and Christian compassion for the victims are not lacking: partial episodes are

---

[73] Ugo Ojetti, 'Contro il romanzo', in *Pègaso* III (1931) 7, p. 90.

[74] Alessandro Luzio (1857–1946), historian of the Risorgimento. Anita was Garibaldi's wife. Ugo Bassi was a patriot shot by the Austrians in 1849. On Bresciani's *Ebreo di Verona* and De Sanctis's essay, see the introduction to this Section.

equably and sympathetically treated, for example the death of Ugo Bassi and the agonizing end of Anita Garibaldi.' But could Bresciani have done otherwise? And in order to form a judgment on Luzio, it should be noted that he praises Bresciani precisely for his jesuitism and his vulgar demagogy.

Q 8 § 104

27 [Inconclusive Debates]

There is a growing number of writings on the separation between art and life. An article by Papini in *Nuova Antologia* of 1 January 1933, one by Luigi Chiarini in *Educazione Fascista* of December 1932. Attack on Papini in *L'Italia Letteraria*. These debates are as boring as they are inconclusive. Papini is a Catholic and an anti-Crocean. The contradictions of his superficial article come from this dual quality. At any rate, this revival of the controversy (several articles in *Critica Fascista*, those of Gherardo Casini and one by Bruno Spampanato against the intellectuals are the most significant and come closest to the heart of the question)[75] is symptomatic and demonstrates the uneasiness being felt over the contrast between words and facts, between neat statements and the reality which contradicts them.

It seems, however, that it is now easier to have the reality of the situation recognized. There is undoubtedly more good will to understand, more impartiality. These are due to the widespread anti-bourgeois spirit, even if generic and of spurious origins. At least there is the desire to create real national-popular unity, although through extrinsic – educational, school-teaching – means, through 'voluntarism'. At least it is being felt that this

---

[75] See G. Casini 'Morte dell'intellettuale' and B. Spampanato, 'Antifascismo della cultura' in *Critica Fascista* XI (1933) 1, pp. 3–4 and pp. 8–9. This debate on the intellectuals was an extension of that on 'contentism' versus 'calligraphism' (see II 15 and introduction to section II). Casini opposed the arguments of Benda (cf. VI 25), criticizing the 'separation between art and life' which comes from intellectuals who 'fear the contamination of the spirit by contact with politics'. Spampanato saw this separation as having set in when fascism moved from its revolutionary phase (1919–22) to its phase of consolidation of power. He argued that the intellectual old guard of pre-fascist days had returned to prominence and that culture could only be revitalized by purging them and injecting a younger, more dynamically fascist personnel into the education system. The other articles referred to here are G. Papini, 'Lo scrittore come maestro', *Nuova Antologia* LXVIII 1459 pp. 30–32, and L. Chiarini, 'Arte e vita', *Educazione fascista* X (1932) pp. 1013–20. See also the pseudonymous article opposing Papini, '"Farfanicchi" e "filistei". Bizze di Papini' in *L'Italia Letteraria* IV (1932) 49.

unity is lacking and that this lack is a national and state weakness. This radically distinguishes the present epoch from that of the Ojettis, Panzinis and co. One therefore needs to take this into account in handling this heading.[76] In any case, the weaknesses are obvious. The first is the conviction that a radical national-popular upheaval has occurred. If it has, this means that no further radical steps need be taken, that it is simply a matter of 'organizing', educating, etc. At most, there is talk of a 'permanent revolution', but in a limited sense, with the familiar meaning that all life is dialectic, military impetus and thus revolution. The other weaknesses are harder to understand. They can only be revealed by an exact analysis of the composition of Italian society, which shows that the large mass of intellectuals belong to that rural bourgeoisie whose economic position is made possible only if the masses of peasants are squeezed to the marrow. If it were to come to passing from words to concrete facts, these facts would mean a radical destruction of the economic base of these intellectual groups.

Q 14 § 35.

---

[76] i.e. 'Father Bresciani's progeny'.

IX

POPULAR LITERATURE

Introduction

Gramsci had borrowed many commercially successful novels from the prison library during his thirteen-month period of incarceration in Milan in 1927–28, and in a letter to Tania of 22 April 1929 he explained that they became interesting 'if one looked at them from the following angle: why are these books always the most read and the most frequently published? What needs do they satisfy and what aspirations do they fulfill? What emotions and attitudes emerge in this squalid literature, to have such wide appeal? (LP, p. 145). In the prison at Turi he wrote nearly fifty notes with the generic heading 'Popular literature', some of which he then rewrote and grouped in a special notebook of 1934–35 (number 21) which he called 'Problems of Italian national culture 1: Popular literature'. Although these notes deal more or less consistently with popular literary taste, they also clearly overlap with and presuppose a number of other subjects in the Notebooks.

They overlap, firstly, with the theme of the non-national-popular character of Italian literature. Gramsci starts from a simple observation: a reading public for popular fiction exists in Italy, but Italian authors do not, with rare exceptions, write the books this public calls for. Most avowedly 'populist' authors appealed to a middle-class readership and were essentially anti-popular in both their style and their politics. Book publishers who issued cheap format novels and newspaper publishers who serialized fiction to increase their circulation therefore tended to satisfy a taste for genres such as crime fiction, romance or adventure by publishing non-Italian writers – French writers in particular. Gramsci's explanation of the continuing appeal in twentieth-century Italy of the French novelists of the '1848 era' is linked to his argument about the failure of a bourgeois revolution to be carried through in Italy and thus the non-emergence of a hegemonic, national-popular stratum of bourgeois intellectuals (see Introduction to Section VI). The reading public in Italy turned instead to the French novelists of seventy or eighty years earlier who had exercised such a hegemonic function. Yet the retard by which these French novelists were still popular in Italy was, to Gramsci, symptomatic precisely of the stagnation and pathological involution of Italy's own political and economic development. It had led after the First World War to a violent twisting of petty-bourgeois demands into the adventuristic forms of early fascism. Gramsci can thus suggest a cultural connection between the popularity in Italy of Dumas' musketeers or Sue's avenging Prince Rodolphe and the fascist squads of 1919–22.

Popular literature is also related in Gramsci's notes to his discussions of language and folklore (see Section V). The still limited diffusion of a unitary Italian language and of literacy in the 1930s makes the concept of popular literature itself a problematic one for Italy at this time. Gramsci recognizes this when he observes the 'absence of a widespread popular literature whether in books or magazines' (X 18). Because many novelists and playwrights were still dialect speakers working with a semi-alien written medium, and because this medium had been used so often to cultivate a high literary style, it was very difficult to write an Italian that did not sound stiff and artificial. Moreover, the 'Brescianist' taste which Gramsci saw as so diffuse among writers in the fascist period served to bolster and preserve a mannered literary language. And then who were the readers of fiction in this period? Official literacy figures for 1931 gave an average of 20 per cent illiteracy for the country as a whole among the population over the age of six, with strong regional variations – the rate for the south was nearly 40 per cent. If one adds semi-literate people, able to read a notice or a form but not a book, then the figures are certainly higher. Rates of illiteracy were greater in rural and peripheral areas than in urban centres, among older people and among the lower social classes, particularly the peasantry. Figures for total book sales were very low in comparison with France, Germany or Britain and a newspaper's daily circulation was reckoned to be high if it exceeded 200,000 in a population of 41 million. In 1930s Italy, therefore, no literature could properly be classed as 'popular' in the sense of being diffused to any great extent among masses of working-class people. The people who read the narrative fiction serialized in the press or printed in cheap novels would have been in the great majority an *urban* proletariat and petty bourgeoisie who had passed through the higher grades of elementary school and probably secondary school of a technical (white-collar) or 'vocational' (skilled manual) type as well. There may also have been a secondary diffusion of popular literature from this reading public to illiterate or semi-literate listeners by reading aloud. In rural areas, where the diffusion of the printed word in any form was much less extensive, 'popular literature' was both different in kind and embodied more in oral transmission. While people in cities read crime fiction, peasants relayed stories or songs in which oral traditions and contemporary realities intersected. Thus a map of popular taste in Italy as a whole in the 1930s, such as Gramsci, writing in prison, could only tentatively sketch out in these notes, revealed different strata reflecting the intervention of different and discontinuous histories in different regional areas.

Gramsci's purpose in mapping popular taste in this way was not to produce a static descriptive picture but rather to explore the relations between dominant and subaltern cultural forms in dynamic terms, as they act upon each other historically. Just as folklore contains the sediments of earlier dominant cultures that have seeped down into subaltern cultures, so Gramsci sees in the popular literature of rural areas residues of earlier dominant literary forms (like romances of chivalry) and scientific conceptions of the world. By a converse process, he sees popular cultural forms being 'raised' into the dominant 'artistic' literature. For instance Dostoyevsky 'passes through' popular serial fiction in order to draw materials for writing artistic fiction. This latter process interests Gramsci because of its bearing on the question of how a dominated class can become hegemonic. As he writes in the note on Paul Nizan (II 5), the essential task is to create a body of writers who can be to the serial novel what Dostoyevsky was to the popular fiction on which he drew. These writers would have to be linguistically accessible – in other words they would have to reject that elaborate Italian that currently passed for good style – and they would have to draw their audience from the existing popular reading public for serial fiction. Gramsci clearly has in mind, in some cases at least, writers of 'left books': he cites as models Giovagnoli's nineteenth-century novel about Spartacus and collections of social poetry.

The fact that Gramsci devotes considerably more space to

narrative fiction than to other popular cultural forms – some of which, like music and cinema, he barely touches on in the Notebooks – might seem odd in view of the relatively restricted diffusion of literature in Italian society. It may to an extent be attributable to inertia on his part and to a very powerful persistence of a 'literary' conception of culture in Italy at the time. More particularly, though, it would seem to be bound up with his emphasis on building hegemony. He tends explicitly to privilege written over spoken or visual cultural forms like radio and film – both of which were rapidly expanding their audiences when he wrote – because the former act 'in depth' (see IX 25). For Gramsci, the mastery of the standard form of the language and the capacity for logical thinking were closely related to one another (see Section V). Moving from a local to a national language, from oral to written culture and from 'simple common sense' to 'coherent and systematic thought' (X 13) were all moments of a process of acculturation which was at the same time a process of self-mastery and political liberation.

1 Influence of French Romantic Serials

I have frequently referred to this 'cultural source' (remember the man of the English privies and mechanical lavatory covers)[1] to explain certain subaltern intellectual phenomena. The argument could be developed more fully and with a broader field of reference. The socio-economic 'propositions' of Eugène Sue are related to certain tendencies of Saint-Simonism, to which the theories of the organic state and philosophical positivism are also connected. Saint-Simonism was also popularly diffused in Italy, both directly (there are publications on the subject that will have to be consulted) and indirectly, through popular novels (such as Sue's) which picked up opinions more or less linked to Saint-

---

[1] This alludes to Mario Gioda (1883–1924), a former anarchist who supported Italian intervention in the war, wrote for Mussolini's *Popolo d'Italia* and became secretary of the Turin Fascio in 1920. In 1912–13 Gioda had written a series of 'exposés' on the Turin underworld for the review *La Folla* under the Balzacian pseudonym 'Vautrin's friend'. Gramsci caricatured Gioda in two articles of 1916 (see CT, pp. 108–9 and 121–22) as displaying character traits of the romantic serial novel tradition. In a 1924 article in *L'Unità* (now in CPC, pp. 367–69) he linked Gioda's name to others with respect to a more widespread 'influence' of Romantic serial literature on anarchism and fascism: 'Mario Gioda . . . must still have in a drawer a thick novel on the Turin slums, a novel like Eugène Sue's *Mysteries of Paris*, a novel in which, with the extensive method of Carolina Invernizio, a peaceful provincial city of honest working people, of peaceful petty-

Simonism via Louis Blanc, etc.[2]

This also serves to show how the political and intellectual situation in this country was so backward that the same problems were being raised as in the France of 1848 and the people raising them were socially very similar to their French counterparts of that time: bohemians, petty intellectuals of provincial origin, etc. (See the chapters 'Revelation of the Mysteries of Political Economy' in *The Holy Family*.) Once again Prince Rodolphe is appointed the regulator of society, but he is a Prince Rodolphe who comes from the people and is thus even more romantic (besides we do not know whether back in the annals of time there may not be blue blood in his pedigree.)

Q3 § 53.

2 'Interest'

Popular national literature. One will have to establish properly what is to be understood by the term 'interesting' in art in general

bourgeois on state pensions, becomes a den of every vice, an aquarium of sea-snakes, a beggars' haven for every social monster. This is what romanticism is, this is the romantic setting in which the fascist mentality was formed. Why was the serial novel, such as that published by Sonzogno, so popular in Italy before the war? Why was *Il Secolo* the newspaper with the highest circulation? Why was Carolina Invernizio the most widely-read novelist? Why are Dario Niccodemi's plays still so successful? . . . Mario Gioda, Massimo Rocca became anarchists reading about Jean Valjean's struggles against Javert . . . French romanticism of 1848 also left some of the petty bourgeoisie on the barricades, alongside the working class; but the working class was still weak, it did not manage to seize power; power was seized by Louis Bonaparte, the romantic petty bourgeoisie turned Caesarist. This is the romantic side of the fascist movement, of fascists like Mario Gioda, Massimo Rocca, Curzio Suckert [Malaparte], Roberto Farinacci etc., etc.; an unbalanced imagination, a quivering of heroic fury, a psychological restlessness which have no other content than the sentiments present in the serial novel of French romanticism around 1848: the anarchists thought of the revolution like a chapter of *Les Misérables*, with its Grantaires, Aigle de Meaux & Co., plus a dash of Gavroche and Jean Valjean; the fascists want to be the "Prince Rodolphes" of the good Italian people. The historical conjuncture has allowed these romantics to become a "ruling class" and all of Italy to become a hack serial novel . . .'

[2] Eugène Sue (1804–75) was converted to a Christian philanthropic socialism just prior to undertaking *The Mysteries of Paris* (1842–43), a novel presenting a panorama of crime and social injustice in working-class Paris. The hero, Prince Rodolphe, roams the Paris underworld in disguise, punishing evil and rewarding virtue. Marx, dealing polemically in *The Holy Family* with Sue's approving Young Hegelian critic Szeliga, noted the way Sue expressed his fear of the class struggle by having Rodolphe 'lame' and 'paralyse' protest by cutting it off at root and substituting it with social reform. Henri de Saint-Simon (1760–1825) was a direct influence on both the positivist Auguste Comte and on Louis Blanc's programme of state workshops for the unemployed. The leading Saint-Simonian, Enfantin, called Sue a true apostle of Saint-Simon.

and in narrative literature and the theatre in particular. The nature of what is 'interesting' changes according to individuals or social groups or the crowd in general: it is therefore an element of culture, not of art, etc. But is it therefore completely extraneous to art, completely separate from it? In any case art itself is interesting, and interesting for its own sake, in that it satisfies a requirement of life. Besides this more intimate characteristic of art, that of being interesting for its own sake, what other elements of 'interest' can a work of art present, for example a novel or a poem or a play? In theory an infinite number. But the ones that are 'interesting' are not infinite: they are, precisely, only those elements that are thought to contribute most directly to the immediate or mediated (of the first degree) success of the novel, poem or play. A linguist can be interested in a play by Pirandello because he wants to find out how many lexical, morphological and syntactic elements of Sicilian dialect Pirandello has introduced or can introduce into the Italian literary language. This is an 'interesting' element that will not greatly contribute to the diffusion of the play in question. Carducci's 'barbarous metres'[3] were an 'interesting' element for a larger circle – the corporation of professional literary men and those who aimed to join it. They were thus a considerable element of immediate 'success' in themselves since they helped to sell a few thousand copies of poems written in barbarous metres. These 'interesting' elements vary according to the times, the cultural climate and personal idiosyncrasies.

The most stable element of 'interest' is undoubtedly the 'moral' one, both positive and negative, for and against. What is 'stable' here is the 'moral category', not a concrete moral content. Intimately linked to this is the 'technical' element, in the particular sense of a means of conveying the moral content, the moral conflict of the novel, poem or play in the most immediate and dramatic way. Thus, in drama we have the *coup de théâtre*, in the novel the dominant 'intrigue', etc. Not all of these elements are necessarily 'artistic', yet neither are they necessarily non-artistic. From the artistic point of view they are in a sense 'indifferent', that is, extra-artistic. They are facts of the history of culture and must be evaluated in this light.

That this happens, that this is the case is proved by so called

---

[3] On Carducci, see footnote 10 on p. 95.

commercial literature, which is a section of national-popular literature. The 'commercial' aspect comes from the fact that the 'interesting' element is not 'naïve', 'spontaneous', intimately fused with the artistic conception, but is sought from without, mechanically, and is doled out industrially, as a sure element of immediate 'success'. Yet this means that even commercial literature must not be disregarded in the history of culture. Indeed it has enormous value precisely in this respect because the success of a work of commercial literature indicates (and it is often the only indication available) the 'philosophy of the age', that is, the mass of feelings and conceptions of the world predominant among the 'silent' majority. This literature is a popular 'narcotic', an 'opium'. Alexandre Dumas's *The Count of Monte-Cristo*, which is perhaps the biggest 'opiate' of the popular novels,[4] could be analysed in this light. What man of the people does not believe he has been treated unjustly by the powerful and does not dream about the 'punishment' to inflict upon them? Edmond Dantès offers him the model, 'intoxicates' him with exaltation and replaces the belief in a transcendental justice in which he no longer 'systematically' believes.

Q5 § 54.

3 [Carlo Linati on 'Interest']

See Carlo Linati's article 'Dell'interesse' in the February 1929 issue of *Libri del Giorno*. Linati asks what the essential quality is which makes books interesting and ends up without an answer. Clearly no precise answer can be found, at least not in the sense intended by Linati, who would like to find the 'essence' in order to be able, or enable others, to write interesting books. Linati says that this has lately become a 'burning' issue. It is true and it is natural that it should be so. There has been a clear re-awakening of nationalistic feelings: it is understandable that one should pose the problem of why Italian books are not read, the problem of why they are considered 'boring' and foreign ones 'interesting'. The

---

[4] On opiates, see footnote 48 below. In *The Count of Monte-Cristo* (1844–45) a young sailor, Edmond Dantès, is framed as a Bonapartist conspirator and imprisoned in the Château d'If. He escapes after fourteen years, comes into possession of a vast treasure hidden on the island of Montecristo and, using this wealth and assuming various personae, systematically carries out his revenge on the three men responsible for his arrest and conviction.

nationalist revival makes one realize that Italian literature is not 'national', in the sense that it is not popular, and that as a people we are subject to a foreign hegemony. The result of which is a series of programmes, controversies and attempts, none of which, however, achieves anything. What would be needed is a ruthless criticism of tradition and a cultural-moral renewal from which a new literature should be born. But that is precisely what does not happen, because of the contradiction, etc.: the re-awakening of nationalism has come to mean the exaltation of the past. Marinetti has become an Academician and is fighting against the tradition of spaghetti.[5]

Q6 § 73.

4 Serial Novels

Compare what I have written about *The Count of Monte-Cristo* as an exemplary model of the serial novel. The serial novel takes the place of (and at the same time favours) the fantasizing of the common people; it is a real way of day-dreaming. One can refer to what Freud and the psychoanalysts say about day-dreams.[6] In this case, one could say that the day-dreams of the people are dependent on a (social) 'inferiority complex'. This is why they day-dream at length about revenge and about punishing those responsible for the evils they have endured. In *The Count of Monte-Cristo* there are all the ingredients for encouraging these

[5] Marinetti was among the first nominees to the Accademia d'Italia, officially inaugurated in October 1929 with the aim of 'promoting and coordinating the Italian intellectual movement in the sciences, literature and the arts, to maintain the purity of its national character according to the genius and tradition of the race', etc. (Inaugural statute). In November 1930, Marinetti launched a campaign against spaghetti declaring that it was 'an obsolete food . . . heavy, brutalizing and gross . . . it induces scepticism, sloth, and pessimism' (quoted in E. David, *Italian Food*, Harmondsworth 1963, p. 93).

[6] For Freud, daydreams were, like dreams, fulfilments of wishes (see Ch. 6 § 1 of the *Interpretation of Dreams*). There are two notes on Freud in the Prison Notebooks (Q 1 § 33 and Q 15 § 74) and a number of scattered references elsewhere. Gramsci's general opinion, based by his own admission mainly on second hand information, was that Freudianism was an attempt to deal with the effects of modern social 'conformism', particularly among the middle classes, and that ideologically it involved a return to eighteenth-century concepts of 'natural man'. On the other hand, he took a sympathetic interest in the psychoanalytical treatment undergone by his wife Julia in the Soviet Union in 1931 (see L, pp. 428 and 477). Freud's *Introduction à la psychoanalyse*, recommended to Gramsci by Piero Sraffa in 1931, was not found among his prison library and is not mentioned in the Notebooks.

reveries and thus for administering a narcotic that will deaden the sense of evil.

Q6§134.

5 [The Heroes of Popular Literature]

One of the most characteristic attitudes of the popular public towards its literature is this: the writer's name and personality do not matter, but the personality of the protagonist does. When they have entered into the intellectual life of the people, the heroes of popular literature are separated from their 'literary' origin and acquire the validity of historical figures. Their entire lives, from birth to death, are sources of interest and this explains the success of 'sequels' even if they are spurious. It may happen, in other words, that the original creator of the type makes his hero die and the 'sequel-writer' has him brought back to life, to the great satisfaction of the public, whose enthusiasm is revived and who recreate the hero's image, extending it with the new material offered to them. The term 'historical figure' should be taken not in a literal sense – although it does also happen that popular readers can no longer distinguish between the actual world of past history and the fantasy world and that they discuss fictional characters as they would those who have really lived – but figuratively in the sense that the fantasy world acquires a particular fabulous concreteness in popular intellectual life. Thus one finds that, for example, the contents of various novels are mixed up because the characters resemble each other. The popular storyteller brings together in one hero the adventures of many and is convinced that this is the 'intelligent' thing to do.

Q8§122.

6 Guerin Meschino

In the *Corriere della Sera* of 7 January 1932, there is an article by Radius with the headings: 'The Classics of the People, Guerino known as "il Meschino".'[7] The heading 'The Classics

---

[7] The *Guerin Meschino* (known also simply as *Guerino*) is a prose romance by Andrea da Barberino (c. 1370 – c. 1431), who also wrote the *Reali di Francia*. Gramsci mentions having read it in prison in Milan in 1927 (L, p. 89). The modern meaning of *meschino* is 'wretched' or 'mean'. It had an older meaning of 'lowly', 'servant'.

of the People' is vague and indeterminate. *Guerino*, along with a whole series of similar books (*I Reali di Francia, Bertoldo*, stories of brigands and knights, etc.), represents a specific kind of popular literature, the most elementary and primitive, which circulates among the most backward and 'isolated' strata of the people: especially those in the South, in the mountains, etc. Those who read *Guerino* do not read Dumas or *Les Misérables*, let alone Sherlock Holmes. There is a determinate folklore and a determinate 'common sense' which corresponds to these strata.

Radius has only skimmed through the book and has little familiarity with philology. He gives a fanciful meaning to *Meschino*; 'the nickname was pinned on the hero because of his humble ancestry'. This is a colossal error which alters the whole popular psychology of the book as well as the psychological and emotional attitude the popular readers have toward it. It is immediately evident that Guerino is of royal blood but that, through misfortune, he is forced to become a 'servant', in other words 'meschino' in the sense the word had in the Middle Ages and as one finds in Dante (in the *Vita nuova*, I recall perfectly well). Therefore, Guerino is the son of a king, reduced to bondage, but who regains his natural rank through his own willpower and means. There is in the most primitive stratum of the 'people' this traditional esteem of birth which becomes 'affectionate' when misfortune strikes the hero and then becomes enthusiasm when the hero regains his social position in the face of his misfortune.

Guerino as an 'Italian' popular poem: from this point of view, it should be noted that the book is very coarse and unembellished, that it has not been worked upon or perfected, given the cultural isolation of the people, left to themselves. Perhaps this is why there are no love affairs or the least bit of eroticism in *Guerino*.

Guerino as a 'popular encyclopaedia': observe how low the culture must be of those strata who read *Guerino* and how little interest they take, for example, in 'geography' for them to be content with *Guerino* and to take it seriously. One could analyse *Guerino* as an 'encyclopaedia' to obtain information about the mental primitiveness and cultural indifference of the vast stratum of people who still feed on it.

Q 6 § 207.

7 Raffaello Giovagnoli's 'Spartaco'

On 8 January 1932, the *Corriere della Sera* published a letter sent by Garibaldi from Caprera to Raffaello Giovagnoli on 25 June 1874, immediately after reading his novel *Spartaco*.[8] The letter is very interesting for this section on 'popular literature', since Garibaldi wrote 'popular novels' too and the letter contains the main principles of his 'poetics' in this genre. Besides, Giovagnoli's *Spartaco* is one of the few Italian popular novels to have also circulated abroad, in a period in which the popular 'novel' in Italy was 'anti-clerical' and 'national', i.e. with strictly indigenous traits and limits.

As far as I recall it, it seems that *Spartaco* would lend itself particularly well to an attempt that, within certain limits, could become a method. One could 'translate it' into modern language: purge it as a language of rhetorical and baroque forms, cleanse it of a few stylistic and technical idiosyncrasies, making it 'current'. It would be a matter of consciously carrying out that process of adaptation to the times, to new feelings and new styles which popular literature traditionally underwent when it was transmitted orally and had not been fixed and fossilized through writing and printing. If this is done in translations from one language to another for the masterpieces of the classical world which each age has translated and imitated according to new cultures, why could it and why should it not be done for works like *Spartaco* and others which have a 'popular-cultural' rather than an artistic value? (Develop this.)

This process of adaptation still occurs in popular music with songs that are widespread among the people. Think of all the love-songs that have gone through two or three re-workings and become political songs. This happens in every country and one could cite some fairly strange cases (for example, the Tyrolese hymn on Andreas Hofer which provided the musical form for the

---

[8] See Raffaello Giovagnoli, *Spartaco*, ed. L. Russo, Florence 1955, where Garibaldi's letter is reprinted in the prefatory material. Giovagnoli (1838–1915) fought with Garibaldi in 1860 and 1863, wrote one of the first histories of the Risorgimento and a book on the Roman revolution of 1848–49. *Spartaco* (1874) deals with the liberation of the slaves by Spartacus and the rebel gladiators in 73–71 B.C. Gramsci's suggestion in this note about republishing a modernized version of the novel was followed to the letter by the PCI in the early 1950s when the review *Vie Nuove* serialized it. The party began serializing fiction in 1949 on the pages of *L'Unità*, polling readers' choices. The first two were Gorky and Jack London.

Molodaia Gvardia).[9]

For novels there would be the obstacle of copyright which today, I think, lasts eighty years from the date of first publication (certain works, however, could not be modernized: for example, *Les Misérables*, *The Wandering Jew* and *The Count of Monte-Cristo*, all of which are too fixed in their original forms).

Q6 § 208.

8 [Aldo Sorani on Popular Literature]

In *Il Marzocco* of 13 September 1931, Aldo Sorani (who has often written about popular literature in various reviews and newspapers) published an article entitled 'Romanzieri popolari contemporanei' in which he comments on the series of sketches on 'Illustrious Unknown Authors' published by Charensol in *Les Nouvelles Littéraires*. 'These are highly popular writers of adventure stories and serials, unknown or almost unknown to the cultured reader but idolized and followed blindly by that larger public which decrees the mammoth circulation of such literature. This public knows nothing at all about literature but it wants to be interested and excited by sensational plots woven out of crime or love stories. For the people, *these are the real writers*. The people feel admiration and gratitude for these novelists which the latter keep nourished by consigning to their publishers and readers a mass of work so continuous and imposing as to appear physically, let alone intellectually, incredible and unsustainable.' Sorani observes that these writers 'have enslaved themselves to an exhausting task and offer a real public service if countless numbers of men and women readers cannot do without them and publishers obtain large profits from their inexhaustible activity.' Sorani uses the expression 'real public service' but he gives it a debased definition, which does not correspond to the one used in these notes. Sorani notes that these writers, as appears from Charensol's articles, 'have become stricter and generally more sober in their manner of life, ever since the by now remote time in which Ponson du Terrail or Xavier de Montépin[10] laid claim to social celebrity and went all out to obtain it. . . , maintaining

---

[9] 'Young Guard': Russian revolutionary song.

[10] Ponson du Terrail (1829–71) and Xavier de Montépin (1823–1902) were prolific serial novelists.

that ultimately it was only their different style which distinguished them from their more academic brothers. They wrote the way people speak, while the others wrote the way people do not speak!'

(Nevertheless, even the 'illustrious unknowns' in France belong to literary clubs, as much as Montépin. Remember also Balzac's grudge against Sue because of the latter's social and financial success.)[11]

Sorani continues: 'A not unimportant aspect of the persistence of this popular literature . . . lies in the enthusiasm of the public. The great French public, that public which some people consider the most shrewd, critical and *blasé* in the world, has remained especially faithful to the adventure story and the serial. High class and high-circulation French newspapers have not been able, or known how, to give up the serial story. The proletariat and the bourgeoisie are still in great masses so naïve (!) as to need an endless number of sentimental and moving, horrifying or tear-jerking stories for the daily nutriment of their curiosity and sentimentality; they still need to take sides between criminal heroes and the heroes of justice and revenge.

Unlike the French public, the English or American public have turned to the historical adventure novel (haven't the French?!) 'or to the detective novel, etc.' (clichés about national character)

'As for Italy, I believe one could ask why popular literature is not popular in Italy.' (This is not phrased accurately; there are no such writers in Italy but there is a multitude of readers.) 'After Mastriani and Invernizio[12] there seem to have been no more of those writers who know how to win over the crowd by horrifying and reducing to tears a public of naïve, faithful and insatiable readers. Why has this type of novelist not continued (?) to thrive among us? Has our literature been too academic of literary even in its lower depths? Have our publishers been incapable of cultivating a plant considered too contemptible? Do our writers not have enough imagination to breathe life into the foot of the page and the supplement? Or is it that we, in this field too, have been and still are satisfied just to import what the other markets produce? We are certainly not teeming like France with

---

[11] Balzac envied Sue's success both as a dandy and as a *feuilletoniste* and attacked him from 1840 in his paper *La Revue Parisienne.*

[12] On Mastriani and Invernizio see footnote 21 on p. 211.

"illustrious unknown authors"; there must be some reason for this deficiency and perhaps it would be worth looking for it.'

Q 21 § 2.

9 Popular Origin of the 'Superman'

Every time one comes upon some admirer of Nietzsche, it is worth asking oneself and trying to find out if his 'superman' ideas, opposed to conventional morality, are of genuine Nietzschean origin. In other words, are they the result of a mental elaboration located in the sphere of 'high culture' or do they have much more modest origins? Are they, for example, connected to serial literature? (And was Nietzsche himself entirely uninfluenced by French serial novels? It should be remembered that this literature, now relegated to the porter's lodge and below stairs was once very popular among intellectuals, at least until 1870, as the so-called 'thriller' is today.) In any case it seems that one can claim that much of the would-be Nietzschean 'supermanism' has its source and doctrinal model not in *Zarathustra* but merely in Alexandre Dumas's *The Count of Monte-Cristo*. The type represented most perfectly by Dumas in *Monte-Cristo* is frequently repeated in his other novels. It can for example be identified in Athos of *The Three Musketeers*, in Joseph Balsamo and perhaps in other characters.

Therefore, when one reads that a person admires Balzac, one must be on guard. In Balzac, too, there is much of the serial novel. Even Vautrin is a superman in his way and what he says to Rastignac in *Père Goriot* is very . . . Nietzschean in the folk sense.[13] The same must be said of Rastignac and Rubempré. (Vincenzo Morello became 'Rastignac' by this kind of . . . popular lineal descent and defended 'Corrado Brando'.)[14]

Nietzsche's success has been very mixed. His complete works

[13] Vautrin is the criminal who in *Le Père Goriot* advises the ambitious young Rastignac to abandon scruples and marry for self-advancement: 'In a million of this herd of human cattle there are ten sharp fellows to be found who climb above everything, even above laws; I am one of them. You, if you're above the common herd, go straight forward with your head high.' (*Old Goriot*, Harmondsworth 1951, p. 130).

[14] On Morello, who used the Balzacian pseudonym 'Rastignac', see footnote 12 on p. 156. Corrado Brando is the superman character in D'Annunzio's play *Più che l'amore* (1905). D'Annunzio subsequently dedicated the play to Morello in recognition of his defence of it. See also SG, p. 179.

were published by Monanni and we all know the cultural and ideological origins of Monanni and his most devoted clientèle.

Vautrin and 'Vautrin's friend' have left a large mark on the literature of Paolo Valera and his review *La Folla* (remember 'Vautrin's friend' from Turin in *La Folla*).[15] The ideology of the 'musketeer', taken from the novel by Dumas, also had a large popular following.

It is entirely understandable that people are somewhat ashamed of mentally justifying their notions with the novels of Dumas and Balzac. So they justify them with Nietzsche and admire Balzac as an artistic writer rather than as a creator of serial-novel type figures. But culturally the real nexus seems incontrovertible.

The type of the 'superman' is Monte-Cristo freed of that particular halo of 'fatalism' peculiar to late Romanticism, and which is even more emphatic in Athos and Joseph Balsamo. Brought into the realm of politics, Monte-Cristo is without a doubt extremely picturesque (the struggle against the 'personal enemies' of Monte-Cristo, etc.)

It can be observed how certain countries, in comparison to others, have remained provincial and backward in this sphere too. While Sherlock Holmes has already become anachronistic for much of Europe, people in some countries are still on *Monte-Cristo* and the works of Fenimore Cooper (cf. the 'savages', 'iron beard', etc.).[16]

See Mario Praz's book *La carne, la morte e il diavolo nella letteratura romantica* (Edizione della Cultura).[17] Alongside of Praz's investigation one should conduct another: into the 'superman' in popular literature and his influence on real life and modes of behaviour. (The petty bourgeoisie and the petty intellectuals are particularly influenced by such novelistic images, which are their 'opium', their 'artificial paradise', in contrast with

[15] On 'Vautrin's friend' (Mario Gioda) see footnote 1 above. *La Folla* (The Crowd) was a Milan periodical, issued in two series (1901–4; 1913–15) and edited by the anarchist publicist Paolo Valera (1850–1926). It was also the title of a novel by Valera (1901).

[16] 'I selvaggi' ('the savages') was the name both of an early fascist group based round Roberto Farinacci and the newspaper *Cremona Nuova* and of the fascists of the Val d'Elsa: see footnote 61 on p. 329. 'Pizzo di ferro' ('iron beard') was the nickname of the fascist quadrumvir and aviator Italo Balbo.

[17] Translated as *The Romantic Agony*, London 1933: a study of the mutations from writer to writer of themes and motifs with an erotic basis in Romantic literature (sadism, vampirism, *femme fatale*, etc.)

the narrowness and pinched circumstances of their real and immediate life.) From this comes the popularity of certain sayings like 'It is better to live one day as a lion than a hundred years as a sheep', particularly successful among those who are really and irremediably sheep. How many of these 'sheep' say: Oh! If only I had power even just for one day, etc.; the desire to be an implacable 'executioner' is the aspiration of someone who feels the influence of Monte-Cristo.

Adolfo Omodeo has observed that there exists a kind of cultural 'mortmain', constituted by religious literature, which nobody seems to want to deal with, as if it had no importance and function in national popular life.[18] Apart from the jibe about 'mortmain' and the clergy's satisfaction with the fact that its special literature is not subjected to a critical examination, there is another section of national and popular cultural life that no one deals with or is concerned about critically: serial literature, both in the strict sense and also in a broader sense (in which one can include Victor Hugo and also Balzac).

In *Monte-Cristo* there are two chapters in which the 'superman' of serial literature is explicitly discussed: the one entitled 'Ideology', when Monte-Cristo meets the attorney Villefort; and the one which describes breakfast at the Viscount de Morcerf's during Monte-Cristo's first trip to Paris.[19] One should see if there are similar 'ideological' inserts in Dumas's other novels. In *The Three Musketeers* Athos is more like the generic 'fatal' man of late Romanticism: in this novel the popular taste for individualism is stimulated rather by the adventurous and extra-legal activity of the musketeers as such. In *Joseph Balsamo* the power of the individual is related to obscure magical forces and to the support of the European freemasons, so the example is less productive for the popular reader. In Balzac the figures are more concretely artistic but are still part of the atmosphere of popular Romanticism. Rastignac and Vautrin can certainly not be confused with the characters of Dumas, which is precisely why

[18] Omodeo's views on religious literature were quoted in an article by Croce (Gramsci's source here): 'La storiografia della filosofia e della religione', *La Critica* XXVII (1929) IV, p. 173.

[19] See *The Count of Monte-Cristo* (London 1909) Volume 1, Chapters 48 and 40 respectively. Monte-Cristo explains to Villefort that he is an 'exceptional being' with a mission to fulfil: he has made a pact with the devil to become an agent of Providence and to dispense rewards and punishments as he chooses. At Morcerf's he is applauded as being 'sufficiently courageous to preach egotism pure and simple'.

their influence can more easily be 'confessed' to, not only by men like Paolo Valera and the collaborators of *La Folla* but also by mediocre intellectuals like Vincenzo Morello who, however, consider themselves (or are considered by many) as belonging to 'high culture'.

The writer to put alongside Balzac is Stendhal with the figure of Julien Sorel and others from his repertoire.

For Nietzsche's superman, as well as the influence of French Romanticism (and in general the cult of Napoleon) one should look at the racist tendencies that culminated in Gobineau and then in Chamberlain and pan-Germanism (Treitschke, the theory of power, etc.)[20] But perhaps the popular 'superman' of Dumas should really be considered as a 'democratic' reaction to the concept of racism with its feudal origin and should be put alongside the glorification of 'Gallicism' in the novels of Eugène Sue.

Dostoyevsky can be called to mind as a reaction to this tendency of the French popular novel. Raskolnikov is Monte-Cristo 'criticized' by a Christian pan-Slavist. For the influence of the French serial novel on Dostoyevsky, see the special number of *La Cultura* dedicated to Dostoyevsky.[21]

There are many theatrical, outward elements in the popular character of the 'superman', with more of the 'prima donna' than the superman about them; a great deal of 'subjective and objective' formalism and childish ambitions to be the 'top of the class', but especially the ambition to be considered and proclaimed as such.

For the relation between late Romanticism and some aspects of modern life (the Count of Monte-Cristo atmosphere) one should read Louis Gillet's article in *Revue des Deux Mondes* of 15 December 1932.

This type of 'superman' is expressed in the theatre (especially French theatre, which in many respects is a continuation of the

[20] Arthur Gobineau (1816–82) treated race, racial inequality and the 'degeneration of the blood' through miscegenation as the key to historical explanation (*Essai sur l'Inegalité des Races Humaines*, 1853–55). His ideas were developed in a pro-Teutonic and antisemitic direction by Wagner's son-in-law Houston Stewart Chamberlain (1855–1927) whose *Die Grundlagen des XIX Jahrhunderts* (1899) influenced Alfred Rosenberg and Hitler. Heinrich von Treitschke (1834–96), historian and theorist of nationalism, envisaged a struggle between strong and weak nations, German expansion and the self-determination of German national minorities outside the fatherland.

[21] See IX 19.

serial literature of 1848): see the 'classical' repertoire of Ruggero Ruggeri, like *Il Marchese di Priola, L'artiglio*, etc. and many of the works of Henry Bernstein.[22]

Q 16 § 13.

10 Various Types of Popular Novel

A certain variety of types of popular novel exists and it should be noted that, although all of them simultaneously enjoy some degree of success and popularity, one of them nevertheless predominates by far. From this predominance one can identify a change in fundamental tastes, just as from the simultaneous success of the various types one can prove that there exist among the people various cultural levels, different 'masses of feelings' prevalent in one or the other level, various popular 'hero-models'. It is thus important for the present essay to draw up a catalogue of these types and to establish historically their greater or lesser degree of success: 1) The Victor Hugo – Eugène Sue (*Les Misérables, The Mysteries of Paris*) type : overtly ideologico-political in character and with democratic tendencies linked to the ideologies of 1848; 2) The sentimental type, not strictly political, but which expresses what could be defined as a 'sentimental democracy' (Richebourg – Decourcelle, etc.);[23] 3) The type presented as pure intrigue, but which has a conservative-reactionary ideological content (Montépin); 4) The historical novel of A. Dumas and Ponson du Terrail which, besides its historical aspect, has a politico-ideological character, but less marked: Ponson du Terrail, is, however, a conservative-reactionary and his exaltation of the aristocrats and their faithful servants is quite different from the historical representations of Alexandre Dumas, even though Dumas has no overt democratic-political tendency but is pervaded by 'passive' and generic democratic feelings and often comes close to the 'sentimental' type; 5) The detective novel in its double aspect (Lecoq,

---

[22] Ruggero Ruggeri (1871–1953), stage (and later also film) actor. Henry Bernstein (1876–1953), French dramatist. Ruggeri was a leading performer of Bernstein's work in Italy.

[23] Émile-Jules Richebourg (1833–98) wrote sentimental popular novels serialized in *La Revue Francaise* and *Le Petit Journal*. Pierre Decourcelle (1856–1926) developed the technique of the sequel or series of sequels.

Rocambole, Sherlock Holmes, Arsène Lupin);[24] 6) The gothic novel (ghosts, mysterious castles, etc.: Ann Radcliffe, etc.);[25] 6) The geographical, scientific adventure novel which can be tendentious or consist simply of intrigue (Jules Verne – Boussenard).[26]

Each of these types also has different national characteristics (in America the adventure novel is the epic of the pioneers). One can observe how in the overall production of each country there is an implicit nationalism, not rhetorically expressed, but skilfully insinuated into the story. In Verne and the French there is a very deep anti-English feeling, related to the loss of the colonies and the humiliating naval defeats. In the geographical adventure novel the French do not clash with the Germans but with the English. But there is also an anti-English feeling in the historical novel and even in the sentimental novel (e.g. George Sand). (Reaction due to the Hundred Years War and the killing of Joan of Arc, and to the defeat of Napoleon.)

In Italy none of these types has had many writers of stature (not literary stature, but 'commercial' value, in the sense of inventiveness and ingeniously constructed plots which, although complicated, are worked out with a certain rationality). Not even the detective novel, which has been so successful internationally (and, for authors and publishers, financially), has found writers in Italy. Yet many novels, especially historical ones, have chosen for their subject Italy and the historical events of its cities, regions, institutions and men. Thus Venetian history, with its political, judicial and police organizations, has provided and continues to provide subject matter for popular novelists of every country, except Italy. Popular literature on the life of brigands has had a certain success in Italy but its quality is extremely poor.

The latest type of popular book is the novelized biography, which at any rate represents an unconscious attempt to satisfy the cultural needs of some of the popular strata who are more smart culturally and are not satisfied with the Dumas type of story. This

[24] Characters invented respectively by Emile Gaboriau (1832–73), Ponson du Terrail, Arthur Conan Doyle (1859–1930) and Maurice Leblanc (1864–1941).

[25] Ann Radcliffe (1764–1823), 'gothic' novelist, wrote *The Mysteries of Udolpho* (1794) and *The Italian* (1797).

[26] On Verne, see IX 16. Louis-Henri Boussenard (1847–1910) wrote numerous adventure novels.

literature, too, has few representatives in Italy (Mazzucchelli, Cesare Giardini, etc.). Not only do Italian writers not compare with the French, the Germans and the English in terms of numbers, fecundity and the gift of giving literary pleasure but, more significantly, they choose their subjects outside Italy (Mazzucchelli and Giardini in France, Eucardio Momigliano in England)[27] in order to adapt to the Italian popular taste formed on historical novels, especially French ones. The Italian man of letters would not write a novelized biography of Masaniello, Michele di Lando or Cola di Rienzo[28] without feeling obliged to cram it with tiresome, rhetorical 'padding', for fear people might think . . . might wonder . . . etc. It is true that the success of novelized biographies has induced many publishers to start running series of biographies, but these books are to the novelized biography what *The Nun of Monza*[29] is to *The Count of Monte-Cristo*. They consist of the familiar, often philologically correct, biographical scheme which can at most find a few thousand readers but cannot become popular.

One should note that some of the types of popular novel listed above have parallels in the theatre and now in cinema. In the theatre the considerable success of Dario Niccodemi is doubtless due to his ability to dramatize ideas and motifs eminently related to popular ideology. This is true of *Scampolo*, *L'Aigrette* and *La Volata*, etc.[30] There is also something similar in G. Forzano's work,[31] but on the model of Ponson du Terrail, with conservative tendencies. The theatrical work – of an Italian character – that has had the greatest popular success in Italy is Giacometti's *La morte civile*,[32] but it has not had imitators of any merit (still

[27] Mario Mazzucchelli wrote about Robespierre and Murat, Eucardio Momigliano about Cromwell and Ann Boleyn.

[28] Leaders of early popular protests (Masaniello with the *lazzaroni* against the Spanish in Naples in 1647, Michele di Lando with the *ciompi* in Florence in 1378 and Cola di Rienzo in Rome in 1347).

[29] See footnote 14 on p. 159.

[30] Gramsci had reviewed two of Niccodemi's plays in his *Avanti!* theatre column. (See LVN pp. 229–30; 355–56). On Niccodemi's relationship with popular serial fiction see also L, p. 270 and the quotation in footnote 1 above.

[31] Gioacchino Forzano was the author of sundry historical dramas and of the libretti of Puccini's two one-act operas, *Suor Angelica* and *Gianni Schicchi*.

[32] Paolo Giacometti (1816–82); *La morte civile* was first staged in 1861.

speaking in a non-literary sense). In this section on the theatre, we might note how a whole series of playwrights of great literary value can be enormously liked by the people as well. The people in the cities greatly enjoy Ibsen's *A Doll's House* because the feelings depicted and the author's moral tendency find a profound resonance in the popular psyche. And what should the so-called *theatre of ideas* be if not this, the representation of passions related to social behaviour, with dramatic solutions which can depict a 'progressive' catharsis,[33] which can depict the drama of the most intellectually and morally advanced part of a society, that which expresses the historical growth immanent in present social behaviour itself? This drama and these passions, though, must be represented and not expounded like a thesis or a propaganda speech. In other words, the author must live in the real world with all its contradictory needs and not express feelings absorbed merely from books.

Q 21 § 6.

11 Popularity of Italian Literature

From *Nuova Antologia*, 1 October 1930: Ercole Reggio, 'Perché la letteratura italiana non è popolare in Europa': 'The slight success of even eminent Italian books among us, compared to that of so many foreign books, should convince us that the reasons for the unpopularity of our literature in Europe are probably the same that make it unpopular in our country; hence, all in all, there is not much point asking of others what we do not expect at home. Even foreigners who are sympathetic towards Italian culture say that our literature on the whole lacks certain modest and necessary qualities, those which appeal to *average man, man of the economists* (?!); and it is because of its prerogatives, of that which makes for its originality as well as its merit, that it does not, and cannot, match the popularity of the other great

---

[33] 'Catharsis' here almost certainly has Gramsci's specialized meaning of 'the passage from the purely economic (or egoistic-passional) to the ethico-political moment, that is the superior elaboration of the structure into the superstructure in the minds of men' ('The term "catharsis"', SPN, pp. 366–67; compare the same use of the term on p. 104 above). The more conventional Aristotelian sense of catharsis with reference to tragedy is probably not relevant despite the fact that Gramsci is talking about theatre. The 1930 draft of this note (Q 3 § 78) reads 'solutions which represent the historical development etc.'

European literatures.'

Reggio mentions the fact that the Italian figurative arts (he forgets music) are, however, popular in Europe and speculates: either there is an abyss between literature and the other arts in Italy which would be impossible to explain, or the fact must be explained by secondary, extra-artistic causes. In other words, while the figurative arts (including music) speak a universal and European language, literature is limited within the confines of the national language. I do not think this objection holds: 1) Because there has been a historical period (the Renaissance) in which Italian literature was popular in Europe; in addition to and even together with the figurative arts: i.e. the whole of Italian culture was popular. 2) Because in Italy, besides literature, the figurative arts are not popular either (whereas Verdi, Puccini and Mascagni are). 3) Because the popularity of the Italian figurative arts in Europe is relative: it is limited to the intellectuals and to a few other sections of the European population; it is popular not as art but because it is tied to classical or romantic memories. 4) Italian music is however as popular in Europe as in Italy. Reggio's article continues along the tracks of the usual rhetoric, although here and there it contains thoughtful observations.

Q6 § 147.

12 [Populist Tendencies]

See Alberto Consiglio's 'Populismo e nuove tendenze della letteratura francese' [Populism and new tendencies in French literature] in *Nuova Antologia*, 1 April 1931. Consiglio takes his lead from the investigation of the 'worker and peasant novel' in *Les Nouvelles Littéraires* (July–August 1930). The article should be re-read if one wants to deal with the subject organically. Consiglio's thesis (more or less explicit and conscious) is this: faced with the growth of the social and political power of the proletariat and of its ideology, some sections of the French intelligentsia are reacting by moving 'towards the people'. This going towards the people is thus interpreted as a renewal of bourgeois thought which does not want to lose its hegemony over the popular classes and which, to exercise this hegemony better, accommodates part of proletarian ideology.

It should be seen whether a phenomenon of this kind may not

also be very historically significant and important and represent a necessary phase of transition and an episode in the indirect 'education of the people'. A list of 'populist' tendencies and an analysis of each of them would be interesting: one might discover one of Vico's 'ruses of nature' – how a social impulse, tending towards one end, brings about its opposite.[34]

Q 6 § 168.

13 The Book Fair

Since the people do not go to the book (to a certain type of book, that of the professional literati), the book will go to the people. This initiative was launched by *La Fiera Letteraria* and by its then editor Umberto Fracchia in 1927, in Milan. The initiative in itself was not bad and did achieve minor results. But the question was not really faced in the sense that the book must become deeply national-popular in order to go to the people and not just 'materially' put onto the streets with bookstalls, etc. In fact there was and is an organization for carrying the book to the people – represented by the 'pontremolesi' [itinerant booksellers] but the type of book circulated in this manner is that of the poorest popular literature, from the *Segretario degli amanti* to *Guerino*. This organization could be 'imitated', enlarged, controlled and stocked with less stupid books and with a greater variety of choice.

Q 23 § 41.

14 Popular Theatre and Novel

The popular drama is called, disparagingly, 'arena drama' perhaps because in some cities there are outdoor theatres called Arenas (the Arena del Sole in Bologna). One should remember what Edoardo Boutet wrote about the classical plays (Aeschylus, Sophocles) which the permanent company of Rome, directed by Boutet, used to perform at the Arena del Sole of Bologna on

[34] Vico's theory of divine providence held that people themselves constructed a world according to a divine plan of which they were not aware. 'For out of the passions of men each bent on his private advantage, for the sake of which they would live like wild beasts in the wilderness, it [providence] has made the civil institutions by which they may live in human society.' *The New Science*, Cornell 1958, p. 62.

Mondays – the day for washerwomen – and about the great success that these performances had. (Boutet's memoirs of the theatre were noted for the first time in the review *Il Viandante* published in Milan by T. Monicelli in 1908–09). It must also be pointed out that some of Shakespeare's plays have always been successful among the popular masses, which shows how one can be a great artist and 'popular' at the same time.

In *Il Marzocco* of 17 November 1929, there is a very revealing note by Gaio (Adolfo Orvieto): '*Danton*, il melodramma e il "romanzo nella vita"'. The note says: 'A recently "formed" theatrical company which has put together a repertory of great popular plays – from *The Count of Monte-Cristo* to *Les Deux Orphelines*[35] with the legitimate hope of getting a few people to come to the theatre, saw its prayers answered – in Florence with a brand new play by a Hungarian author about the French revolution: *Danton*.' The play is by De Pekar and it is a 'pure pathetic fable with extremely free imaginative details.' (For example, Robespierre and Saint-Just attend the trial of Danton and engage in argument with him.) 'But it is a fable, cleverly written, which uses the old infallible methods of the popular theatre, without dangerous modernistic deviations. Everything is elementary, limited, and well proportioned. The sensational actions and the uproars alternate with opportune moments of a quieter tone and the audience relaxes and consents. Clearly the audience is enthusiastic and is being entertained. Is this the best way to bring people back to the playhouse?' Orvieto's conclusion is significant. So in 1929 one must perform *The Count of Monte-Cristo* and *Les Deux Orphelines* in order to attract an audience and in 1930 in order to get the people to read the newspapers one has to serialize *The Count of Monte-Cristo* and *Joseph Balsamo*.

Q21§7.

15 Statistics

How many novels by Italian authors have been published by the popular periodicals with the widest circulation, such as *Il*

---

[35] *Les Deux Orphelines* (1874), a hugely successful play by Eugène Cormon (1810–1903) and Adolphe Dennery (1811–99).

Romanzo Mensile, Domenica del Corriere, Tribuna Illustrata and
Mattino Illustrato? The *Domenica del Corriere*, during its entire life
(about thirty-six years), perhaps none out of about a hundred
novels published. The *Tribuna Illustrata* a few (recently a series
of detective stories by Prince Valerio Pignatelli); but it must be
noted that the *Tribuna* has a far smaller circulation than the
Domenica. It is not well edited and offers a poorer type of novel.

It would be interesting to look at the nationality of the authors
and the type of adventure stories published. The *Romanzo Mensile*
and the *Domenica* published many English novels (though French
ones must predominate) and detective stories (they published
Sherlock Holmes and Arsène Lupin) but also German and
Hungarian (Baroness Orczy is very common and her novels on
the French Revolution have often been reprinted even in the
Romanzo Mensile, which also must have a wide circulation) and
even Australian novels (by Guy Boothby which have gone
through various editions).[36] The detective story or kindred type
is undoubtedly predominant, imbued with a conservative and
reactionary conception or based on pure intrigue. It would be
interesting to know who on the editorial staff of the *Corriere della
Sera* was responsible for selecting these novels and what
instructions were given, since on the *Corriere* everything was
judiciously organized. *Mattino Illustrato*, although it comes out in
Naples, publishes the same type of novels as the *Domenica* but lets
itself be guided by financial questions and often by literary
pretensions (thus, I believe it has published Conrad, Stevenson
and London). The same can be said for *Illustrazione del Popolo*
of Turin. The administration of the *Corriere* is, relatively and
perhaps absolutely, the centre of the widest circulation of popular
novels. It publishes at least fifteen a year with a very large
circulation. Next must come the Sonzogno publishing house
which must also publish a periodical.

A historical study of the publishing activity of Sonzogno would
give an approximate enough picture of variations in the popular
public's taste. The investigation is difficult because Sonzogno
does not print the year of publication and often does not number
its reprintings, but a critical examination of the catalogues would

---

[36] Emmuska Orczy (1865–1947), Hungarian-born baroness, wrote the immensely
popular *Scarlet Pimpernel* (1905) and two less successful sequels (1908 and 1933). Guy
Boothby (1867–1905) was an Australian writer who settled in England in 1894, producing
some fifty novels in ten years.

yield some results. Even a comparative study of the catalogues of fifty years ago (when the *Secolo* was at its height) and those of today would be interesting.[37] The entire genre of the tearful-sentimental novel must have fallen into oblivion, except for a few 'masterpieces' that must still endure (like *The Blackcap of the Mill* by Richebourg). Besides, this does not mean that such books are not read by certain strata of the population in the provinces, where the 'open-minded' still 'enjoy' Paul de Kock and where lively discussions are held on the philosophy of *Les Misérables*.[38] It would also be interesting to follow the publication of novels in weekly parts, as well as novels published as speculative ventures which cost a considerable amount and are tied to prizes.

Edoardo Perino and, more recently, Nerbini have published a number of popular novels, all with an anti-clerical setting and linked to the Guerrazzi tradition.[39] (One need not even mention Salani, publisher of popular literature *par excellence*.) A list of popular publishers should be compiled.

Q 21 § 8.

16 Verne and the Scientific-geographical Novel

In Verne's books nothing is ever completely impossible. The 'possibilities' that Verne's heroes have are greater than those which actually exist at the time, but not too much greater and above all not 'outside' the line of development of the scientific conquests already made. What is imagined is not entirely 'arbitrary' and is therefore able to excite the reader's fantasy, which has already been won over by the ideology of the inevitability of scientific progress in the domain of the control of natural forces.

It is different with Wells and Poe in whose work the 'arbitrary' for the most part dominates, even if the starting point is logical and is inserted into a concrete scientific reality. In Wells and Poe the human intellect dominates; hence Verne has been more popular, because he is more comprehensible. At the same time,

[37] The Milan publishing house Sonzogno, established in 1818, founded the daily paper *Il Secolo* in 1866 (see footnote 41 on p. 411).

[38] Paul de Kock (1794–1871), French popular novelist.

[39] On Guerrazzi, see footnote 11 on p. 95.

though, this balance in Verne's novelistic constructions has come to restrict his popularity (leaving aside his low artistic value). Science has overtaken Verne and his books are no longer 'psychic stimulants'.[40]

Something similar can be said of detective adventures, for instance Conan Doyle. In their day they were exciting, now hardly at all and for a number of reasons: because today the world of crime detection is better known, while Conan Doyle was largely responsible for revealing it, at least to a large number of law-abiding readers. But particularly because in Sherlock Holmes there is a (too) rational balance between intelligence and science. Today we are more interested in the individual contribution of the hero and the 'psychical' technique in itself, and therefore Poe and Chesterton are more interesting.

In his article 'Impressioni da Giulio Verne', in *Il Marzocco* of 19 February 1928, Adolfo Faggi writes that the anti-English character of many of Verne's novels is traceable to the period of rivalry between France and England which culminated in the Fashoda episode.[41] The assertion is wrong and anachronistic. Anti-British sentiments were (and perhaps still are) a fundamental element of the psychology of the French people. Anti-German feeling is relatively recent and less deep-seated than anti-British. It did not exist before the French Revolution and it became embittered after 1870, after defeat and the painful impression that politically and militarily France was not the strongest nation in Western Europe because Germany had beaten her – and alone, not in coalition. Anti-English feeling goes back to the formation of modern France, as a unitary and modern state, and thus to the Hundred Years War and the response of the popular imagination to the story of Joan of Arc. It was reinforced in modern times by the wars for hegemony on the continent (and in the world), culminating in the French

---

[40] This contrast is elaborated in Q 5 § 84: 'In Verne we are generally in the realm of verisimilitude and ahead in time. In Wells the starting-point is implausible, whereas the details are scientifically exact or at least verisimilar. Wells is more imaginative and ingenious, Verne more popular. But Wells is a popular writer too in all the rest of his output: he is a "moralist" writer, and not just in the normal sense but also in the inferior one. However, he cannot be popular in Italy and the Latin countries generally and in Germany: he is too bound to the Anglo-Saxon mentality'. See also the comments on Wells in L, pp. 498–99.

[41] Anglo-French conflict over the occupation of Egyptian Sudan came to a head when their respective troops met at Fashoda in 1898, precipitating the threat of war.

Revolution and Napoleon. The Fashoda episode, while very serious, cannot be compared to this imposing tradition which is evidenced in all of French popular literature.

Q 21 § 10.

17 The Detective Novel [i]

The detective novel was born in the margins of the literature dealing with 'causes celèbres'. Moreover the novels like *The Count of Monte-Cristo* are also connected to this literature. Are we not dealing here too with fictional 'causes celèbres', coloured by the popular ideology concerning the administration of justice, especially if it is interlaced with political passion? In *The Wandering Jew* is not Rodin a type of organizer of 'villainous plots', who does not blanch at any crime or murder?[42] And is not Prince Rodolphe, on the contrary, the 'friend of the people', the one who thwarts intrigues and crimes? The transition from this type of novel to those of pure adventure is marked by a schematizing of the plot, which is purged of every element of democratic and petty-bourgeois ideology. There is no longer the struggle between the people – good, simple and generous – and the obscure forces of tyranny (Jesuits, secret police linked to reason of state or the ambitions of single rulers, etc.), but only the struggle between professional or skilled criminals and the forces of private or public order, on the basis of written law. The celebrated French collection of 'causes celèbres' has had its correlative in other countries. At least part of it was translated into Italian for the trials famous all over Europe, like that of Fualdès for the murder of the courier from Lyons.

People have always been interested in 'judiciary' activities and still are. Public attitudes to the apparatus of justice (always in discredit, hence the success of the private or amateur detective) and towards the criminal have often changed or at least been variously coloured. The great criminal has often been represented as superior to the judicial apparatus, even as the representative of 'true' justice: the influence of Romanticism, Schiller's *The Robbers*; the tales of Hoffmann, Ann Radcliffe and

---

[42] In Sue's *Le Juif Errant* (1844–45), Rodin is a Jesuit agent who hunts down and schemes against the descendants of a persecuted Protestant to stop them inheriting the latter's fortune.

Balzac's Vautrin.

Types like Javert in *Les Misérables* are interesting from the point of view of popular psychology.[43] From the point of view of 'true justice', Javert is wrong, but Hugo represents him in a sympathetic way as a 'man of character' who is faithful to 'abstract' duty. With Javert perhaps a tradition is born according to which even the policeman can be 'respectable'. Ponson du Terrail's Rocambole. Gaboriau continues the rehabilitation of the policeman with 'M. Lecoq' who paves the way for Sherlock Holmes. It is not true that in the 'judiciary' novel the English represent the 'defence of the law', while the French exalt the criminal. In reality there is a 'cultural' passage due to the fact that this literature also circulates among certain educated strata. Remember that Sue, widely read by the middle-class democrats, contrived a complete system for the repression of professional crime.

There have always been two currents in this detective literature: one mechanical – intrigue – the other artistic. Today Chesterton is the major representative of the 'artistic' current as Poe once was. With Vautrin Balzac dealt with the criminal but he is not 'technically' a writer of detective novels.

Q 21 § 12.

18 The Detective Novel [ii]

See the book by Henri Jagot, *Vidocq* (Berger-Levrault, Paris 1930). Vidocq provided the suggestion for Balzac's Vautrin and for Alexandre Dumas (there is also a bit of him in Hugo's Jean Valjean and particularly in Rocambole). Vidocq was condemned to eight years as a counterfeiter, after a careless mistake; twenty escapes, etc. In 1812 he enrolled in Napoleon's police force and for fifteen years commanded a squad of police agents created especially for him. He became famous for his sensational arrests. Dismissed by Louis-Philippe, he founded an agency of private detectives, but with little success: he could only work in the ranks of the state police. He died in 1857, leaving behind his *Memoirs*, which were not written just by him and contain many exaggerations and boasts.

[43] In Victor Hugo's *Les Misérables* (1862), Javert is the diligent police officer who continually reappears on the traces of the reformed ex-convict Jean Valjean.

2) See Aldo Sorani's article 'Conan Doyle e la fortuna del romanzo poliziesco' [Conan Doyle and the fortunes of the detective novel] in *Pègaso* of August 1930, notable for its analysis of this kind of literature and the different forms it has assumed up to the present. In dealing with Chesterton and the Father Brown stories, Sorani fails to consider two cultural elements which seem, however, essential: a) He does not refer to the grotesque atmosphere present especially in *The Innocence of Father Brown*, yet this is the artistic element which heightens Chesterton's detective stories when their expression has come off perfectly (which is not always). b) He does not refer to the fact that the stories of Father Brown are 'apologias' of Catholicism and the Roman clergy – trained to know all the wrinkles of the human soul, by practising confession and functioning as a spiritual guide and intermediary between man and the divinity – against the 'scientism' and positivistic psychology of the Protestant Conan Doyle. In his article Sorani discusses the various (in particular Anglo-Saxon) attempts of major literary importance to perfect the technical aspects of the detective novel. The archetype is Sherlock Holmes, with his two fundamental characteristics, that of the scientist and that of the psychologist. It is one of these or both of them together that writers try to perfect. Chesterton has stressed the psychological element in the game of inductions and deductions with Father Brown, but he seems to have exaggerated in this direction with the poet-policeman type Gabriel Gale.[44]

Sorani sketches a picture of the unprecedented success of detective novels in all ranks of society and tries to identify its psychological origin. He sees it as an expression of revolt against the mechanical quality and standardization of modern existence, a way of escaping from the pettiness of daily life. But this explanation can be applied to all forms of literature, whether popular or artistic, from the chivalric poem (does not Don Quixote also try to escape, even in a practical sense, from the pettiness and standardization of daily life in a Spanish village?) to the various kinds of serial novels. Is all poetry and literature therefore a narcotic against the banality of everyday life? At any rate, Sorani's article is indispensable for a more organic subsequent investigation of this kind of popular literature.

---

[44] Gabriel Gale is the protagonist of Chesterton's novel *The Poet and the Lunatics* (1929).

The question 'Why is detective literature widely read?' is only one aspect of a more general problem: why is non-artistic literature widely read? Undoubtedly, for practical and cultural (political and moral) reasons. This generic answer is, with its limits of approximation, the most precise. But does not artistic literature also circulate for moral and practical or political reasons and only indirectly for reasons of artistic taste – to seek and enjoy beauty? In reality one reads a book because of practical impulses (and one should find out why certain impulses are more general than others) and one re-reads for artistic reasons. The aesthetic emotion hardly ever comes on the first reading.[45] This is even truer of the theatre, where the aesthetic emotion is a minimal 'percentage' of the spectator's interest. On the stage other elements are at work, many of which are not even of an intellectual order, but merely of a physiological one, such as 'sex appeal', etc. In other cases the aesthetic emotion in the theatre does not derive from the literary work, but from the interpretation of the actors and the director.[46] In these cases, though, the text of the play which provides the pretext for the interpretation must not be 'difficult' or psychologically over-refined, but 'elementary and popular', in the sense that the passions represented must be the most deeply 'human' and derive from immediate experience (revenge, honour, maternal love, etc). Therefore, even in these cases the analysis becomes complicated.

The great traditional actors were more acclaimed in *Morte civile*, *Les Deux Orphelines* and *Les Crochets du père Martin* than in complicated psychological intrigues. In the former case, the applause was unbounded; in the latter, it was colder and aimed at separating the actor whom the public loved from the work performed.[47]

There is an article by Filippo Burzio on Alexandre Dumas' *The Three Musketeers* (published in *La Stampa* of 22 October 1930 and reprinted in *L'Italia Letteraria* of 9 November) which gives a similar explanation to Sorani's of the success of popular novels. Like *Don Quixote* and *Orlando Furioso*, Burzio considers *The Three*

---

[45] On rereading, compare II 16 and IX 19.

[46] Compare II 16, III 2 and IV 1.

[47] On *La morte civile* and *Les Deux Orphelines* see respectively footnotes 32 and 35 above. *Les Crochets du père Martin* (1858) is by Eugène Cormon and Eugène Grandé (1810–87). Cf. Gramsci's article on the actor Ermete Novelli in LVN, p. 233.

Musketeers a very successful personification of the myth of adventure, 'in other words of something essential to human nature, which seems to be progressively and seriously drifting away from modern life. The more rational existence becomes' – or rather rationalized by coercion, which though it may be rational for the dominant classes is not so for the dominated and which is connected to economic-practical activity so that the coercion is exercised, albeit indirectly, even on the 'intellectual' strata? – 'and the more organized it becomes, the more severe becomes social discipline and the more precise and predictable' – but not predictable for the ruling class as is shown by crises and historical catastrophes – 'becomes the task assigned to the individual, so the margin of adventure is correspondingly reduced, like the common woodland encroached on by the suffocating garden walls of private property. . . Taylorism is a fine thing and man is an adaptable animal, but perhaps there are limits to his mechanization. If they were to ask me for the deep reasons of the anxiety in the West, I would answer without hesitation: the decline of faith (!) and the deadening of adventure. Which will win, Taylorism or the Musketeers? This is another matter and the answer, which seemed certain thirty years ago, is best held in suspense. If the present civilization does not collapse, perhaps we will witness interesting mixtures of the two.' The question is this: Burzio does not take into account the fact that the activity of a large part of humanity has always been Taylorized and rigidly disciplined and that these people have always sought to escape through fantasy and dreams from the narrow limits of the organization that was crushing them. Is not religion, the greatest collective adventure and the greatest 'utopia' collectively created by humanity, a way of escaping from the 'terrestrial world'? Is not this what Balzac means when he talks about the lottery as the opium of poverty, a phrase subsequently taken up by others?[48] What is most significant is that alongside Don Quixote there is Sancho Panza, who does not want 'adventures' but security in

[48] See Q 16 § 1, where Gramsci quotes a passage from Balzac's story *La Rabouilleuse* (1841) referring to lotteries: 'Cette passion, si universellement condamnée, n'a jamais été étudiée. Personne n'y a vu l'opium de la misère.' He comments: 'The passage in Balzac may also be linked to the expression "opium of the people" used in the *Critique of Hegel's Philosophy of Right* published in 1844 (check the date) [in fact 1843] whose author [Marx] was a great admirer of Balzac . . . It is probable that the passage from the expression "opium of poverty" used by Balzac for the lottery to the expression "opium of the people" for religion was aided by reflection on Pascal's wager, which makes religion like a game of chance, like betting.'

life, and that a large number of men are obsessed precisely by the 'unpredictability of tomorrow' and by the precariousness of their daily lives, in other words by an excess of probable 'adventures'.

In the modern world the question takes on a different hue than in the past. The coercive rationalization of existence is increasingly striking the middle and intellectual classes to an unprecedented degree. Yet even for them it is not a matter of a decline of adventure but of a daily life that is too adventurous, too precarious, along with the conviction that there is no single way to contain such precariousness. Thus people aspire to the adventure which is 'beautiful' and interesting because it is the result of their own free initiative, in the face of the adventure which is 'ugly' and revolting, because due to conditions imposed by others and not proposed.

The explanation of Sorani and Burzio can also be used to explain the sports fan; in other words it explains too much and therefore nothing. The phenomenon is at least as old as religion and is polyhedric not unilateral. It also has a positive aspect, the desire to 'educate oneself' through contact with a way of life considered superior to one's own, the desire to elevate one's personality by proposing ideal models (compare the remarks on the popular origin of the superman [IX 9]), the desire to know more about the world and about people than is possible under certain conditions of life, snobbery, etc. (The point about popular literature as an opium of the people is referred to in a note [IX 2] on Dumas' other novel, *The Count of Monte-Cristo*.)

Q21 § 13.

19 Cultural Derivatives of the Serial Novel

See the issue of *La Cultura* in 1931 dedicated to Dostoyevsky. An article by Vladimir Pozner correctly maintains that the novels of Dostoyevsky are culturally derived from serial novels such as those of Eugène Sue.[49] It is useful to keep this derivation in mind for writing this section on popular literature, because it shows how certain cultural currents (moral interests and motives, sensibilities, ideologies, etc.) can have a double expression: the

---

[49] Vladimir Pozner, 'Dostojevskij e il romanzo d'appendice', *La Cultura* X (1931) II, 128–50. Pozner showed how Dostoyevsky transformed elements of both the gothic novel (Radcliffe, Lewis) and the historical novel (Scott), into social and contemporary narrative.

merely mechanical one of a sensational intrigue (Sue and others) and a 'lyrical' one (Balzac, Dostoyevsky, and in part Victor Hugo). Contemporary readers are not always aware of how poor some of these literary expressions are. This was partly the case with Sue who was read by all social groups and who 'moved' even 'cultured' persons, but who then declined to being a 'writer read only by the people'. (The 'first reading' gives purely, or almost purely 'cultural' sensations, those of content, and the 'people' are first readers, acritical, moved by sympathy for the general ideology of which the book is often an artificial and forced expression.)

For this same subject see: 1) Mario Praz's book *La carne, la morte e il diavolo nella letteratura romantica*, La Cultura, Milan-Rome (see Luigi Foscolo Benedetto's review of it in *Leonardo* of March 1931:[50] it seems that Praz has not made a clear distinction between the various levels of culture, whence a number of objections by Benedetto, who, however, seems himself not to have grasped the historical nexus of the literary-historical question); 2) Servais Etienne's *Le Genre romanesque en France depuis l'apparition de la 'Nouvelle Héloïse' jusqu'aux approches de la Révolution*, published by Armand Colin; 3) [Alice Killen's] *Le Roman terrifiant ou 'Roman noir' de Walpole à Anne Radcliffe, et son influence sur la littérature française jusqu'en 1860*, Champion; and Reginald W. Hartland's *Walter Scott et le 'roman 'frénétique'* (same publisher). (Pozner's statement that Dostoyevsky's books are 'adventure novels' probably derives from an essay by Jacques Rivière on the 'adventure novel' perhaps published in the *NRF*), where the term is taken to mean 'a broad representation of actions which are both dramatic and psychological', as Balzac, Dostoyevsky, Dickens and George Eliot conceived it.) 4) An essay by André Moufflet on 'Le style du roman feuilleton' in the *Mercure de France* of 1 February 1931.

Q 21 § 14.

20 [André Moufflet on the Serial Novel]

According to Moufflet the serial novel was born because an infinite number of people leading drab restricted lives felt, and

---

50 See footnote 17 above.

perhaps still feel, the need for illusion, as if to break the wretched monotony to which they see themselves condemned.

A general observation: this can be done for all novels and not only serial ones: one must analyse the *particular illusion* that the serial novel provides the people with and how this illusion changes through historical-political periods. There is snobbery, but in the classic serial novel there is also an underlying stratum of democratic aspirations. The Gothic novel à la Radcliffe, the novel of intrigue, that of adventure, the detective novel, the thriller, the underworld novel, etc. The snob sees himself in the serial novel that describes the life of the nobility and the upper classes in general, but women and girls also enjoy it, especially the latter who think that they can gain entry to the upper class by way of their beauty.

For Moufflet there are 'classics' of the serial novel but this is understood in a particular way: it appears that the classic serial novel would seem to be the 'democratic' one, with various nuances that range from Victor Hugo to Sue to Dumas. Moufflet's article should be read, but it must be borne in mind that he examines the serial novel as a 'literary genre' (for its style, etc.), as the expression of a 'popular aesthetic'. This is false. The people are 'contentist', but if the popular content is expressed by great artists, these will be preferred. Remember what I have written about the people's love of Shakespeare, the Greek classics and, in modern times, the great Russian novelists (Tolstoy, Dostoyevsky). The same for Verdi in music.[51]

In the article 'Le mercantilisme littéraire' by J.H. Rosny senior, which appeared in *Les Nouvelles Littéraires* of 4 October 1930, it says that Victor Hugo wrote *Les Misérables* inspired by Eugène Sue's *The Mysteries of Paris* and by its success, a success so great that even forty years later the publisher Lacroix was still astonished by it. Rosny writes: 'In the intentions both of the editor of the newspaper and the serial writer, the serials were products inspired by public taste and not by the taste of the authors.' This definition, too, is one-sided. Indeed, Rosny only writes a series of observations on 'commercial' literature in general (thus including pornography) and on the commercial aspect of literature. It is not by chance that this 'commercial'

---

[51] The reference is to IX 23 below, 'Popular literature: Opera', where, however, no mention is made of the Russian novelists.

aspect and a given public 'taste' coincide. Indeed the serials written around 1848 had a specific socio-political line which still makes them sought after and read today by a public with the same feelings as in 1848.

Q 17 § 29.

21 [Novelized Biographies]

If it is true that novelized biographies continue, in a certain sense, the type of popular historical novels of Dumas *père*, it can be said that from this point of view and in this particular sector, in Italy 'a gap is now being filled'. See what is being published by Corbaccio and a few other publishers, especially the works of Mazzucchelli.[52] It should be noted, however, that the novelized biography, although it has a popular public, is not fully popular in the way the serial novel is. It is addressed to a public that has or believes it has pretensions to a higher culture, to the rural and urban petty bourgeoisie that thinks it has become the 'ruling class' and the arbiter of the state. The modern type of popular novel is the detective story, the 'thriller', and in this sector there is nothing. Likewise, there are no adventure novels in the broad sense, either like those of Stevenson, Conrad and London or like the contemporary French type (Mac-Orlan, Malraux, etc.).

Q 14 § 17.

22 The Operatic Conception of Life[53]

It is not true that a bookish and non-innate sense of life is only to be found in certain inferior strata of the intelligentsia. Among the popular classes, too, there is a 'bookish' degeneration of life which comes not only from books but also from other instruments of diffusion of culture and ideas. Verdi's music, or rather the libretti and plots of the plays set to music by Verdi, are responsible for a whole range of 'artificial' poses in the life of people, for ways of thinking, for a 'style'. 'Artificial' is perhaps not

---

[52] See footnote 27 above.

[53] 'Melodrammatica' in the original: 'melodramma' is a normal Italian word for grand opera, which Gramsci is referring to in this and the following two notes.

the right word because among the popular classes this artificiality assumes naïve and moving forms. To many common people the baroque and the operatic appear as an extraordinarily fascinating way of feeling and acting, a means of escaping what they consider low, mean and contemptible in their lives and education in order to enter a more select sphere of great feelings and noble passions. Serial novels and below-stairs reading (all that literature which is mawkish, mellifluous and whimpery) provide the heroes and heroines. But opera is the most pestiferous because words set to music are more easily recalled, and they become matrices in which thought takes shape out of flux. Look at the writing-style of many common people: it is modelled on a repertory of clichés.

However, sarcasm is too corrosive. Remember that we are not dealing with superficial snobs, but with something deeply felt and experienced.

Q8 § 46.

23 Popular Literature: [Opera]

In another note I have mentioned the fact that in Italian popular culture music has to some extent substituted that artistic expression which in other countries is provided by the popular novel and that musical geniuses have had the kind of popularity which writers have lacked.

It should be seen: 1) Whether the rise of opera coincides in all its phases (i.e. not as an individual expression of single great artists, but as a historico-cultural fact) with the rise of the popular epic represented by the novel. I think it does. The novel and the opera originate in the eighteenth century and blossom in the first half of the nineteenth. In other words, they coincide with the appearance and expansion of national-popular democratic forces throughout Europe. 2) Whether the expansion of the Anglo-French popular novel in Europe coincides with that of Italian opera.

Why did Italian artistic 'democracy' have a musical and not a 'literary' expression? Can the fact that its language was not national but cosmopolitan, as music is, be connected to the lack of a national-popular character in the Italian intellectuals? At the same moment that a strict nationalization of indigenous intellectuals occurred in every country, and this phenomenon also took place, although to a lesser extent, in Italy (even the eighteenth century in Italy, especially the second half, is more 'national', than cosmopolitan), the Italian intellectuals continued their European function through music. It might be observed that the plot of the libretti is never 'national', but European, in two senses. Either because the 'intrigue' of the drama takes place in all the countries of Europe, and more rarely in Italy, using popular legends or popular novels. Or because the feelings and passions of the drama reflect the particular sensibility of eighteenth-century and Romantic Europe. This European sensibility nevertheless coincides with prominent elements of the popular sensibility of all countries, from which it had in any case drawn its Romantic current. (This fact should be connected to the popularity of Shakespeare and the Greek tragic dramatists, whose characters, overcome by elementary passions, jealousy, paternal love and revenge, are essentially popular in every country.) It can thus be said that the relationship between the Italian opera and Anglo-French popular literature is not critically unfavourable to the former, since the relationship is popular-historical, not artistic-critical. As an artist, Verdi cannot be 'compared' to Eugène Sue, even though Verdi's popular fortunes can be compared only to Sue's (although for the aristocratic – Wagnerian – aesthetes of music, Verdi occupies the same place in the history of music as Sue in the history of literature). Second-rate popular literature (Sue and followers) is a politico-commercial degeneration of national-popular literature, whose models are precisely the Greek tragedians and Shakespeare.

This view of opera can also be used as a criterion for understanding why Metastasio was popular, especially as a librettist.[54]

Q9 § 66.

24 Popular Literature: Operatic Taste

How can one combat in Italy the operatic taste of the man of the people when he comes into contact with literature, especially poetry? He thinks that poetry is characterized by certain external

[54] Pietro Metastasio (1698–1782), dramatic poet and librettist for Gluck and others.

traits, largely rhyme and the hammering of metrical accents, but above all bombastic solemnity, oratory and operatic sentimentalism, a theatrical rendering coupled with a baroque vocabulary. One of the causes of this taste is to be sought in the fact that it has been formed not through private and individual meditations on poetry and art but through the collective expressions of oratory and theatre. 'Oratory' does not just refer to the notorious popular assemblies of the past but to a whole series of urban and rural instances. In the country, for example, funeral oratory and that of the local magistrate's court and law-courts is closely followed. All of these manifestations have a popular audience of 'fans' and, for the law-courts, an audience made up those waiting their turn, witnesses, etc. In certain district magistrate's courts, the hall is always full of these people who memorize the turns of phrase and the solemn words, feed on them and remember them. It is the same for the funerals of important people which always draw large crowds, often just to hear the speeches. Lectures in the cities have the same function and likewise the law-courts. Popular theatres, with what are called arena performances (and today perhaps sound films, but also the subtitles of old silent films, all done in an operatic style) are of the utmost importance for the creation of this taste and its corresponding language.

This taste can be combated in two principal ways: by ruthlessly criticizing it, and by circulating books of poetry written or translated in non-'elevated' language, where the feelings expressed are not rhetorical or operatic.

See the anthology compiled by Schiavi; Gori's poems.[55] Perhaps translations of Marcel Martinet and other writers who are more numerous now than before: sober translations, like Togliatti's versions of Whitman and Martinet.[56]

Q 14 § 19.

25 Oratory, Conversation, Culture

In his essay 'On the Athenian orators' (check the source), Macaulay attributes the facility with which even the most

---

[55] Alessandro Schiavi (ed.) *Labor. Fiorita di canti sociali*, Milan 1924. Pietro Gori was an anarchist.

[56] Togliatti's translations appeared in *L'Ordine Nuovo* from 1919–20. See also I 6.

educated Greeks let themselves be dazzled by almost puerile sophisms to the predominance of live and spoken discourse in Greek life and education.[57] The habit of conversation and oratory generates a certain ability to find very quickly arguments that are apparently brilliant and that momentarily silence one's adversary and leave the listener dazed. This observation can also be applied to certain phenomena of modern life and to the ephemeral cultural preparation of some social groups like the urban workers. This partly explains why the peasants are distrustful of intellectuals speaking at political meetings. The peasants spend a long time chewing over the statements they have heard and whose sparkle has temporarily struck them. But, after the emotion stirred up by the words has cooled and their good sense has regained the upper hand, they see the deficiencies and the superficiality and become distrustful as a matter of course.

There is another important observation by Macaulay that is worth recalling. He reports a remark by Eugene of Savoy, who said that those who ended up being the greatest generals were those who were suddenly put in charge of the army and thus had to concern themselves with large-scale operations and manoeuvres.[58] In other words, he who by profession has become a slave of trivial details is the victim of bureaucracy. He sees the tree, but loses sight of the wood; he sees the regulation and not the strategic plan. Yet the great captains could take care of both: the soldiers' rations as well as large-scale manoeuvres, etc.

One might add that the newspaper comes very close to oratory and conversation. Newspaper articles are usually written in a hurry, improvised, and are almost always like speeches made at public meetings because of the rapidity with which they are conceived and constructed. Few newspapers have specialist editors; when they do, their work is largely improvised. Specialization helps one to improvise better and more rapidly. Especially in the Italian newspapers there are no pondered and detailed periodical reviews for such sectors as the theatre and the economy. The contributors only partially make up for this and, lacking a unified approach, do not leave much of a mark. The solidity of a culture can thus be measured in three principal

[57] Thomas Babington Macaulay, 'On the Athenian orators' [1824] in *Miscellaneous Writings*, London 1870, pp. 56–63.

[58] Ibid. p. 58.

degrees: a) the culture of those who only read the newspapers, b) of those who also read magazines (not the variety ones), c) of those who read books – not to mention all those people (the majority) who do not even read the newspapers and who form their handful of opinions by attending occasional public meetings, such as those held in election periods, where they hear speakers of widely differing levels. Observation made in prison in Milan, where *Il Sole* was available: most of the prisoners, including politicals, read *La Gazzetta dello Sport*. Among about 2,500 prisoners, eighty copies at the most of *Il Sole* were sold. After the *Gazzetta dello Sport* the most read publications were the *Domenica del Corriere* and *Il Corriere dei Piccoli*.[59]

It is evident that for a very long time the process of intellectual civilizing has especially taken an oratorical and rhetorical form, in other words one with no or too few written aids. The recollection of notions expounded by word of mouth was the basis of any education (and still is in some countries, for example Abyssinia). A new tradition began in the Humanist period when the 'written exercise' was introduced into schools and teaching. But already in the Middle Ages, with scholasticism, there was an implicit criticism of the tradition of teaching based on oratory and an effort to supply the memory with a firmer and more permanent skeleton. It can be seen, on reflection, that the importance given by the schools to the study of formal logic is in fact a reaction against the old loose style of exposition in teaching. Errors of formal logic are especially common in spoken arguments.

The art of printing then revolutionized the entire cultural world, giving to memory an aid of inestimable value and allowing an unprecedented extension of educational activity. Another kind of extension is thus implicit in this research, that of the qualitative as well as quantitative modifications (mass extension) brought about in ways of thinking by the technical and mechanical development of cultural organization.

Even today, spoken communication is a means of ideological diffusion which has a rapidity, a field of action, and an emotional simultaneity far greater than written communication (theatre, cinema and radio, with its loudspeakers in public squares, beat all forms of written communication, including books, magazines,

---

[59] The *Gazzetta dello Sport* (daily), the *Domenica del Corriere* (a Sunday magazine) and the *Corriere dei Piccoli* (a children's magazine) all still exist.

newspapers and newspapers posted on walls) – but superficially, not in depth.

The academies and universities as organizations of culture and means for its diffusion. In the universities: oral lectures, seminars and workshops, the role of the great professor and the assistant. The role of the professional assistant and that of the 'old men of Santa Zita' in the school of Basilio Puoti, mentioned by De Sanctis,[60] namely the formation in the class itself of 'voluntary' assistants, spontaneously selected from among the students themselves, who help the teacher and give follow-up lectures, teaching others by practical example how to study.

Some of the preceding observations have been suggested by reading the *Popular Manual of Sociology*,[61] which is imbued with all the deficiencies of conversation, the superficial argumentation of oratory, and the weak structure of formal logic. It would be interesting to use this book as an example of all the logical errors indicated by the schoolmen, recalling the very true observation that even ways of thinking are acquired and not innate and that, once acquired, their correct use corresponds to a professional qualification.[62] Not to possess them, not to be aware of not possessing them, not to raise the problem of acquiring them through 'apprenticeship' is like claiming to be able to build an automobile while knowing that one must rely on the workshop and the tools of a village blacksmith. The study of the 'old formal logic' has now fallen into disrepute, and to an extent with good reason. But the problem of putting people through an apprenticeship in formal logic to act as a check upon the loose expository manner of oratory reappears as soon as one raises the fundamental problem of creating a new culture on a new social base, which does not have traditions in the way the old class of intellectuals does. A 'traditional intellectual bloc', with its

[60] In his essay 'L'ultimo dei puristi' (1868) De Sanctis recounted how his former teacher Basilio Puoti used to be surrounded by a group of veteran pupils who had been with him for five or six years and to whom he jokingly referred as 'gli anziani di Santa Zita' (the phrase is from Dante, *Inferno* XXI, 38). See also SPN, p. 29.

[61] For Gramsci's analysis of Bukharin's *Popular Manual of Marxist Sociology* see SPN, pp. 419–72.

[62] Gramsci is alluding to a passage in the preface to the second edition (1885) of Engels' *Anti-Dühring*: 'the art of working with concepts is not inborn and also is not given with ordinary everyday consciousness but requires real thought, and . . . this thought similarly has a long empirical history, not more and not less than empirical natural science'. In Q 11 § 44, Gramsci discusses the importance of this concept for the philosophy of praxis.

complex and capillary articulations, is able to assimilate the 'apprenticeship in logic' element into the organic development of each of its individual components without even needing a distinct and specialized apprenticeship (just as the children of educated parents learn to speak 'grammatically', in other words they learn the language of educated people, without even having to go through specific and tiring grammatical exercises, unlike the children of parents who speak a dialect or Italian mixed with a dialect). But not even this occurs without difficulty, friction and loss of energy.

The development of the technical-professional schools in all the post-elementary grades has posed this problem anew in other forms. According to Professor G. Peano, even in the Polytechnic and the higher institutes of mathematics the students from grammar schools are better trained than those from the technical institutes.[63] This better training is due to the overall 'humanist' instruction (history, literature, philosophy) as is more amply demonstrated in other notes (those dealing with the 'intellectuals' and the problem of education).[64] Why cannot mathematics (the study of mathematics) give the same results, if it is so close to formal logic that it can be confused with it? As occurs in matters of teaching, if there is a similarity there is also an enormous difference. Mathematics is essentially based on the numerical series, on an infinite series of equivalences ($1 = 1$) that can be combined in infinite ways. Formal logic tends to do the same, but only up to a point: its abstractness is maintained only at the beginning of the learning process, in the immediate and basic formulation of its principles, but it becomes concretely operative in the very discourse in which the abstract formulation is made. The language exercises that one does in the grammar school make it apparent after a time that in Latin-Italian and Greek-Italian translations there is never identity between the terms of the languages placed side by side, or at least that what identity there seemed to be at the beginning of the exercise (Italian 'rosa' = Latin 'rosa') becomes increasingly cómplicated as the 'apprenticeship' progresses, moves increasingly away from the mathematical scheme and arrives at a historical judgement or a

---

[63] Giuseppe Peano (1858–1932) mathematician, a founder of symbolic logic, was a professor at Turin University when Gramsci was a student there.

[64] See the two sections 'The Intellectuals' and 'On Education' in SPN pp. 5–43.

judgement of taste, in which nuances, 'unique and individualized' expressiveness, prevail. And this occurs not only when one compares two languages, but also when one studies the history of a single 'language', where it emerges how a single sound/word varies semantically through time and how its function in a clause (morphological, syntactic and semantic as well as phonetic changes) varies too.

Note. An experiment made to demonstrate the evanescent impact of the 'oratorical' method of instruction: twelve well-educated persons repeat one to another a complex fact and then each person writes down what he has heard. Often, the twelve versions are amazingly different from the original account (which is written down as a control). Repeated, this experiment can be used to show that the memory which is not trained with appropriate methods should not be trusted.

Q 16 § 21.

X
JOURNALISM

Introduction

Gramsci's purpose in the notes on journalism is twofold: to understand how the bourgeois press is organized and to plan the organization of a Communist press. The opening note in this section announces the double project. On the one hand Gramsci wants to see 'how the ideological structure of a dominant class is actually organized' and he concentrates on the press as its 'most prominent and dynamic part'. On the other he asks what resources an 'innovative class' – in other words the proletariat – can oppose to this 'formidable complex of trenches and fortifications of the dominant class' and how it can spread these resources to 'the classes that are its potential allies' (X 1).

The notes on the bourgeois press are based mainly on Gramsci's own recollections of the pre-fascist period when he himself was a journalist in Turin. Despite the fact that the Italian press was regionally-based rather than truly national – each major city had one or two main newspapers – and despite circulation figures that were low in world terms (the *Corriere della Sera*'s circulation in 1913 was 300,000), the newspapers were a powerful ideological and political force. The pre-1919 state had a very narrow social base: essentially it was constituted out of powerful minoritarian groups – ministerial coalitions, big industrial and agrarian interests, the big banks. The major newspapers intersected with these groups and voiced their interests. This convergence between the press, finance capital and the political class had mainly occurred in the period after 1900 when the costs of new technologies such as telephone and wire services forced newspaper owners to seek increased financial backing from local business interests. These institutional shareholders then exerted pressure on the editors to follow a specific line. Through these same economic interests, the newspapers became tied to the political clienteles and ministerial factions which served as their mouthpieces in parliament. *La Stampa* was linked to Giolitti, the *Giornale d'Italia* to his opponent Sonnino, and so on. Newspapers thus had a crucial function of articulating policy and organizing consent around particular issues: as in the First World War, when almost the entire Italian press, with the exception of *La Stampa* and the Socialist *Avanti!*, functioned as a pro-war lobby. It is in this sense that Gramsci calls the newspapers the 'real parties' in the late liberal era. Between 1919 and 1922 a large part of the Italian press passed into the hands of trusts and banks which were favourable to fascism. Although it was not till 1926 that the press was fully 'fascistized' (i.e. subjected to Press Office censorship and staffed by loyal personnel) the support of its major shareholders for fascism had already led to conflicts with editors who had adopted an anti-fascist line. Thus, in the crisis of 1924 following the murder of the Socialist deputy Matteotti by fascists, the editors of the *Corriere della Sera* (Albertini) and *La Stampa* (Frassati and Salvatorelli) denounced the murder and defended press freedoms. Their respective financial backers, the Crespi and Agnelli families, declared their no-confidence in the editors and permitted fascistization to take place. By the time Gramsci wrote these notes the entire Italian press was controlled in tandem by the fascist state and the big economic interests that supported it, and since 1927 all journalists had been required to be members of a fascist journalists' union.

In the notes dealing with the Communist press, Gramsci tries to think out a situation which is nearly antithetical to this one. Rather than newspapers functioning as organs of capitalist interests – whether as political parties unto themselves or coercively overseen by an authoritarian state – they must function as the articulations of the interests of a mass democratic movement and serve to reach the widest possible readership. His planning is meticulous. In effect he constructs a scale model of a party press, divided into newspapers, magazines and almanacs according to different functions and different readerships, a model that is accurate down to such details as visual layout, the subdivision of a publication into sections, the training of journalists. Again, his experiences as a journalist lie behind these notes. The practice he mentions of culling and commenting on articles from other publications was one he had adopted as editor of *Il Grido del Popolo* in 1917. His concern with the precise format, linguistic 'level', range and circulation of Communist Party publications was already in evidence in a number of his letters dating from 1923–26 dealing with a new series of *L'Ordine Nuovo*,

and with the party daily *L'Unità*. And his emphasis on discipline
in X 3 probably harks back to an acrimonious exchange of
September 1926, just prior to his arrest, with Alfonso Leonetti
and the other editors of *L'Unità*, whom he accused of
undisciplined management in allowing a telephoned article of his
to be printed in a mangled form which altered the meaning of
whole passages.

Many of these notes actually look rather unpolitical and
unspecific because their language is more than usually Aesopic.
Gramsci was evidently anxious that they bypass the prison
censor's scrutiny, and he tends to use innocuous-looking phrases
when writing such politically sensitive material. Thus the
Communist Party and the party press are referred to here as 'a
group which wants to spread an integral conception of the world'
(X 6), a 'unitary cultural organism' and a 'homogeneous cultural
centre' (X 13). The 'élite' in X 12 which has 'distinguished and
detached itself' likewise refers to the Communist Party which,
after the split with the Socialists, must now 'recreate the unity'
of the working-class movement under Communist leadership.
These phrases should nevertheless not be treated as mere
circumlocutions. Like other Gramscian formulas – for instance
'philosophy of praxis' – they also indicate specific features of his
idea of Marxism. Thus when he writes of a 'group that aims to
spread an integral conception of the world' he is not merely
talking about the party and Marxism but about a *specific notion* of
the party and Marxism: an integral 'conception of the 'world' and
a 'norm of conduct' are recurrent shorthand in the notebooks for
the twin aspects of the 'intellectual and moral reformation' which
he sees historical materialism as stimulating on a mass scale.

More specifically, these notes on the Communist press provide
important indications of Gramsci's conceptions of the relations
between party, class and class allies during his imprisonment.
This is because the relations between a party press and its readers
are also the relations between the party centre and its rank and
file and allied groups: the press is a crucial means by which
information is relayed to supporters and new members are won
over. It is clear from these notes that Gramsci conceives of these
relations in a dynamic, expansive way. He defines what he calls
'integral journalism' (the subject of special Notebook 24,
reproduced here as X 11 – X 19) as one which is able to 'create
and develop' its readers' needs and 'progressively enlarge' its

readership (X 11). This expansive process will be paralysed if the organization of the press becomes bureaucratized. It is essential, rather, that the press should stimulate the needs of its readers and develop their potential. In this way, 'the association [the party] does not set itself up as something fixed and definitive, but as tending to widen itself out towards a whole social grouping, which in turn is conceived as tending to unify the whole of humanity.' (X 3).

1 Cultural Themes: Ideological Material

A study of how the ideological structure of a dominant class is actually organized: namely the material organization aimed at maintaining, defending and developing the theoretical or ideological 'front'. Its most prominent and dynamic part is the press in general: publishing houses (which have an implicit and explicit programme and are attached to a particular tendency), political newspapers, periodicals of every kind, scientific, literary, philological, popular, etc., various periodicals down to parish bulletins. If this kind of study were conducted on a national scale it would be gigantic: one could therefore do a series of studies for one city or for a number of cities. A news editor of a daily newspaper should have this study as a general outline for his work: indeed, he should make his own version of it. Think of all the wonderful leading articles one could write on the subject!

The press is the most dynamic part of this ideological structure, but not the only one. Everything which influences or is able to influence public opinion, directly or indirectly, belongs to it: libraries, schools, associations and clubs of various kinds, even architecture and the layout and names of streets. It would be impossible to explain the position retained by the Church in modern society if one were unaware of the constant and patient efforts it makes to develop continuously its particular section of this material structure of ideology.[1] Such a study, done seriously, would be very important. Besides providing a living historical

[1] In 1916 Gramsci had written of the array of titles in a Catholic bookshop window in Turin: 'I admire and envy the priests who succeed in obtaining such visible results with their cultural propaganda. In reality, we do not pay much attention to this slow process of intellectual stagnation by the clergy. It is something impalpable, which slides along like an eel, limp, which does not seem solid, and yet it is like the mattress that resists cannonades better than the walls of Liège' (CT, p. 132; SM, pp. 39–40).

model of such a structure, it would accustom one to a more cautious and exact estimate of the forces acting in society. What resources can an innovative class set against this formidable complex of trenches and fortification of the dominant class? The spirit of scission,[2] in other words the progressive acquisition of the consciousness of its own historical personality, a spirit of scission that must aim to spread itself from the protagonist class to the classes that are its potential allies – all this requires a complex ideological labour, the first condition of which is an exact knowledge of the field that must be cleared of its element of human 'mass'.

Q3 § 49.

2 Italian Intellectuals

Comparison between French cultural concentration, which is summed up in the 'Institut de France', and the lack of co-ordination in Italy. Italian and French cultural reviews (such as *Nuova Antologia* and *Revue des deux mondes*). Italian daily newspapers are much better done than the French. They fulfil two functions: they give information and general political direction and they express a political, literary, artistic, and scientific culture that has no widespread organ of its own (the little review for average culture). In France on the other hand even the first function has been divided among two series of dailies: the newspaper of information and the newspaper of opinion which, in turn, may be directly dependent on a party or may have an appearance of impartiality (*Action Française, Temps, Débats*). In Italy, due to the absence of organized and centralized parties, one cannot overlook the newspapers: it is the newspapers,

---

[2] The term 'scission' (sometimes translated as 'cleavage') is drawn from Sorel, who wrote in the *Reflexions on Violence* (Chapter 6 § 1) of 'the scission between classes, the basis of all socialism'. It derives from his analogy between socialism and primitive Christianity. For Sorel, Christianity made a distinct 'scission' or 'rupture' from Judaism while at the same time inheriting its compatible elements. In the same way socialism, in its scission from capitalism, would keep the heritage both of capitalist science and technology and of the 'morality of the producers' (i.e. the proletariat), formed through trade union solidarity and struggles (see *Le Système historique de Renan*, Paris 1905, p. 71). Compare Gramsci's statement of 1920: 'Every revolution which, like the Christian and the Communist revolutions, comes about and can only come about through a stirring within the deepest and broadest popular masses, cannot help but smash and destroy the existing system of social organization' (SPW I, p. 331).

grouped in series, that constitute the real parties.[3] For example, after the war Giolitti had a series of newspapers that represented the various currents or fractions of the democratic liberal party: *La Stampa* in Turin which sought to influence the workers and had at intervals marked reformist tendencies (the lines taken by *La Stampa* were always fluctuating, intermittent, depending on whether Giolitti was in or out of power);[4] *La Tribuna* in Rome, which was tied to the bureaucracy and to protectionist industry (while *La Stampa* was more for free trade – more markedly so when Giolitti was not in power);[5] *Il Mattino* in Naples, which was linked to the Giolittian clique in the South, along with other minor organs.[6] (For some of its articles and some information services, *La Stampa* was at the head of a journalistic cartel which included in particular *Il Mattino*, *La Nazione* and also *Il Resto del Carlino*.)[7]

[3] Compare the *Ordine Nuovo* article of September 1920 in which Gramsci deals with the break-up of the old Italian party system after the 1919 elections: 'As a political force, capitalism has been reduced to a corporate association of factory owners. It no longer possesses a political party whose ideology also embraces the petty-bourgeois strata in the cities and the countryside, and so ensures the survival of a broadly-based legal state. In fact, capitalism can find political representation today only in the great newspapers (a print-run of 400,000; a thousand voters) and in the Senate . . .' (SPW I, p. 336). See also the remarks on newspapers and political parties in SPN, pp. 148–49.

[4] From 1900 to 1920 *La Stampa* (founded Turin 1867) was edited by Giolitti's associate Alfredo Frassati. It backed Giolitti's 'leftist' policies of wartime neutrality and gradual absorption of the working-class movement into the liberal state, using (from 1919) an ex-*Avanti!* writer like Francesco Ciccotti to advocate collaboration with bourgeois democracy. Gramsci had remarked in 1919 that '*La Stampa's* "socialism" will probably yield no results, because *La Stampa* does not believe in socialism' (ON, p. 299). He defined the paper's politics as 'freedom through order, balance between the internal needs of the country and those of international politics, a just proportioning of energies and aims to the means available, maximum audacity in reforms, solidarity between all social classes, etc., etc.' (ON, p. 289). From 1920–25, under Luigi Salvatorelli, *La Stampa* sought a broad-based liberal-democratic opposition to fascism. In 1926 it was fascistized under the editorship of Andrea Torre and passed into the financial hands of Fiat.

[5] *La Tribuna* (founded Rome 1883) was edited from 1910–23 by Olindo Malagodi and funded by the Banca Commerciale and a group of Giolittian financiers. Malagodi was a mouthpiece of the rightest elements in Giolittism (strong hierarchical state, opposition to PSI maximalists) and the nationalist-imperialist line on the paper was represented by the staff writer Vincenzo Morello ('Rastignac': see IV 9) and the contributions of D'Annunzio. After 1923 the paper came out in favour of fascist 'normalization' and merged in 1925 with Roberto Forges Davanzati's organ *L'Idea Nazionale* (see footnote 22 on p. 103).

[6] *Il Mattino* (founded Naples 1892), vehicle of aggressive colonialism, represented by nationalist 'aesthetes' like D'Annunzio and Borgese. Its editor Edoardo Scarfoglio took a typically southern Italian view of expansionist foreign policy as the basis for creating a 'bloc of consciousness and will' against Lombard materialism.

[7] *La Nazione* (founded 1859), Florence-based paper backed by the steel industry. *Il Resto*

The *Corriere della Sera* formed a current by itself which tried to be in Italy what *The Times* is in England, custodian of the nation's values above and beyond individual currents.[8] In reality it was linked to the Lombard textile (and rubber) export industry and was therefore more consistently in favour of free trade. After the war the *Corriere* was to the right of Nittism (after having backed Salandra).[9] Nittism, too, had its chain of newspapers: the *Corriere* on the right, the *Carlino* on the centre right, (*Il Mondo* to the centre left), *Il Paese* to the left. Nittism had two aspects: plutocratic, linked to protected industry; and leftist. The *Giornale d'Italia* occupied a separate position, connected as it was to protected industry and to the big landowners of Emilia, the Centre and the South.[10] It is interesting to note that the large newspapers that represented the tradition of the Action Party – *Il Secolo* in Milan, the *Gazzetta del Popolo* in Turin, *Il Messaggero* in Rome, *Roma* in Naples – had from 1921 to 1925 a different attitude from that of *La Stampa*, the *Corriere*, the *Giornale d'Italia*, *La Tribuna*, *Il Mattino* and also *Il Resto del Carlino*.

The *Corriere* was always against Giolitti, as I have explained in an earlier note.[11] At the time of the Libyan war, too, the *Corriere* remained neutral until a few days before war was declared, when

---

del Carlino (founded 1885), Bologna-based paper backed by the sugar industry and local agrarians.

[8] The *Corriere della Sera* (founded Milan 1876) became Italy's highest circulation daily by 1900 (75,000) after getting the financial support of the Lombard cotton magnate Crespi in 1885 and the industrialists De Angeli (textiles) and Pirelli (rubber) in 1895. Luigi Albertini (1871–1941) became principal shareholder and editor in 1900 and rapidly reshaped both the paper's technical production and its political line, which emerged as a coherent opposition to Giolitti's policies (electoral management, overtures to Catholics and socialists, wartime neutrality) and a defence of the liberal-conservative tradition of the old Right. By 1920 circulation had risen to 400,000 and Albertini called for a strong government of national reconstruction. Initially favourable to fascism when he thought it could be contained by the state, from late 1924 Albertini took an openly anti-fascist line which led to his removal in 1925. The *Corriere* retained the merest veneer of its old liberalism under fascist control.

[9] Francesco Saverio Nitti (1868–1953): economist (early spokesman on the 'southern question') and premier from June 1919 to June 1920. Antonio Salandra (1853–1931): premier from March 1914 to June 1916.

[10] The *Giornale d'Italia* had been founded (Rome 1901) and part-financed by Giolitti's rightist opponent Sonnino. By 1920 it had the highest circulation in the centre-south and represented the nationalist agrarian bourgeoisie. It espoused fascism in 1921–24 and in 1926 was taken over by an editorial group which included Enrico Corradini.

[11] Q 1 § 43 (not translated). The relevant section was rewritten as Q 19 § 26 (R, pp. 95–104).

it published the strident and blundering article by Andrea Torre.[12]

Nittism was still a nascent pólitical formation then. Nitti, however, lacked some of the essential skills of the statesman; he was too timorous physically and too indecisive. He was very cunning, but this is a subaltern quality. The creation of the Royal Guard is his only important political act.[13] Nitti wanted to create a French type of parliamentarism, but there was the problem of the armed forces and a possible *coup d'état* (remember how Giolitti always sought to create extra-parliamentary crises: with this 'trick' Giolitti wanted to maintain formally intact the royal prerogative of nominating ministers outside or at least alongside parliament. In any case, he sought to prevent the government from being too linked or exclusively linked to parliament). Since the *carabinieri* depended politically and disciplinarily on the Ministry of War and thus on the general staff (even if they were financially dependent on the Ministry of the Interior), Nitti created the Royal Guard as an armed force dependent on parliament, as a counterweight against any designs for a *coup d'état*. By a strange paradox, the Royal Guard, which was a full professional army, i.e. of a reactionary type, was to have a democratic role, as the armed force of the national parliament against the possible attempts of irresponsible and reactionary forces. One should note the secret struggle in 1922 between nationalists and democrats over the *carabinieri* and the Royal Guard. The liberals, under the mask of Facta, wanted to reduce the corps of *carabinieri* or incorporate a large part of it (50 per cent) into the Royal Guard. The nationalists reacted and General Giardino spoke in the Senate against the Royal Guard and had its cavalry disbanded.[14] (Remember *Il Paese*'s comic and pitiful defence of this cavalry, the prestige of horses, etc., etc.)

Nitti's directives were very confused: in 1918, when he was minister of the Treasury, he carried out an oratorical campaign

[12] Torre's first article supporting war in Libya appeared in the *Corriere* on 10 September 1911. He wrote five more leaders on the same theme during the month. War was declared on 29 September.

[13] Nitti formed the 25,000-strong paramilitary Guardia Regia to check the internal disturbances of 1920. It was disbanded in 1923 and replaced by the fascist Milizia volontaria per la sicurezza nazionale (MVSN).

[14] See on this episode Gramsci's *Ordine Nuovo* article 'Il sasso nello stagno,' 14 March 1922 (SF, p. 470).

in support of an accelerated industrialization of Italy. He talked a lot of nonsense about the country's wealth of iron and coal deposits. (The iron was that of Cogne, the coal Tuscan lignite. Nitti went so far as to maintain that even after Italy's industry had expanded tenfold there would still be enough of these minerals for export. On this subject, see *L'Italia in rissa* by F. Ciccotti.)[15] Before the armistice he supported the 1,000 lire insurance for the combatants, thereby winning the sympathy of the peasants. Significance of the amnesty for deserters (Italians abroad would no longer have sent remittances, of which the Banca di Sconto had a near monopoly). Nitti's speech on the technical impossibility of a revolution in Italy, which had a dazzling effect on the Socialist Party (see Nitti's speech together with Serrati's open letter of November or December 1920).[16] 90 per cent of the Royal Guard was made up of southerners. Nitti's programme for the mountain basins in southern Italy which produced so much enthusiasm.

The death of General Ameglio, who committed suicide after a public altercation with General Tettoni, entrusted with an administrative inspection of the colonial rule of Cyrenaica (Ameglio was the commander in chief of the Royal Guard).[17] The tragic nature of Ameglio's death must be connected to the suicide of General Pollio in 1914. (In 1912, when the Triple Alliance was renewed, Pollio had signed the naval-military agreement with Germany which took effect on 6 August 1914. I think it was precisely on the basis of this agreement that the *Emden* and the *Göschen* were able to take refuge in the port of

[15] Nitti's 'favourite creatures are his schemes for Italian industrialization which offer him a pleasing picture of our country bristling with factory chimneys, resounding with workshops and cloudy with the smoke of steelworks': Francesco Ciccotti, *L'Italia in rissa* (1921) pp. 57–58.

[16] Nitti addressed parliament with the new government's programme on 10 July 1919: 'Revolution in those countries which produce raw materials or which are largely self-sufficient can be, and is, an evil. In countries which lack sufficient raw materials and are unable to subsist, it would be like a huge attempt at suicide'. Serrati's open letter, 'Risposta di un comunista unitario al compagno Lenin', appeared in the Piedmontese *Avanti!* on 16 December 1920. Gramsci commented in *L'Ordine Nuovo* of 19 March 1922 (SF, p. 482): 'Serrati chose to break with Lenin rather than break with Turati, because he too had been persuaded by Nitti's propaganda on the technical impossibility of a revolution in Italy'.

[17] Giovanni Ameglio (1854–1921), veteran general of the Libyan campaign and from 1913–18 governor of Cyrenaica, the Libyan province ceded with Tripolitania to Italy in 1912. Giolitti put Ameglio in command of the Royal Guard in 1920. Rumours (probably unfounded) circulated that Ameglio had taken his own life after quarrelling with Tettoni.

Messina: on this subject see the articles by 'Rerum Scriptor' in the *Rivista delle Nazioni Latine* and *L'Unità* of 1917 and 1918, which I summarized in the *Grido del Popolo*.)[18] In his memoirs Salandra mentions the 'unexpected' death of Pollio (he does not say it was suicide): the famous 'Memorandum' of Cadorna, which Salandra claims to have had no knowledge of, must reflect the views of the general staff under Pollio's command and dependent on the Agreement of 1912.[19] Salandra's declaration that he did not know about it is extremely important and says much about Italian politics and the real situation of the parliamentary element in the government.

In a study of newspapers functioning as a political party, one should take single individuals and their activity into account. Mario Missiroli is one of these.[20] But the two most interesting types are Pippo Naldi and Francesco Ciccotti. Naldi began as a young Borellian liberal[21] – contributing to little liberal reviews – and became editor of *Il Resto del Carlino* and *Il Tempo*. He was a very important agent of Giolitti and Nitti and was connected with the Perrone brothers and certainly with other big businessmen.[22] His activity during the war is shrouded in mystery. Ciccotti's activity is highly complex and difficult, although his personal value is mediocre. During the war he

[18] 'Giolitti, la guerra e la pace' in *Il Grido del Popolo* 14 August 1918 (SG, pp. 293–97). Rerum Scriptor was the pen name of Gaetano Salvemini. Gerratana's critical edition notes that Gramsci makes factual errors here in recalling the date of the naval pact (in fact June 1913) and the names of the two German navy units.

[19] Alberto Pollio was army chief of staff until his death in July 1914; he was succeeded by Luigi Cadorna. Rumours of his suicide were not officially confirmed.

[20] Mario Missiroli (1886–1974) journalist, at first a liberal influenced by Sorelian syndicalism, moved from the anti-fascist to the fascist camp after 1922. He was editor of *Il Resto del Carlino* in 1918–21.

[21] Giovanni Borelli (1867–1932) was editor of *L'Idea Liberale* and founder in 1901 of the conservative-monarchist Young Liberals' party (PLGI). The party controlled local newspapers in several northern Italian cities but gained no seats in parliament and began to break up after 1910. From 1922 Borelli advocated collaboration between liberals and fascists.

[22] Filippo Naldi, ex-editor of a nationalist periodical, took over *Il Resto del Carlino* in 1913 with the financial backing of a group of sugar manufacturers. Naldi in turn secured funds from pro-war and anti-socialist industrialists to enable Mussolini to launch *Il Popolo d'Italia* in 1914. Naldi edited the Rome paper *Il Tempo* in 1921–22. The brothers Pio and Mario Perrone, owners of the industrial giant Ansaldo and principal shareholders in the Banca di Sconto, had close links with Nitti. Francesco Ciccotti (1880–1937), socialist who had shifted from a pro-war to an anti-war line, from 1915 to 1919 took a Giolittian position.

adopted disparate stances. Was he always an agent of Nitti or did he work for Giolitti for a certain period? In Turin in 1916 and 1917 he was wholly defeatist; he invited immediate action. If it is possible to speak of individual responsibility for the events of August 1917,[23] Ciccotti should have been considered the most responsible. Instead, he was barely interrogated by the investigating judge and there were no proceedings against him. I remember his speech of 1916 or 1917, after which a hundred youths and adults were arrested for having shouted 'Long live Austria!' I do not believe that anyone did actually shout this, but after Ciccotti's speech it would not have been odd if somebody had. Ciccotti began his speech by saying that a serious fault lay at the door of the Socialists: that of having affirmed that the war was capitalistic. According to Ciccotti, this amounted to ennobling the war. With a remarkably subtle skill in arousing elementary popular feelings, he then elaborated a vivid tale of skulduggery which began more or less like this: on a certain evening, Vincenzo Morello (Rastignac), Senator Artom and a third person whom I do not remember met at the Caffè Faraglino...; the war was due to the conspiracy of these three men and the money of Barrère.[24] I recall having seen some workers, whom I knew to be very calm and temperate, leave the room after the peroration in a state of incredible excitement. The next day *La Stampa* published an unsigned article, written by Ciccotti, in which he asserted the need to form a bloc between Giolitti and the workers so that the government apparatus would not fall completely into the hands of Salandra's Apulian

---

[23] Spontaneous rioting and a general strike were sparked off in Turin on 22–26 August 1917 by inflated food prices and a prolonged bread shortage. The agitation and sacking of bakeries took the form of an anti-war protest but lacked political leadership. Approximately fifty demonstrators were killed in the brutal repression by police and troops. The local socialist leaders were rounded up and the Boselli government (see footnote 27 below) was strengthened overall by the episode. Minister of the Interior Orlando sacked the prefect of Turin, Edoardo Verdinois, and the director general of public security, Giacomo Vigliani. The report of the events in *Il Grido del Popolo* ('Le cinque giornate del proletariato torinese') was seized at the printers. (See CF, pp. 286–95 for the text of the original proofs.) On the arrests following Ciccotti's speech, see Gramsci's article of 4 November 1916 in CT, pp. 610–11. See also I 18.

[24] On Vincenzo Morello see footnote 12 on p. 156. Ernesto Artom (1868–1935), Italian diplomat involved in pre-war negotiations with the Austrians in 1915, had sought a neutralist solution through cession with compensation of the disputed border territories. Camille Barrère (1851–1940), French Ambassador to Rome, played a key role in pre-war diplomacy, encouraging intervention alongside France. French political circles had provided finance for Mussolini's interventionist *Popolo d'Italia*.

henchmen. A few days later, *La Giustizia* in Reggio Emilia published the summary of a speech delivered by Ciccotti at Reggio, where he had praised Prampolini.[25] I remember showing this newspaper to a few 'hard-liners' who were infatuated with Ciccotti and wanted people to support a campaign to give *Avanti!* to Ciccotti (certainly on the instigation of Ciccotti himself). No one has yet thoroughly investigated the events of August 1917 in Turin. It is certain that the events were spontaneous and caused by a prolonged lack of bread, which in the previous ten days had brought about the complete shortage of all the workers' staples (rice, polenta, potatoes, vegetables). But the problem is precisely this: how does one explain this absolute shortage of provisions? (Absolute: in the house where I lived, three meals in a row were skipped, after a month in which the meals skipped were becoming more frequent – and this was a house in the centre.) Prefect Verdinois in a statement of self-defence published in 1925 does not give sufficient information. Minister Orlando only administratively reprimanded him and in his speech to the Chamber he came off badly himself; in the meantime, no inquest at all was made. Verdinois accuses the workers, but his accusation is inept. He says the events were not caused by the lack of bread because they continued even when bread made with flour from the military warehouses was put on sale. For twenty days, however, the *Gazzetta del Popolo* had been predicting that the shortage of bread would lead to events like these and warned daily that bread should be provided before it was too late. Naturally, it changed its tune afterwards and spoke only of foreign money. How was it possible to let a bread shortage occur in a city whose province has scarce wheat cultivation and which had become a huge workshop for the war, with a population increased by more than 100,000 munitions workers?

I was convinced that the lack of bread was not an accident but was due to the sabotage of the Giolittian bureaucracy and, in part, to the ineptitude of Canepa who was neither fit for office nor able to control the bureaucracy that depended on his commissariat.[26] The Giolittians were seized by an incredible Germanophile

---

[25] On Prampolini see I 4.

[26] Giuseppe Canepa (1865–1948), reformist socialist member of Boselli's coalition, was head of the General Commissariat of Provisions and Foodstuffs at the time of the 1917 riots.

fanaticism. They knew that Giolitti could not yet take power, but they wanted to create an intermediate link, Nitti or Orlando, and overthrow Boselli.[27] The mechanism was late in functioning, when Orlando was already in power, but the situation had already been prepared to bring down the Boselli government in a pool of Turin blood. Why was Turin chosen? Because it was almost completely neutral, because its people had gone on strike in 1915, but above all because events were especially important in Turin. Ciccotti was the principal agent of this affair. He used to go too often to Turin, and not always to address the workers, but also to talk with *La Stampa*. I do not believe that the Giolittians were connected with Germany: that was not indispensable. They were aroused because of the events in Rome in 1915 and because they thought that the hegemony of Piedmont would have been strongly shaken or even shattered, they were capable of anything. The trial at Portogruaro against Frassati and the affair of Colonel Gamba demonstrate only that these people had lost all control.[28] It is necessary to have seen the satisfaction with which the editors of *La Stampa*, after Caporetto, spoke of the panic that had seized the Milanese leaders and of the *Corriere*'s decision to remove its entire plant, to understand what they were capable of. Undoubtedly, the Giolittians had been afraid of a military dictatorship that would put them up against the wall. They spoke of a plot for a *coup d'état* between Cadorna and Albertini: their eagerness to reach an agreement with the socialists was incredible.

During the war, Ciccotti served as a go-between in order to publish in *Avanti!* articles by the English Union of Democratic Control (the articles were received by Signora Chiaraviglio).[29] I remember Serrati's description of his meeting in London with a lady who wanted to thank him in the name of the Committee and the poor man's astonishment. Caught between these intrigues, he

---

[27] Paolo Boselli (1838–1932) became Prime Minister after Salandra fell in June 1916, backing a trenchantly pro-war line and a policy of national unity. His coalition included radicals and reformist socialists. Vittorio Emanuele Orlando, who as Boselli's Minister of the Interior had been attacked by army chief Cadorna and the right for his soft line towards the neutralists and socialists, succeeded Boselli to the premiership after the military defeat at Caporetto in September 1917 (not before August as Gramsci suggests).

[28] At a military tribunal in Portogruaro in 1915, it was revealed that Quirino Gamba, military columnist on Frassati's *La Stampa*, was in league with an officer of the German high command. The trial fuelled accusations of collaboration by the Giolittian neutralists.

[29] See footnote 41 on p. 318.

did not know what position to adopt. Another anecdote recounted by Serrati: Ciccotti's article against the Banca Commerciale was allowed to be published, while his article against the Banca di Sconto was censored.[30] Ciccotti's comment on a speech by Nitti which at first was censored but then allowed after a telephone call by Ciccotti recalling a promise of Nitti's; it was not published by Serrati. But the most interesting episode is that of the Jesuits who, through Ciccotti, tried to bring an end to the campaign for the Church of the Holy Martyrs:[31] what could the Jesuits have given to Ciccotti in exchange? But in spite of everything, Ciccotti was not expelled because he had to be granted journalistic indemnity. Another of these types was Carlo Bazzi.[32]

Q1 § 116.

3 Types of Periodical: Dilettantism and Discipline

Necessity of severe and rigorous internal criticism, with no lapses into conventionalism or half measures. There exists a tendency in historical materialism which stimulates (and supports) all the worst traditions of middle-level Italian culture and seems to correspond to certain traits of the Italian character: improvisation, 'flair', fatalistic laziness, mindless dilettantism, lack of intellectual discipline, moral and intellectual irresponsibility and disloyalty. Historical materialism destroys a whole set of prejudices and conventionalities, false senses of duty, hypocritical obligations; but it does not for this reason justify falling into scepticism and snobbish cynicism. Machiavellism had a similar result, because of an arbitrary extension or confusion between political 'morality' and private 'morality', between politics and ethics, though this confusion

[30] The Banca Commerciale and the Banca di Sconto were tied respectively to the rival cartels Ilva and Ansaldo who made massive profits out of wartime arms production. See also footnote 22 above.

[31] In May 1916, the parishioners of the Santi Martiri in Turin appealed to the local council against the threatened suppression of their parish (in fact a move by the Jesuits to regain control of the church). On this episode and the significance of Jesuit infiltration into education and the pulpits in Turin, see Gramsci's articles 'L'infiltrazione gesuitica a Torino' (1916) and 'La rinascita gesuitica' (1917) in CT, pp. 399–401 and 701–4.

[32] Carlo Bazzi, interventionist journalist on *L'Internazionale*.

certainly did not exist in Machiavelli himself, far from it, since his greatness precisely consists in having distinguished politics from ethics. No permanent association can exist and retain a capacity for development if it is not sustained by certain ethical principles, which the association itself establishes for its single components in the interests of internal compactness and the homogeneity needed to achieve its ends. This does not mean that these principles are devoid of a universal character. Such would be the case if the association had itself as its end, if it were a sect or a criminal conspiracy (in this case only does it seem to me possible to say that politics and ethics are indistinguishable, precisely because the 'particular' is raised to a 'universal'). But a normal association thinks of itself as an aristocracy, an élite, a vanguard, and thus linked by a million threads to a given social grouping and through that to the whole of humanity. Therefore the association does not set itself up as something fixed and definitive, but as tending to widen itself out towards a whole social grouping, which in its turn is conceived as tending to unify the whole of humanity. All these relationships give a tendentially universal character to the group ethic, which has to be conceived as capable of becoming a norm of conduct for humanity as a whole. Politics is conceived as a process out of which a morality will emerge; that is to say, it is conceived as leading towards a form of social coexistence in which politics and morality along with it will alike be superseded. (Only from this historicist point of view can one explain the widely felt anguish about the contrast between private morality and public/political morality; this anguish is an unconscious and sentimentally uncritical reflection of the contradictions of contemporary society and of the absence of equality of moral subjects.)

But one cannot talk of élite/aristocracy/vanguard as if it were an indistinct and chaotic collectivity, into which, by intercession of a mysterious holy spirit or some other mysterious and metaphysical unknown deity, is poured the grace of intelligence, ability, education, technical preparation, etc.; and yet such a way of thinking is widespread. We find reflected here on a small scale what happened on a national scale when the state was conceived as something abstracted from the collectivity of citizens, as an eternal father who thought of everything, arranged everything, etc; hence the absence of a real democracy, of a real national collective will, and hence, as a result of this passivity of individuals, the necessity of a more or less disguised despotism of the bureaucracy. The collectivity must be understood as the product of a development of will and of collective thought attained through concrete individual effort and not through a process of destiny extraneous to individual people; hence the need for an inner discipline and not just an external and mechanical one. If there have to be polemics and splits, there is no need to be afraid of confronting them and getting beyond them; they are inevitable in these processes of development, and to avoid them only means putting them off until they indeed become dangerous and even catastrophic, etc.

Q6 § 79.

4 Types of Periodical: The Final Evolutionary Being

Anecdote on Professor D'Ercole's history of philosophy course and the 'final evolutionary being'. For forty years he spoke of nothing but Chinese philosophy and Lao-tse. Each year there were 'new recruits' who had not heard the previous year's lectures so he had to start again. Hence for generations of students the 'final evolutionary being' became a legend.[33]

In certain cultural movements which enlist their personnel from among people who are only embarking on their own cultural life, the rapid expansion of the movement itself in winning over new members and the lack of personal cultural initiative on the part of those already won over make it impossible ever to move on from the basics. This has serious repercussions on journalistic activity in general, newspapers, weeklies, reviews, etc., which are apparently destined never to get beyond a certain cultural level. Moreover, the failure to take this kind of requirement into account explains the labour of Sisyphus of the so-called 'little reviews', which are addressed to everyone and no one and after a while become entirely useless. The most characteristic example was that of *La Voce*, which at a certain point split into *Lacerba*, *La Voce* and *L'Unità* with a tendency in each of these to split *ad infinitum*.[34] If the editorial boards are not tied to a disciplined

[33] See I 4.

[34] *La Voce* was founded in 1908. Salvemini left in 1911 to found *L'Unità* and Papini and Soffici in 1913 to found *Lacerba*. From 1914 to 1916 *La Voce* appeared in white wraps as a literary review, edited by Giuseppe De Robertis. A separate *Voce politica* (edited by Prezzolini and then De Viti De Marco) ran from May to December 1915.

rank and file movement, they tend either to become cliques of 'unarmed prophets' or to break up in accordance with the disorderly and chaotic movements occurring among various groups and strata of readers.

It must therefore be explicitly recognized that reviews are sterile in themselves if they do not become the motive and formative force of cultural institutions of a mass associative type, i.e. not of closed cadres. This also needs to be said for party reviews. It should not be thought that the party constitutes in itself the mass cultural 'institution' of the review. The party is essentially political and even its cultural activity is of a politico-cultural kind. The cultural 'institutions' need to be not only institutions of 'cultural policy' but also of 'cultural technique'. Example: a party contains illiterate members and the party's cultural policy is the fight against illiteracy. A group for the struggle against illiteracy is not exactly the same thing as a 'school for the illiterate'. A school for the illiterate teaches people how to read and write; a group for the struggle against illiteracy prepares all the most effective channels for eradicating illiteracy from the great mass of a country's population.

Q 6 § 120.

5 Types of Periodical: [Critical Information]

Individually nobody can follow all the literature published on a group of topics or even on a single topic. The provision of critical information, for the benefit of a public of average culture or just entering cultural life, with a coverage of all the publications on the group of topics likely to be of greatest interest to it, is a necessary service. Just as those in power have a secretariat or a press office which keeps them informed daily or from time to time about everything published that they need to know about, so a similar service will be provided for its public by a periodical. It will define its task, it will limit it, but this is its task; this requires, however, that an organic and complete body of information is provided – limited, but organic and complete. Reviews should not be casual and occasional, but systematic: and they also need to be accompanied by retrospective 'surveys' that 'sum up' the most essential topics.

A periodical, like a newspaper or a book or any other mode of didactic expression that is set up with a certain average public in view – readers, listeners, etc. – cannot satisfy everyone to an equal degree, be equally useful to everyone, etc.: the important thing is for it to be a stimulus to everyone, since no publication can replace the individual thinking mind or establish from scratch intellectual and scientific interests where people are only interested in café chit-chat or think that the aim of life is enjoying oneself or having a good time. So there is no need to be worried about the multiplicity of criticisms: indeed the multiplicity of criticisms is the proof that one is on the right road. When on the other hand, the tenor of the criticisms is uniform, it is something that needs thinking about: 1) because it may point to a real weakness; 2) because one may have been mistaken about the 'average' level of the readership being addressed, and therefore be working in a void, 'for eternity'.

Q 8 § 57.

6 Journalism: Almanacs

Since journalism, in the notes devoted to it, has been considered as the manifestation of a group which aims to spread an integral conception of the world through various journalistic activities, the publication of an almanac can hardly be left aside. Almanacs are basically annual periodical publications which examine the complex historical activity of each year from a certain standpoint. The almanac is the 'minimum' of periodical 'advertising' that can be given to one's own ideas and judgements on the world, and its variety shows how much each single moment of this history has been given a special role in the group, just as its organic quality shows the degree of homogeneity the group has come to acquire. Of course, to get its circulation the almanac has to keep in mind specific needs of the group of buyers it addresses, a group which often cannot spend money twice on the same need. The content therefore needs to be chosen: 1) for those parts which will make it superfluous to buy another almanac; 2) for that part which seeks to influence readers so as to guide them in a predetermined direction. The first part will be reduced to the minimum necessary to satisfy the given need. The second part will emphasize those subjects considered to be of the greatest educative and formative importance.[35]

Q 14 § 60.

7 Journalism: Readers

The readers must be considered from two main points of view: 1) as ideological elements, philosophically 'transformable', ductile, malleable, capable of transformation; 2) as 'economic' elements, able to buy and make others buy the publications. The two elements are in fact not always separable, since the ideological element is a stimulus for the economic act of buying and distributing. However, in working out a publishing plan the two aspects should be kept apart so that the calculations are realistic and not based on wishful thinking. In any case, in the economic sphere, people's possibilities do not correspond to their will and ideological impulse, and provision therefore needs to be made for the possibility of 'indirect' purchase, i.e. paid for by services (distribution). A publishing enterprise produces different types of reviews and books, graded according to different cultural levels. It is hard to establish how many possible 'customers' there are at each level. One needs to start from the lowest level where the 'minimum' commercial plan can be established, i.e. the most realistic estimate, bearing in mind however that the activity can (and must) modify the starting point. Not only can (must) the sphere of buyers be extended, but a

---

[35] For this note, compare Gramsci's statement in a letter from Vienna of 20 December 1923 to the PCd'I executive committee (reproduced in *Rinascita* 22 January 1966, p. 23; on this correspondence see introduction to this section): 'I want to propose that a kind of yearbook of the working class be compiled. This should contain in brief everything that might interest a party member or sympathiser. I have already drafted a plan of its contents and have thought about how the work on each chapter should be distributed. It could come out in the second half of 1924 in a 600 or 700 page book. In thirty or so chapters one could provide: a review of the international political and trade union movement; an examination of the Italian situation from all angles (economic, political, military, labour, finance, etc.). Part of the volume should be devoted to Marxism and its history, particularly in Italy; another part to Russia, its political organization, its economic situation, the history of the Bolshevik party, etc. There should be a chapter summarizing the theory and tactics of the Comintern as they have developed through its congresses, the enlarged Executives and the most important work of the Executive Committee. I think that after three years of civil war, when it has been very hard systematically to follow the party newspaper and other publications, a large number of workers, particularly among the emigrants, would be pleased to have at their disposal a volume like the one whose contents I have just sketched out'. On 'yearbooks' and 'almanacs' see also X 15 below.

hierarchy of needs to be satisfied and activities to be carried out can (must) be determined. One can obviously remark that the enterprises existing up till now have become bureaucratized, they have failed to stimulate needs and organize ways of satisfying them. This has often meant that a chaotic individual initiative has yielded better results than the organized one. The truth in the latter case was that there was neither 'initiative' nor 'organization' but merely bureaucracy and a fatalistic fad. Instead of energizing a collective effort the so-called organization was often a narcotic, a depressant, even a blockading or a sabotage. Besides, one cannot speak of a serious journalistic publishing business if the element of organization of the buyers is absent. Being particular kinds of customer (at least in the mass) they need a particular organization, strictly linked to the ideological line of the 'commodity' being sold. It is a commonplace observation that modern newspapers are really run by the managing editor and not by the editor.

Q 14 § 62.

8 Journalism: Intellectual Movements and Centres

It is the duty of journalistic activity (in its various articulations) to follow and monitor *all* the intellectual centres and movements which exist or are formed in the country. *All of them*. Those which have an arbitrary or lunatic quality can just about be left out; though even these should at least be registered, with the tone they deserve. Distinction between intellectual *centres* and *movements* and other distinctions and gradations. Catholicism for instance is a large centre and a large movement: but within it there are partial movements and centres which tend towards a transformation of the whole, or towards other more concrete and limited ends which need to be taken into account. It seems that before all else one should 'draw' the intellectual and moral *map* of the country, in other words circumscribe the big movements of ideas and the large centres (although there are not always large centres corresponding to the large movements, at least with the qualities of visibility and concreteness one usually attributes to this word: the typical example is the Catholic centre). Next one must take account of the innovative *pressures* around, which do not always germinate, i.e. develop into anything, but which must not for this reason be any the less followed and monitored. Besides, at its beginnings a movement is always uncertain, its future in doubt, etc.; does this mean one needs to wait till it has acquired all its force and consistency before dealing with it? Nor does it have to possess the qualities of coherence and intellectual profundity: it is not always the most coherent and intellectually rich movements which triumph. Indeed, a movement often triumphs precisely because of its mediocrity and logical elasticity: anything goes, the most blatant compromises are possible, and may well themselves be the cause of the triumph. Read the reviews produced by the young intellectuals other than those which have already made a name and represent serious and definite interests. The Bompiani *Almanacco letterario* for 1933 (pp. 360–1) lists the basic programmes of six of these reviews which ought to represent the pressures of movement in our culture: *Il Saggiatore, Ottobre, Il Ventuno, L'Italia vivente, L'Orto, Espero.* They do not seem particularly clear, with the odd exception. *Espero* for example proposes 'in philosophy to publish the *post-idealists*, who are conducting a careful critique of idealism, and only those idealists who manage to take account of this critique.' The editor of *Espero* is Aldo Capasso, and being a post-idealist is a bit like being 'contemporary', i.e. nothing. *Ottobre* has a clearer programme, perhaps indeed the only clear one. Nevertheless, all these movements require examination, snobbery aside.

　　Distinction between *militant* movements (the most interesting) and 'rearguard' movements of accepted ideas which have become classic or commercial. Should *L'Italia Letteraria* be counted among these? It is certainly not militant or even classic! The most apt and accurate thing to say would be that it is just a shambles.[36]

Q 14 § 71.

9 Journalism: Types of Periodical: [External Appearance]

Comparison of the first number of the review *Leonardo* published by Sansoni in Florence with those published by Treves. The difference is quite considerable, and yet Treves are not typographically the most up to date of publishers. The surface

---

[36] On *L'Italia Letteraria* see VIII 13 above and footnote 13 on p. 96.

appearance of a review is of great importance both commercially and 'ideologically' (to secure fidelity and affection). In this case it is in fact hard to distinguish the commercial from the ideological aspect. Factors: page, including setting of margins, spacing between columns, column width (length of line), compactness of columns, i.e. number of letters per line and face of each letter, paper and ink (attractiveness of headlines, sharpness of the characters depending on how worn the type-moulds or hand-set letters are, etc.). These elements are important not only for reviews but also for daily papers. The fundamental problem for every periodical (daily or otherwise) is that of ensuring fixed sales (if possible continually increasing), which means the ability to establish a commercial plan (in expansion etc.). Clearly, the fundamental element for a periodical's success is the ideological one, the fact that it does or doesn't satisfy specific intellectual-political needs. But it would be a serious mistake to think that this is the only element and particularly that it is valid 'in isolation'. Only in exceptional conditions, in specific periods of boom in public opinion, does it occur that an opinion is successful whatever the outward form in which it is presented. Generally the manner of presentation has a great importance for the stability of the business and this importance can be positive but it may also be negative. It is not always 'good business' to give something away for nothing or at half price, just as it is not good business to charge too much or give 'too little' for 'one's money'. At least in politics. The public distrusts an opinion which costs nothing in print: they see through the trap. And, conversely, they distrust 'politically' whoever is not adept at administering the funds contributed by the public itself. How could a party which does not possess or (what amounts to the same thing) is incapable of choosing the personnel to administer a newspaper or review properly be deemed capable of administering power in the state? By the same token, a group which knows how to achieve valuable journalistic results with limited means shows by this ability alone that it will know how to administer well more extensive organizations, etc.

This is why the same attention must be paid to the 'external' appearance of a publication as to its ideological and intellectual content. In reality the two things are inseparable, and rightly so. A good principle (though not always) is to give the outward form of a publication a characteristic which by itself gets it noticed and remembered: a form of free advertising, as it were. Not always, because it depends on the psychology of the particular readership one wants to win over.

Q 14 § 73.

10 Journalism: Types of Periodical: [Political Education]

Gentile's review *Educazione Politica*, which later changed its name.[37] The title is an old one: Arcangelo Ghisleri edited a review with the same name and it was more in line with the goal proposed.[38] But how many reviews did Ghisleri edit and, aside from the man's honesty, with what real effect? It is true that education can be arranged on different planes to obtain different levels. Everything depends on the level the 'chief' thinks he is at, and it is natural for a chief editor to think he is always at the highest level and to present his position as an ideal to the readers of the lower orders.

Q 14 § 80.

11 [Integral Journalism]

The type of journalism considered in these notes is one that could be called 'integral' (the meaning of this term will become increasingly clear in the course of the notes themselves), in other words one that seeks not only to satisfy all the needs (of a given category) of its public, but also to create and develop these needs, to arouse its public and progressively enlarge it. If one examines all the existing forms of journalism and the activities of newspaper writing and publishing in general, one sees that each of them presupposes other forces to be integrated or to be co-ordinated with 'mechanically'. For a critical and comprehensive treatment of the subject, it seems more opportune (for methodological and didactic purposes) to presuppose another situation: that there exists, as the starting point, a more or less homogeneous cultural grouping (in the broad sense) of a given

---

[37] Its title was changed in 1927 to *Educazione Fascista* and again, in 1933, to *Civiltà Fascista*.

[38] Arcangelo Ghisleri (1855–1938) was a radical republican journalist.

type, of a given level and especially with a given general orientation; and that one wants to use such a grouping to construct a self-sufficient, complete cultural edifice, by beginning directly from ... language, from the means of expression and reciprocal contact. The whole edifice should be constructed according to 'rational', functional principles, in that one has definite premisses and wants to arrive at definite results. Of course, the premisses will necessarily change during the elaboration of the 'plan' because, while it is true that a given end presupposes given premisses, it is also true that during the actual elaboration of the given activity, the premisses are necessarily changed and transformed. One's knowledge of the end, as it widens and becomes more concrete, reacts back upon the premisses, 'shaping' them increasingly. The objective existence of the premisses allows one to think of given ends, i.e. the given premisses are such only in relation to certain ends that can be conceived concretely. But if the ends begin progressively to materialize, the initial premisses necessarily change, which in the meantime are no longer ... initial, and therefore the conceivable ends change too. This connection is rarely considered, even though it is immediately obvious. We see it manifested in businesses with 'planned' management, which do not function as pure machines but depend on a mode of thinking in which freedom and the spirit of enterprise ('doing deals') play a far greater part than the official mouthpieces of abstract (or maybe too 'concrete') 'freedom' and 'enterprise', stuck as they are in their present roles, would care to admit. This connection is therefore a real one, yet it is also true that the initial 'premisses' continually reappear, though under other conditions. Just because the new intake into a school learns its ABC, it doesn't mean that illiteracy disappears once and for all. Every year there will be a new intake which will have to be taught the ABC. Nevertheless it is clear that the rarer illiteracy becomes among adults, the less difficult it will be to get 100 per cent attendance in the elementary schools. There will always be 'illiterates', but they will tend to disappear above the normal age of five or six.

Q 24 § 1.

12 [Types of Newspaper]

Here is how the various types of newspaper are described in the 1926 *Annali dell'Italia Cattolica*, with reference to the Catholic press

> In a broad sense, the 'Catholic' newspaper (or rather that 'written by Catholics') is that which does not contain anything against Catholic doctrine and morality and follows and defends its norms. Within such lines the newspaper can pursue political, economic-social or scientific goals. In the strict sense, however, the 'Catholic' newspaper is that which, in agreement with the Ecclesiastical Authority, has as its direct purpose an effective Christian social apostolate, in the service of the Church and as an aid to Catholic Action.[39] It bears, at least implicitly, the responsibility of the Ecclesiastical Authority, but it must also follow its norms and directives.

This is really a distinction between the so-called newspaper of information, without explicit party allegiances, and the newspaper of opinion, the official organ of a given party; between the newspaper for the popular masses or 'popular' newspaper and that dedicated to a necessarily restricted public.

In the history of journalistic technique the *Piccolo* of Trieste can in certain respects be considered 'exemplary', at least according to Silvio Benco's book[40] on the history of this newspaper (as regards the Austrian legislation on the press, the position of Italian irredentism in Istria, the formal legalitarianism of the imperial and royal authorities, the internal conflicts between the various fractions of irredentism, the relation between the national popular mass and the political leadership of Italian nationalism, and so on).

In other respects, the *Corriere della Sera* was most interesting in Giolitti's time or in the liberal period in general, if one bears in mind the politico-cultural and journalistic situation in Italy, so different from the French situation and in general from that of

---

[39] Catholic Action was an organization set up after the Unification to counteract the secularization of civil society, and was an important channel for shaping Catholic political consent in the years of the papal *non expedit*. Having granted Catholic Action a degree of autonomy by the 1929 Concordat, Mussolini in 1931 forced Pius XI to curtail its effectively dissident activities among youth groups. It was nevertheless an important training ground during the regime for the leaders of postwar Christian Democracy.

[40] Silvio Benco, '*Il Piccolo' di Trieste, Mezzo secolo di giornalismo*, Milan-Rome 1931.

other European countries. The clear division in France between popular newspapers and newspapers of opinion cannot exist in Italy which lacks a centre as populous and culturally predominant as Paris (and where the political newspaper is less 'indispensable', even among the upper and so-called educated classes). Furthermore, one should note that the *Corriere*, although the most widely read newspaper in the country, has never been explicitly ministerial except for short periods of time and in its own way: on the contrary, in order to be at the service of the state', it had to be almost always against the government, thereby expressing one of the most notable contradictions of our national life.

It would be useful to seek in the history of Italian journalism the technical and politico-cultural reasons for the success that the old *Secolo* of Milan had for a certain time.[41] It appears that in the history of Italian journalism two periods can be distinguished. The first was a 'primitive' one of generic indistinctness, in politico-cultural terms, which made possible the large circulation of the *Secolo* on a programme of a vague 'secularism' (against clerical influence) and a vague 'democratism' (against the preponderant influence of rightist forces in the life of the state). Furthermore, the *Secolo* was the first 'modern' Italian newspaper with foreign services and ample information and news on Europe. Then there was a subsequent period in which, through transformism, the rightist forces 'nationalized' themselves in a popular direction and the *Corriere* replaced the *Secolo* as the high circulation daily. The vague democratic secularism of the *Secolo* became in the *Corriere* a more concrete national unitarianism; the secularism was less plebeian and vulgar and the nationalism less popularized and democratizing. It should be noted that none of the parties which broke away from the shapeless popularism of the *Secolo* attempted to re-create the democratic unity on a higher and more concrete politico-cultural plane than the earlier primitive one. This task was abandoned almost without a struggle to the conservatives of the *Corriere*. And yet this should be the task

[41] *Il Secolo* was founded in 1866 by the Milan publishers Sonzogno. By 1872 it had the highest circulation in Italy (30,000) and was noted for its popularizing slant and its pioneering use of wire services and foreign correspondents. It was overtaken in the 1880s by its Milan rival the *Corriere della Sera*. After 1918 *Il Secolo* took a democratic-reformist line, exhorting the workers to make piecemeal demands and avoid escalations into Bolshevism. The paper was fascistized in 1923 and ceased publication in 1928.

after every process of clarification and differentiation: to re-create the unity, broken during the progressive movement, on a higher level in the hands of the élite which has succeeded in winning out of the generic indistinctness a more concrete personality by exercising a directing function over the old complex from which it has distinguished and detached itself. The same process was repeated in the Catholic world after the formation of the Popular Party,[42] a democratic 'breakaway' that the rightist parties succeeded in subordinating to their own programmes. In both cases the petty bourgeoisie, although they formed the majority of the leading intellectuals, were overpowered by elements of the fundamental class. In the lay camp the industrialists of the *Corriere*, in the Catholic camp the agrarian bourgeoisie in alliance with the large landowners overpowered the political professionals of the *Secolo* and the Popular Party, although the latter represented the great masses of the two camps, the urban and rural semi-proletariat and the petty bourgeoisie.

Q 24 § 2.

13 Types of Periodical

Three fundamental types of review can roughly be distinguished, characterized by the way in which they are compiled, the type of reader they aim at, and the educative goals they want to achieve. The first type can be established by combining the editorial elements found in a specialized way in B. Croce's *La Critica*, in F. Coppola's *Politica* and C. Barbagallo's *Nuova Rivista Storica*.[43]

[42] The Italian Popular Party (PPI) was a mass Catholic party (precursor of the present DC) founded by Luigi Sturzo in January 1919. It emerged in the elections of that year (the first with both manhood suffrage and proportional representation) as Italy's second largest party after the PSI. After Mussolini took power, the PPI was progressively isolated by the fascists and the Catholic right (Vatican, Jesuits) before being suppressed, like the other political parties, in 1926.

[43] The format of Croce's *La Critica* (1903–44, continued to 1951 as *Quaderni della 'Critica'*) was outlined in a letter from Croce to Karl Vossler in 1902; '1) Retrospective articles on what has been done in Italy in the last forty years in the fields of literature, history, criticism, philosophy etc., in order to prepare a history of the philosophy and literature of united Italy; 2) critical articles on the Italian and foreign literature of the day, but only on the *significant* books of good or bad tendency.' Francesco Coppola (1878–1957) leading nationalist, set up and edited *Politica* in 1918 with Alfredo Rocco. Corrado Barbagallo (1877–1952) founded the *Nuova Rivista Storica* in 1917, remaining editor until 1930 when it was taken over by Gioacchino Volpe.

The second type, 'critical-historical-bibliographical', by combining the elements that characterized the best issues of L. Russo's *Leonardo*, Rerum Scriptor's *L'Unità* and Prezzolini's *La Voce*. The third type by combining some elements of the second type with the English type of weekly like the *Manchester Guardian Weekly* or *The Times Weekly*.[44]

Each of these types should be characterized by a highly unitary and non-anthological intellectual line; it should in other words have a homogeneous and disciplined editorial staff. Hence only a few 'principal' contributors should write the essential body of each number. The editorial line should be highly organized so as to make an intellectually homogeneous product, while respecting the necessary variety of styles and literary personalities. The editorial staff should have a written statute which, for what it is worth, can prevent incursions, conflicts and contradictions (for example, the content of each number should be approved by the majority of the staff before publication).

A unitary cultural organism which offered the three above-mentioned types of review to the various strata of the public (and a common spirit should in any case be present in all three types), backed up by a corresponding book publication, would satisfy the needs of a certain mass of readers, a mass which is intellectually most active, but only in the potential state, and which it matters most to develop, to make it think concretely, to transform it and homogenize it through a process of organic development that can lead it from simple common sense to coherent and systematic thought.

The critical-historical-bibliographical type: analytic study of the material, carried out from the viewpoint of the reader of reviews who generally cannot read the works themselves. A scholar who examines a definite historical phenòmenon in order to build up a general overview must carry out a whole series of preliminary investigations and intellectual operations of which only a small part end up being used. Such a labour would, however, be used for this average type of review, put in the hands of a reader who, in order to develop intellectually, needs to have access both to the overview and to the whole work of analysis which led to that particular result. The ordinary reader does not

[44] Gramsci had received the weekly supplements of *The Times* and the *Manchester Guardian* in prison. On Russo and *Leonardo* see footnote 32 on p. 215. 'Rerum Scriptor' was the pen-name of Gaetano Salvemini.

and cannot have a 'scientific' habit of mind, which is acquired only through specialized work. It is therefore necessary to help him obtain at least a 'sense' of it through an appropriate critical activity. It is not enough to give him concepts already elaborated and fixed in their 'definitive' form. Their concreteness, which lies in the process that has led to that form, escapes him. One should therefore offer him the whole process of reasoning and the intermediate connections in a well defined way and not just by referring to them. For example: a complex historical movement can be broken down in time and space and also into various levels. Thus, although Catholic Action has always had a single and centralized leadership, it displays great differences (and also contrasts) in regional attitude in different periods and according to the specific problem encountered (e.g. the agrarian problem, trade-union line, etc.).

In reviews of this type certain sections are indispensable or useful: 1) a political-scientific-philosophical encyclopaedic dictionary, in this sense: in each number one should publish one (or more) short encyclopaedic monographs on the political, philosophical and scientific concepts that come up time and again in the newspapers and the reviews and which the average reader has difficulty in understanding or actually misinterprets. In reality, every cultural current creates a language of its own, i.e. it participates in the general development of a determinate national language, introducing new terms, giving a new content to terms already in use, creating metaphors, using historical names to facilitate the understanding and judgement of specific contemporary situations, etc., etc. These monographs should be 'practical', related to needs that are really felt, and should be written with the average reader in mind. If possible, the compilers should be aware of the more frequent errors and should trace them back to their sources, which are the publications of scientific trash, like the 'Biblioteca Popolare Sonzogno' or the encyclopaedic dictionaries (Melzi, Premoli, Bonacci, etc.) or the most widely circulated popular encyclopaedias (Sonzogno, etc.). The monographs should not be presented in organic form (e.g. in alphabetical order or grouped according to subject matter), nor should they be allotted a pre-established space, as if a comprehensive work were already in view, but they should be immediately related to the subjects discussed in the review itself or in its more advanced or more elementary sister publications.

The length of the treatment should be determined in each case not by the intrinsic importance of the subject but by its immediate journalistic interest (all this is stated as a general rule and with the usual grain of salt). In short, the encyclopaedic section must not be presented as a book published in instalments but, in each case, as a treatment of subjects that are interesting in themselves, from which a book might derive but not necessarily.

2) Linked to the preceding section is the one dealing with biographies, to be understood in two senses: both in that a person's whole life can be of interest to the general culture of a given social stratum and in that an historical name can become part of an encyclopaedic dictionary because of its association with a particular concept or event. Thus, for example, one might need to mention Lord Carson in order to allude to the fact that the crisis of the parliamentary regime already existed before the world war and precisely in England, in the country where this regime appeared the most efficient and substantial. This does not mean that a full biography of Lord Carson has to be provided. A person of average culture is interested in only two biographical facts: a) in 1914, on the eve of the war, Lord Carson was in Ulster where he enlisted a very large armed corps in order to oppose, through an insurrection, the application of the Irish Home Rule Act, approved by Parliament which, according to the English saying, 'can do everything except make a man into a woman'; b) Lord Carson not only was not punished for 'high treason' but he became a minister a little later, on the outbreak of war. (It might be useful to present complete biographies in a separate section.)

3) Another section can include political-intellectual autobiographies. If these are well put together, with sincerity and simplicity, they can be of the utmost journalist interest and can have a great formative effectiveness. The way in which one has succeeded in freeing oneself from a given provincial or corporate environment, as a result of what external impulses and with what internal conflicts, so as to achieve a historically superior personality, can suggest, in living form, an intellectual and moral course, besides being a document of cultural development in given epochs.

4) A fundamental section can be the critical-historical-bibliographical examination of the regional situations (meaning by region a differentiated geo-economic organism). Many people would like to know and study local situations, which are always

interesting, but they do not know how or where to begin. They do not know the bibliographical material or how to research in libraries. One would therefore need to provide the general framework of a concrete problem (or a scientific theme) by listing the books that have dealt with it, the articles in specialized reviews, as well as the material that is still in a raw state (statistics, etc.), in the form of bibliographical summaries, with a special circulation for publications that are unusual or in foreign languages. In addition to regions, this work can be done from various points of view for general problems, cultural problems, etc.

5) A systematic culling of data from newspapers and reviews for whatever is relevant to the fundamental sections: simply citing authors and titles, with brief remarks on their general tendency. This bibliographical section should be compiled for each number, and for some subjects it also needs to be retrospective.

6) Book-reviewing. Two types. A critical-informative type: on the assumption that the average reader cannot read the book in question, but that it is useful for him to know its content and conclusions. A theoretical-critical type: on the assumption that the reader has to read the book in question; therefore it is not simply summarized, but the critical objections that can be brought against it are voiced, its most interesting parts are stressed, points that have been sacrificed in it are developed, etc. This second type of book review is more appropriate to the higher level of periodical.

7) Critically presented bibliographical data, arranged by subject matter or groups of topics, on the literature concerning authors and the fundamental questions for the conception of the world underlying the reviews published: for Italian authors and for Italian translations of foreign authors. This critical bibliography should be very detailed and meticulous, since one must remember that only through this work and this systematic critical elaboration can one arrive at the genuine source of a whole series of erroneous concepts put about without control or censorship. One must keep in mind that in every region of Italy, given the very rich variety of local traditions, there exist groups of different sizes characterized by particular ideological and psychological elements: 'each town has or has had its local saint, hence its own cult and its own chapel.'

The unitary national elaboration of a homogeneous collective consciousness demands a wide range of conditions and initiatives. Diffusion from a homogeneous centre of a homogeneous way of thinking and acting is the principal condition, but it must not and cannot be the only one. A very common error is that of thinking that every social stratum elaborates its consciousness and its culture in the same way, with the same methods, namely the methods of the professional intellectuals. The intellectual is a 'professional', a skilled worker who knows how his own specialized 'machines' function. He has an 'apprenticeship' and a 'Taylor system' of his own. It is childish and illusory to attribute to everyone this acquired and not innate ability, just as it would be childish to believe that any unskilled worker can drive a train. It is childish to think that a 'clear concept', suitably circulated, is inserted in various consciousnesses with the same 'organizing' effects of diffused clarity: this is an 'enlightenment' error. The ability of the professional intellectual adroitly to combine induction and deduction, to generalize without falling into empty formalism, to transport from one sphere of judgement to another certain criteria of discrimination, adapting them to new conditions, is a 'specialization', a 'qualification'. It is not something given to ordinary common sense. This is why the premiss of 'organic diffusion from a homogeneous centre of a homogeneous way of thinking and acting' is not enough. When a ray of light passes through different prisms it is refracted differently: if you want the same refraction, you need to make a whole series of rectifications of each prism.

Patient and systematic 'repetition' is a fundamental methodological principle. But this must not be a mechanical, 'obsessive', material repetition, but an adaptation of each concept to the different peculiarities and cultural traditions. The concept must be repeatedly presented in all its positive aspects and in its traditional negations, arranging each partial aspect into the totality. Finding the real identity beneath the apparent contradiction and differentiation, and finding the substantial diversity beneath the apparent identity, is the most delicate, misunderstood and yet essential endowment of the critic of ideas and the historian of historical developments. The educative-formative work that a homogeneous cultural centre carries out, the elaboration of a critical consciousness that it promotes and favours on a specific historical base which contains the concrete premisses for such an elaboration, cannot be limited to the simple theoretical enunciation of 'clear' methodological principles: this would be to proceed merely in the manner of the eighteenth-century 'philosophes'. The work needed is complex and must be articulated and graduated. It requires a combination of deduction and induction, formal logic and dialectic, identification and distinction, positive demonstration and the destruction of the old. And not in the abstract but in the concrete, on the basis of the real and of actual experience. But how can one know what the most widespread and entrenched errors are? Evidently, it is impossible to have 'statistics' on ways of thinking and single individual opinions, with all the combinations of them found in larger and smaller groups, statistics that give an organic and systematic picture of the real cultural situation and the ways in which the 'common sense' is really manifested. The only alternative is the systematic review of the literature that is most widely circulated and most accepted by the people, combined with the study and criticism of the ideological currents of the past, each of which 'may' have left a deposit, combining variously with the preceding and successive layers.

A more general criterion enters into this same order of observations: changes in ways of thinking, in beliefs, in opinions do not occur through rapid, simultaneous and generalized 'explosions'. Rather, they are almost always the result of 'successive combinations' determined by the most disparate and uncontrollable 'formulas of authority'. The illusion that there are 'explosions' comes from a lack of critical penetration. Methods of traction did not develop directly from the animal-drawn coach to the modern electric express train, but passed through a series of intermediate combinations, some of which are still in existence (such as animal traction on rails, etc.), and railway stock which has become outdated in the United States is still used for many years in China and represents a technological advance there. Likewise in the cultural sphere the different ideological strata are variously combined and what has become 'scrap iron' in the city is still a 'utensil' in the provinces. Indeed, in the cultural sphere 'explosions' are even less frequent and less intense than in the technological sphere where, at least at the highest level, an innovation spreads with relative rapidity and simultaneity. The 'explosion' of political passions accumulated in a period of technological transformations, which lack correspondingly new forms of adequate juridical organization but which instead are immediately accompanied by a degree of direct and indirect coercion, is confused with cultural transformations, which are slow and gradual. Whereas passion is impulsive, culture is the product of a complex process of elaboration.[45] (The reference to the fact that at times what has become 'scrap iron' in the city is still a 'utensil' in the provinces can be usefully developed.)

Q 24 § 3.

14 [Types of Periodical: Moralizing Reviews]

Gozzi's *Osservatore* constitutes a typical review, of a type of moralizing periodical peculiar to the eighteenth century (which reached its perfection in England where it had originated with Addison's *Spectator*).[46] It had a certain historical-cultural significance in propagating the new conception of life, acting for the average reader as a bridge between religion and modern civilization. Today the type, in a degenerate form, is preserved especially in the Catholic camp, whereas in the camp of modern civilization it has been trasformed and incorporated into the humorous reviews which, in their own way, would like to offer a 'constructive' criticism of morals. Publications like *Fantasio* and *Le Charivari* have no counterparts in Italy (the primitive *Asino* of Podrecca and *Il Seme*, written for the peasants, were something of the kind).[47] In certain respects some of the local and crime

[45] The terminology here draws on Croce's distinction between politics as 'passion' and cultural and moral life as ethico-political history. See Q 10 II § 41 V for Gramsci's discussion of Croce's concept of 'passion'.

[46] On Gasparo Gozzi, see footnote 97 on p. 267. *L'Osservatore Veneto* appeared from 1761–62, inspired by the model of Addison and Steele's *Spectator* (1711–14).

[47] *L'Asino* was an illustrated weekly founded in 1895 by Guido Podrecca. It ceased publication in 1925. *Il Seme*, a Socialist party paper for the peasants, ran from 1901 to 1914. Writing on 27 March 1924 to Togliatti, Gramsci had made a proposal which 'for the moment at least, will serve only for the preparation of our future movement. I thought that our party could revive on its own behalf the old PSI paper *Il Seme* as a fortnightly or a monthly. It should be done like the old one, with a modernized content, but of the same type. It should cost no more than one soldo [20 soldi = 1 lira] so that it can circulate among the poorest peasants, and it should have many simple cartoons, short articles etc. It should be directed at popularizing the slogan of the workers' and peasants' government, at reviving the anticlerical campaign because I think that four years of reaction must have thrown the masses in the countryside back into superstitious mysticism, and also spreading our own general propaganda'. (In Togliatti (ed.) *La formazione del gruppo dirigente del PCI nel 1923–24*, Rome 1974, p. 257.)

news pages of the daily papers and the cultural or topical commentary sections derive from the eighteenth-century moralizing type of review.

Baretti's *La Frusta Letteraria* is a variety of this type:[48] a review of encyclopaedic and universal bibliography, it criticized contents and it tended to moralize (it criticized manners, attitudes and outlooks, drawing not on life and on events, but on books). Papini's *Lacerba*, in its non-artistic part, belonged to this type and some of its aspects were very original and seductive. Its 'satanistic' bent (Papini's 'Gesù peccatore' [Jesus the sinner], 'Viva il maiale' [Long live the pig], 'Contro la famiglia [Against the family], etc.; Soffici's 'Giornale di bordo' [Ship's diary]; the articles by Italo Tavolato, 'Elogio della prostituzione' [In praise of prostitution], etc.) was forced and too often its originality was artificial.[49]

One can say that the general type belongs to the sphere of 'common sense' or 'good sense' because its aim is to modify average opinion in a given society by criticizing, suggesting, mocking, correcting, modernizing and, in the last analysis, by introducing 'new commonplaces'. If well written, with verve and a certain sense of detachment (so as not to sound like a sermon), yet with sincere interest in average opinion, reviews of this type can have a large circulation and exert a profound influence. They must not have any 'haughtiness', either scientific or moralistic, they must not be 'philistine' or academic, nor appear fanatical or excessively partisan. They must place themselves in the camp of 'common sense' itself, detaching themselves from it just enough to permit a teasing smile, but not one tinged with contempt or overweening superiority.

'La Pietra' and the 'Compagnia della Pietra'. Motto from Dante's Pietra poems: 'I want to be as harsh in my speech'.[50]

Every social class has its own 'common sense' and 'good sense', which are basically the most widespread conception of life

---

[48] *La Frusta Letteraria* (1763–65) was also influenced by the precedent of the *Spectator*; Giuseppe Baretti (1719–89) made it the vehicle of his flair for polemic and a watchdog against literary elitism.

[49] On *Lacerba* see footnote 23 on p. 46. 'Against the family' probably refers to 'Appunti sulla famiglia' in the issue of 15 July 1914 (by Soffici, not Papini).

[50] It is not clear what the 'Compagnia della Pietra' refers to. The quotation from Dante ('Così nel mio parlar voglio essere aspro') is from a set of four lyrics known as the 'rime pietrose' which are renowned for their technical difficulty.

and man. Every philosophical current leaves a sedimentation of 'common sense': this is the document of its historical reality. Common sense is not something rigid and stationary, but is in continuous transformation, becoming enriched with scientific notions and philosophical opinions that have entered into common circulation. 'Common sense' is the folklore of philosophy and always stands midway between folklore proper (folklore as it is normally understood) and the philosophy, science, and economics of the scientists. Common sense creates the folklore of the future, a relatively rigidified phase of popular knowledge in a given time and place.

Q 24 § 4.

15 Yearbooks and Almanacs

The type of review like *Politica* or *La Critica* requires from the outset a body of specialized editorial staff capable of providing at regular intervals a scientifically elaborated and selected subject matter. A group of editors of this kind, who have reached between themselves a certain level of cultural homogeneity, is far from easy to bring into existence and it represents the point of arrival in the development of a cultural movement. This type of review can be replaced (or anticipated) by the publication of a 'Yearbook'. These 'Yearbooks' should have nothing in common with an ordinary popular 'Almanac' (the compilation of which is qualitatively tied to the daily newspapers, and is pre-arranged with an eye on the average newspaper reader). Nor should the Yearbook be an occasional anthology of writings that are too long to be used by another type of review. It should be prepared organically, according to an overall plan, so as to be like the prospectus of a definite programme of a review. It could be dedicated to a single subject or divided into sections and deal with an organic series of fundamental issues (the constitution of the state, international politics, the agrarian problem etc.). Each Yearbook should be self-contained (it should not have articles that are to be continued) and should be equipped with bibliographies, analytical indexes, etc.

Study the different types of popular 'Almanacs' (which, if well done, are little Encyclopaedias of topical subjects).

Q 24 § 5.

16 [Cattaneo]

For a general exposition of the principal types of reviews, one should remember the journalistic activity of Carlo Cattaneo.[51] The *Archivio Triennale* and the *Politecnico* should be studied very attentively (and alongside the *Politecnico* the review *Scientia* founded by Rignano).

Q24§6.

17 Original Essays and Translations

This problem arises especially for reviews of the average and elementary type. They too should be made up predominantly of original writings. There must be a reaction against the traditional habit of filling the reviews with translations, even if the writings are by 'authoritative' people. Nevertheless, the contribution of foreign writers cannot be abolished: it has its cultural importance, as a reaction against provincialism and shallowness. Possible solutions: 1) obtain a set of original contributions; 2) summarize the principal writings of the international press by compiling a section like the 'Marginalia' in *Il Marzocco*: 3) compile periodical supplements of entirely translated material, under a somewhat different title, with separate page numbers, which can obtain an organic, critical-informative selection of foreign theoretical publications. (See the popular type like Minerva, and the type like the *Rassegna della Stampa Estera* published by the Ministry of Foreign Affairs.)

Q24§7.

18 Science Columns

The Italian type of daily newspaper is determined by the totality of organizational conditions of the cultural life of the country: absence of a widespread popular literature whether in books or

[51] Carlo Cattaneo (1801–69), Risorgimento democrat, one of the political leaders of the 'five days' insurrection in Milan 1848, ran two series of the review *Politecnico* (1839–45; 1860–65). The review was multi-disciplinary (natural science, economics, technology, education, the arts to a small extent) and was subdivided into three parts: original contributions, reviews, news of ideas and recent publications. The *Archivio Triennale delle Cose d'Italia* (3 vols. 1850–56) was a collection of documents on the years 1846–48 with Cattaneo's comments appended.

magazines. The reader of the dailies therefore looks to his newspaper for a reflection of all the aspects of the complex social life of a modern nation. It should be observed that the Italian newspaper, relatively better produced and more serious than that of other countries, has ignored scientific information, while there was a notable body of journalists specializing in economic, literary and artistic literature. Even in the most important reviews (like *Nuova Antologia* and the *Rivista d'Italia*) the part dedicated to the sciences was almost non-existent (today conditions have changed in this respect and the *Corriere della Sera* has a notable set of contributors specializing in scientific issues). Specialist scientific reviews have always existed but there has been a lack of popular reviews. (See *L'Arduo*, published in Bologna under the editorship of S. Timpanaro;[52] *Scienza per Tutti*, published by Sonzogno, had a wide circulation, but to form an opinion on it one need only recall that it was edited for many years by . . . Massimo Rocca.)[53]

Scientific information should be an integral part of every Italian newspaper, both in the form of a scientific-technological bulletin and in that of a critical exposition of the most important scientific hypotheses and opinions (the part on health and sanitation should constitute a column to itself). More than others, a popular newspaper should have this scientific section in order to control and direct the culture of its readers, which is often imbued with 'witchcraft' or fantasies, and in order to 'deprovincialize' current notions.

The difficulty of finding specialists who know how to write for the people: one could go systematically through the general and specialist reviews of professional culture, the acts of the Academies and foreign publications, compiling extracts and summaries in special appendices, carefully selecting themes and subject matter with an understanding of the cultural needs of the people.

Q 24 § 8.

[52] *L'Arduo* appeared in two series, 1914–20 and 1921–23. Sebastiano Timpanaro senior was a physicist.

[53] Massimo Rocca, former journalist on *Avanti!* (under the pseudonym Libero Tancredi), left in 1914 to support intervention on *L'Iniziativa* and subsequently sided with the first *fasci*. *La Scienza per Tutti* was a small newspaper of general information. Rocca published *Idee sul fascismo* in 1924. He broke with fascism before 1926. See also footnote 1 on pp. 345–46.

19 Schools of Journalism

An article by Ermanno Amicucci with this title was published in *Nuova Antologia* of 1 July 1928 and it may have been subsequently republished in a volume with some of his other pieces. The article is interesting for the information and suggestions it offers. It should however be pointed out that in Italy the issue is much more difficult to solve than appears from reading the article, and it would seem that the educational initiatives have had very significant effects (at least as far as journalism in the technical sense is concerned; the schools of journalism are probably schools of general political propaganda). The principle, however, that journalism must be taught and that it is not rational to leave journalists to learn on their own, casually, through crude practical experience, is vital and will increasingly spread as journalism gradually becomes a more complex industry and a more responsible civil institution in Italy too. The limitations in Italy come from the fact that there are no large concentrations of journalists, because of the decentralization of national cultural life, and that there are very few newspapers and the mass of readers is meagre. The number of journalists is very small and the profession is therefore fed through its own hierarchy: the less important newspapers (and the weeklies) serve as a school for the more important newspapers and vice versa. A second-rate sub-editor on the *Corriere* becomes editor or chief sub-editor of a provincial newspaper, and a sub-editor who has proved himself first rate on a provincial daily or on a weekly is absorbed by a large newspaper, etc. In Italy there are no centres like Paris, London or Berlin, which number thousands of journalists, constituting a real broad professional category of economic importance. Moreover, in Italy the average pay is very low. In some countries, like the German-speaking ones, the number of newspapers published in the entire country is impressive, and to the concentration in Berlin there corresponds a wide stratification in the provinces.

The question of local correspondents, who can rarely (only in the big cities and in general where important weeklies are published) be professional journalists.

For certain types of newspaper the problem of the professional school must be solved in the newspaper office itself, by transforming or integrating regular staff meetings into organic schools of journalism. Young people and students from outside should be invited to attend lectures there along with the staff, so that eventually real politico-journalistic schools are formed, with lectures on general topics (history, economics, constitutional law, etc.) which might also be entrusted to competent outside experts who are able to take into consideration the needs of the newspaper.

One should start from the principle that every sub-editor or 'reporter' should be enabled to put together and direct all sections of the newspaper, just as every sub-editor should immediately acquire the qualities of a 'reporter', that is, give all of his activity to the newspaper, etc.

As regards the number of Italian journalists, *L'Italia Letteraria* of 24 August 1930 carries the data of a census conducted by the Secretariat of the National Union of Journalists: by 30 June, there were 1,960 journalists in the Union, of whom 800 were affiliated to the Fascist Party. They were distributed as follows: Bari, 30 and 26; Bologna, 108 and 40; Florence, 108 and 43; Genoa, 113 and 39; Milan, 348 and 143; Naples, 106 and 45; Palermo, 50 and 17; Rome, 716 and 259; Turin, 144 and 59; Trieste, 90 and 62; Venice, 147 and 59.

Q24 §9.

CONCORDANCE TABLE

The following table is designed to let the reader trace each of the texts translated in this volume to an Italian source and vice versa. For section I ('Proletarian Culture') the first column gives, where applicable, the page numbers of an article in the critical edition of the pre-prison writings, *Scritti 1913–1926*, in course of publication by Einaudi in their NUE series. The second column gives a source in the older editions. The two sets of page numbers for LVN refer respectively to the original Einaudi edition (1950) and (in brackets) to the Riuniti reprint of the same edition with a different pagination (1971). For sections II to X, all from the Prison Notebooks, the right-hand side of the table shows four columns. The first column gives, in each case, the number of a *notebook* followed by that of a *note*, according to the numbering of Valentino Gerratana's 1975 critical edition (Q). The heading of the first and second columns uses Gerratana's designation of each of Gramsci's prison notes as either A, B or C texts. An A text is a first draft, a C text a second version and a B text a unique draft. All the translations here have been made from B or C texts: hence the first column lists either a C text (in which case the second column gives, in square brackets, its corresponding A text or texts) or a B text (in which case the second column is blank). The third and fourth column give (as with the last part of section I) the corresponding page numbers of the first Einaudi edition of the notebooks in six volumes (1948–51) followed in round brackets by those of the 1971 Riuniti reprint. Titles in square brackets have been supplied, in order to aid identification, for all cases where Gramsci either left a note or article untitled or where he gave it a merely generic 'tag' heading common to several notes, like 'Popular literature' or 'Italian intellectuals'. In most cases the titles are those of the Platone edition, though we have occasionally substituted our own. Unbracketed titles are the original ones. Abbreviations of titles of volumes are as listed on p. XV above. An asterisk designates a text published for the first time in the critical edition; n = footnote, e = extract from a longer text.

I PROLETARIAN CULTURE

	Critical edition	Previous editions	Einaudi	Riuniti
Politics and Culture				
1 For a Cultural Association (1917)	CF 497–500	SG 143–5		
2 Philanthropy, Goodwill and Organization (1917)	CF 518–21	SG 145–7		
3 A Single Language and Esperanto (1918)	CF 668–73	SG 174–8		
4 Culture and Class Struggle (1918)	NM 48–51	SG 238–41		
5 Serial Novels (1918)	NM 60–1	SG 243–5		
6 [Communism and Art] (1919)		DP 385–7		
7 The Problem of the School (1919)		ON 255–6		
8 [Questions of Culture] (1920)		SC 217–19		
9 Party Art (1921)		PV 143–5		
Futurism				
10 The Futurists (1913)	CT 6–8	PV 6–8		
11 Marinetti the Revolutionary? (1921)		SF 20–2		
12 [A Letter to Trotsky on Futurism] (1922)		SF 527–8		
Theatre Criticism				
13 Theatre and Cinema (1916)	CT 802–4		LVN 248–50	(305–7)
14 The Theatre Industry [i] (1917)	CF 911–13		LVN 288–90	(353–5)
15 The Theatre Industry [ii] (1917)	CF 915–18		LVN 290–2	(355–8)
16 The Chiarella Brothers Again (1917)	CF 919–21		LVN 292–4	(359–61)
17 The Theatre Industry [iii] (1917)	CF 922–4		LVN 294–7	(361–3)
18 Continuation of Life (1917)	CF 927–8		LVN 297–8	(364–5)

		Critical edition		Einaudi	Riuniti
		B/C text	A text		
10	Criteria of Literary Criticism	15/38		LVN 11–12	(26–8)
11	For a New Literature (Art) through a New Culture	6/133		LVN 10	(25)
12	[Individualism and Art]	14/28		LVN 64–5	(89–90)
13	Criteria of Method	23/36	[3/41]	LVN 19–21	(36–9)
14	[The Writer's Attitude]	8/9		LVN 89–90	(120–1)
15	Non-National-Popular Characteristics of Italian Literature ['Contentism' and 'Calligraphism']	15/20		LVN 79–81	(107–9)
16	[Languages of the Arts]	6/62		LVN 22–4	(40–2)
17	Neology	23/7	[9/132]	LVN 24–6	(42–4)
18	Sincerity (or Spontaneity) and Discipline	14/61		LVN 26–8	(44–6)
19	Cultural Themes. 'Rationalism' [i]	14/67		PP 175–7	(229–32)
20	Popular Literature. [Rationalism(ii)]	14/2		LVN 29	(48)
21	Popular Literature. [Rationalism(iii)]	14/1		LVN 29–30	(48–9)
22	Popular Literature. ['Functional' Literature]	14/65		LVN 28–9	(46–8)
23	The New Architecture	3/155		LVN 30–1	(49–51)
24	Justification of Autobiography [i]	14/59		PP 174	(228–9)
25	Justification of Autobiography [ii]	14/64		PP 174–5	(229)
26	Some Criteria of 'Literary' Judgement	23/5	[4/36]	LVN 31–3	(51–2)
27	Methodological Criteria	14/5		LVN 33	(52–3)

VI PEOPLE, NATION AND CULTURE

		Critical edition		Einaudi	Riuniti
		B/C text	A text		
	Giovanni Papini [iii]	8/98		LVN 161–2	(205)
	[iv] Papini as a Jesuit Apprentice	8/105		LVN 162–3	(206)
	Giovanni Papini [v]	8/160		LVN 163	(207)
	Giovanni Papini [vi]	17/13		LVN 164	(208)
	Giovanni Papini [vii]	17/16		LVN 162	(205–6)
	Giovanni Papini [viii]	17/24		LVN 161	(205)
6	Giuseppe Prezzolini [i]	23/31	[1/142]	LVN 164–5	(208–10)
	Giuseppe Prezzolini [ii]	1/90		LVN 165–6	(210)
	Giuseppe Prezzolini [iii]	23/24	[9/20]	LVN 166	(210–11)
7	Curzio Malaparte [i]	23/14	[1/42]	LVN 169–70	(214–15)
	Curzio Malaparte [ii]	23/22	[9/10]	LVN 170–1	(216)
8	Luca Beltrami (Polifilo)	23/42	[3/94]	LVN 166–7	(211)
9	Leonida Répaci [i]	23/13	[1/39]	*	
	Leonida Répaci [ii]	23/26	[9/48]	*	
10	Giovanni Ansaldo	23/23	[9/11]	LVN 168–9	(213–14)
11	War Literature	23/25	[9/43]	LVN 148–50	(189–91)
12	The Academy of Ten	3/9		LVN 171	(216–17)
13	La Fiera Letteraria	1/102		LVN 171–2	(218–19)
14	Bontempelli's Novecentismo	23/29	[1/136]	*	
15	Novecentismo and Super-country	23/30	[1/137]	LVN 173	(219)
16	Super-city and Super-country	6/27		LVN 173	(219–20)
17	Jahier, Raimondi and Proudhon	23/34	[3/10;1/94]	LVN 175–6	(221–3)

IX POPULAR LITERATURE

INDEX